Philadelphia, Richardson & co.

Richardson & co.'s Unclaimed Money Register of Great Britain and Ireland

A descriptive index of 20,000 names of heirs and next of kin, British subjects who have died intestate in Australia, Tasmania, New Zealand, America, and the Cape of Good Hope

Philadelphia, Richardson & co.

Richardson & co.'s Unclaimed Money Register of Great Britain and Ireland
A descriptive index of 20,000 names of heirs and next of kin, British subjects who have died intestate in Australia, Tasmania, New Zealand, America, and the Cape of Good Hope

ISBN/EAN: 9783337270407

Printed in Europe, USA, Canada, Australia, Japan

Cover: Foto ©Suzi / pixelio.de

More available books at **www.hansebooks.com**

RICHARDSON & CO'S
UNCLAIMED MONEY REGISTER

OF

GREAT BRITAIN AND IRELAND.

A DESCRIPTIVE INDEX OF

20,000 NAMES

OF

HEIRS AND NEXT OF KIN

BRITISH SUBJECTS WHO HAVE DIED INTESTATE IN AUSTRALIA,
TASMANIA, NEW ZEALAND, AMERICA, AND
THE CAPE OF GOOD HOPE.

TOGETHER WITH

HANCERY AND OTHER ADVERTISEMENTS FOR HEIRS, LEGATEES, AND
PERSONS WANTED,

AND

UNCLAIMED ARMY AND NAVY PRIZE MONEY

From 1665 to Date.

PHILADELPHIA:

RICHARDSON & CO.

No. 711 Sansom Street.

1880.

RICHARDSON & CO'S
UNCLAIMED MONEY REGISTER

OF

GREAT BRITAIN AND IRELAND.

A DESCRIPTIVE INDEX OF

20,000 NAMES

OF

HEIRS AND NEXT OF KIN

BRITISH SUBJECTS WHO HAVE DIED INTESTATE IN AUSTRALIA,
TASMANIA, NEW ZEALAND, AMERICA, AND
THE CAPE OF GOOD HOPE.

TOGETHER WITH

CHANCERY AND OTHER ADVERTISEMENTS FOR HEIRS, LEGATEES, AND
PERSONS WANTED,

AND

UNCLAIMED ARMY AND NAVY PRIZE MONEY

From 1665 to Date.

PHILADELPHIA:
RICHARDSON & CO.
No. 711 Sansom Street.

1880.

Entered according to Act of Congress in the year 1880, by RICHARDSON & Co., in the office of the Librarian, at Washington.

CONTENTS.

Fees, - - - - - - - viii
Next of Kin, Advertisements for - - - - 1
Chancery, " " - - - 78
Legatees, " " - - - - 105
Persons Dying Intestate in the Colonies, - - 133
Addenda to General Index, - - - - 151

UNCLAIMED PROPERTY.

$285,000,000.

In the Court of Chancery alone, the amount of money and other property unclaimed and awaiting legal owners, is said to be about *two hundred and eighty-five million dollars.* The rightful heirs to this large sum are scattered throughout the world, and, it is reasonable to suppose, that a majority of such are residents of the United States and British Colonies.

This property has been left principally by persons who have died intestate. In the Treasury alone, the money taken possession of by the Government, amounts to many millions of dollars, although advertisements have been inserted in the public papers for the proper claimants. Not only in Great Britain, but in India and the British Colonies large amounts are awaiting ownership.

BANK OF ENGLAND DIVIDENDS.

An extract from the *London Times,* speaking of one branch of this subject, says: "The unclaimed dividends handed over to the Commissioners for the Reduction of the National Debt, and by them invested in the public funds, amounted at the close of the last fiscal year, to no less than $14,000,000 stock. There is also in the hands of the Commissioners, more than half a million stock, on which no dividends have been claimed for upwards of ten years." Thus we have in this single item of unclaimed bank dividends, nearly *three million of dollars,* the rightful claimants to which are doubtless unaware that they are entitled to any part thereof.

In INDIA, the amount of money left by British subjects who have died there within the last hundred years is large, all of which is recoverable, on producing proper proofs of relationship to the various deceased persons.

Other large amounts have been left by persons who have died intestate in AUSTRALIA within the last thirty years.

ARMY AND NAVY PRIZE MONEY.

Another important item seldom noted, is *Unclaimed Prize Money*. On the 31st of December, 1862, this amounted to about $6,000,000.

One would scarcely believe that so respectable an amount of money, the legal property of England's defenders and their legal heirs, should thus be forfeited and unclaimed; but the wonder will partly cease, when we consider the long period that is usually allowed to elapse before distribution of such funds.

RICHARDSON & CO'S
Unclaimed Money Registry,

For the Recovery of Claims in all Parts of the World.

OFFICE, 711 SANSOM STREET, PHILADELPHIA, PA.

Office Hours from 10 to 4 o'clock.

To facilitate the work for which our REGISTRY has been established, we have, at considerable trouble and expense, secured the valuable information within; but we would further inform inquirers, who believe themselves entitled as rightful claimants to such interests, that we have secured access to still further information, when wanted, to the extent of over one hundred thousand names, through correspondence with similar registries in Great Britain, of twenty years' experience, and possessing every facility for searching and tracing the rights of claimants, as far back as 1665.

All persons who believe themselves entitled to claims for such property or moneys, or who wish investigation to be made for the same, are respectfully requested to make application to our Registry, where every facility will be afforded for aiding them in the matter at a comparatively trifling cost.

Wills of persons who have died in Great Britain, Ireland, India, and other parts of the world, since the year 1600, searched for and obtained; also copies of advertisements, and all other documents requiring search in the matter of Unclaimed Estates, Dividends in the Bank of England, and Unclaimed Prize Money, &c.

FEES.

1. Search for name not in index, with abstract.......... $ 2 00
2. Copy of advertisement for heirs....................... 6 00
3. Search for Will.. 10 00
4. Copy of Will in proportion to length, given when found.
5. Search and examination of proceedings relating to any chancery suit, and report thereon... 25 00
6. Special investigations dependent upon the nature thereof, and expense attending the same.

NOTE—Applications and letters requiring answer, must be accompanied by return postage, to require prompt attention.

All remittances must be by Post Office order, and all correspondence be addressed to

RICHARDSON & CO.,
711 Sansom Street, Philadelphia, Pa.

Anderson, Thomas, Wm. *d* abrd 1858
" David ⎱ brothers of Wm.
" Nathl. ⎰ A. of America &
" Thomas ⎱ London 1795
" Francis ⎰ cousins of Wm.
" Mary G. ⎱ A. of America &
" Overton ⎰ London 1795
Andoird, George, *d* abroad
Andrews, Hannah, of Essex, *d* 1812
" John, of Norfolk *d* abroad 1847
" Rev. Jno. of Glo'ster, *d* 1811
" Marg. of Dorsetshire, *d* 1833
" Mary, Somers Town
" Mordecai, of Essex, *d* 1812
Angrer, George, *d* in Soho
Angus, John, *d* Aberdeen 1836
Anson, Charlotte, of Hampstead
Anthony, John, of Beaconfield 1800
Antram, Thos., of Clerkenwell 1802
" William, of 32d Regt. Foot
Antram or ⎱ Eleanor, of Epson, *d* in
Antrim ⎰ Kent 1845
Applebye, Christopher, Surrey 1751
Appleton, Daniel, of London 1775
Applebee, William, of Westminster
Applebee, James
Apsland, Elizabeth
Appleby, Wm. *d* in Surrey 1810
Arnold, Richard, of London 1758
Arthur, James, of Yorkshire 1786
Armstrong, Thomas, of Hants
Arnold, Lumley, of Northamptonshire
Armstrong, Edmund, of London
Arlidge, Thomas, of London
Archdall, Richard, of Madeira, 1811
Archdall, Eliza, of Exeter
Armstrong, Emma, *dau* of Henry
Arnold, Henry, of Bath
Arbouin, Francis, of London 1763
Arnold, John, servant
Arnett, Thomas B. *d* Stafford 1863
Arden, Edward H.
Armstrong, George, Middlesex 1826
Arbuthnot, Elizabeth, *d* Dorset 1824
" Jno. & Co. Peterhead 1814
" Robt, of Edinburgh 1809
Archael, Isabella, *frmly* Day
Archer, Charles, of Perth 1810
" George, of Birmingham
" George, surgeon 17th Regt.
" Joseph, of Suffolk
" Wm., *d* in Southwark 1864
Ardesoif, Ann, *frmly* Buckie
Armsby, Fred. seaman M S

Armstrong, Archibald N. Paddington
" David E. Capt. Scotland
" Elizebeth, *d* at Paris 1830
" James, seaman
" Mary, *w* of capt. Philip,
" Peter, seaman M S
Arnold, David, *d* in Liverpool
" Elizabeth, *o'wise* Ashcroft, *d* 1824
" Hannah, of Shrewsbury
" Richard, mariner, Portsea
Arnott, Mary, *d* in Hants 1842
Arthur, John, of London 1770
" Dr. John, Army
Arundell, Briant W., Kensingt'n 1827
Ashwell, Mary, of Exeter
Ashby, Hannah M., of London
Ashworth, John, of Lancashire
" James, of Bacup
Asquith, Amos, *d* Surrey
Ashworth, John, of Liverpool
" Rev. John Harvey
Ashford, Eliza, of Pimlico.
Ashton, Arthur, of London 1812
Aspinal, Benjamin, of London 1812
Astle, Thomas, son of Thomas
Ashley, Sarah, of Pimlico
Ashburner, George, of Kensington
Ashcroft, Elizabeth, *frmly* Arnold
Ashkettle, Mary, London, *d* 1829
Ashton, John, of Cheshire, *d* 1846
Ashworth, Rebecca, Dublin, *d* 1812
Ask, William, seaman R N
Askew, Elizabeth, *frmly* Batterson
" George, of Lancashire
Askey, Edward, of London
" Hannah
Aston, Thomas, carpenter, Coventry
Astor, John J. *d* in New York
Atwell, Henry, *d* Holland 1788
Atkinson, Robert ⎱ of Cumberland
" Margaret ⎰
Atkinson, Lieut. *d* abroad
Atkins, John, *d* Middlesex
Atkinson, John, of Sidmouth
Atkins, Anna, of Brittany
Atkinson, Capt. G. P.
Atherton, John, *d* in India 1821
Atkins, Joseph, seaman R N
" Robert, *d* at Norwood 1861
Atkinson, Ann, *frmly* Grewer
" Ann, *d* Whitechapel 1858
" John, merchant 1807
Atkyns, Charlotte, of Norfolk, *d* abd
" Richard, California
Atwick, Rev. Geo. *d* Edmonton 1849

GENERAL INDEX.

Aubrey Family, of Bath
Auchmutty, Capt. Warren
Austen, George, of Surrey
Audinet, James, of London
Austin, Robert, of Middlesex
" George } of London
" Edward }
" Mary C. of Dublin
Aulsebrook, Alex. *d* Middlesex
Aubrey, Charles L. *d* in Surrey 1836
" Peter, of Westminster
Auchenlech, William, *d* in India
Austiss, William, butler
Auston, Robert, of Dartford
Averill, Thomas, *d* in America
Aves, William, *d* at Hammersmith
Avill, Mary, Clapham, *d* 1861
Ayray, Richard, of Limerick
Ayscough, James }
" Thomas } sons of Jas. A.
" William }
Axford, Dorothy, of London

B

Barrett, Mrs. Frances
Bartram, Alfred, painter
Batley, R., of London
Barbor, Robert, of London 1834
Barry, Herbert, of London 1853
Baker, Elizabeth, housekeeper
Baldery, John, Milbank, warder
Bashford, Thomas Augustus
Barnett, James, *d* Scotland
Bate, Mary, *d* 1848
Banks, Mary, *frmly* White
Barker, Richard, of Bucks
Barlow, Richard, of London
Bartles, Susannah, of London
Baldwin, John, of Worcestershire
Barlee, Dorothy, Thorp Mandville
Barker, Henry, of Chiswick
Barnard, Ramsden, of Yorkshire
Bance, John, of Berkshire
Bayley, Francis, of Middlesex
Batten, Walter, of Essex
Barton, Mary, of Gravesend
Barnes, John, of London
Barnes, Cornelius, of Hants
Bart, John, of Dunkirk
Barlow, Sophia, of Yorkshire
Baker, Miriam, *formerly* Pedingham
Barrett, Elizabeth, *formerly* Hook
Basnett, William, *d* Middlesex
Baber, Frances, of Worcestershire

Bache, John, *d* London
Bambridge, James, *d* London
Barnevelt, Robert, *d* London
Baker, Frances, *frmly* Griffin
Barton, Rev. Philip, of Bucks
Barter, William, of the New Forest
Bates, Robert, Middlesex, *d* 1741
Battely, Rev. Charles, of Suffolk
Badger, Ann, of Gloucester
Bargean, John } relatives
" Joseph } of
" Francis } Mary Le Reux
Bayne, John, *d* Middlesex
Baker, Jeremy, of Gloucester
Ball, Ann, of Wiltshire
Baynes, Rev. Thomas, of Suffolk
Banks, William, of Lancashire
Banks, Elizabeth, *d* Lancashire 1863
Bainbrigge, Thomas, *d* Staffordshire 1818
Baker, Joshua, *d* London 1787
Bateman, Josiah, of Staffordshire
Bayfield, William, *d* Norfolk 1821
Barratt, Samuel, of Lothbury
Baker, James, of Chichester
Barry, Daniel, nephew of Mrs. Payne
Barton, Matthew, left London 1849
Baker, Samuel, mariner, 1851
Baron, Catharine, Lancashire, *d* 1861
Baker, Mrs. A., of City-road, 1852
Barby, Edwin V., son of Nancy
Barrett, Mary Ann, of Norfolk
Balsdor, Mr, tailor
Barnard, James, of London 1799
Bassett, William, of London 1800
Baldwin, Samuel
" Catherine, *frmly* Palmer
Bailey, Maria, *frmly* Haines
Badderley, Robert, *d* London 1799
Baker, John, of Linton, Kent
Barnes, John, *otherwise* Baker
Balderson, Catherine, of Woodstock
Barrow, James, of Whitehall 1821
Bayfield, George C., of Norfolk
Barwick, George, carpenter
Banks, Major Roger, d 1834
Ball, Wm, of Covent Garden 1839
Barr, Alfred, left England 1850
Barker, Thomas, builder, Clapham
Bateman, Thomas Major, E I C S
Balme, John, of Leeds
Barbone, Angelina S , Surrey, *d* 1867
Baird, Mary, } mother and sister of
" M. J., } J. T. Baird
Bagnall, Ann, *w* Gloucestershire
Barge, William, brother to John

NEXT OF KIN. 5

Ball, Charles Edmund
Band, William, seaman M S
Barnett, William, seaman M S
Baird, Mary A., *frmly* McNeilance
Banks, Mary ⎫ sisters of Elizabeth
Barnes, Sarah ⎭ Flatters
Bachons, Richard, of Clerkenwell
Ballaine, John, of Jersey
Baker, Hannah, of Warwickshire
Barton, Thomas, of Marlow, Herts
Barton, Henry, tailor, of Greenhythe
Barker, J., *d* abroad 1864
Bartlett, G., *d* abroad 1864
Barber, John Vaughan
Barrow, Samuel, *d* Australia 1854
Bant, J., *d* abroad 1865
Bates, Ann, Somers Town
Bates, Thomas, of London 1723
Batchelor, Amey, of Hadley
    " Isaac, *d* in China 1857
    " Eliza, *o'wise* Brown, *d* 1851
Bates, Joseph, of Canada West
Batho, Mary, of Bees, Salop
Batten, John, seaman M S
Batterson, Elizabeth, Westmoreland
Batting, Eliz., of Yewcrofts, Bucks
Battiscomb, Robert, of London 1723
Bathurst, Dorothy F., of Wilts
Baxter, Alex., surgeon, R N *d* 1812
    " Alfred, of London, *d* 1834
    " Isabella, *frmly* Watson
Bayley, Eliz., of Guildford, *d* 1863
Baylie, Richard, of Walworth
Baylis, Thomas, of Stepney
Baynes, Thomas, Captain, *d* in India
Barlow, Joseph, of London 1812
Bacon, Joseph, of London 1812
Band, John, of Bond-street 1836
Bavley, Peter, of Kennington 1814
Ball, Ellen M. ⎫ children of Charles
    " Matilda ⎭ Edmund Ball
Barker, William, servant
Bailey, John ⎫ relatives of William
    " Joseph ⎬ Bailey, of Ports-
    " Mary ⎭ mouth 1792
Barrow, Gustav, of Stockholm 1850
Bailey, Charles, *d* Sussex 1865
    " Dinah, of Heckfield
    " Mary, *o'wise* Moore
    " Barnard, of Hammersmith
Bassett, Mrs., *frmly* Henson
Baker, Thomas
    " Edward
Barker, Thomas, of Yorkshire
Backhouse, Elizabeth, daughter of Richard

Back, Mary, Hadley, Middlesex
Backhouse, Thomas, of Bucks
Backler, Margaret, Hoxton
Bacon, William, seaman R N
Badaley, Joseph, *d* Staffordshire 1785
Baddeley, James, *d* West Malling 1795
Badiffe, James, living 1717
Bailey, Benjamin, of London 1800
    " Elizabeth, of Marylebone
    " Jane, *frmly* Twigg, *d* 1800
    " John, of London 1800
    " Mary, *frmly* Wyart, *d* 1825
    " Sarah, *o'wise* Leferre
    " Thos., Greenwich pensioner, *d* 1852
    " William
Baines, Thomas ⎫ descendants of
    " Susannah ⎭ wanted
Baillie, James, of Scotland 1794
Baird, John, mariner
    " William, of Westminster 1724
Baker, Ann, of Finsbury 1852
    " John, *d* in Kent
    " John, seaman R N
    " John, of Devon, *d* 1821
    " John, seaman M S, *d* 1836
    " Juliet, *w* of Major James
    " Margaret, London
    " Mary Eliza, *d* 1857
    " Mary, London
    " Ursula, Bucks, *d* 1870
    " William, of Greenwich 1818.
Balantyne, Rob't, of Edinburgh 1809
Ball, John, ship carpenter
Ballard, Elizabeth ⎫ children of
    " John ⎬ John B. gro-
    " Nancy ⎬ cer, London,
    " Thomas ⎭ 1750
Balmanno, Alex., *d* Kensington 1839
Bamblet, William, *d* Australia 1858
Bamford, Mary, *d* London
Banck, Frances M., *o'wise* Harper
Banks, William, marine Navy
Banks, William, *d* in India
Bannerman, Elizabeth, *d* Richmond
Bannister, Martha, of Wigan, *d* 1783
Barber, Charles, *d* in London 1799
    " Francis, seaman M S
Barclay, George, Capt,, *d* India 1811
Barford, Hugh, of Surrey, *d* 1860
    " Richard ⎫ married 1782
    " Phœbe ⎭ lived at Lichfield
    " Mary, *o'wise* Bradbury
Barge, Benjamin ⎫ of London 1810
    " Caroline ⎭

GENERAL INDEX.

Barker, William, butcher, M S
" Sam'l, of Manchester, d 1834
" Mary, frmly Bond
" Caroline A., of Brixton
Barlow, A., d abroad
" Ann, of Turnham 1731—90
" Catharine
" Frederick, of London 1804
" Frederick, London 1823
Barland, John, of Scotland 1810
Barnard, David, of Norfolk, d 1808
Barnes, William, seaman Navy
" John, of Cumberland
" Sarah, Berkshire, d 1853
Barnett, William, of Hereford
Barnewall, George, Captain Army
Barr, Jane, d at Chelsea 1826
" Alfred, of Australia 1850
Barratt, Thomas H., of Ewell, Surrey
Barrett, Mary A., of Norfolk
Barrow, Ann, of Acton, Warwick
Barron, Patrick, of Aberdeen 1800
Barry, David, seaman Navy
" Michael, " "
" Elizabeth, o'wise Wyeth
Bartlett, William, of Weymouth
Bartington, John, of London
Bartholomew, Ann, frmly Walls
Barton, Benjamin, seaman M S
" T., d abroad 1863
" Thomas, of Marlows, Herts
" Henry, tailor, Greenhithe
" Sarah, frmly Emere
Barston, Jeremiah
" Dorothy
Barnett, Catharine, London
" William, seaman M S
Bassett, M., frmly Fish, of Jamaica
Bates, Ann, frmly Hopkins, d 1862
" Edward, d in China
Baumont, John William
Bellamy Family
Besley, Elsie Burrow, dau of Emma
Beeby, William, d Cumberland 1817
Bellew, F. J , d Cheshunt 1868
Bean, Henry, of Luton
Bennett, Ann, of Norwich
Benson, Joseph, of Windermere
Bettle, Jonathan, of Woolaston
Benwell, John, of Cambridge
Bernes, Andrew, d Chelsea
Beake, Mary, d Westminster
Beeby, Abraham, of London
Beaumont, William, of Suffolk
Beeke, Thomas, of Lincoln
Beale, Richard, of London

Beard, Charles, d London 1744
Beale, William, d Middlesex
Bethell, Elizabeth, o'wise Henshaw
Bennett Family, of Bristol
Benson, Miles, of Hants
Bell, Nathaniel, of London
Bevan, Elizabeth, Carmarthen 1787
Bennett, Carrington, of Surrey
Beadon, Rev. Edward, of Devon
Beaven, Rev. John, of Monmouth
Beswell Family
Bond Family
Beswell, Edward, of Surrey
Bell, Richard, London 1834
Beaumont, Thos. R., Southwark 1814
Bennett, Thomas, Bath 1857
Bell, Dr. William, d abroad 1868
Bellamy, Ann, frm'y Bailey
Beattie, George, of Southwark
Belfit, Richard, of Marylebone 1867
Bezely, Sarah, o'wise Webster
Bennett, —, a butler
Benham Family, 1785—1798
" Francessa
Beard, John, of Kingston, Surrey
Bealson, Mary, of Aldersgate 1811
Bennett, William } of Carshalton,
" Richard } Surrey 1800
Benton, Joseph, seaman M S
Bell, Maria S. C., o'wise Arnold
Bedwell, Henry, of Llandillo
Bernardi, Casimirro, d Pimlico 1860
Bennett, Estevan, d abroad
Benson, Joseph, Windermere d 1828
Beer, Samuel, d Devonshire
Bentley, Abraham, of Yorkshire
Beckman, William, seaman M S
Berry, Michael, seaman M S
Bennett, Elizabeth, of Manchester
Benn, Anthony, of London 1719
Beauclerk, Charlotte, London 1812
Bevis, Mary, w, Cornwall d 1865
Beel, James, went to Sydney 1853
Beagley, Thomas, of Somers Town
Beale, Ann, frmly Minett
Bear, Mary, of Durham
Beard, Jane, native of Stirling
Beauchamp, Robert, Captain, d India
Beaumont, Edward, of London, 1828
Beavis, James, seaman M S d 1828
Beazely, Thomas, footman
Becber, Charles C., of London 1816
Beckman, John, seaman Navy
Bedell, Thomas, of London 1720
Bedingfield, J., of London
Beechy, Blackman, of 65th Regt.

Begg, James, of Edinburgh, *d* 1805
Belcher, George, seaman M S
Belin, Peter, of London *d* 1786
" Elizabeth, *o'wise* Brown, *d* 1784
Bell, Alexander, *d* abroad 1838-9
" Charlotte, Mrs., *d* in Middlesex
" Charles, of Perth 1810
" Elbth., *o'wise* Hunt
" John, of Perth 1810
" Malcolm, *d* in India
" Mary, niece of C. Graham
" J. F. G., *d* in Prussia
Bellas, Sarah, *o'wise* Smith, *d* 1841
Bellier, James, of Ireland, *d* abroad
Bellingham, J. G., Captain, *d* in India
Bellman, Vincent
Benbow, Daniel, of Glamorgan *d* 1828
" Mary *d*, London
Bending, Hy., master mariner, *d* 1854
Bendix, Matilda, Stepney, *d* 1827
Bennett, Charles, surgeon 1779
" Charles, of Essex 1830
" Charles, mercer in 1800
Bennett, Estevan, *d* in Mexico
" C. E., Mile End, London
" Frances, *frmly* Edwards
" John, of Cornwall, *d* 1833
" Margaret, *d* London
" Maria D., *d* 1856
" Mary, *w* of John, *d* 1859
" Mary, of Croydon, Surrey
" Sarah, *frmly* Lawrence
" Sarah, living in 1836
" Wm., Capt., *d* abroad 1812
Benning, Lieut., *d* in China 1864
Benoist, Mary M., Westminster 1788
Benson, Henry, ship-carpenter, *d* 1830
Benson, Peter, seaman Navy
" George, Captain, *d* abroad
Bentinck, William, seaman Navy
Bentley, William, seaman Navy
" Thomas, of America 1783
Benwell, Joseph, *d* in India
Berridge, Cath., *o'wise* Horwood 1844
Berry, Samuel, plumber, Croydon
" Elizabeth, Croydon
Bert, Margaret F., *o'wise* Markham
Bertram, Jane, *o'wise* Ferguson, 1786
Berton, Sarah, *o'wise* Kaye, *d* 1834
Bestman, Frances A., London *d* 1863
Bethinger, Francis, *d* abroad 1760
Bethune, Hugh, of London 1809
Bettle, James, of Hale Weston, Hunts
" Thomas, ⎱ of Northampton-
" William, ⎰   shire
Betty, Rachel W., London

Betts, George, of London 1804
Bird, Joseph, *d* Croydon
Biscoe, Fanny, of Kentish Town
Birch, John, of Mansfield
Billingley, Elizabeth, Kidminster
Bickley, Brune, of Surrey
Bird, H. C. W., *d* Middlesex
Binmer, John, of London
Birket, C. J. W., of Berks
Biddlecombe, Charles, of Surrey
Bicknell, Elizabeth, *d* London 1838
" William, of Berks 1830
Binham, Esther, *d* Exeter 1866
Bissett, Ann, *formerly* Wheeler
Bill or Bills Family
Bishop, John, *formerly* of Bath
Binks, Alfred Ephraim
Bishton, Ann, *formerly* Clark
Bishop, Harry George, *d* abroad
" Thomas, Manchester, *d* 1844
Brimes, John, living 1840
Billing, Arthur J., 17th Lancers
Bishop, Robert, of Gloucestershire
Bittleston, John, of London
Bickley, Edward ⎱   living from
" Elizabeth ⎰   1750—1780
Bissett, Elizabeth, *d* 1865
Bickley, Dr. B., of Surrey *d* 1749
Biddell, Mary, Chelsea *d* 1838
Biddulph, Henry, seaman Navy
Bigg, Hester, *d* Camberwell 1829
Biggert, Sarah, Paisley N B
Biggs, Elizabeth, *d* Southampton 1830
Bignell, John, servant
Bignell, Mary, of Tunbridge Wells, *d* 1851
Bigot, Anthony, of Leeds & Brighton
Bincliff, Rev. Jonathan, Derby *d* 1815
Binder, Thomas, seaman M S
Binton, Joseph, seaman M S
Birch, John, yeoman Hants
" Hannah, *d* Staffordshire 1807
" William, of Birmingham *d* 1840
" Joseph ⎱ nephews of Joseph,
" William ⎰   Showell
" Joseph, *d* at Hammersmith 1812
" Wm., went abroad 1800
Bird, James B., of London
" Jane, of Tyburn, 1840
" Joseph, of Ratcliffe 1802
" Richd. J., Lieut. *d* in India
" William, ⎱ of Newton Abbott,
" Bridget, ⎰   Devon
Birkbeck, David, draper, Finsbury
Birkett, Thomas, of Cumberland
" Henry, *d* in Australia

Birrell, Dr., surgeon, Army
Birwood, John, of Devonshire
Bishop, Thos., of Manchester *d* 1844
" Martha, of Deptford
Bispham, Margt., Lancashire *d* 1830
Blethin, William, of Monmouth
" Timothy
" Temperance ⎫ all living
" Margaret ⎬ 1730
" Annie ⎭
Blackshaw, Elizabeth ⎱ of Covent
" Edward ⎰ Garden
Blacklow, Thos., of London 1838
Blew, John, *d* Blomsgrove 1819
Blofield, Thomas, of Norfolk
Blackford, William, of Latchford
Blunt, William, of Essex
Blosse, John, of London
Blue, Joshua, *d* London
Blecheynden, Carter, of Kent
" Thomas, of Essex
Blackall, Thomas, of Oxford
Blum, Anthony, of Germany
Blomely, Ann
Blenkinsop, Henry
Blunt, Thomas, of London
Blay, Charles, of Iffley
Blackbourne, Wm., *d* London 1840
Blue, John, seaman M S
Blissett, Thomas ⎱ of Southwark
" Sarah ⎰
Blissett, Mary
" Harriet ⎫
' Catherine ⎬ children of
" Susannah ⎬ Thomas and
" Thomas ⎬ Sarah Blissett,
" William ⎬ of Southwark
" Richard ⎭
Bloxham, Rev. C., of Wilts
Blazely, William, of Norfolk
Blight, James H., of Canton 1835
Blacklock, Elizbth., of Finsbury 1831
Blatch, William Henry, of Andover
Black, Chas. W., *d* in India 1824
" Samuel, *d* in Canada 1841
" Wm., *d* at Hammersmith 1829
Blackall, Richd., of Hampstead 1776
Blackie, James, seaman 1793
Blackiston, R., Capt. R. N.
Blackman, Ann, of Kingsland Road
Blackmore, John F., London *d* 1827
Blackstock, Jas., of Whitehaven
Bladen, Wm., seaman, M S
Blades, John, of London 1823
Blagden, Francis E., *d* S America
Blair, James, *b* at Wapping 1778

Blair, James, of Ayr, N B
" Maria, *otherwise* Hardcastle
Blake, Catherine M., *s*, Hants, *d* 1845
Blackwood, Rev. Robt., of Aberdeen
Blake, Ann, *w*, Bethnal Green
Blakeley, Robert, Pentonville
" Jane, of Southend, Essex
Bland, Harriett, Kensington, *d* 1840
Blanchard, Sarah, *d* Norwood
" John, seaman, Navy
Blandford, Mrs., of London
Blankett, Rear-Admiral, *d* 1801
Blazely, William, printer, Norwich
Blay, James, seaman, Navy
Blaney, Thomas, of Worcestershire
Bleckley, Jas., *d* Godmanchester 1843
Bletso, Elizabeth *otherwise* Cheyre
Blomfield, Sarah, of Norwich
Bloomfield, Robert, of Essex
" Robert, of N. York, 1833
Blouse, William, *d* at Sydney 1820
Blowfield, Mathw., of London, *d* 1815
Blunden, John, Chelsea pensioner
Blundell, Ann, *w* of Henry
" Archd., Lieut. Army, 1795
Blyth, Thos., seaman M S., *d* 1841
Boydell, Dr. Josiah
Doyle, J., *d* abroad 1869
Boby, Ann, of Ipswich
Boyes, Craven, *d* Yorkshire 1836
Bodell Family, Ireland
Bowes, George, of Northampton
Bowden, John, of London
Bodens, Meliora, *d* Middlesex
Bowers, Robert, of Berks
Bolton, John, of Jamaica
Bottomley Family, of Yorkshire
Booker, John, *d* Canterbury
Bourke, Michael, *d* Middlesex
Boyce, Lieut., *d* abroad
Bolney Family,
Bowis, John, of Lincolnshire
Bouillon, Francis, *d* Middlesex
Bowes, Thomas, of Yorkshire
Bowden, David, *d* Lisbon
Boardman, Martha, *frm'ly* Andoe
Bodfield, Mr., of London
Boileau, John J. M., of Marylebone
Bond, John, of Bristol, *d* 1827
" Sarah, of Hackney
Bowis, Peter, of Peterborough 1860
Bowles, Michael, seaman, Royal Navy
Boreman, Ambrose, of Surrey
Bowen, Eliza, Croydon
Bowtell, Thomas, of Deptford, *d* 1822

NEXT OF KIN. 9

Bourne, Elizabeth ⎫
" Lucy ⎬ all lived near
" Sophia ⎬ Enfield
" Charlotte ⎭
Bolton, Frances, Liverpool, *d* 1866
Booker, George, of Liverpool, *d* 1866
Borthwick, Walter, of London 1720
Brown, John, native of Notts
Bolcherly, Mr., living 1842
Boaring, John, of Yorkshire
Bownas, John, seaman, M S
Bodicote, John, *d* 1783—1796
Bottom, Hannah, *o'wise* Strudwick
Boast, William, left Yorkshire 1855
Boyle, A., master-mariner 1864
Bolton, Robert, of London 1828
Bodkin, Joseph, *otherwise* Jeffries
" Ann, *otherwise* Jeffries
Boyse, Rev. Richard, Wexford, *d* 1864
Bond, Elizabeth ⎫
" Mary ⎬ brothers and sisters all living in 1800
" Sarah ⎬
" William ⎭
Bonnery, John, seaman, *d* 1812
Bonus, James, clothier, London
Boon, Maria, *frmly* Price
Booth, Jeremiah, of Croydon, *d* 1805
" Samuel, *d* in America
" Sarah, *frmly* Whitaker
Boothe, James, surgeon, 12th Regt
Bostock, Sarah, *frmly* Yeomans, *d* 1833
Bosville, Margaret, of Hammersmith
Bouchier, Rev. Richd., of Berkshire
Boucher, Sarah E., *d* abroad 1825
Boughton, Edwd. of Gloucester, *d* 1830
Bourn, Aaron, of Wolverhampton
Bourne, Elz'th *o'wise* Lipscombe, 1808
" Elzbth., ⎫ chil. of George B.
" Lucy, ⎬ of Enfield, Midx.
" Charl'te ⎭ who *d* 1746
Bourke, John, of Liverpool
Bourton, Sarah, *o'wise* Concanen
Bowater, John, of Woolwich, Kent
Bowber, John, *mar* Mary Jones 1802
Bowen, Rev. Thos. of London, *d* 1800
" Elzbth., Upcot, Herts
Bowers, William, seaman, Navy
" W. H., seaman, M S, *d* 1837
Bowes, George, agent, Chelsea
Bowler, Charles, of Harmondsworth
Bowman, Mary, Hackney, *d* 1861
" John, seaman, M S
Bowyer, Hannah, *w*, London, *d* 1814
Bourn, Sam'l, of Marylebone, *d* 1834
Box, John, of Woolwich, *d* 1827
Boyce, Charles, seaman, *d* 1850

Boyd, Cathcart, of Edinburgh, 1810
" John, *d* in Wales 1826
" John A., *d* at Bayswater 1858
" Robert, quartermaster R N
" Thomas, *d* at Hull 1808
" William, surgeon R N, *d* 1809
" William C., *d* in India
Boyter, Alexander, seaman, 1793
Boyton, Michael, of Dover
" William, Lieut., *d* in India
Boswell, Eleanor, of Newington
Bruce, Alexander, of Edinburgh
Broad, Maria, *d* Middlesex 1867
Brown, Robert, of Ratcliff
Bryan, Jane, *d* Devonport 1866
Brown, Mary Ann, *frmly* Ekin
Brown, Margaret, wife of Ebenezer
Brown, Edward Johnson
Briggs, John G., *d* 1868
Brent Francis, *d* Surrey
Brown, Martin, merchant, *d* 1711
Brewster Samuel
Bromley, James, of Staffordshire
Brightwell, Thomas, *d* London
" Benjamin, *d* London
Briscoe, William, of Herts
Bradshaw, Ellerker, of Yorkshire
Brewer, Mary, *d* Middlesex
Bridgman, Elizabeth, *d* Gloucester
Brooks, Jeremiah, *d* Middlesex
Brock, Philip, of London
Brent, Humphrey, of Somerset
Bright, Mary, *o'wise* Bull
Brunsden, Elizabeth, *o'wise* Burgess
Brethengham, Thomas, of Norfolk
Brimble, Albertus, *d* Ely 1773
Browning, Frederick, *d* London
Brighton, Mary, of Clapham
Brooke, Samuel, of Kent
Browning, John, of Chelsea
Bromley, William, of Warwickshire
Brain, John, of Lancashire
Brown, Thomas, of Somerset
Brown, Margaret, *d* Middlesex
Bridges, Ann, of Hampshire
Bradley, Joseph, of Hampshire
Bridgen, William, of Shropshire
Broughton, John, of Surrey
Bradley, Ralph, of Durham
Brown, John, of Suffolk
Brown, William, of Hampshire
Bradley, Joseph, of Lincolnshire
Branham, John, of Yorkshire
Brander, Alexander, *d* London
Broadment, Katherine
Brown, Margaret, *d* London 1782

GENERAL INDEX.

Brown, Francis, Leicester, d 1814
Braithwaite, Mary, frmly Griffith
Bryant, Ann, frmly Russell
Brown, Thomas, seaman, E I C S
" John, quartermaster, E I C S
" Thomas, tailor, London
Brand, Mrs. Ann Eliza
Bridges, Edmond, of London 1754
Bryan, Jane, frmly Hayes
" John, gunner R N, d 1830
" John ⎫ formerly of coun-
" Lawrence ⎭ ty of Wexford
Brown, Charles, Hackney, d 1849
Bradbury, Chas., Manchester d 1861
Broster, Enock, Lancaster, d 1854
" Emma, Lancaster, d 1866
Brough, Letitia, of Bayswater
Breacher, William, living 1750
Brooks, James, of Oxford
Brown, Elzbth., ⎫ children of Wm.,
" Ann, ⎭ of Liverpool, 1825
Broughton, Elizabeth, of Norwich
Brodrick, Alesia, daughter of James
Bray, Michael, of London 1813
Brown, Elizabeth, o'wise Lavis
Browning, James, London, d 1861
Bradshaw, Peter, Lancashire, d 1857
Brown, George, of Willesden
" Adam, of Edinburgh
Brakin, Harris Carr, staff-surgeon
Brown, Eliza Ellen, sister of Louisa
Bridges, William, of Wilts
Bradley, William O., d Durham 1860
Brice, Mary, living 1840
Bryant, Ann, of Lenham, Kent
" Mr., of Cambridge
Broome, Thomas, of Stratford, Essex
Brown, Henrietta E., d 1838
Brooks, James, of Oxford
Bradley, Joseph, of Ashbourne
Brime, Charles ⎫ living from 1750-80
Brice Thomas ⎭
Breeze, H., d abroad 1865
Brown, Charles, d Middlesex 1849
Brooks, Charles J., of Oxford Street 1835
Bruce, J. M., d abroad 1868
Brown, Thos. Edward, London, 1809
Browne, Rev. Thomas, d 1868
Brown, Catherine, frmly Williams
Brown, Eliza Ellen, o'wise Tennent
Brady, Jane ⎫ of Paddington or
" Mary Ann ⎭ Marylebone
Bruce, Mary Ann, London
Brealey, John, d Middlesex 1852
Brereton, Margaret, o'wise Harrison

Brereton, Randall
Bradshaw, Charlotte, o'wise Willats
Brealey, Albert, of London
Bradford, Alex., native of Ireland
Bradfield, Mary, of Glasgow, 1793
Bradley, Thos. H., d in America 1826
" William, seaman, Navy
Bradshaw, John, Capt., d London
" William, d abroad 1812
Bracken, John, of London
Bragg, Daniel, of London
Braid, Robert, seaman, 1793
Braine, Francis, of Swansea, d 1834
Brake, Dan. Excise Officer, Stockport
Brameld, George, farmer, Yorkshire
Brand, Ebenezer, d Bedford 1823
Brandt, John, seaman, M S
Branigan, James D., d abroad 1860
Brayfield, Esther, of Clapham, 1772
Brayn, Joseph, d Greenwich 1809
Breithamp, Christopher, d India
Bremar, John ⎫
" Francis ⎬ children of John
" Henry ⎬ of Kensington,
" Anna ⎭ b 1780-90
" Anna, o'wise Young, d 1859
" Henry, d in America
Breman, James, d London 1848
" John, of Ireland, d abroad
Brett, Mary, d at Peckham 1836
Brewer, James T., mariner, d abroad
" Rebecca, London 1810
Briant, Charles, of Tattenden, Berks
Brickenden, Eleanor, o'wise Davies
Brickwood, Mary, o'wise Edgar
Bridgetower, Mary, d abroad 1807
Briggs, James, mariner, d 1839
Bright, Mary, Abingdon, d 1834
Brissington, John, d in N. America
Bristow, Ann, w Hounslow, Middlesex
" Henry, of Hersham
" George, Capt., d 1828
Broadbelt, Rev. Campbell
Broadhurst, Richard ⎫ of London
" William ⎭ about 1795
Brock John, d in India 1835
Brooke, Letitia, frmly Harding, d 1823
Brooker, Elizabeth, d Pimlico 1861
Brooks, Benjamin, of Portsmouth
" Elizabeth ⎫ of London 1810
" John ⎭
" James, of Oxford
" Sydney, of London 1788
Broomes, Thomas J, d in India
Broughton, Henry, d abroad 1807
Bromley, James, of Glascow, d 1795

Bromley, Benjamin ⎫
" Henry ⎬ uncles of Benj.
" Jeremiah ⎭ Pryce
Brown, Agnes, *frmly* McWhinnie
" Ebenezer, of Edinburgh
" George, seaman M S
" Harriett E., *d* 1838
" Henry B, of Dover
" James, of Lond.& Manchest'r
" James, baker, London 1827
" James, seaman M. S
" Jane, *frmly* Spencer
" John, seaman M S
" John, of Bermondsey, Surrey
" Joseph, gunner M. S
" Maria, *d* 1831
" Margaret, Hackney Road
" Margaret, *d* New York
" Margaretta S., London 1841
" Mary A., Kensington
" Mary, *dau.* of Wm. of London
" Peter, *d* at sea 1843
" Ralph, merchant, *d* abroad
" Samuel, seaman M S
" Samuel, of Kensington
" Sarah Mrs., *d* London 1815
" Rev. Stephen W., *d* 1832
" Thomas, *d* Exeter 1851
" Thomas, of Pintol, Devon
" Thomas, seaman M S
" Thomas, of London
" Thomas, *d* Chepstow 1844
" William, seaman M S
" William, of Stepney, *d* 1829
" William, mariner Navy
" William, of Devonshire
" William, farmer, Derby *d* 1795
Browne, Sir Anthony, living 1540
" Dr. of 52d Regt. Foot
" John, of Brodden, *d* 1835
Brunt, John, of London
Brunet, John, seaman M S
Bryan, Mary, Peckham, 1781
" Frances, *o'wise* Keene, *d* 1819
Bryant, Rob't, jeweler, Camden Town
Bryer, John, *d* in London
Brydges, Edmund, of Strand, 1753
Brashier, Wm. of Birmingham, 1832
Braund, Alice, *d* 1802
Breacher, William, living 1750
Bucke, W H., went abroad 1860
Bushe, Kendal
Burton, Lieut. R. W. J.
Butler, Johanna, of Hastings.
Budd, Mary, *d* Herts 1720
Bull, Martha, of Berkshire

Burton, Rev. L. of Brackley
Butler, Nicholas, of London
Burder, Thomas, of London
Bush, James, of Kent
Burgoyne, William, of London
Butler, William, of Carnarvon
Burrough, Richard
Burrough, Robert
Bull, Mary, *frmly* Bright
Burgess, William, of Wilts
Buckeridge, Lewis, of Herts
Bunting, Tomlinson, of York
Bunting, Elizabeth, of Durham
Burney, Edward, of Wrexham
Burrough, James, of Chelsea
Burnell, Darcy, of Notts
Butler, Joseph, of Abingdon
Burton, Bartholomew, *d* London
Bushell Thomas, of Kent
Burleigh, Samuel, of Durham
Butler, James, *d* Surrey
Burton, Richard, of Wakefield
Bulmer, Christopher, of Yorkshire
Burroughs, William, of Wilts
Buchinger, John, of London
Burcham, William, *d* Liverpool
Burns, Jane, of Edinburgh
Burbey, Richard, of London
Buad, Mary, of Wiltshire
Button, John, of Chippenham 1820
Burdimore, Elizabeth
Bull, Charles, of Whitechapel 1838
Burton, Mary, Clapham, *d* 1868
Burgh, Eliza
Burgh, Matthew T., *d* Cheltenham
Buttersby, J., *d* abroad 1868
Buckingham, Robert, *d* Cheltenham
Buckingham, Philip
Butler, Edward, saddler
Bull, Eleanor ⎫
Bull, Eliza ⎬ of Brompton 1862
Butcher, John, of Prittlewell
Bull, James, of Market Deeping
Burnham, John D., native of Hull
Burkhardt, Christian, of Carlsruhe
Bull, Joseph S., *d* London 1837
" William, civil engineer 1836
Burton, James Richard, law stationer
Buckley, Edmond, Merioneth, *d* 1867
Burnett, Colonel John, E I C S
" Captain C. J., *d* abroad
Burrell, William, *d* abroad 1840
Bulcraig, Hannah, Durham, *d* 1864
Burton, Mary, Middlesex, *d* 1865
Butt, Elizabeth E. A., of Calne
Burden George, *d* Essex 1832

Burrows, John
Butts, Rev. Eyton, Ireland, d 1779
Buckenden, Eleanor, o'wise Davies
Buckney, David
Burslem, James S., of Surrey
Bury, John, left Lond. as a cabin boy
Butler, Jane, formerly Sidden
Burchmore, Elizabeth, of Walworth 1861
Burton, Hannah, frmly Blay, d 1852
Burdy, S., of Liverpool 1839
Burman, Isaac, son of Richard
Burbey, Richard, London, d 1861
Bunbury, W. H. Lieut. Col., d 1833
Bunn, Sarah, Lichfield, d 1831
Bunyan, Elbth., of Shoreditch, d 1834
Burchett, —, frmly of London
" Benj., of Shadwell 1770
Burcham Robert, of Ipswich, d 1814
Burchall, John, of Wilts, b 1715
Burch, Richard, of Cheshire
Burdell, Emma, d New York 1862
Burham, Robert, seaman, d 1839
Burke, Jane J., d at Bath
" Olivia, o'wise Cain
Burn, Georgina, d abroad
Burns, Elizabeth, d at Hoxton
" John, d India 1806
" George, d abroad
" Henry, seaman M S
" John, seaman M S
Burnett, Lilias, Montrose, N B
" Robert, d abroad 1861
Burgess, Peter, of Holland, 1730
Burrell, Samuel, of Chelsea
" Thomas, of Steyning
" Jane, o'wise Marshall
" William, of Durham, d 1836
Burridge, Sarah, frmly Amory, d 1816
" John, Ensign, d India
Burroughs, Mary, o'wise Batho
" Hannah ⎫
" Sarah ⎪ sisters and
" Daniel ⎬ brothers of
" Nathaniel ⎪ Mary Burroughs, o'wise
" Richard ⎪ Batho, of
" Thomas ⎪ Shropshire.
" William ⎭
Burrow, James, of Yorkshire
Burrows, Ann J., o'wise Roberts
" Dennis
" Edwd. T. ⎫ ch of Dennis B.
" Eropa P. ⎪ who marr'd H.
" Ann P. ⎬ Pitman, at
" Mary A. C. ⎪ Gloucest'r,1726
" Wm. P. ⎭

Burt, James, of Winfield, Sussex
" James, surgeon Army
" William, seaman Navy
Burton, Elzbth, Birmingham d 1859
" Hannah, of St. John's Wood
" Henrietta, o'wise Cutters
" Richard, of Newington
" Philip, of London 1800
Bury, J., surgeon Army
Bussell, Agnes
" Ellen
" Frances Louisa
" John Garratt
" Louisa Jacune
" Lenox
" Mary
" Mary Yates
" William
" William M.
Bussey, Ann, d at Chelsea
Buswell, John, of Westminster, d 1818
Butler, Sarah, frmly Scott, d 1860
" Thomas, of London 1757
" Samuel, master mariner
" Ann, d London
" Mrs. H. H. of Clapham 1834
" Edward, seaman M S
" Nicholas, d London 1864
" Francis, of Marylebone
Butter, Jane, frmly Wooley, d 1803
Butterfield, Catherine, Durham
Buxton, Hannah, frmly Blay, d 1852
Bye, Samuel, seaman Navy
Bynon, Elzbth, of Glamorgan, d 1805
Bystrom, William, seaman M S
Bywater, George, of London, d 1840
Byne, Francis B. d Cork 1866
Byde, Barbara, d 1715
Byerley, Elizabeth, d Middlesex
Bylett, Susannah, of Sunderland
Byers, Peter, of Northumberland.

C

Carlan, George, of Lanarkshire
Caley, Helena Johanna
Carter, Mary, d Herts, 1869
Carter Families
Calder, Mary, o'wise Elmslie
Cary, William Frederick
Carter, Caroline, d Sussex 1865
Carter, William ⎫
Carter, Edward ⎬ of Clerkenwell
Caines, George, d Liverpool 1869
Callaway, Stephen, of Wilts
Cary, John, of Somerset

Carter, Humphrey, of Hereford
Card, Andrew, of Middlesex
Carter, Robert, of Middlesex
Campion, Mary, *o'wise* Green
Canning, Francis, of Warwick
Campbell, Sarah, *d* abroad
Carter, Frances, *d* Essex
Cary, Richard, of Oxford
Carey, John, of Glo'stershire
Cadogan, Scirefind, of Yorkshire
Cantram, Mary, *d* Suffolk
Cahill, Edward, *d* Middlesex
Caldwell, Tracey, of Hereford
Cargill, Daniel, of Aberdeen
Casson, Elizabeth of London
Carter, Thomas, of Middlesex
Cameron, Major Donald, *d* 1797
Camps, Joseph, of Norfolk
Cantwell, Joseph, of Middlesex
Carrington, B. of Surrey
Carroll, Denis, *d* Chelsea 1790
Cassuas, Michael, of London 1840
Card, John, of London 1824
Campbell, Major John, 76th Regt.
Campbell, Barbara S. Edinburgh
Campbell, Isabella, *d* Peebles 1867
Carmichael, Alex., *d* abroad 1854
Carleton, Mary
Carter, John S. C. surgeon, *d* 1851
Canning, Mr. G. of Stockwell
Carlisle, Christopher, clerk
Campbell, Marianne, *o'wise* Walters
Campion, Amelia M., *o'wise* Lloyd
Campbell, John A., formerly of Jamaica
Carpenter, Daniel, of Horningham
Carmichael, Dugald, *d* India
Carrol, Mrs., *w*, York 1768
Castle, Robert } of Kingston-upon
" Jane } Hull
Capper, Elizabeth, *d* Kensington
Catermole, John, *d* Portsea 1798
Carnan, Mary A. *w*, London, *d* 1863
Cattell, William, of Southwark
Cain, Olivia, *frmly* Burke
Cave, Joseph, of Luton, Beds
Cartes, Mary Ann, *dau.* of Maria
Capp, William Hugh
Capron, Richard, of Dalston
Calderhead, John, native of Edinboro'
Callaghan, Francis, native of Ireland
" Peter } brothers of
" Patrick } Francis, of
" James } Cavan, Ireland
" Thomas }

Carter, Thos. W., Maidstone, *d* 1838
Campbell, Major K., *d* in India
Cain, Mary, of Torkvill
Capon, Jane, Yarmouth 1841
Carr, Henry, *d* Middlesex 1860.
Carter, John, of Camberwell 1838
Carnley, Daniel, of London
Cabil, John, draper, Kingsland
Cahil, Elizabeth, of Edmonton
Caldicott, Richard, of Lincoln, *d* 1862
Callum, Miss, *d* Ramsgate 1859
Came, Barbara, *frmly* Opie, *d* 1727
Cameron, Ann, Bath
" Duncan, of Scotland 1832
" John, *d* London 1814
" John, of Scotch Regt. 1749
Cambridge, Elzbth, of Glo'stershire
Camfield, Elizabeth, *frmly* Thurley
Campbell, Agnes, of Ayrshire 1803
" Adyne
" Alexander, *d* India 1783
" Colin, Perthshire, *d* 1827
" Caroline, of Ayrshire 1803
" Duncan, *d* abroad 1852
" Daniel, seaman
" E. C. Lieut. *d* abroad 1820
" H.F. Ensign, *d* abroad 1824
" John, *d* Birmingham 1820
" John P. Lieut. R N
" Maria, *frmly* Wilson
" Mary
" N. S. surgeon 56th Regt.
" Patrick, of Ayrshire, 1803
" Peter, steward M S
" Robert B. Captain R N
" W. F. of Brompton, Midx.
Campe, John, clerk London
Camper, James, of Rochford, Essex
Cannell, Elizabeth, of Essex
Canning, John, mariner, *d* 1840
Canning, William, of Quendon, Essex
Canochan, Margaret, of Baltimore
Caplen, James, quartermaster Army
Canter, John B. of Bristol, *d* 1862
Card, John, seaman Navy
Carey, Elizabeth, of London 1730-90
Carman, Thomas, of Kent, *d*, 1830
Carmichael, John, *d* abroad 1781
" T. Lieut. *d* 1819
Carpau, Basil, *d* at Edmonton
Carpenter, Ann P. }
" Edward } of London 1810
" John P. }
" J. of Greenwich, *d* abd.
" Henry, of London, *d* 1837
" Nathaniel, *d* America 1778

Carpenter, Coryndoa ⎫ relatives of
" Bushrod ⎬ Dr. Nathaniel
" Nathan'l ⎪ C. who d in
" Wm. F. ⎭ America 1778
Carr, Jane, w, Guernsey
" Jane, of Southend, Essex
" John, d Ratcliff
Carroll, W. seaman Navy
" Anthony, d in India
Carry, Michael, d South America
Carston, Jacob, of Middlesex d 1848
Carter, Mrs. Ann, of Middlesex, 1830
" Carolina, o'wise Mooby
" Henry, of London, d 1837
" Isaac, seaman, M S
" John, of Durham, d 1835
" John, farmer, Yorkshire
" John, Mariner M S
" John, of Gloucester, d 1802
" Joshua, of Whitechapel 1800
" Samuel, of London 1800
" Susannah, of Bloomsbury
Cartwright, Thomas, of London
Carver, George, of Peckham, d 1847
Case, Richard, of Worcestersh, d 1767
" William, of Willoughby, d 1817
Cass, J., d abroad 1863
Cassin, Peter M., d India 1810
Castiron, Thomas, d abroad
Caston, Mary, of London, d 1828
Castle, Mary, of Wapping
Castry, John, d abroad 1847
Cator, Thomas, of London
Child, George, of Bristol
Cheer, James, of Bucks, d 1869
Chapman, Mary E., frmly Playle
Church, John B., of London 1834
Chambers, Dorothy
" Simon
Chadwick, Robert, d Kent
Charie, James, of London
Cheesebrough, Chris., of London
Challen, Stephen, of Sussex
Cheek, Robert, of Essex
Chamberlain, Eliza, of Chester
Chichester, John, d America
Chapman, Elizabeth, d London
Cheeseman, Alice, frmly Draper
Church, Richard, d Bombay
Choak, Ellen A., d Stepney 1866
Chapman, Thomas, of Liddington
Cheyney, Levin ⎫
" William ⎬ related to Ann
" James ⎪ Levin, London
" George ⎪ 1756
" Ann ⎭

Chequers, Daniel, of Lockeridge
Cherry, Matthew ⎱ of Northampton-
" Bridget ⎰ shire
Cheeseman, Thos. of Walworth, d, 1833
Chambre, Major Alan, Twickenham
Chiene, John, d abroad 1837
Champion, James Henry
Charles, Thomas, of Devon 1822
Chitty, Philip, d Tasmania 1840
Charleton, Mrs., of Regent's Park
Cheeseman, John ⎫ brothers and
" William ⎬ sisters of
" Mary ⎪ Thomas, who
" Frances ⎭ d 1833
Charnock, Miss, of Westbourne Grove
Chrisman, George, corn merchant
Chambers, Richard, of Lincoln 1775
Chapman, Mary, d 1838
Church, Janetta, of Wimpole Street
Charters, Benjamin, London 1805
Chifney, Sarah Mary
Chittock, Wm., d Westminster 1865
Chapman, Jane
Chalmers, Robt., of Vauxhall 1827-37
Chambers, Thos., of Hackney Road
Cheek, Solomon, of Westminster
Chadwick, Wm., of Plymouth 1845
Chalk, James, of London 1823
Chalmers, John, of Edinburgh 1796
" Mary, of Berkshire
" John, quart.mast. E I C S
" James, of Perth 1810
Challet, Ann, o'wise Crookshank
Challoner, William, of Yorkshire
Chamberlayne, Alice, of Hadfield
Chambers, Matthew, seaman, Navy
" Thomas A., d abroad
Chamness, Js. of Twickenham, d 1802
Champion, Alex., of London 1800
Channing, T., d abroad 1851
Chapman, Mary, o'wise Davis
" Joseph, Capt. 42nd Regt.
" Joyce, Mrs., of Lambeth
" Elzth. of Walworth, d 1837
" Geo., shipwright, Portsea
Charles, Richard, of Dublin
Charleton, Mat. N'thumberland 1862
Chatfield, W. B., son of Rev. John C.
Chatterton, Esther, London 1787
" James, of London 1750
Chauncey, William, d 1765
" Richd. of London 1750-80
Cheese, Thos., of Bodenham, d 1836
Cherriman, Gregore, d India
Chesney, Alex., victualler, Liverpool
Chesterfield, Robt. of Devon, d 1854

NEXT OF KIN. 15

Chorus, Maria A. J., *d* Chelsea 1822
Chorley, John, draper, London 1754
Chilman, Robert, of Paris
Chrichton, Jas. mast. mariner, *d* 1838
Christie, John, seaman M S
" James, *d* Southwark
Christmas, Mary, *frmly* Gostelow
Cheyne, Elizabeth, *frmly* Bletso 1790
Church, William, *d* India 1795
Churchill, John, mariner
" Thos., of Chertsey, *d* 1782
" Ann, *w* of Thomas
" Elizab'th, mother of Thos.
" Dorothy, half-sist. of Thos.
Churchman, John, of London 1680-8
Clarke, Mary Jane
" James, of Stepney
Clark, John, *m* C. Laundry
Clapperton, James, of Dysart
Clark, Sarah, *o'wise* Knowler
Clifford, Rev. Edward, *d* Sussex
Clarke, John, of Cockermouth
Clark, Ann, of Rochester
Clapham, Jolly, *d* India
Clayton, Jonathan, *d* Middlesex
Clifford, Loftus, of Mansfield
Clement, John, of Glamorgan
Clarke, John, of West Wycombe
Clinton, John, of London 1815
Clarke, Mich'l, Warwickshire, *d* 1865
" Hannah, *frmly* Huskins
Clark, John, married M. S. King
" James, of Stepney
" Richard, of London
" Thomas, of Tooting
" William, London 1836
" Benj., of Kingston, Surrey
" Margaret, Clifton
" George, of Norfolk
Cluley, John, of Moxley 1863
Clay, Reginald G. M. } sons of
" William T. M. } K. M. Clay
Cliquet, R. E. Celestine
Clemens, ——, *d* abroad 1863
Clinton, James, *d* Cheltenham
Clegg, Thomas, of Wakefield
Clowes, William, Henley, surgeon
Clark, James, son of Edward
Clement, Mary } natives of
" Ann } Herefordshire
Clifford, Susan C. } grandchildren
" Alice C. } of George
Clark, Louisa, formerly Wright
" Thomas, *d* Sunderland 1864
" Julia, *o'wise* Sullivan
" James, of Stepney

Clifford, Thomas, of Walworth
" Susan }
" Maria } children of
" John } Thomas
" Selina }
Claer, Jas., of Leatherhead, *d* 1814
Claggett, Grace, *d* 1807
Clark, Ann, *o'wise* Smith, *d* 1823
" Alexander, mariner, *d* 1832
" Charles B., of Pembrokeshire
" Fred'ck, Lieut-Col., *d* abroad
" Hannah, Mrs.
" Jane, of Portsmouth 1810
" John, of London 1800
" Joseph, of Peterborough 1819
" Julia, *d* New York
" Margaret, *d* London 1833
" Mary, *d* America
" Mich'l M., Chelsea pensioner
" Paulina, lady's-maid
" Sarah, Lambeth, *d* 1819
" Sarah, Bristol, *d* 1786
" Sarah, of Newington, Surrey
" Thomas, attorney, London
" Thomas, *d* at Greenwich
" Thomas, *d* at Sunderland 1864
" Thomas, schoolmaster, *d* 1864
" William, of London 1823
" William, of Blackfriars 1804
" Mary, of Godstone, *d* 1839
" James }
" Samuel } brothers & sisters
" Henrietta } living in London
" Hester J. } about 1804
" Jane V. }
Clarke, Ann, of Gloster
" Ann, *frmly* Axtell, *d* 1810
" Ann, *frmly* Griffith, *d* 1860
" Elizabeth, Chislehurst, Kent
" Lieut. E., *d* in India
" James } seamen M S
" John }
" John, of Wisbeach, *d* 1748
" Maria A. of Marylebone, *d* 1850
" Mary, *d* in London
" Patrick, surgeon R N, *d* 1825
" Susannah, London, *d* 1808
" Thomas, *d* in Durham 1864
" Thomas, marine Navy, *d* 1813
" Thomas, Army surgeon
" Thomas, hairdres'r, Norwich
" Thomas, Worcester, *d* 1826
" James } descendants of
" Richard } Meece Beau-
" Meece B. } champ, W. Indies
" Elzbth. } and living in 1782

Clarke, W. J., servant, *d* 1840
Clarkington, Chas. photographic art.
Clarkson, David, of Yorksh., *d* 1827
" Sarah, York, *d* 1858
Clary, John, native of Ireland
Clay, Ann ⎫ children of Geo. C.,
" Elzbth. ⎬ of Rotherithe,
" Susanna ⎭ living 1825
" Martha, Loughton, *d* 1803
Claydon, Rich., of Cropedy, Oxford
Clayton, Elzb., native of Newcastle
Clegg, Edmund B., of Salford, *d* 1859
Clements, Sarah K., *d* 1815
Cleveland, Mary II., of Islington
" Mary M, Bath, *d* 1846
Clunes, Rich., Lieut., *d* abroad 1819
Coldstream, John, living 1820
Collins, John, native of Mayo
Cottrill, Wm., *frmly* of Worcester
Coles, Ann, *o'wise* Inglis
Cornish, Gertrude, *d* Surrey 1869
Cope, Francis, of Staffordshire
Cooper, Rebecca, *frmly* Thornby
Colbach, ——, married H. Sherwood
Collinridge, Augustus, of Brompton
Connor, Louisa, of Hampstead Road
Colley, James, of Somerset
Compton, Thomas, of Somerset
Couchman, Edward, of Cranbrooke
Coffins, Thomas, mariner
Coates, John, of Yorkshire
Cook, John, of London
Cox, Samuel, of Herts
Coomes, Joshua, of London
Colson, Robert, of Bombay
Colston, John, of Suffolk
Cook, Thomas, of Sussex
Corp, Ann, *d* Bristol
Cooper, John, of London
Coates, Charles, of Gloucestershire
Copley, Mary G., *o'wise* Brown
Cooke, Joseph, of London
Conron, Arthur, *d* Middlesex
Cooper, John, *d* Middlesex
Collins, Treby, *d* London
Cowell, Jane, *d* Middlesex
Cotterell, John, of Liverpool
Cockell, Mary, of Yorkshire
Cooper, William, of Antigua
Cooke, Elizabeth, *frmly* Wilkinson
Cooksey, Holland, of Worcestershire
Corbin, William, of Flintshire
Court, Samuel, of Essex
Cock, Mary, *d* Surrey 1839
Cole, John, *d* Surrey
Cook, Anna M., *d* Middlesex

Cooke, Joseph, *d* Middlesex
Cooper, George, of Witney
Coupar, Alexander, of Scotland
Cox, John, *d* Ipswich 1837
Cock, Ambrose, of Shadwell 1827
" John
" Deane
" Thomas
Cole, Frederick L., London 1844
Coney, Frederick, of Paris 1847
Cottle, Richard John, of London 1825
Conway, Henry, of Marlborough
Cooper, Thomas, *d* Middlesex 1867
Coates, Richard, *d* Croydon 1868.
Collins, Mary
Corbett, Fred. A., of Birmingham
Corney, J. W., *d* abroad 1866
Collingwood, Mrs. Eliza, Charlton
Cook, Matilda, of Gloucestershire
Coates, Jane, of Ripon
Cookes, John, of Barnes
Cox, Richard, of Shepherd's Market
Connell, Daniel
Cotton, John, of Deptford
Cowell, Duncan, mariner
Cowen, Duncan, seaman M S
Cordy, Thomasine, of Suffolk 1796
Coupar, Andrew, surgeon
Conolly, Mary, of Dublin
Cohen, Hester, of Manchester
Cooper, James, *d* Pendleton
Costin, Thomas, of Berkhampstead
Cowling, Edward, of Shoreditch
Coston, Mr. ⎫ of Dalston 1823-24
" Mrs. ⎭
Collins, M., stockbroker 1824
Colley, Emma, *dau* of Ann
Cody, Richard ⎫ of Ballycurren
" John ⎭
Collett, Susannah, Luton
Cox, Catherine, Wilts, *d* 1865-6
Collins, Dennis, R H Artillery,*d* abd
Coulthard, Edward, *d* London 1864
Cousens, William, of Yorkshire
Cook, Jemima, of Somerset
Collins, William, of Antigua
Coupland, Agnes, *o'wise* Whitbrook
Cooper, George, of California 1856
Coles, Daniel
Copping, David K.,Bolesdale,Suffolk
Cook, Sarah, *frmly* Leighton
Collins, Daniel, of Hinton, Suffolk
" Sarah, of Chelsea
Cooke, George, *d* Middlesex
Coalpeper, Jane, of Devonshire
Coalman, Mary, Hanwell

Collins, Patrick, Brighton, *d* 1866
" John, Armagh, *d* 1860
Coleman, Herbert, son of Elizabeth
Cooper, Saml., *d* North Walsham 1861
Collins, Eliza, of Maidstone
Connell, A., quartermaster, *d* India
Coates, Mr. W., of Regent's Park 1859
Coape, Henry Coe
" James
Cousins, George
Colquhoun, Archibald Yorkshire
Coombs, Mary, of Blackwater
Constable, William
Collins, James
Comber, Thos., Cambridge, *d* 1829
Cowley, Mary, *d* Cheltenham 1865
Cochrane, Wm. S., of Islington 1836
Cox, William Matthew
Collett, Frederick, of Ipswich
Cook, Ann Maria, Middlesex 1858
Cox, E., lived at Harrow
Corney, Geo. W., of the R Navy
Cole, John W., of Bayswater
Cope, Thomas, of Staffordshire
Cox, Philip, brewer 1832
Coombe, Francis, of Herts, *d* 1641
" Barbara, *frmly* Ewer
" Ann, *frmly* Greenhill
Cobb, Charles, of London, *d* 1810
" Susannah, *frmly* Norton
Cocke, Sarah, London
" Captain Richard, *d* India
Cocker, Lieut. F. W., *d* 1827
Cockerill, Alice, Queenhithe 1782
Cockerill, Joseph, of North Shields
Cockburn, Mr., *d* abroad 1863
Cochrane, Peter, *d* London 1825
Coane, Lieut. Montgomery, *d* 1806
Coghlan, Lieut. James, Army 1821
Coke, Christopher, merchant, 1709
Colburn, William, *d* India 1852
Cole, Hannah, *w* of John
" Samuel, seaman M S
" Arthur, H. E I C S, *d* India
" William R., of Blackwall
Colebatch, M., of Lower Bellingham
Colebeck, Elimes, *d* at Hayes 1798
Colgate, John, of Tunbridge
Colles, Lieut. William, *d* Ireland, 1825
Collier, Benjamin, *d* in India
" Penelope, Maidenhead, *d* 1860
" Thomas C., traveller, *d* 1838
" Wm., of Knightsbridge 1835
Collingwood, John, of Rotherhithe
Collington, Nathaniel, *d* in America
Collings, Capt. Elias, *d* India

Collingridge, Ensign Samuel, *d* India
Collins, Charles, of London
" Charles, seaman M S
" Benjamin, son of Hannah
" Ann, *o'wise* Ward
" Jane, *frmly* Beard
" Mary, *frmly* Mayo, *d* 1863
" Robert, of London
" Sophia, Richmond, *d* 1815
" Rev. William, of Hereford
" Henry ⎱ of Yeovil, Somer-
" Philip ⎰ set, 1800
Collis, George, *d* abroad 1838
Collyer, Thomas, servant
" Joseph, of London, 1600-90
Colson, Wm., seaman M S, *d* 1808
Comber, Ann, Brentford, 1800-6
Compton, William, *m* J. Dave 1785
" Wm., of Northampton 1795
Combrune, Louisa, *d* 1834
Comyn, James, of London 1752
Condie, John, of Glasgow, *d* 1860
Concanen, Sarah, *frmly* Bourton *d* 1861
Condie, John, of Burnfoot, N B
Conning, Wm., of Glasserton, N B
" Wm, *d* London about 1780
Conner, Lieut. Richard H., R N
Connop, Newel, of Enfield 1800
Conollys, Mary, of Dublin
Conrad, Christopher, seaman
Constantine, J., of London, *d* 1799
Connor, James H., *d* in America
Conway, Susannah, *w*, Bloomsbury 1836
Cook, Ann, *d* London 1837
" Charlotte, of Bloxham, Oxford
" Charles A., tailor, Hertford
" Edward, of Haversham
" Frances, Shadwell
" George, purser Navy, *d* 1817
" Jno., of Tottenham-court Road
" Lieut.-col. John W.
" Sarah, of London 1802
" Elizabeth ⎱ of Suffolk, *d* in
" John ⎰ London
" George, of London 1763-91
" Johana, of London, 1722-91
Cooke, Jane, of Shoreham
" Joseph, of Bow, Middlesex
" Mary, Marylebone
" Mary, of Horsham, Sussex
" Nancy, *dau* of Mary
Cookson, Lieut. G. P., *d* abroad 1811
Coombe, Ann, *m* R. Evered
" William, of London 1811
Coombs, Hester, Somerset, *d* 1800

GENERAL INDEX.

Coombs, Capt. John, d India
Cooper, Frances, York, d 1803
" George, of Skelton
" John, of London
" Nicholas, seaman M S
" Rachael, Whitechapel
" Sarah, Dover, d 1820
" William P., d 1845
" William, of Kingston, d 1861
Coopley, James, of Bristol, d 1851
Coote, Charles E., of Bristol 1853
Copland, Thomason, Westminster
Cope, Richard ⎫ brothers and sisters
" Joseph ⎬ of James C., of
" Ann ⎬ Wadeby, Stafford-
" Maria ⎭ shire
Corbett, George, Barrister, 1752
Cork, Mary, frmly Langstoth
Cornfute, James, of Perth 1810
Cornelius, Margaret, b 1766 d 1842
Corner, Lieut. Richard B., R N
Cornelia, Peter, of New York
Cornish, William B., of Exeter
" Benjamin
" Daniel
" Benjamin ⎫ children of Ben-
" Charles ⎬ jamin and
" Mary ⎬ grandchildren
" William ⎭ of Daniel
" Sarah, frmly Abbott
Corser, Thomas, d New Zealand
Corre, Sarah, d Marylebone
Coster, Francis, mariner M S
Coston, Angelina, of Pentonville
Cottain, Sarah, o'wise Burroughs
Cotton, Nathaniel, chaplain, d India
" Mary, d in Herts, b 1765
" William, grandson of Thomas
" Brighton, of Drury Lane 1820
" Richard, of Leeds 1787
Coulter, J., d abroad
Coulson, Joseph, of London, d 1799
Coumbs, Wm., of Devonshire, d 1860
Coupar, David, mariner, London
Courtney, Jane W., Portsea, Hants
Courvisoir, Cath., Stoke Newington
Coutts, Alex., of Montrose, d 1805
" Thomas, of London 1768
Couzens, Wm., of Newcastle-on-Tyne
Covenant, Capt. John M., H E I C S
Coventry, Chas., of Glasgow, d 1858
" And., brother of Charles
" Catharine, o'wise Smeaton
" Margaret, o'wise Black
Covert, John
" Martha

Covert, Mary, m D. Walker
Cowan, Lieut. William, R N, d 1818
Cowell, Esther, d Liverpool 1860
Cowpland, William, merchant, d 1783
Cowell, Rich., yeoman, York, d 1861
Cowper Family, of Dorset
Cowper Family, of London
Cowperthwaite, Elizabeth, b 1795
Cox, William, of Calne, Wilts
" Joseph, surgeon, d India
" E., servant at Harrow
" John, of London 1800
" William, schoolmaster
Coxhead, Sir Thos., of London 1800
Coyle, Jno., of Sydney and Liverpool
Colt, Sarah, d America about 1800
Cozens, Charles, of London
Coals, Mary, Bristol
Coates, Elizabeth, frmly Lumley
" James, d in India
Craven, Frederick, d Middlesex 1868
Craig, John, of Scotland
Crowdace, James, of Gateshead
Crane, Mr. J., of London
Crickmore, Mary, of Hampstead R'd
Crane, Hugh, of the Isle of Man
Crosse, Thomas
Craghill, John, of Carlisle
Creake, Sampson, of Kent
Cross, Trevill, of Devonshire
Cross, Thomas, of Hants
Crutcher, Elizabeth, d Surrey
Cracroft, Robert, of Lincoln
Crowton, Mary, of Stamford
Crutcher, Ralph, d. Surrey
Crawford, Robert, of London 1842
Crompton, Charles, of London 1846
Crowden, John P., of London 1826
Craddock, John, of Lincolnshire
Crosley, Mrs., frmly Hadfield
Croome, Mrs., frmly Hadfield
Creak, Mary, Norwich, d 1824
Critchell, M. A. M. R., Middlesex
Crawford, John, of Manchester
Crawford, Henry, d India
Crummer, George, d Herts 1821
Crispin, George R., Surrey
Creet, Samuel, d London 1866
Criss, Walter, d in America
Craig, John B., d in America
Craister, Maria, Exeter 1865
Creser, Thomas, son of William
Crabtree, John ⎫ sons of Charles
" Thomas ⎭
Crook, Benoi P., of Gloucester 1847
Cresswell, Charles, of London 1844

Crabball, Elizabeth, Denbighshire
Cracroft, Major Charles, *d* in India
Cragie, Captain C. W., *d* in India
Craig, James, of Patrick
" Alex., farmer, *d* Edinburgh
Crane, Henry, ship carpenter
Craseau, Harriet, of Walworth
Craven, John, of Yorkshire, *d* abroad
Crawford, Rt. C., master-mar. *d* 1858
" John, of Bloomsbury, 1817
" John, Esq.
" Marg.L., *o'wise* DeMalizan
Cray, Samuel, of Tideswell
Creed, Robert, of Norfolk, *d* 1862
Cree, Lieut. David, R N, *d* 1820
Creak, Thomas, native of Norfolk
Cresswell, Mary, native of Shropshire
Crichton, Strahan & Co., Dundee 1800
Crick, James, of London, *d* 1824
Cripps, John D., of London, *d* 1840
Croft, James, *d* in Surrey 1862
" Mary, servant, Cheshunt
Crogham, Christopher, *d* abroad
Crompton, Wm., of London, 1720–80
" Lieut. H.T., Army, *d* 1862
Croome, Mary, *d* London 1863
Croombe, Mary, of Marylebone
Crookshank, Ann, Grenada, *d* 1841
Crosbie, James, of London 1800
Cross, Ann, *frmly* Cope
" Thomas, grocer, Dorset
Crosby, George, seaman M S
Crosswell, Hannah B., *o'wise* Douglas
Crottey, Timothy, of Dublin
Crouch, Charles, of Antigua
" Joan, of Sopley, Hants
" Samuel, of Sussex, *d* 1835
Crowther, Joshua, of Yorkshire
Crutchley, Jas., *d* Westminster 1841
Crutchley, Mr., of Western Australia
Crucifix, J. H., *d* in India 1805
Crump, Mary, of Rotherithe *d* 1782
Crussell, John, of Colchester
Crozier, William, of Southwark
Cushing, Catharine, milliner
" Kate, of London 1850
Cullern, Charlotte, *d* Berks 1869
Cunliffe, Blandina, *o'wise* Topsfield
Cubit, Thomas } of Norfolk
" John }
Culliford, Richard, of Chelsea
Cuppage, Walter, of London
Cunyngham, Walter, of Scotland
Cunliffe, Ann, *d* Middlesex
" Nicholas, of Middlesex
Cull, Stephen, of Gloucester

Cudjoe, Frederick, of Ireland
Curwen, Henry, of Cumberland
Cunningham, Archibald, *d* Kent
Cullingfor, Sarah, *d* London
Cunningham, Thomas, *d* Norfolk
Cundrie, Isabella, *d* Liverpool 1838
Curl, W. H. R., *d* India
Cutting, Hannah, *d* Essex 1843
Currie, William, *d* India
Cumming, Robert, seaman
Curry, Susan, *d* Surrey 1867
Curran, Mary Ann
Cundall, William, *o'wise* Morgan
Curtis, James, of Dalston
Cullen, Rich'd, *d* Lincolnshire 1834
Cullum, Elizabeth, *frmly* Turner
Cumberland, Sally, Sussex
Cummings, C. J. F., *d* Paris 1837
Cumyns, Right Hon. and Rev.
Cunningham, Sophia, *frmly* George
" Susanna, of Ireland 1805
Curran, Margaret, *d* Manchester 1858
Currie, Ann, *d* Kennington 1800
" William, of Inverkeithing
" William, *d* Edinburgh 1862
Curry, Andrew, *d* Southwark 1857
Curtis, Timothy, of London 1800
" John, of Bristol
Cuthbertson, Jas., *d* Wolverhampton
Cusic, Mary, London
Cussen, R. J., *d* abroad 1852
Cundy, Wilcox N., engineer

D

Dalton, Ellen, of Newhall
Davis, Emily, lived at Birmingham
Davis, Paul, of Monmouth 1730
David, Mr., *frmly* of the Strand
Dallas, Robert, of London 1800
Daniel, Edward, of Middlesex 1840
Dawson, Elizabeth, *d* Yorkshire 1868
Dargent, James, of London
Davis, Thomas, of London
Darby, Richard, of London
" Sarah, *o'wise* Underwood
Dance, William, of Wilts
Dalzell, Robert, *d* Middlesex
Day, John, of Norfolk
Darley, Vincent, of Cornwall
Darwent, Sarah, *frmly* Sawney
Dance, Richard, of London
Da Costa, Rebecca M., *d* London
Davy, William, *d* Gloucester
Da Costa, Benjamin de M.
" Raphael de M. M.

GENERAL INDEX.

Da Costa, R. De B. M.
Darke, Absolam, of Great Yarmouth
Dancer, Francis, d Middlesex
Darrett, James, d Middlesex 1850
Dawson, Harriett, d London 1858
Day, Ann, of London
Davis Thomas ⎫
 " Richard ⎬ of Priors Marstin,
 " John   ⎪ Warwick.
 " Edward   ⎭
Davies, Mary
 " Ada
Dashwood, William, d 1834-5
Davidson, John, d in Australia
 " Charles, d in Australia
Dale, William D., of Essex
D'Amboise, Eliza, frmly Beston
Dawson, Richard, of Yorkshire
David, C. J., d abroad 1835
Davies, Louisa, London 1857
 " George, of Gloucestershire
Davis, Mrs., sister of Major Humfray
Day, William, of Collingwood street
Davis, Sarah, of Spain, 1865
 " Jemima, s Chelsea, d 1859
 " E., d abroad, 1864
Darsie, Thomas W., of Sudbury
Daiscol, Jeremiah, Spitafields 1842
Day, Elizabeth, of Holborn 1848
Dawes, Frederick, of Norfolk
Davison, Robert, son of Thomas
Davis, John, Liverpool, d 1860
Dargie Stewart C., of Forfarshire
Daniel Charles ⎫ supposed to have
 "   John   ⎬ been born in Notts
Day, Eliza, of Brompton, 1862
Damylaville, Madame
Davis, D., frmly of Stratford
Dalmigavie Family, Inverness
Dawkins, Ann, of Lewis
Dacre, Joseph, of Cumberland
Daniels, John   ⎫ nephews of
 "   George   ⎬ Thomasin Fagg
Darley, John, Esq
Davies, William, of Elleswell
Daniel, Edward, of London 1839
Da Silva, Baron H. J., merchant 1848
Dawson, William, of Bristol 1827
Davis, William, d Epping 1867
Davison, Mary, Yorkshire, d 1842
Davis, Charles G. H., d abroad 1868
Davies, John Thomas, of Wrexham
Darbyshire, Hannah, frmly Williams
Dawson, Sarah, of Cheshire
Day, Benjamin, d in Jamaica
 " Samuel, clerk, 1744

Day, Lieut. Thomas, R N, d 1819
 " George, seaman M S
 " John, farmer, Kent, d 1832
 " John, d London
 " Susannah, frmly Dennis
 " Mary, of Somerset
Darley, Hill, of London, d 1817
Darman, William, victualler, London
Dart, William, coachman, d 1859
Dauber, Elizabeth, of Olney, Bucks
David, C. J., d abroad 1835
Davidson, Elizabeth, d London
 " William, d London 1816
Davies, Eleanor, w of Archdeacon D.
 " George, seaman, M S
 " Hannah, o'wise Burroughs
 " John, of London
 " Joseph, of London, 1600-1700
 " Louisa, d London 1857
 " Robert, of Mold, Flintshire
 " Thomas, of Windsor, d 1797
 " William, of London, d 1833
Davis, Capt. Evan, d India 1827
 " James, d Pembroke 1827
 " James, d London
 " Josiah, of London 1700
 " John, seaman, d 1842
 " George, of London, d 1841
 " Isaac, mariner, d 1823
 " Henry, of Oxford
 " Louisa, of Holborn 1857
 " Mary, of Oxford, d abrd 1826
 " Mrs. Mary, of Sussex
 " Richard, mariner, Bermuda
 " Thomas, d in London 1790
 " Charles ⎫ brothers of Mary
 " George ⎬ D. of Tyldesly,
 " William ⎭ Lancashire
Datton, Richard, d Oxford 1812
Davey, John, of London, d 1835
 " Mary, of Chelsea
Dawe, Geo. Rd. of Marylebone, d 1829
Daws, Alice, native of Plymouth
Dailey, William, d America 1812
Daldy, Ephraim, d Kent 1822
Davill, John, d Surrey 1815
Deacle, Sophia, frmly of Chichester
Dean, Elizabeth, o'wise Kohler 1756
Debbeig, Hugh, clerk Exchequer Office
De la Tour, William, London
Delahay, Thomas, of London 1725
Delannoy, Peter, of London 1700
Delap, Wm., surgeon, Ireland, d 1842
Dempster, Wm., of Montrose, N B
 " Francis, brother to Wm.

Denderson, Thomas, seaman, *d* 1843
Denis, Mary, of the Isle of France
De Bray, Elizabeth, of London
De Gregorio, Coza Cazar
Dewick, James, of London 1831
Desormeaux, Ann, *d* Middlesex
Dent, Joseph, *d* Essex
Deards, William, of London
Denne, Benjamin, of Westminster
Deere, Mary, of Glamorgan
De Pinna, Isabella Louisa, *d* abroad
Dean, Sarah, *o'wise* Fisher
Descudigan, Phillip, *d* Middlesex
" Esther, *d* Jersey
Dewdney, Jane, *s*, London, *d* 1847
De Lancey, Susan, *s*, Cheltenham, *d* 1866
De Pontes, A. T. D., *d* Ryde, 1865
De Lavaux, Leon
Delaporte Ann, of Newington
De Jonge, Jacob Isaac, London
Deacon, James W. of Hyde Park 1858
Dennis, John, groom
Devine, Mrs., of India
Deszabo, Imre, merchant, *d* 1865
Deyell, Thomas, *d* in America
Dermer, Elizabeth, *d* Vienna 1861
" Charles, of Madgeburg
DeCourcy, Henry L. A., *d* New York
Deacon, Joseph, of Shoreditch 1857
D'Estriband, Harriett Julia
Dennison, Maria B., *w*, Surrey, *d* 1867
De Franca, Jos. H., Greenwich 1831
De Maltzan, Baroness, *d* abroad
Dennis, Elizabeth, of Westminster
De Haum, Henry, *d* Westminster
Delamore, Richard, *d* abroad 1812
Denison, P., Esq., of Dublin 1769
Dean, Thomas A., of Lambeth 1832
De Bray, Jacob, of London 1805
De Saintonge, Eliza, Charlton
Deir, William
Delafield, William, of London
Dennis, Mary, *w*, *d* Soho 1824
" Susannah, *o'wise* Peasgood
Denvon, Donald, of Leith 1850
Densham, Joseph, of Kingsland 1810
Denston, Rev. John, of Warwick
" Richard, brother to John
Denton, Jane, *w*, Suffolk 1787
Devereux, Capt. Wm. P., *d* 1861
Devey, William, of London, *d* 1836
Devies, Benjamin, of Southwark
Devinny, John, *d* abroad
Dewell, Lieut. Thomas, *d* 1825
Dexter, Jn. of Southgate-grove, *d* 1858

DeEsterre, Eleanor, *s*, *d* Isle of Wight
Dickson, Alfred, son of John
Dickson, John, of London 1832
Dickenson, Sarah, of Surrey
Dickenson, Elizabeth, *d* Middlesex
Dickson, William, mariner
" Henry, of London 1823
" John, of London 1843
Dixon, John, *d* Middlesex 1845
" Franklin
Dinning, Deborah, of Exeter 1830
Dixon, Henry, of North Shield
Dickson, Alexander L., *d* abroad
" Alexander L., *d* abroad
Dick, David, shoemaker, Glasgow
" Douglas } sons of David, of
" Forbes } Glasgow
" William, *d* at Windsor
Dickens, Thomas, of London, *d* 1814
" Wm., of Manchester, *d* abd
Dickenson Wm., surgeon, London
Dickie, Wm., tailor, of Devonport
Dickson, William, of Perth 1810
" Major Jos., *d* abroad 1805
" Captain J., *d* India 1808
Dillon, Ann, *s*, born Dublin 1759
" Mary, *frmly* Wood
" Eliza, *o'wise* Archambad, *d* 1857
Dinham, A. M. G. C., *s*, of Spalding
Dipple, Thomas, of Islington, *d* 1859
Ditchburn, John, of New Castle-on-Tyne
Dixon, Joseph, draper, Holborn
" Margaret, Mrs., of Southwark
" Richard, of Yorkshire, *d* 1832
Dove, Eliza, *widow*
Doughton, Hannah, *d* Kent 1870
Donaven, Patrick, of Ireland
Dobyn, William, of Monmouth 1737
Downe, John, of London
Docksey, Hope, of Derbyshire
Doolittle, Elizabeth, *frmly* Billingsley
Doidge, Henry, of Fulham
Dobell, William, of Sussex
Dobbins, Phillip, *d* London
Dow, William, *d* Middlesex
Dodson, George, of Cresage
Doyle, Ann, *d* America
Donaldson, John, *d* London 1836
Donald, Mary, *o'wise* Blair
Domett, Judith, of Devonshire
Dowdall, Granville, Hockridge
Dolier, Isabella, of Liverpool
Dolier, Edward, of London
Dobbing, Anthony, of Sunderland
Dobie, George S., son of James

Dolphin, William, toll-gate keeper
Don, a medical gentleman
Dobie, George S., Scotland, *d* 1864
Dobson, George, native of Northumberland
Dolman, J. G. C.
Downton, George
Doyle, James, *d* Lambeth 1865
Douglass, Hannah B., *frmly* Cresswell
Doe, Susan *d* Switzerland 1861
Dove, William, *d* Tasmania
" James ⎫ brothers of William
" Thomas ⎭
Dobson, Lieut. Geo., 45th Regt. Ft.
" Henry P., of Jamaica
" Sir Richard, Australia
Dodd, Rev. Rd., of Camberwell 1804
Dodge, Elzbth., *d* Paddington 1840
" George, *d* abroad 1861
Doherty, Margt., Monmouth, *d* 1837
Dolbeare, Thos., of Boston, America
Dolan, Maria C., *d* abroad, 1864
Dolman, Samuel, seaman, Navy
Dolman, Samuel, seaman, Navy
Donelan, Henry, *d* India, 1858
Donaldson, James ⎫ of Borrostown,
" Agnes ⎭ Scotland
Donohue, Miss Hannah, of Dublin
Dorkins, Wm., steward M S, *d* 1835
Doran, Capt. William, *d* abroad 1851
Dorsdell, Richard, master mariner
Dorville, W. and G., of London 1811
Dott, Thomas, seaman 1793
Douglas, Maj. Alex., *d* Limerick 1828
" Harriet B., *d* Derby 1852
" Hugh M., *d* about 1852
" James, mariner, *d* 1835
" Mrs. Mary, of Kelso
" Ensign, William N., *d* 1824
" William, of Scotland 1799
Douse, Joseph, surgeon, Vauxhall
Dowland, Captain, John, *d* 1860
Dowles, Charles, *d* London 1854
Dowling, John, *d* abroad 1859
" Catherine, *d* London 1862
Downe, George, of London, *d* 1806
" Richard, of London 1820-9
Downes, Rich., of Stockwell 1700-20
" Elizabeth, niece of Richard
Downey, Ensign, Robert, *d* abroad
Downham, A., *o'wise* Molineaux
Downing, Capt. John, *d* abroad 1823
Doyle, Arthur, of Waterford, *d* 1841
" John, seaman M S, *d* 1842
" Mary, *dau*. Elzbth. of Dublin
" Michael, *d* abroad 1859

Drake, Elizabeth, *frmly* Goss
Draper, Comfort, of Worcestershire
Drage, John, of Cambridgeshire
Dressler, Maria, *d* abroad 1820
Draper, Mary, Somerset
" Edward, *d* in Surrey 1827
Drayton, Ann ⎫
" Benjamin ⎬ of London
" Sarah ⎭
Drew, Charles, *d* Suffolk 1740-50
Driver, George, serjeant, *d* abroad
Dromford, Jane, of Chelsea and Bris.
Drummond, Margaret, *d* Farnham
" James, W. S. 1801
" Miss C., Edinburgh 1799
" Peter, of Edinburgh 1796
Drybutter, James, of London 1800
Duncombe, Henry Stuart
Duncan, Robert, of Middlesex 1826
Duke, Richard, of Devonshire
Dunbar, George, of London
Duer, John, of Middlesex
Duffield, Francis, of Bucks
Dunstall, John, *d* London
Dunce, Joseph, of Reading
Duffield, Michael, *d* Chelsea
Dudley, Thomas, of Shropshire
Dutton, Charles, *d* Middlesex 1866
Dunch, William
" Dudley
Duncan, Ann, *d* Fifeshire
Dunderdale, Henry ⎫ merchants,
" W. T. ⎭ London 1820
Dufty, Thomas, *d* abroad 1865
Dudley, George, living 1770
Dunant, William, Yorkshire 1823
Duff, J., of Genoa 1849
Dunning, Mrs. of Exeter
Duncan, John F., London, *d* 1865
Dunleary, Hugh Francis, valet
Dunn, Joseph, of Lincolnshire 1805
Dubois, James, living 1800
Duffy, James, surveyor
Dwindell, Martha, *d* France
Dunn, Thomas, of Roxburgh 1759
" Isabella, daughter of Thomas
" Thomas, miller, 1790
" John, *d* in Canada
" James, *d* Canada 1837
Durham, Nathan, *d* Warwick 1867
Duffield, Francis, of Bradford
Duckett, Samuel, of London 1764
Ducket, Sir George, Bart.
Dudley, Robert, of Bethnal Green
Dudie, Captain Thos. A., *d* at Poole
Duff, Alexander M., of Banff 1804

Duffy, Hugh, *d* in London 1830
Dudgeon, Robert, of Edinburgh 1798
Dugdale, Robert, of Dorsetshire
Duke, Robert, draper, Colchester
" Capt. Charles, of Quebec 1800
Duffield, Job, *d* Islington 1850
Dunbar, W. G. C., *d* India 1812
" Mary, of Torquay, &c.
" Margaret, *d* London 1844
Duncan, William G., *d* India 1858
" John, of Bristol, *d* 1853
" David, seaman M S
Dunlop, James, baker, Beith N B
Dunn, Ann, Marylebone 1814
" Elzbth. *frmly* Althorpe, *d* 1809
" George, of Milton, *d* 1814
Dunstone, Jas., master-mariner 1813
Durant, William, soldier, *d* abroad
Durndell, Martha, *d* in France
Durward, James, master-mariner
Dupree, Ann, *d* London 1855
Duguid, James, of Edinburgh
Dutton, Joseph, of London 1770
" John ⎱ sons of Joseph, of
" Henry ⎰ London
Duval, Ann, Hoxton
" David, of Lond. and America
Dyott, John, of Lichfield
Dyer, William, *d* Birmingham 1827
Dyke, John, *d* Lymington
Dyble, John, marble mason
Dyke, Hester, *d* Somerset 1865
Dyer, John, *d* London 1791
Dyle, Frances, servant, *d* 1855
Dyer, Elizabeth ⎱ daughters of Thos.
" Sarah ⎰ of London
Dyett, Mr., of London, *d* abroad 1843
Dynley, Lieut. Wm., *d* in London

E

Earp, Edward, *d* Coventry 1868
Eaton, Christopher, *d* Norfolk 1799
Early, John, son of William
Eades, Ann, of Woolwich 1723
Easton, William, son of Charles
Eagle, William, *d* Middlesex 1867
Ealand, Robert G., *d* Middlesex
Eadnell, Richard, attorney, London
Eagles, Capt. Edward, of India 1777
Earlesman, Richard, of Salisbury
Earp, Thomas, of Withyham, Sussex
East, James, groom, *d* 1832
" Thomas, *d* abroad 1858
Easthope, Jane, native of Salop

Eaton, Ann, *d* Ormskirk 1822
" Benj. of Rotherithe, *d* 1815
" Elizabeth A., *d* London 1810
" George, of Pimlico
Eckford, Robert, *d* Jersey 1865
Eccles, Lieut. G. W., *d* India 1812
Eckford, Alexander, *d* 1858
Edwards Family
Edwards, John, *d* Kent 1851
Edmunds, C. H., of Oxford
Edge, Richard, of Lancashire
Edwards, William, *d* Kensington
Edwin, Catherine, of Bedford
Edmonds, Giles, of Wiltshire
Edmonds, John, merchant 1750
Edes, Edward, of Bermondsey
Edes, John, of Egham
Edgar, John, *d* London 1797
Edwards, Frances
" Elizabeth
" Mary
" Robert, *d* in New Zealand
Edmonds, Luther, Bishopsgate
Edgar, Edward, of London 1827
Edney, Harriet, wife of John
Edmonds, Edgar, Barnwell
" Eldred Alfred
Edwards, Mary, London
" George, of Dorset
Edmond, James, Glasgow 1832
Edmondson, Richard
Edge, Thomas F., *d* Edinburgh 1843
Edhouse, Sophia, Knightsbridge 1780
Edie, Robert, of Dundee 1847
Edmond, James, of Glasgow 1832
Edmonds, John, of Bristol, *d* abroad
" Mary E., *d* London
Edridge, William, of Bermondsey
Edwards, Edward, of London, *d* 1810
" Frances, *o'wise* Bennett
" Lieut. John, *d* abroad 1838
" John, of Newgate, *d* 1832
" Joyce, Isleworth 1720
" Isaac, *d* London
" Maurice, Cirencester, *d* 1848
" N., sister to E. Houghton
" Samuel, of Birmingham
Effringham, John, *d* Surrey 1739
Egan, Joseph B., *d* abroad
Egan, Colonel, of Surrey
Eiffert, Philip P., *d* London 1793
Ekins, Mary, *o'wise* Brown
Elmslie, Mary, *d* Surrey 1868
Ellis, Mrs. Ann
Elburn, Sarah, of London 1797
Elmes, Sarah, *o'wise* Young

Elliott, Robert, *d* London
Eldred, John, of Suffolk
Elwick, George G., of Kent
Ellerker, John, *d* Doncaster
" Alice, *d* Doncaster
Ellis, James, E I C service
Elvin, Joseph, *d* London 1870
Ellard, Martha, *frmly* White
Ellis, Mary, of Kent
Elisha, Sarah, *frmly* Whitehouse
Elmore, W., *d* abroad 1866
Ellison, Capt., Knight of Windsor
Elliott, Samuel, of Southampton
" Alice
Elger, Thomas, of Islington
Elstob Family
Ely, Mr., of Bury
Eliot James, *d* Middlesex 1858
Elsey Rosina, *w* of John
Ellis William, *d* in India
Elkins Mary Ann, *frmly* Evans
Eldridge Thomas, of Stock, Essex
Elkin Thomas, of Hanbury, Stafford
Elley John, station-master, *d* 1861
Ellinett, Lt. Geo. P. Royal Marines
Elliott, Lt. Edmund, *d* abroad 1841
" Fleming, born London, 1750
" George, *d* London 1857
" Grace, *d* Devon 1844
" Mrs. H. J., of Paddington
" John, of Smithfield 1790
" John, of London
" J. B., *d* abroad 1857
" Mary, *s*, Dorchester
" Mary, of Derby, *d* aged 92
" Ensign Robert, *d* abroad
" William, of London
Ellis, Mrs. Ann, of Hamstead
" Eliza, *frmly* Smith, *d* 1858
" James, seaman Navy
" Jeremiah, *d* abroad 1810
" John, of Yorkshire, *d* 1860
Elmes, Thomas, *d* in Kent
Elmer Thomas } of Wallaton, Not-
" Ann } tinghamshire
Elms, Richard, of Sussex, *d* 1804
Ellison Susanh, *s*, Marylebone, *d* 1820
Else, William, of Herefordshire
" George, cousin to William
Elson John C., of Laleham, *d* 1833
Emes, Joseph, of London
Empson Mary, *frmly* Barford
Embleton, Luke, *d* Surrey 1865
Emmett, Mary, *o'wise* Ravensham
Ensley, Ann, of Bedford
Ensor, Felix, of London

Ennis, Edward, born 1798
England, Ann S, *d* Bath 1063
England, Richard, *d* 1812
English, C. N., army surgeon
" Thomas, *d* Halifax
Ennis, John C., *d* abroad
" Charles J., *d* abroad
Erly John, of Ireland
Erratt, Joseph, *d* abroad 1834
Erskine, James, *d* abroad
Escourt, Thomas, of Wilts
Estcourt, Edmund, of Gloucester
Essell, Edward John, *d* abroad 1805
Essary, Lucy, *o'wise* Graham
Essery, Lieut. John, Royal Navy
" Mary, *frmly* Palmer
Esten, James, merchant, *d* 1774-5
Etches, Thomas, of London
Evans, Charles B., of Cheltenham
" Thomas Diamond
" Mary, *d* Somerset
" Samuel, *d* London
" David, *d* Middlesex
" Absolam, *d* Middlesex
" William, *d* Middlesex
" Mary Ann, of Yorkshire
Everett, Amelia, of Southampton
Evans, John, of London 1840
Etheridge, Mr., of Somerset
Etherington, Elizabeth, Northamp'n
Everett, Ann, *frmly* Greening
Evans, James, *d* abroad 1865
" James, *d* America
" Henry, son of G. W. Evans
" Arthur
" Jessie
Ewer, Barbara, living 1600
Ewing, Phœbe, Exeter, *d* 1860
Evans, Elizabeth, *d* London 1825
" Elizabeth, *d* Bristol
" George, master-mariner
" Richard, of Somerset 1821
" Sarah, of Paddington
" Sophia, *d* London 1829
" Lieut. William, *d* abroad 1799
" William, brother to Richard
Evered, Ann
" Robert
Everett, John, of Beccles, Suffolk
Everson, Mark, *d* abroad 1811
Ewer, Samuel, clerk, *d* 1804
Ewbank, Henry, *d* Kingsland 1847
Eyare, Jemima, *d* Surrey
Eyre, Ann, of Yorkshire, *d* 1833
" Elizabeth F., Bath, *d* 1820
" Mary, cousin to Daniel

F

Fairey, John, of St. Neots
Farrell, Margaret, of Melbourne
Farrer, John, *d* Yorkshire 1832
Farmer, Edward, *d* London
Faything, Richard, *d* London
Fayers, John, of Norfolk
Farrah, John, of Southwick
Farnsworth, John, of Lincolnshire
Farmiloe, William C. } of North
" Alexander H. } Nibley
Faulkener, Samuel, of Bath, *d* 1813
Farmer, George W., of London
Fallowfield, William } children of
" Margaret } William
" William, *d* abroad 1819
Fayers, Thomas, Norfolk, *d* 1841
Falconer, Jane, *w* of Sylvester
Fayers, John, of Snettisham
" Thomas, of Cambridge
Farnsworth, John, of Lincolnshire
Farren, John G., *d* Denbigh
Farr Family, Inverness
Fairfield, George, of Calcutta
Fabian, A. A. C., *d* in Middlesex
Fairclough, Mrs. Eliza'th, *d* Scotland
Fall, Wm. N., of Yorkshire
Fancy, George, painter, *d* London
Fantham, John, Farrier
Farborough, Sarah, *o'wise* Nicolls
Farman, W. H.
Farmer, R. S. W. *d* Whitechapel 1826
Farquhar, J., *d* abroad 1863
Farr, John, of London 1765
" William, of Monmouth, *d* 1835
Farrer, Josiah, of London 1780
" Richard F., of Leeds, *d* 1846
" Thos., merchant, Liverpool
" Jane, *w* of Thomas, *d* 1852
Farrell, Edward, *d* London 1842
Farthing, Robert, master-mariner
Fatio, Cornet John E., *d* India
Fay, Eleanor, of Paddington 1822
Fetching, Hans Caspar, *d* Middlesex
Feldman, Henry, *d* Westminster
Fennell, George, of the Royal Navy
Fenn, Elizabeth, of Cambridgeshire
Feillett, Elizabeth, *d* 1794
Fenwick, Peter, of Hawick
Ferguson, Mr., of Finsbury
Feegan, John J., *alias* Capt. F.
Ferguson, Henry, native of America
Ferrior, Mary, of Pembrokeshire
Ferrers, George J., mariner

Fenton, Jane, *o'wise* Falconer
Fetherston, James } children of
" Margaret } Joseph
Ferne, Edward, of Southwark 1810
Fearn, John, of Sheffield, *d* 1862
Feaston, F. T., of London 1814
Felix, Mary, Chelsea, *d* 1838
Fell, Sarah, Chelsea, *d* 1813
Felton, William, seam'n Navy, *d* 1810
Fenn, Charles, master-mariner
Fennell, William, sergt. Army, *d* 1846
Fenner, Henry, of Middlesex, *d* 1860
Fenwick, Lieut.-Colonel Robert
Ferguson, Cecilia, of Edinburgh
" Cecilia } daughters of
" Henrietta } Hy. of Glasgow
" Henry, *d* Glasgow 1786
" James, cooper, Liverpool
" James, writer, Glasgow
" James G., of Hoxton
" John, seaman M S
Ferris, Francis, of the R. N. 1800
Forth, Nathan } of London 1780
" William }
Few, John, of Pottern, Wilts
Fitzharris, Andrew, of America
" Patrick, of Dublin
" James, of London
" Michael } of Liverpool
" Catharine }
Fitchew, John
Field, Mr. H., of London
Fisher, John M., of London 1846
Filchett, Richard, of London 1843
Fitzpatrick, Ann, *d* Liverpool 1869
Fisher, James, of Whitehaven
Fisher, Mary, of Devonshire
Fish, Charlotte, *d* Middlesex
Fidkin, James, of London 1820
Fisher, Madeline, of Edinburgh 1788
" P., *d* in Australia
Firth, John, formerly of Naples
Fitzpatrick, *d* abroad 1864
Fisher, Abraham, *d* Cumberland 1864
" John, father of Abraham
" Thomas
Field, Daniel, of Marylebone 1794
Fitzgibbon, Michael, London 1851
Files, Stephen, of Georgia
Finley, Jane
" Margaret } of Londonderry
" Ann }
Finigan, Elizabeth
Fillingham, John J. A., *d* 1862
Fisher, James, merchant, Liverpool
" Isabella, married E. Dolier

Firth, Joseph, of Yorkshire
Finch, Joseph, d India 1815
" Justin, d India 1861
Field, John, of Birkenshaw
Fiddes, Alexander, of Scotland, d 1833
Field, Mary, of Tottenham
" Frances A., of Paris 1844
Fielder, Joseph ⎰ living in London
" Thomas ⎱ 1790
" Thomas ⎱
" Martha ⎰ of London 1790
" Ebenezer ⎱ children of
" John ⎰ Thomas
Fieldsend, J. C., d abroad 1853
Filer, Edw., of Lincolnshire, d 1853-4
Fillingham, Susannah, *frmly* Dennis
Finch, William G., d London 1826
" Hon. Rev. Ed., d abroad 1830
" Henry, builder, Walmer
Finlay, Mary, Durham d 1805
Fish, Lieut. Nathaniel, R N
" Charlotte, London 1800
Fishbourne, J. M., Army surgeon
Fisher, John, of Whitehaven
" Mary, Brompton
Fitch, Mr., d at Cork 1850
Fitzgerald, Patrick, d Westminster
" Lieut. M. G., d abroad
" Thomas ⎱ seamen Navy
" Patrick ⎰
Fitzgibbon, Michael, d London 1851
Fletcher, William, d Middlesex
Floyer, Margaret, of Dorchester
Flower, Edward, of Essex
Fletcher, Sarah M., d Suffolk
Fletcher, Mrs., of Regent's Park
Flett, Andrew, of Orkney
Flatters, Elizabeth
Fletcher, Susannah, *o'wise* Curry
" Richard, of Walworth
Fleetwood, Cornelius, mariner, d 1770
Flack, William, of Copford, Essex
Fleaureau, C., *o'wise* Syfret
Flemming, Archibald, d London 1838
" John, E I C S
Fletcher, Mary A., of Essex, d 1849
" Elizabeth
" Mary
" Harriet
" Jane
" Richard John
" Charles Orlando
Flinn, Richard, master-mariner
Flint, Thomas A., servant 1818
" Mrs. H., of Epsom, Surrey
Flower, Jane, *w* Bethnal Green

Folds, James, d Lancashire 1820
Fortune, William, of Scotland
Forster, John, of Northumberland
Fosse, Ann, of Ilfracombe
Forster, James, d London
Fortrey, James, of Cambridgeshire
Fowke, Mary, *frmly* Wrotte
Foster, Elmes, d Northamptonshire
Forster, Alice, d Middlesex
Foster, Michael, d Essex
Foljambe, Henry, d Surrey 1788
Forrest, James, d abroad 1821
Fosbrook, Anthony D., d Norfolk 1861
Foster, Albert B., d in Russia
" Frances A., *dau* of Robert
Foley, George, Yorkshire d 1863
Forrest, William, of Glasgow
Foster, William C., son of Lawrence
Foulds, Mary, Lancashire d 1817
Fontaine, Charles, d in America
Fox, Francis, of Falmouth
" William, d Woolwich 1864
Ford, J., mariner, d 1865
Foyle, James, went to America
Fort, Eliza, Leeds, d 1862
Foot, Malachi, of Clerkenwell
Ford, Susannah, daughter of James
Fowler, Richard, ironmonger, 1831
Forster, Andrew, seaman M S
" Thompson, Notts, d 1830
Fox, Mr., of City Road
Fogg, William, merchant d abroad
Forbes, Dr. James
" William, of Aberdeen d 1863
Ford, Thomas, seaman Navy
" Thomas, of Southwark 1800
Forest, Thomas, of Westminster 1759
Forrester, Sarah, *o'wise* Fry
Forsyth, David, seaman M S
Forster, John, d abroad 1813-14
Forsant, Peter, d London 1791
Fortune, John, quartermaster, d 1813
Fosbery, F., d abroad 1863
Foster, John, d Greenwich 1854
" Chas., of Somers Town, 1810
" Elizabeth, *o'wise* Berry
" Joseph, seaman 1841
" Lucy, of Plymouth 1803
" Mary, living 1780
" Nanny, of Settle, York
" Phœbe, *frmly* Whitehouse
" Samuel, d at Birmingham
Fotheringham, Samuel, d abroad
Fouracre, Mary, Hoxton, d 1841
Fowle, Elizabeth, Norfolk, d 1839
" Nicolas, of Kent 1715

Fowler, Joseph, *d* in America
" Joseph, solicitor, London
" Mr., attorney, Cornwall
" Mary A., *o'wise* Carman
" William, of Pimlico *d* 1848
Fox, Charles, seaman *d* 1814
Freeman, Fielder, E I C S
Fryer, Robert ⎫ of Newcastle-
" Stephen ⎭ on-Tyne
Frank, Isaac, of Leighton Buzzard
Fruin, William *d* Rochester
Freeman, Barbara, *d* Essex
Frost, Eliza, *dau* of William
Franks Family
Fraser, James, of Brighton
" Elizabeth, of Edinburgh
" John, son of Hugh
Francis, Vincent, *d* Middlesex
" John, of London 1846
Fry, John, of London 1845
Frost, John L., of London 1832
France, Thomas, of London
Freer, Thomas C., *d* abroad 1866
Frost, Eliza, of Nottingham
Fraser, Agnes, of Edinburgh
" Hugh, of Aberdeen
Freeman, Martha, *frmly* Rickard
Fryer, George H., *d* Kingsland
Frazer, Alexander, of Perthshire
" Archibald, *d* Australia
Freeman, Alfred, went abroad 1854
Fraser, Capt., 4th Light Dragoons
Frost, Charles H., *d* Southwark 1866
Freeman, J., clerk 1857
Frampton, James A., *d* Middlesex
Freer, Thomas C., *d* abroad 1866
Franklin, Henry, surgeon *d* 1864
" Henry, of Canada 1851
Freeman, Mary, Chipping Norton
French, William G., of Marylebone
Friend, William, merchant, London
Fries, Elizabeth *d* Essex 1809
Frill, Hugh, sergeant *d* 1840
Frisby, Richard, merchant London
Frobisher, Ann, *w*, London 1820
Fromow, Mrs., *w* of Peter
Frost, John L., of London
" Michael, of Barkston, Lincoln
" James, son of Michael
Fry, Sarah, *w* Chatham 1829
" Francis, yeoman, Hants
Franckland, Joseph
" Jane
" Mary
Franklin, Arthur, of Rotherithe
" Lydia, Chichester 1829

Francis, Harriet, *d* London, 1844
Francis, Albina, *o'wise* Curtis
" John, of Poplar, *d* 1835
" Thomas, *d* London 1787
Frampton, Sarah, *o'wise* Turner
Fraser, Alex., *d* in Surrey 1806-7
" Mary
" Jean, of Aberdeen, N B
" Alex., of Inverness *d* abd 1848
" Lieut. Thomas D., *d* abroad
Frazer, William, seaman Navy
Frederick, Charles, seaman *d* 1850
Freeman, David, servant *d* 1824
" John, seaman Navy
" Robert, of Norfolk 1805
" Samuel, *d* 1819
" William, of Westminster
French, Elizabeth ⎫ living 1820
" George ⎭
" Elizabeth, *w* of George
" Mary, *d* Newbury 1835
" Mary, *o'wise* Clements
" Richard, seaman *d* 1846
Fulcher, Mary, *d* Middlesex 1866
Fuller, John Proctor, *d* London
Furnivall, Sarah, of Middlewich
Fuller, Thomas, *d* Essex 1662
Furley, Phillip ⎫ of Clerkenwell
" Robert ⎭
Fuller, Miss Mary Ann
Funnell, Edward H., courier
Fudge, George, shoemaker, London
Fuller, Sarah, *w* Southwark
Fulwood, John, of Southwark
" Mary, *o'wise* Gregory
Fulton, Charlotte, *o'wise* Surrey
" Charles, of Luton, *d* 1832
" Thomas, of Picton, Herts
" Elizabeth, *o'wise* White
Fusedale, Alice, *s*, *d* Surrey 1859
Fyfe, George, of Dundee 1841

G

Gaskin, Eliza Sarah, *o'wise* Nudd
Gardner, Miss Henrietta A.
Gascoigne, Fred'k H., London 1854
Gauden, Gilbert, of Scotland
Galbraith, James, *d* Scotland 1794
Gater, Richard, of Sussex
Gardiner, William, *d* Middlesex
Garth, John, of Durham
Gall, William, *d* Whitehaven
Garrett, William, *d* Hampshire
Gace, Mary, *d* Greenwich

GENERAL INDEX.

Gartside, Sarah, *o'wise* Teaton
Gauldie, Ann, Edinburgh, *d* 1866
Garlic, Sarah, Yorkshire, *d* 1866
Gayard, Charles, of Lincoln, *d* 1856
Galiffe, Benjamin, of Yorkshire
Galloway, Mary, *o'wise* Collier
Garston, John, seaman M S
Gay, Mr., *d* abroad 1867
Gardener, Richard, of London 1831
Gabain, George, of London, 1854
Gardner, Henry, of London 1820
Gadd, Ann, wife of William
Garner, Harry, son of Matthew
Gahagan, James, of Grenada 1798
Gale, Sarah, of Berkshire
" Jonathan, *d* Manchester 1844
Galloway, Wm., of Edinburgh 1801
Gant, Richard, of London 1759
Gardiner, Rev. John, of Surrey
" Lucy, of Essex, *d* 1742
Gardner, Edward, *d* New Zealand
" Hannah, *o'wise* Stears
" Susannah C., *s* living 1802
" Robert, *d* 1818
Garlie, Benjamin, of Albany
Garnatt, Wm., of Tadcaster, *d* 1840
Garner, Thomas, surgeon, *d* 1762
Garnett, Thomas, attorney 1770
Garratt, Jas., quartermaster, *d* 1809
Garwood, John E., of London
Gasner, James, of Rochester 1804
Gates, Elizabeth, of Brighton
Gay, Ann, *frmly* Nice
Gerrard, William, of Stirling
Genet, Ann, *o'wise* Jean
Gellatly, Betsy L, of Gravesend
Gedge, John, of Middlesex, 1839
Gerrans, Rev. B., *d* Surrey 1825
Gethings, Ann
Geldhart, Richard, of Liverpool
Gerard, George, of London
Gentle, Eliza, Hoxton, *d* 1865
Genet, Anthony } living 1810
" Ann }
Geddis, Miss Jane, of London
Gedney, John, *d* Yorkshire 1809
Geed, Charles, mariner, *d* abroad
Geer, George W., *d* abroad
George, Richard, of Wilts, *d* 1795
" Lieut. John, *d* abroad 1803
" Geo. C., of Cornwall, *d* 1830
" Hannah, *frmly* Taylor
" Sylvester, seaman Navy
" Thomas, seaman Navy
Gepp, Harriet M., *w* London, 1849
Gibson, Frederick, *d* abroad 1866

Ginman, Elizabeth, servant
Giddins, William, carpenter
Giffard, Sarah E., *o'wise* Phillips
Giles, William, of Croydon
Gilding, Abigail, *d* London
Giles, John, *d* Middlesex
Girdler John S., *d* Middlesex
Gibson, Ann, *o'wise* Blundell
Gill, Hannah, Marylebone
" John, of Rotherhythe
Gillet, Sophia E. C., *b* at Paris
" Christopher, of Lincolnshire
Giles, Thomas, Somerset, *d* abroad
Gibson, Robert, E I C S 1848
Ginstimani, J. P., of London
Gibson, Matthew, London
Gipps, Henry P., of Hythe
Giddings, Simon, Somerset
Gibbs, Sarah, *frmly* Skinner
Giddings, James, son of Matthew
Gibbs, William John, *d* abroad
Gill, Thomas, *d* Sydney
Giles, William, seaman M S
Gilbert, John, waiter, London
Gibbs, William, of Southwark
Gibbs, Sarah, *frmly* Skinner
Gillespie, Peter, of Scotland 1740
Gilbert, John, of London 1838
Gill, George, of London 1807
Gilbert, Joseph, of Islington 1831
Gibberson, George, *d* abroad 1856
Gibb, Lieut., *d* abroad 1864
Gibbon, Sarah, Sunderland
Gibbons, Joseph, of Lambeth 1808
Gibbs, Betsy, *d* Camberwell 1841
Gibson, James, of Edinburgh 1795
" Jas., of Shrewsbury *d* 1840
" James, seaman M S
" M. A. M. P., *o'wise* Critchell
" Peter, of Edinburgh, 1797
" William, *d* abroad 1807
" William, of Weardale, *d* 1840
Gifford, Lieut. John, *d* abroad
" Nathaniel, of London 1700
Gilbert, Dorothy, of Durham
" Thomas, of London 1750-60
" Mrs. Alice, of London
Gilding, John, of Staffordshire, *d* 1858
Gill, Thos., solicitor, London, *d* 1837
" William, tailor, Marylebone
Gillette, Sarah, *o'wise* Cotton
Giles, Sarah, of Twickenham
Gilson, Lawrence, of Marylebone
Gisbey, George, *d* in Essex 1763
Glover, William, ship steward, *d* 1848
Glenn, Richard, Bowness, *d* 1865

Glanford, J., *d* abroad 1864
Glassier, Elizabeth, *frmly* Penny
Glasenkamp, Franz Frederick
" Elizabeth
" Maria
Glazier, Richard, *b* 1756
" Samuel, of Lincolnshire
Glasgow, Major Geo., of Quebec 1800
" Robert, *d* abroad 1862
Glass, Alexander P., surgeon, *d* 1862
" Donald, of Ross, *d* 1844
Glasse, Anna A., *d* abroad 1857
Glen, Andrew, merchant, Glasgow
" William, *d* abroad 1863
Glencross, Sam'l, left Scotland 1730-40
Glencross, Elzbth., *dau.* of Saml., *d* 1815
Gloster, Elizabeth, *d* London
Glover, James, master-mariner 1848
Glyn, Martha, of Newington, Surrey
Goss, Thomas, *d* Devon 1868
" Elizabeth, *o'wise* Drake
Goodwyn, Daniel, *d* Westminster
Good, William, of Demerara
Goode, Ann, *frmly* Patterson
Goundes, James, of Dudingstone
Goodchild, William, seaman
Goddard, Morris Matthew
Goff, Hannah, Herts, 1840
Gough, Henry T., *d* Westminster
Goreham, Amherst, *d* 1823
Gorrie, Daniel, Liverpool, plumber
" Catherine, *o'wise* Duncan
" Ann, *o'wise* Wild
Gootch, William, Islington *d* 1866
Goodson, John, London, 1814
Gordon, Margaret, Glasgow
Goodman, Thomas, Stoke-on-Trent, *d* 1866
Goodenough, William, *d* 1837
Goleborn, Thomas L., Bedford 1835
Good, Mrs. Jane
Goodlad, Jarvis, of Sheffield
Gordon, Mrs. Robert
" Lieut. F. D.
" Margaret, Glasgow
Goard, James } sons of Captain
" John } Benjamin G.
" William }
Goddard, Henry, *d* at Chatham
Godden, Elizabeth, of Devonshire
Godly, Lieut. 60th Regt. Foot
Goff, Hannah, Marylebone, *d* 1849
" Joshua, master-mariner
" Martha, *frmly* Corbett
Goll, Catharine, *d* Clapton 1829
Gogerly, Jacob, *d* London 1829

Gold, John, of Camberwell
" Clement C., of Kent
Goldham, Thomas, *d* Middlesex 1847
Goode, Ann, Warwickshire, *d* 1798
" Mr., surgeon, Leominster
Goodrich, Lieut. Thos., *d* abroad 1813
Goodwin, Elijah, seaman M S
Gordon, Alexander, *d* abroad, 1811
" Alexander, of Scotland 1835
" Thomas, of Gloucestershire
Gordinge, Wallinger, of Wiltshire
Gorham, Christopher, of Kent
Gorman, Mary, *dau.* of John
Gorwood, Wetwang, *d* London 1814
Gough, Frances, of Cliffe
Gowers, William, *d* Westminster 1828
Gowlan, Thomas, of London 1797
Gowlett, Sarah, *o'wise* Laver
Graham, William, of London
" George, *d* London
Greville, Ann }
" Elizabeth } of Bristol
" Mary }
Green, Mary, *frmly* Campion
Greene, Nicholas, of Falmouth
Griffin, Francis, *d* India
Graves, Timothy, *d* Cambridge
Grove, Henry, *d* West Indies
Gregg, Catharine, *d* Portsmouth
Greatorex, Samuel, of Essex
Gray, William, *d* Middlesex
Green, Mary Ann, *d* Grantham
Greig, Woronzow, *d* Surrey, 1865
Grey, William, of London, 1829
Greenaway, Mary, *o'wise* Carter
Grace, Henry, of Lancashire
Green, John, *d* Hants, 1799
Gregory, Martha, *d* Middlesex
Griffith, John, of Bexhill
Grentrex, J. H., photographer 1860
Greenhill, David } of London
" Joseph } 1760-80
Green, Alexander E., Warwickshire
Greening, Ann, *o'wise* Steadman
Graene, Elizabeth, wife of Charles
Green, B., *d* abroad, 1863
Griggs, William, *d* abroad 1823
Griffiths, William, *d* Shropshire 1861
Graveson, Henry, of Notts 1824
Griffiths, Richard
Gray, Thomas
Green, Harriett, *d* Middlesex
Graham, Robert, of Fyfeshire 1796
Grant, Alexander, *d* India 1860
" William Henry
" John, of London 1825

Grieffenberg, Joseph, d Norwich 1862
Graham, Laura, d 1862
" Robert C., Liverpool 1839
Greatrex, Ellen J., London 1854
Green, Thomas, Scotland, d abroad
Grosso, Robert F., d London 1857
Green, Thomas, Leeds
Grove, Caroline E., Acton
Green, John, accountant 1853
Grinsell, William, Woolwich
Greenhill, Ann, living 1600
Griffiths, Charlotte, d Durham
" Edward, of Carnarvon
Griffin, George, of Brighton
Gregson, John S. } of Rochford,
" Jane } Essex 1811
Grain, Frances, of Surrey 1803
Grace, Henry
" Jane
Graham, Andrew, of Edinburgh 1793
" Agnes, wife of William
" Colin P.
" David, son of William
" Douglas C., d abroad 1855
" Wm. of Collier-row, Bottern
Grange, James, upholsterer, London
Grant, Capt. Alex. d abroad 1860
" C., army surgeon
" Duncan, d at Putney
" John, surgeon, d abroad 1814
" Sarah, Somers Town, d 1816
" William, d Demerara 1794
Gray, Andrew, living 1795
" Elizabeth, dau of Joseph 1770
" Elizabeth, o'wise Oaks
" John, brother to Elizabeth
" Martha, frmly Bannister 1853
" Mary, o'wise Morrell
" Phœbe, Mayfair, London
Green, Captain James, R N
" John, of London
" Joseph, seaman
" James, seaman Navy
" Jane, formerly Brown 1816
" Capt. Francis, d abroad 1813
Greenhill, Robert, of London
Greening, Thomas, of Chelsea, d 1809
Greenlaw, Lieut., d abroad 1864
Greenough, Jane, formerly Blackitter
Greenslade, William, d in India
Griffith, Charlotte, Dublin, d 1837
" Lieut. Charles, d abroad
" Maria A. Southwark, 1823
Grove, Edward, of Lambeth
" Mary, formerly Luff
" George A., d London 1813

Grubb, Mary, born about 1772
" Richard
" Jane }
" Nelly } sisters to Richard
" Nancy }
" George, of London, d 1833
Greenway, Alice }
" Henry } of London
" Sarah } 1750-80
Greenwood, Thos. of Bensing, d 1846
" Phillis, d in Kent
Gregory, Ann, London, d 1853
Grice, Mary, of Limehouse
Grier, Mary A., of London 1798
Grierson, Joseph, clerk, d 1862
Grieve, Andrew, H E I C S, d 1844
Griffin, Sophia, d Middlesex 1843
Griffith, Eliz'h, sister to Mary Cumley
Grint, John, of Wandsworth
Grant, Henry E., of Edinburgh
Grittors, Lieut. H., d Chatham
Grant, George, of Walworth
Groen, Margaret, frmly Heath
" Louisa, dau of Charles
Graham, Eliz'bth M., frmly Campbell
Granet, Dr. B., of Chelsea 1835
Greaves, J. B., of London 1836
Green, John, of Horselydown 1853
Grinsell, William, of Woolwich 1860
Grover, Thomas, London 1836
Gurney, Catharine, d Bermondsey
Guest, Robert, of Shropshire
Guyard, Caroline, d Middlesex 1868
Gurney, Caroline, d Surrey 1867
Gutzlaffe, Jacob, d abroad
Guest, Robert, of Shropshire
Grimes, Sir Thomas
Gunter, James, b 1790
Guest, Elizabeth }
" Henrietta } of Bristol
Guthurie, Julia, frmly Wilkinson
Gurr, Jane, of Ramsgate
Guest, William V., London 1851
Gwyn, Thomas T. }
" Mary A. } of Shropshire
Gwynne, Thomas } of Rees, Shrop-
" Mary } shire
Gwillin, Catharine, of London
Gunn, Elizabeth, d Hoxton 1826
Gunner, Sarah, of London
Gunning, Richard, hatter, London
Gurr, John, of Kent, d 1803
Gutcher, Thomas, d about 1861
Gwinnett, Ann, o'wise Bourn 1781
" Batton, d Wolverhampt'n
" Emilia, of Glamorgan

Gye, Samuel, *d* Gosport
Gwynn, John, *d* Worcester

H

Harrison George, *d* Yorkshire 1867
Hamilton, Maurice
Handcock, Captain Elias R
Harrington, S., of Kingston
Hales, Julia Emma, of London
Halliday, Margaret, of Walworth
Haynes, Ann, of Finsbury 1817
Hamond, Miss, of Gravesend 1864
Havens, Sophia
Hargrave, Matilda, *d* Wakefield 1865
Hartley, Ralph, *d* Manchester
Hall, William, *d* London
Hackett, Elizabeth, *frmly* Harman
Harrison, Henry, born about 1662
Harvey, Richard, of Glostershire
Hardwicke, Edward, *d* Middlesex
Hay, Richard, *d* Middlesex
Hayes, Jacob, *d* Somerset
Halley, Thomas, *d* Colchester
Hall George, *d* Surrey 1843
Hall, John R., of Ludlow
Hall, John, *d* Daventry 1829
Hamilton, Marg'ret,*d* Chichest'r 1824
Hanley, Elizabeth, *d* Essex
Harrison, William, of London
Haward, Searl E., *d* Surrey 1766
Haward, Edward, of Surrey 1809
Hall, Esther, sister of Mrs. Ennis
Hawes, Sarah
Hawes, Jane, married Mr. Johnson
Hawes, Francis, of London
Hawes, Matthew, son of Francis
Haworth, Sarah, of Chester
Hards, Ann, *d* 1842
Hardman, Catherine
Harford, Mary, servant 1810
Hale, Ann, Brompton, *d* 1839
Hales, Robert, of Norfolk
Hardman, Sarah, *w* Hadfield
Hall, William, seaman, *d* 1845
Harland, Robert, of Southwark
Harris, Richard
Halsey, Mary, of Middlesex
Harris, Mark S., of London, 1793
Hartwall, James, *d* Somerset 1866
Hammond, Robert, of London
Hamp, Alfred, brother to Edward
Haynes, James, went abroad 1852
Hampshire, Mary, of Whitechapel
Hargreaves, William, of Lancashire

Hayes, Jane, *o'wise* Hambley 1807
Harvey, William, of Falmouth
Hassell, John, *d* Staffordshire 1822
Haley, Martha, *frmly* Hassell
Harpe, Grace, *frmly* Hassell
Hassell, Elizabeth, sister of John
Harrison, Lauristina, *d* abroad 1862
Harries, Elizabeth
Harris, William, blacksmith
Hampton, John, servant
Hassen, Jane, married Mr. Cook
Hall, William G., of Bombay
Halford, Joseph *b* at Utah
Harris, Susannah, of Chemlsford
Hartshorn, Mary, Bilston, *d* 1843
Haine, Madame R., of Antwerp 1856
Harrison, A. W., of Wolverhampton
Harper, Frances, Surrey, *d* 1861
Haigh, Mr., trustee of Elizabeth Waskett
Harris, Henry, *o'wise* Hunt
Harding, John, Surrey, *d* 1842
Harding, William ⎱ brothers and
  " Thomas ⎰ sisters of John,
  " Elizabeth ⎱ of Surrey
Harrison, Mr., of Liverpool
Hams, Robert P., *d* Liverpool
Haines, Maria, *o'wise* Bailey
Harrington, Richard, Warrington, *d* 1863
Haynes, Susannah, *o'wise* Maltwood
Hanlon, J., *d* abroad
Harris, Edward, of Clerkenwell
Haley, Robert, of London 1814
Harrap, Harriett, *frmly* Legood
Harriss, W. T. O., of City Road 1854
Harvey, Kate, of Brompton
Haynes, Ann, of Finsbury 1820
Hayes, Charles, wine merchant 1815
Hagarty,Marg'ret, of Shoreditch 1866
Haggison, John, seaman M S
Hartley, Bernard, *d* Yorkshire
Hardy, Lucretia C., Middlesex
Hardman, Daniel, of London
Harvey, Susannah, *b* 1757
Handen, Mary, Middlesex
Hall, Ann, *d* in Paris
Hamilton, John J., *d* Ventnor 1866
Hackett, Charles A., living 1835
Hawkins, James, son of Robert
Hammond, Mr.
Hartley, William, left England 1835
Hardy, Elizabeth, Sussex, *d* 1860
Haynes, Benjamin
Hammond, Robt., went abroad 1854
Hardy, S. C., *w* of Admiral John H.

Hardy, Sarah, of London
Harrington, Joseph, of Isle of Wight
Hamilton, Henry, d abroad 1808
" Rev. Andrew, of Ireland
" Rev. Edmund, of Ireland
Hammond, Sarah
" Martin, mariner, d 1794
" Rev. James, living 1820-33
" John, d in America
Hampton, John, d 1859
Hand, Elizabeth, o'wise Miller
" Richard G., d at Chelsea
Handley, Frances, Birmingham
Hankins, Mary, of London 1840
Hannaford, Geo., mariner, d 1827
Hannay, Martha, of Westminster
Hannington, Lieut. J. G., d abroad
Hanson, Cath, of Westminster
Hansen, J., d abroad 1863
Harbut, Delia, Lincolnshire 1838
Harcourt, M. R. G., *frmly* Stracey
Hardcastle, Maria, *frmly* Blair
Harden, Mary, *frmly* Seaman
Harding, Elizabeth, Somerset
" Joseph, solicitor
" Maj. Richd., d abroad 1808
Hart, Sarah, of Sussex
" Frederick, of London
Haslane, Sarah, London
Hassell, Sarah, of Brighton 1854
Hatton, John, d 1855
Hawkins, Henry, of London
" Lieut. William, d 1816
Hay, Francis, seaman Navy
" James Scott, d abroad
" Sarah, Paddington, d 1837
" Wm., of Northumberland 1796
Hayley, Thomas J., d abroad 1809
Haynes, Elizabeth, of Shropshire
" Sarah, Southwark, d 1821
" William, of London
Hayward, Jane, o'wiss Wake
" John, brother to Thomas
" John, d 1858-60
" Phœbe, o'wise Boyes
" Thomas, of Portsea, Hants
" Mrs. Margaret, of Somerset
Hamer, John, of Southwark 1817
Hamilton, John, of London 1820
Hayes, Charles, of London 1816
Haynes, Ann, of Finsbury 1817
Harrison, Charles, of Lambeth 1819
Haines, Nathan T., of London 1815
Harrison, Mary G., Lancashire d 1867
Haring, John, of London 1820
Hayman, C., d abroad 1868

Hart, Martha, o'wise Andoe d 1849
Harvey, John, went to America 1796
" Mary York, dau. of John
Hammond, William, d Devon 1833
Hatton, Elizabeth, *frmly* Paine, d 1868
Hancock, John, of Shropshire
Harris, Edward, of Clerkenwell
Hadfield, George, architect 1782
Harborne, Edward, of Solihull
Harrison, Margaret, Liverpool 1811
Harris, Captain Edward W., d 1837
Hare, William, of Stratford, d 1864
Harper, Thomas, of London
Hayden, William, of Wandsworth
Hazlefoot, William Henry, of Chelmsford
Haase, Mary, w of F. B. H., who d 1770
Haddon, Wm., d abroad 1837
Hadkinson, John, d London 1826
Hagan, James, of Ireland, d 1800
Haggar, Mary, of Bedford
Haines, George J., of London
" John, of Southwark 1825
" Sarah, wife of Thomas
Haldoine, Lieut. W., d abroad
Halfpenny, Cornelius, d 1852
Hall, Ann, d Brixton 1856
" Ann, of Newington, Surrey
" Betsy, d at Brighton
" Catharine, of Notts 1804
" Dorothy, *frmly* Robinson
" Edward, of E I C S, d 1831
" Elizabeth, d in Bloomsbury
" Isaac, seaman Navy
" John, of Notts, d 1811
" Rev. John, of Yorkshire 1760
" Mary, d London 1833
" Richard, of Ifield, Sussex
" Sarah, Alnwick
" Thomas, cordwainer, Lewes
" Thomas, of Bungay, Norfolk
" William, seaman M S
Hallett, Mary, London 1823
Halliday, Ann, Westminster, d 1830
Hallmarke, Jos. of Gt. Yarmouth 1799
" James, native of Cheshire
Halsey, Samuel, of London
Hamilton, Cath., Dublin, d 1777
Harrison, Elzbth., Yorkshire, d 1818
" Lieut. Geo. L., d abroad 1816
" Henry
" Jane, Philadelphia
" Lieut. John, d abroad
" John, native of Manchester
" Mary Ann, d London
" Rich., of Warrington, d 1863

Harrison, Ralph, of Greenwich, Kent
" Susannah, *frmly* Deighton
" Thomas
" Thos. butcher, Westminst'r
" William, of London 1750
Hart, Alexander, *d* abroad
Hartley, Hannah, of Surrey
Hartson, James, *d* abroad 1858
Harsley, Charles, of Yorkshire
Harvey, Jane, *d* Dublin 1845
" Susannah, daughter of John
" Richard ⟩ of Wallingford,
" Hannah ⟨ Berks
" Robert, merchant 1830
Harvie, Sophia, of Hertford 1856
Hardress, John, of Canterbury 1700
" Tomlinson, wife of John
Hards, Richard, of Sussex, *d* 1805
Hardy, Ann, *frmly* Spencer
" Alexander, *d* abroad 1851
" William, of Dorset, *d* 1853
" Wm., surgeon, *d* abroad 1820
Hardyman, Elizabeth, Somers Town
Hargraves, Ann, Grantham, *d* 1846
Harkness, John ⟩ of Lisbon,
" Jane ⟨ Portugal
Harling, Hy., of Bethnal Green, *d* 1828
Harmer, John, of Greenhithe, Kent
Harnes, John, seaman M S
Harper, Captain Wm., *d* abroad
" Frances M., *frmly* Bauch
Harradin, Elizabeth, of Whitehaven
Harrington, Andrew, seaman Navy
" Lieut. J. G., *d* abd 1820
" Mary, of Westminster
" Peter, seaman Navy
Harris, Lieut. Alex. M., *d* 1851
" Ann P., *o'wise* Josling
" George, *d* Surrey 1838
" Henry G., *d* Kennington 1847
" James, *d* Bloomsbury 1826
" Jane, of Brighton
" Jane ⟩ of or near Woolwich,
" John ⟨ 1820
" John, of Herefordshire
" Susannah, Chelmsford, *d* 1825
" Wm., of Dagenham, *d* 1859
Heddington, Ann, of London
Heyworth Family
Herbert, Joseph, *d* abroad 1837
Heather, Michael, of London 1860
Heasman, John, of Sussex
Heath, Matthew, of Wiltshire
Hesse, John A. F., *d* Paddington
Heath, James, of Berkshire
Hemment, Ann, of Whittlesey

Henshaw, Thomas, *d* Blackley 1810
Herbert, William, *d* Chelsea
Heslop, Thomas, of Whitehaven
Heath, Margaret, of Staffordshire
Hebden, George, of Leeds
Hegley, William, of London
Herbert, William, of Oxfordshire
Heywood, John P
Hewson, Ann, Gainsborough
Heeson, Christopher, of Cornwall
Henzell, Ann, Cheapside 1838
Henderson, William, surgeon R N
Henville, M E., Hants, *d* 1866
Hengham, Robert K., *d* abroad
Heeley, Martha, *frmly* Hassell
Heath, Mary, *frmly* Russell
Healum, George, valet 1859
Hemment, Ann, Isle of Ely, *d* 1804
Heale, G. W., of Greenwich
Hering, W. H., Esq., Tamworth
Heath, Mary, *dau* of Moses, *d* 1810
" John, of Gloucester
Henderson, Ann M. S., Portsea
Hegginbottom, George, living 1846
Hely, Henry Parnell
Hearne, Francis, *d* in America
" John B., of Surrey
Heyes, William, of Mold
Heighington, Jessica, Mrs.
Hemmens, Jane E., of Bristol
Heath, William, of 15th Hussars
Henningham, Mrs. E., of Woolwich
Henningham, J. G. C. D.
Heathcote, Thos. of Berkshire, 1823
Hernon, Elizabeth, of London 1832
Hewitt, Dan'l Chas., of London 1847
Henfry, Benjamin ⟩ brothers of John
" George ⟨ of Sheffield
Henson, —, otherwise Bassett
Heath, Henry B.T., of Edgware Road
Herring, John, of Lambeth, *d* 1813
" Joseph, of London, *d* 1763
Head, Charles, *d* abroad 1832
Heapy, Elizabeth, Islington, *d* 1790
" Esther, Rotherhithe
Heard, William, gardener, Essex 1846
Heath, Thomas, of London
" Colonel Robert T., *d* 1813
Hedley, Hannah, Durham *d* 1840
Hedges, Mrs. Susannah, *d* 1838
Helm, —, of Germany, *d* abroad
Hemans, Mrs., of London
Hemming, Samuel, of London 1760
Heming, Capt. George, *d* abroad
Henderson, James, surgeon R N
" Marian, of Southwark

Henderson, Rev. R., *d* abroad 1839
" William, of Elgin N B
" William II. J., *d* 1860
Hendrick, Elizabeth, *d* London 1829
Hendry, Elizabeth of Portsmouth
Heney, Mary, Bristol, *d* 1846
Henley, Edwd., of America, 1760-80
" Lady B., of Hants 1709
" Elizabeth ⎫
" James ⎬ of Hailsham,
" Mary ⎭ Sussex
" William
Henry, Charles, *d* abroad 1857
Hepburn, Col. David, *d* 1854
Hepworth, Thomas, *d* about 1857
Herdsman, Richard, of Somerset 1815
Herne, Jane ⎫
" Jacob ⎬ of London, 1750-60
" Thomas ⎭
Herring, Charlotte, of Richmond
" Hester, *o'wise* Howe, *d* 1846
Hester, Jno., of Surrey, *d* abrd 1830
Hewlett, Martha, *o'wise* Hanning
Hewson, Henry, seaman M S
" Mary A., Hammersmith
Hewston, James, of London 1806
Heyes, Elizabeth, of London 1807
Heynault, Francis, of London 1793
Hill, Louisa, of Poplar
Hill Family
Hill, William, *d* Middlesex 1868
Hills, Charles, *b* London 1803
Hiort, Mary A. G., *d* Grantham 1860
Hicks, J. H., *frmly* of Fulham
Hitchcock, Thomas
Highstreet, Andrew, *d* Westminster
Hickes, William, *d* Hamburgh
Hirst, Joshua, *d* Yorkshire
Hindley, Susannah, *d* Alcester
Hill, John D., of Bradford
Higginbottom, Geo., of London 1846
Hill, Mary ⎫
" John ⎬ living 1821
Higgs, Thomas, *d* Kidlington 1844
Hill, William, *d* Middlesex
" Thomas, of London, 1802
" Margaret, *d* Edinburgh 1866
Hindmarsh, Thomas, *d* abroad
Hillier, John ⎫ of the Isle of
" Caroline ⎭ Wight
Hill, Thomas
Hickman, Sophia, *frmly* Upsall
Higson, Mary, *o'wise* Balshaw
Hirst, Hannah, *o'wise* Vickerman
Hicks, Richard, of Southwark
Hill, Arthur, went to Sydney 1821

Hibbard, Richard, of Sleaford
Hill, George, Notts, farmer, *d* 1863
" Sarah, of Hemel Hampstead
" Hannah, *w* of George
Hibble, Ann, *frmly* Merry, *d* 1833
Hibbert, Margaret, of Twickenham
Hibble, Ann, *s*, *d* London
Hickes, George, of London
Hicks, Jno., of Godmanchester, *d* 1827
Higginbotham, John, of London
Higgin, John, yeoman, Wilts
Higgins, Harriet *s*, *d* Torquay
" Joseph, *d* India
" Mrs. M., of Southampton
" Thomas B., of London 1843
" William, of Radnor
" Matthias, living 1804
Hill, Benjamin, of Northampton
" David, *d* Edinburgh, 1860
" Esther, Mrs., of Clapham, 1772
" Francis, of Walworth, *d* 1790
" Major George, *d* abroad 1809
" Jane, of Walworth, *d* 1790
" John, *d* Sheerness 1824
" Joseph, purser R N, *d* 1808
" Joseph, of Northampton
" Mary, *o'wise* Wood, *d* 1700
" Mary, *o'wise* Barrow
" Mary, of Yorkshire, *d* London
" Mrs., of Marylebone, 1767
" Sarah, *d* in Russia
" Thomas, *d* in London
Hilliard, James, of Walworth, *d* 1800
" John, of Liverpool, *d* 1836
Hillier, Hannah, *frmly* Taylor
" William, of Bloomsbury, 1784
Hills, John, of Wicker, Cambridge
Hinchcliff, William ⎫ of Harwich,
" Ann ⎭ Essex
Hind, Sarah, *s*, native of Gloucester
Hinkley, Maria ⎫ of Kent, went to
" Barbara ⎭ Scotland
Hinckesman, Anthony ⎫ stationers,
" Richard ⎭ London
Hinley, Daniel, of London, *d* 1812
Hines, Thos., of Pinner, Middlesex
Hinton, Ann, *b* 1760, *d* abroad
Hitchcock, Giles, *d* London
" Wm. G., *d* in America
" Henry, *d* London
Hitching, Ann, *w*, Pembroke, *d* 1833
Hitchin, Elizabeth, *w*, Westminster, 1814
Higgs, John, of Berkshire, *d* 1799
Holbrook Family
Hooper, Mrs., of Paddington

Holmes, Mary, *widow*
Hotchkiss, Thomas, of Shropshire
Hopkins, Elizabeth, *d* Clifton, 1863
Holton, Daniel, *d* abroad 1869
Horrock, Sarah, *widow*
Hodgius, Sarah, *d* Surrey 1869
Hooper, Miss
Holmes, John F., of Ayr, N B
Houblon, Peter, *d* London 1707
Howell, Richard, of Kent
Hockenwall, John, of Cheshire
Housson, William, *d* Kent
Hollins, Sarah, *d* Hanbury
Hollins, William, *d* 1864–5
Holloway, John, *d* Middlesex, 1821
Holmes, Dorothy, of Yorkshire
Honeyman, Elizabeth, of Middlesex
Holt, Sarah, *frmly* Jones
Howell, Henry } of Chelsea
" Martha
Horn, James, brother to Lawrence
Hopley, William } uncles to John
" Samuel
Hornby, John, of Lancashire
Hoskin, Jane, *d* Middlesex
Holyfield, William, London
How, Hester, Middlesex, *d* 1846
Hookes, William, of Canterbury
Horwood, Mary S., *d* 1840
Hogg, Archibald, of Scotland
Hollins, Ann, *o'wise* Rogers
Horton, Elizabeth, Bath, *d* 1844
Holmes, James, of Brixton 1850
Hodges, William, painter 1834
Hodgson, Isaac, of Wapping 1827
Holland, George, of London 1835
Holloway, John, of London 1841
Howell, Thomas, of London 1810
Howorth, Mrs., *frmly* Rider
Houlding, Mary A. R., of Uxbridge
Hobber, Jane, of Brompton 1842
Holland, James
" Annie } of Stepney 1842
" Henrietta
Hodgson, Robert, of London
Hood, Nathaniel, of Greenwich
Holman, Mr.
Homewood, William
Honeyman, John, of Glasgow
Howell, Sarah, *o'wise* Porch
Howard, Ann, Surrey, *d* 1868
Houlden, sister of John Henfrey
Horne, Frederick W., mariner
Howell, William } of Pembroke
" Mary   1770–80
Horwood, Henrietta S., Islington

Holmes, Robert Alexander
Howard, C., mariner, *d* abroad 1866
Horgan, Jeremiah, Australia, farmer
Holton, Mrs. of Marylebone
Houston, Elizabeth, Dublin
Hornby, Elizabeth } of Yorkshire
" John
Hopley, John, of Occlestone
Holm Family, of Inverness
Hogarth, Hannah, otherwise Johnson
Horton, John, left England 1864
Hopkins, John, of Somerset
Howell, John, Cambridge, *d* 1867
Hopkins, Ann, otherwise Bates, *d* 1862
Holder, William W., Worcester
" Mary Ann, of Worcester
Hopkinson, Miss, aged about 80
Hollaway, James, of Bristol
Horne, Miss, *dau.* of Frederick W.
Hobbs, Sarah, *w* of George
Howe, Balwin W., of Kent
Hobbs, Frances, *frmly* Irish
Hockett, William, army surgeon
Hobson, Charles, *d* in Dorsetshire
Hodkinson, Samuel, *d* abroad
" Thos., of Birmingham
Hodson, James, farmer, Cambridge
Hoffman, John, of Cambridge, *d* 1797
Hogarth, George, of Scotland 1796
" Robert, of Berwick, 1801
Hogg, George B., *d* 1854–5
" Wm., surgeon, *d* abroad 1820
" Archibald, *d* London 1861
Hogan, Margaret, *w*, Somers Town
Holden, Wm., of Yorkshire *d* abrd
Holdon, William, *d* London
Holland, Ambrose, of Essex
" Harriet, *s*, Dublin, *d* 1835
" Richard, of Leominster
Hollis, Martha, *s*, Essex, *d* 1841
" John, of Eling, Hants
Holliday, John, of Essex
Hollaway, Mrs. Jane, of Wiltshire
Holme, John, *d* Preston, 1863
" John, of Gilling, Yorkshire
Holmes, William, cook, M S, *d* 1843
" Mary, *frmly* Little
" Joseph, of Dublin, *d* 1829
" Thomas, *d* in London 1827
Holt, Wm., banker, London 1823
Homer, Mrs. } of Clerken-
" Miss Amelia } well
Hooke, Esther, living 1701
Hook, Lawrence, seaman, *d* 1810
Hooper, Stephen, of Ramsgate
Hooton, Rich., of Nottingham, *d* 1851

Hope, Susannah, s, Bath
" Mary A., s, d London 1863
" William F., d Chatham 1856
Hopkins, Wm., native of Canterbury
" George, of Gloucestershire
Hopkinson, Benj., of London, 1821
" Benj., solicitor, d 1835
Hopley, John, seaman, d 1843
Hopper, Benjamin, sergeant, d abrd
Horah, John A., d about 1861
Horldon, George, of Canada
Horn, Lawrence, d Middlesex 1808
Hornby, Elizabeth, s, d London 1823
" John, d in America
Horne, A. E. R., w, d Battle 1859
Horsey, Samuel, of Surrey, 1781
Horsefield, Elizabeth, frmly Booth
Horsenail, Lieut. S., R N, d 1794
Horwood, Elizabeth M. N., d 1849
Hough, John, of Chester
Houghton, Cath., wife of Richard
Houlston, James, seaman, Navy
Hounsham, A., d America 1853
Houston, Alex., of Glasgow 1800
" Robt., d in S. America
Houstown, Geo. II., of Southwark
Howard, Elizabeth, s, d Bloomsbury
" Henry, of Bermondsey
" Isaac, d in America
" Henry, attorney, d 1806
" Robert, seaman M S
" R. F., master-mariner
" William, of London, d 1774
How, Joseph, solicitor's clerk
" Rich'd., of Market Harborough
Howe, Elizab'h L., o'wise Underdown
" John, of London, d 1817
" Mary, frmly Weston, d 1835
" Edward L., merchant, d abd
Horwick, Henry } of North Chapel,
" Thomas } Sussex
" James } of Denton,
" William } Sussex
Howlett, Henry, of London
" Samuel, seaman Navy
Howorth, Robert, of Essex, d 1819
" Ann } daughters of
" Sarah } Robert
Honett, Anna, s, d in Kent 1840
Hunt, Hannah, d abroad
" John, mariner
Hutchings, John, d London
Hurst, Edward, d London
Hunter, John, d America
Hutchinson, Robert, d Carlisle
Hurst, Jane, frmly Smith .

Hunt, Thomas, d **Surrey 1841**
Hunter, John, son of **William**
Hunt, Elizabeth
" Jane
Hutchinson, Mary, of Winton
" Isabella, of Winton
Hummell, Sarah, of Hammersmith
Hunter, Thomas, Westminster 1846
Hudson, Justice, of London 1823
Hunt, John, living 1817
" Thomas, of Madras;
Hullins, George, master-mariner
Hutt, George E., d Middlesex 1867
Hutchins, Chas. J., of Liverpool d 1868
Hubbard, Richard, chair-maker
Huskins, Hannah, o'wise Clarke
Hunt John, son of Amos
" Thomas, d at Peckham
Hughes, James, d London 1868
Humfreys, John, d abroad 1824
Hunter, Elizabeth, frmly Nielson
Hughes, John, d Middlesex 1820
" Helen M., Taunton 1837
Hurrell, Thomas, of Suffolk 1814
Hunt, Henry H., of Lambeth
Hutchinson, John, d abroad 1861
Hume, William, of Liverpool
Humfray, Major Samuel, d abroad
Hudson, William, Yorkshire, d 1864
Huckin, Henry, d Colney Hatch 1863
Hudson, Robert
" Market Gilbert
Hunt, Isabella, d at Brixton
Hudson, John
" Elizabeth, o'wise Lowe
" Ann, of Kilkenny
Hutchinson, John, of Lazenby
Huggins, William F., living 1835
Hughes, Richard, of London
Humbus, Ann C., d Brugen 1813
Hunter, William, of Ayr, N B
Hume, Jane
" Annie }
" Mary } children of Wil-
" Margaret } liam Hume, of
" James } Liverpool
" Joseph }
Hudson, Henry, of Hayling Isle
" Geo., gardener, Lancashire
" Susannah, niece of R. Sheldon
Huett, Sophia H., London 1810
Huff, Andrew B, seaman, d 1818
Huggett, Abraham, d London 1818
Hugh, Aaron, of Brecon
Hughes, David, d London 1840-4

Hughes, Elizabeth, servant
" Hester, Bristol, d 1836
" Mr. H. A., d abroad
" John, of Bermondsey, d 1827
" John, seaman M S
" Thomas, stationer, London
" Thos., of Penyfrith, d 1852
" Thomas, d in Lancashire
" William, servant, d Bath
Huke, James, of Bloomsbury 1816
Hull, Elizabeth, frm'ly Bell
" John D., living 1810
" Charles Edward, of London
Hulme, George, d London 1813
Humber, John, of Dorset
Humes, William, seaman Navy
Hume, J. R., army surgeon
Hume, Priscilla, frm'ly Elkin
Humphreys, Mary P., o'wise Young
" Samuel J. G., d abroad
" John, clerk R N
Hunt, Lieut. George M., d abd 1810
" Sir Thomas
" Mary, o'wise Stephens 1796
" Samuel, of London 1796
" Samuel, d abroad 1824-25
" William H., d abroad
Hunter, Ann, of London, 1776-90
" Thomas, d abroad
" George, seaman Navy
" James, d abroad 1858
" William, soldier, d abroad
" Captain William, d abroad
" Bridget, d abroad 1821
Huntle, John, seaman, d 1842
Huntley, Israel, d London 1838
Huntingdon, Jane, of Cumberland
Hurley, John, seaman Navy
Hussey, Edward, d Noxton 1858
Hutchinson, Wm., d abroad 1863
Hutchins, Jane, of Bath and London
Hutchinson, Thomas, seaman Navy
" Capt. W. F., d abroad
" Rev. Walter, of Worcester
Huton, Mrs. Ann, of London
Hullmandel, C. J., of Westminster
Hyde, Charles, d Stockport
" Ann, d Surrey, 1814
" George, d abroad 1827
" John, of Worcestershire
" William, d London 1820

I

I'ans, Michael
Irish, John Arthur, d Shropshire

Ireland, Edward, d London
Imison, Joseph, of Knaresborough
Ireland, John, of London
Ivie, Ann, o'wise Le Sueur
Ingram, Samuel, d Exeter
Ingles, John, of Stanton, d 1762
" Ann, d 1767
" Culpeper, living 1757
" Richard, d Burford 1803
" Catharine, d Burford 1816
Ireland, Edward C., of Cardiff
Ibbottson, William, d York 1796
Innes, Mary, d Russia 1864
Irving, John Crockford, d Derby
Ilsley, Martha, Cowes, d 1866
Inglish, George, alias J. Smith
Ibbottson, James, Middlesex, d 1845
" Sarah, d 1847
Israel, Samuel, merchant, Hamburgh
Infield, John, brother to Caleb
Innes, George, native of Aberdeen
Ilett, William
Ingram, Adam
Ikin, Jonathan, of London 1822
Inster, Archibald, native of Shetland
Ireland, John A., d London
Irvine, William, seaman
" Lieut. John, d abroad
Irving, Geo., underwriter "Lloyd's"
" Mary, d Carlisle 1860
Isaac, George Frederick, of London
Ives, Elizabeth, frmly Stabbs, d 1813
" William, seaman Navy
Ivie, Lieut. Thomas, d abroad
Ivory, Charlotte, Southwark, d 1820
Ivyleafe, James, of Essex
Imlach, Chas. J. F., surgeon, d 1857
Infield, Lieut. Caleb, R N, d 1829
Inglis, Walter, seaman Navy
" William, d Surrey 1802-3
Inglish, Mary, Marylebone, d 1808
Innes, Lieut. Chas. D., d abroad 1857
" George, mariner, M S
" Gilbert) of Aberdeenshire,
" Jean) Scotland
" James, d Jamaica 1798
" Judith, of Plymouth, d 1814
" William, d London 1794

J

Jarvis, Anna, of Feltham
Jackson, William
Jackson, John
Jackson, Mary
Jarrold, Matthew, of Suffolk

38 GENERAL INDEX.

Jarrett, William, of Sussex
Jacobs, John, *d* Gloucestershire
Jackson, Honoria, of Yorkshire
James, Thomas, of Pembrokeshire
James, Edward, of E I C S
Jacob, William, *d* Colchester
James, John, *d* abroad 1831
Jay, Sir James, of Bath
James, James, *d* Middlesex 1844
Jaques, Edward R., of Essex
Jardine, John, *d* abroad 1821
Jarrett, John, *d* Kent 1861
Jackson, William, of Liverpool
" Wm., of Yorkshire, *d* 1820
" Isaac, *d* Middlesex 1868
James, John, of Piccadilly 1838
" Joseph, of London 1820
Jackson, William, York, *d* 1848
James, Mary, Bristol, *d* 1865
Jackson, Sarah, Middlesex, *d* 1866
" George, of New Kent Road
Jacques, Louisa, Essex, *d* 1862
Jamieson, James, *d* America
Jackson, Martha, *frmly* Hallow 1824
" Mrs. Catherine, 1853
" William, sergeant, 1834
" John Miles
" Thomas } of Cumberland
" Joseph
James, Elizabeth Ann, *d* Surrey 1848
" Alexander
Jackman, William, *d* about 1859
Jackson, William, of Liverpool
James, Elizabeth, London, *d* 1837
Jarram, Lucy, left Sheffield 1837
Jackson, Oliver, Esq.
" Charles, seaman Navy
" Henry *d* London
" Jane, *o'wise* Farrer, *d* 1852
" John, *d* America
" John, mariner
" John, *d* in S. America
" John, son of John
" Sarah, Westminster, *d* 1852
" William, of Nova Scotia
" William, of Bristol, *b* 1757
" William, of London 1780
James, Abraham, seaman M S
" David, seaman M S
" Elizabeth, Lambeth 1776
" John, of Brentford, *d* 1813
" Philip, seaman M S
" Richard, *d* America
Jameson, John, seaman, *d* 1847
Jamieson, William, *d* in Jamaica
" John, *d* in America

Jennings, Thomas, of Deptford
Jefferson, Thomas, *d* Cumberland
Jenkins, Richard, of Bath
" Emma
" Sarah
" Elizabeth
Jenning, Henry, carver
Jeffe, James, of Harrow
Jerningham Family
Jenks, Sarah O., of France
Jennens, William ⎫
" John
" Sarah
" Mary
" Elizabeth ⎬ living 1700
" Ann
" Humphrey
" Robert ⎭
Jeffcot, Arthur, of Camberwell 1839
Jefferd, William, wine merchant
Jenkins, Thomas, of America 1861
Jennings, Eliza, *o'wise* Thorn
Jeffries, Ann, *o'wise* Bodkin
Jenkins, Mary, daughter of Edward
Jerrom, Rev. Thomas
Jennings, Thomas, of Somers-town
Jeeves, Catherine } of Hampstead,
" John } Middlesex
Jeffrey, Alexander, of Alloa, N B
" Lieut. W. N., *d* abroad 1819
Jeffries, Michael, of Paddington
Jefferson, Fanny, Cockermouth
Jefferies, Mr., jeweller, London
Jenkins, Capt. Chas. K. *d* abrd 1805
" Capt. Thos., *d* abrd 1814-15
" Jane, wife of John
" E. A., army surgeon
" Rev. Wm., *d* London 1764
Jenkinson, Edna, Manchester, *d* 1845
Jennings, Ann, Westminster
" Elizabeth, *o'wise* Fisher
" Humphrey, of Suffolk
" Jane, Somerset, *d* 1834
" John, seaman M S
" John, of Enfield, *d* 1805
" Mich'l A., *d* Jamaica 1808
" Sarah, of Staines, Middle'x
" William F., seaman
" William, of Suffolk, *d* 1798
" Wm., of Bristol & London
Jermy, John, *d* London 1818
Jephson, Lieut. John, R N
Jenvy, Jane, of Lymington Hants
Jones, Mrs. Elizabeth
Johnson, William R.
Johnson, Eliza

Johnson, John, *d* Cambridgeshire
Jones, Frederick H. S.
Jordan, Miss Jane
Jove, Mrs. Elizabeth
Jones Family
Jones, Hugh D., *d* abroad
Jordan, Oliver, *d* West Indies 1712
" Elizabeth, *w, d* 1713
Johnson, Henry C., *d* India
" Elizabeth, *d* London
Jones, John, *d* London
" Arthur, *d* Middlesex
Jolly, John, merchant, Madras
Johnson, Alexander, mariner
" Thos. of Northamptonshire
" Samuel, of Suffolk
" Alexander, *d* Middlesex
" James, of London 1812
" Charles, of Wapping 1825
" William, London 1846
" Isaac, of London
Johnstone, Rosina, Islington, *d* 1866
Jones, Henry, native of Galway
" Joseph, of Haselmere
Jobson, Joseph, of Shrewsbury
Jones, Samuel, left Shropshire 1825
" William, of Sheffield
Johnson, Mary A., *frmly* Carter
Jones, Ann, wife of William
" William, of Birmingham
Jowett, Benjamin, of Bermondsey
Jones, Mary, Kensington, *d* 1861
" Richard, of London
" Ann, Denbigh, *d* 1862
" John, native of Denbigh
Jordan, William, J., Croydon, *d* 1862
" Timothy, Whitechapel, *d* 1824
Joseph, Henry, Algoa Bay 1758
Johnson, Adam, *d* in America
Jones, Mary, of Carmarthen
Jordan, Caroline A., *o'wise* Bakewell
Johns, Elizabeth, *frmly* Wales
Jones, William ⎱
" John ⎰ of Carmarthen-
" Evan ⎱ shire
" Hesther ⎰
Johnson, John, surgeon
Joslin, Caroline, of Canada
Johnstone, Capt. John M., *d* 1857
Joyce, George, *d* Bristol 1866
Jones, Mrs., *frmly* Piercey
" William, *d* Sydney 1826
Johnson, Jacob, seaman M S
" Hannah, *o'wise* Schofield
" Geo. Travers, *d* abroad 1836
" Peter, *d* abroad 1823

Jocelyn Elzbth, *o'wise* Parry, *d* 1843
Johnstone, Rob., of Houndsditch 1851
Jocelyn, H. B., *d* abroad 1858
Johnson, Alexander, seaman Navy
" Ann, wife of James, Sussex
" Benjamin, seaman Navy
" David, of Dublin 1780
" David, son of James
" Elizabeth, of Marlebone
" Elbth., *o'wise* Evans, *d* 1823
" Francis, Marylebone
" Geo. W., private 12th Regt.
" Capt. James, M R M, *d* 1815
" Jane, of City Road, London
" John, seaman Navy
" John, *d* Worthing 1841
" John of Stepney 1800
" Joseph, *d* Calcutta 1821
" Lawrence, seaman M S
" Mary, *frmly* Taylor
" Sarah, *o'wise* Hay *d* 1837
" Thomas, *d* abroad
" Thomas, seaman, *d* 1833
" William, seaman Navy
" Wm. of Norfolk, *d* abd 1806
Johnston, Henry ⎱ seamen Navy
John ⎰
Jolly, Sarah, *frmly* Steel, *d* 1808
Jones, Alexander, of London 1771
" Ann, *frmly* Hodkinson
" Ann, *d* Highgate 1809
" Ann, wife of Thos. of Ratcliffe
" Arabella, living 1785
" Benjamin, seaman M S
" Cath., Birmingham *d* 1858
" Colonel of the Royal Artillery
" David, seaman M S
" Elbth., cousin to Wall Family
" Elizabeth, *d* London
" Elzbth. *dau* of Samuel 1775
" Edmund, *d* abroad 1848
" Grace, living 1785
" Griffith, *d* 1778
" George, Bishop of Kildare
" Henry L., native of Wales
" John, *d* in America
" John of London, *d* abroad 1843
" John, son of Samuel 1775
" Joseph, seaman M S
" Mary, *dau.* of Samuel 1775
" Mary, *frmly* Perryman
" Mary, *dau.* of David
" Mary, *o'wise* Bowbeer
" Martha, *w* London
" Owen, mariner
" Rev. Pryce of Carmarthen

GENERAL INDEX.

Jones, Robert G., of Marylebone
" Robert, seaman Navy
" Robert J., of Yorkshire
" Richard, of Knightsbridge
" Richard H., *d* abroad 1845
" Samuel, *d* previous to 1775
" Samuel, son of Samuel 1775
" Sarah, *dau.* of Samuel 1775
" Sarah, *dau.* of John and Ann
" Sarah, *o'wise* March
" Sarah D., of Lambeth
" Thomas, of Cheshire
" Thomas, living 1785
" Thomas, of Hedgerley, Bucks
" William, builder, London
" William, clerk, London
" William, seaman M S, *d* 1839
" William, *d* London 1852
Josling, Ann P., *frmly* Harris
Joules, Cath. H., Staffordshire 1824
Jowse, Mrs. Mary, *d* Surrey 1797
Joyce, Rev. Jeremiah
" Mary, Clifford, York
Judson, Elizabeth, *d* Middlesex
Jupps, Charles, builder
Judd, Rebecca, of Waltham Abbey
Judge, Joseph, of London 1811
Jubb, George, of London
Julian, George, of London
Judson, Sydney, of Ireland
Juniper, Samuel C., of Sussex
Julia, Rebecca, of Lincoln

K

Kane, Charles, Chelsea pensioner
" Thomas, of Brentford, *d* 1846
Kay, James, of Rochdale
" William
Kaye, John, of Essex, *d* 1826
" Sarah, *o'wise* Benton, *d* 1834
" Joseph, of Netherton, York
" John } cloth-dressers, of
" Peter } Yorkshire
" William }
Katinska, Anna, *frmly* Thompson
Keiling, Thomas
Kearney, Ellen, *d* Middlesex 1867
Kemble, John, *d* Dublin 1856
Kenyon, James, *d* Lancashire 1860
Keating, Arthur Saunders 1838
Keys, Alexander, *d* in America
Kearney, Richard, of Kildare
" Mary, *o'wise* Flood
Kerton, John } went to America
" Sarah } 1848

Keveney, Mrs., of Mayo, Ireland
Keen, Mrs., of Stratford-place
Kenworthy, Hugh, Leeds, *d* 1854
Keld, Henry, mariner, Yorkshire
Keith, John, *d* in Australia
Keating, Ann, of Essex, 1830
Keaquick, John, of Bristol 1844
Keating, Eliza E., Birmingham
Keate, George, living 1815
Kennedy, Emily Jane
Ker, James, of Ayton, N B 1781
Kenward, Mary, Sussex, *d* 1867
Kennington, Thomas, of Soho 1826
Kenny, Peter, surgeon, *d* abd 1845
Kent, John, gardener, Kent, *d* 1809
" William, of Teddington
Kenworthy, John, of London 1754
Kerby, Eleanor, Bloomsbury, *d* 1824
Kerr, James, seaman M S
Kerrison, Wm., gardener, of Wales
Kerry, Thomas, of Shropshire
Kesterton, Sarah, of Wandsworth R'd
Kettlewell, Catherine
" Thomas
Kew, William, of America 1837
Key, William, cork-cutter, London
" Harriet, Glo'stershire
" Mary, *d* in Sussex 1861
Keys, David W., native of Canada
Keau, Farmer, *d* London 1830
Keane, Mary, of London
" Michael, *d* abroad 1858
Kease, Mary, London
Keeler, Thomas, farmer, Kent
Keene, Frances, Marylebone 1819
Keilly, Lieut. Augustus T. P., *d* 1834
Keith, James, seaman Navy
" James, merchant, Banff 1788
Kelby, James, seaman Navy
Kelliam, John, *d* in London
Keller, Eliza, of London
Kelly, Ann, Lewisham
" Cornelius, *d* S. America
" Elizabeth, *d* London 1842
" Edward, of Piccadilly, *d* 1820
" James, seaman Navy
" Jane, *d* London 1847
" Gibbons, clerk, London 1823
" John, son of John and Bridget
" Thomas, seaman Navy
Kelly, Colonel Thomas E., *d* 1858
" William J., of the Navy 1813
Kelway, Henry, of Plymouth, *d* 1730
Kemp, Catherine, of Bristol, 1840
" Elizabeth, of Deptford
" Elizab'h, *frmly* Seabrook 1820

Kemp, John T., clerk, *d* London
Kempe, Lucretia, Yorkshire, *d* 1823
" Wm., *d* in Wiltshire 1859
Kempson, Ann ⎱ of London,
" Samuel ⎰ 1770-90
Kendall, Francis, *d* America 1820
" Lieut. Thos., *d* abroad 1813
Kendrick, John, of Whitechapel 1771
Kenknight, William ⎱ of Cliffe,
" Mary ⎰ Kent
Kennedy, James, seaman M S
Kennett, Capt. John, *d* abroad 1815
" Thomas, of Portsea, *d* 1842
Kennin, Oswald, of Cumberl'd, *d* 1818
Kendrick, Charles, of Winchcomb
Kingsby Family
King, Samuel, *d* Surrey
Kidd, W. J. P., *d* Gleneig 1870
King, John, of Westminster 1854
Kitchen, Elizabeth, *d* London
Kidley, Elizabeth, *frmly* Howorth
Kilpatrick, Samuel, *d* abroad
Kirk, John, of Islington
Kingston, Henry, of Lincolnshire
Kimber, William, of Berkshire
Kirton, John, *d* London 1833
Kinshott, Mary
Kinlock, Charlotte G. S., *d* Surrey 1835
" Adine ⎱ children of
" Georgiana ⎰ John
Kite, Hannah, lived at Exeter
King, Walter ⎫
" Feilder ⎟ nephews and niece
" George ⎬ of William King,
" Charles ⎟ of Surrey, *d* 1864
" Ada K. ⎭
Kirby, Elizabeth, Greenwich
King, William, Godalming, *d* 1864
" George, Buckingham, *d* 1864
" Mary Ann, *o'wise* Price
Kirchner, Edward, *d* abroad 1863
Kirkpatrick, W. G., Isleworth 1825
King, Edward, of Brighton
Kirk, John ⎱ of Marylebone
" Charlotte ⎰
Kirwan, Henry, of Dublin
Kidd, James, *d* in America
Kidney, Benjamin, of London, *d* 1817
Kidney, Sarah, of London
Kilgour, Peter, of Scotland, *d* abroad
King, Ann, *d* Southampton 1842
" Andrew, of Chelsea, *d* 1823
" Elizabeth, *frmly* Stackhouse
" Ensign George F., *d* 1815
" Lieut. Henry P., *d* abroad
" John, seaman M S

King, John, of Halifax, York
" Lieut. John, *d* abroad 1812
" Kesia A., *d* in Lambeth
" Mary, *frmly* Baker
" Mary, of Bungay, Suffolk
" Mary, *w* of Thomas
" Samuel, seaman, *d* 1834
" Sophia D., Chelsea, *d* 1846
" Thomas, *d* in Middlesex 1860
" Richard, solicitor's clerk
" William, of Maidstone
Kingston, William, of Hants, *d* 1853
Kinkade, Thomas, *d* in London 1835
Kinnersley, Mary, *frmly* Holmes
" William, *d* in London
Kirby, Bartholomew, *d* abroad 1814
Kirke, Anna M., of Bampton, Oxford
Kirton, George, solicitor, London
Kittridge, William, of London
Knight, Isaac, of Bristol
Knott, Jeremiah, *d* America
Knowles, Thomas, of Sowerby
Knightsbridge, Alice, *d* Westminster
Knott, John, *d* Surrey
Knudson, Colonel Christopher
Knight, Elizabeth, *d* London 1869
Knowler, Sarah, *frmly* Clark
Knight, Henry, of Lambeth
Knight, Stephen, of Fulham
Knee, P., station-master, Bombay
Knight, Henry, of Limehouse
" James, of Wigan, *d* 1833
" Jeremiah, of London, *d* 1822
" Sir Joseph, R'r-Admiral 1775
" Ralph, of Wigan, *d* 1837
" Rich'd, of Lincolnshire 1740
Knox, Andrew, of Montrose 1803
" Maria, *frmly* Webb
Knowles, James, of London, 1808
" Richard ⎱ of Peckham,
" Martha ⎰ Surrey, 1783
Kowing, William, native of Hanover
Krake, Ann C., *d* at Holloway 1827
Kynaston, Lieut. Chas. T., *d* abroad
" Thomas, of Harley, Salop
Kyte, Henry, *d* India

L

Lavis, Elizabeth, *o'wise* Martin
Law, Henry, *d* abroad
Lavender, Selina, of Essex
Lawes, Maria, *o'wise* Wilby
Laing, James, master-mariner
Lancaster, Elizabeth
Large, Peter, *d* abroad 1694

42   GENERAL INDEX.

Lawrenson, Joseph, *d* London
Lawrence, William, *d* Gloucestershire
"   Richard, *d* Westminster
"   Robert, *d* Norfolk
"   Thomas, *d* Deptford
"   Edward, *d* Dorset
"   Thomas, *d* America
"   Richard, *d* Hants
Langston, John, *d* Africa
Lambe, Thomas, *d* Northampton
Lambert, Richard, *d* London
La Beaume, Melchier, *d* Carlisle
Latour, Caroline, of Hoxton, Beds
Large, Ruth W., *frmly* Sparks
Lawley, Alice S., London, *d* 1861
Lakin, John, Durham, *d* 1829
Large, William
"   Matilda
"   Jane
Lawson, Ann, Whitehaven, *d* 1867
Lawrence, Reginald, son of Henry
Lacey, Thomas, of London 1830
Lamont, John, of Radcliffe 1847
Langston, Thomas, of London 1817
Lay, Mark, of Deptford 1813
Lane, Arthur, son of William
Lawriston, Colonel A., *d* 1821
Lamb, John, draper
Lane, William, of Worcester, *d* 1867
Ladbroke, Felix, of London
Laing, William, gunner Navy, *d* 1812
Lamb, Dr. James, *d* London 1830
"   Peter, of London, 1730-80
Lambert, Mary, Worcester, *d* 1851
"   Allan, of Surrey, *d* 1827
"   Elizabeth, of Surrey, *d* 1830
"   Mary, *frmly* Wadham, *d* 1820
Lambertson, Fanny, *frmly* Oakes
Lambell, Elizabeth, *d* Lambeth, 1835
Lane, John, of Salisbury
"   Giering, of London 1800
"   Lieut. George, *d* abroad
Lang, Robert, of Accrington
Lang, Henry D., of Cheshunt
Langford, Robert, of Mold, Flint
Langan, John, merchant, *d* abroad
Langley, Samuel
"   Caroline, Homerton
Lanigan, Charles, of Birmingham
Langmore, Mary, *frmly* Abbott
Lapsley, James, of Scotland
Lascelles, Jane, *frmly* Lumley
Laud, Ann, *d* London 1811
Laughlin, Eliza A., *d* America
Laurie, James D., of Edinburgh
Laver, Mrs. Sarah, of Essex

Laverick, John, mariner, *d* 1818
Lawler, Bridget, Middlesex 1838
"   Elizabeth, London 1840
Lawrence, John, *d* America 1814
"   Mary, of Bath
"   Sarah, *o'wise* Bennett
"   William, cooper, *d* abroad
Lawson, Joseph, mariner, *d* 1800
"   William, *d* Liverpool 1842
Lawton, Sarah, Litchfield
"   John, *d* abroad 1857
Lawson, Christopher, *d* 1834
"   Henry, seaman Navy
Laxton, Stephen, brother to Hannah
"   Thomas, of Everton, *d* 1816
"   S., of Cattismore, Rutland
Laycock, John, of Bramley, Leeds
Leach, Lieut. William, *d* abroad 1804
"   Elizbth., niece of D. Marshall
"   Mary A., *d* abroad 1862
Lesley, Charles, butler, 1815
Le Pennell, George
Leigh, Elizabeth, of Yorkshire
Legg, William } formerly of Bath
"   Frederick }
Leiven, John, *d* London
Lemon, William, *d* Surrey
Lemon William, *d* Truro
Leggett, Samuel, *d* Norfolk
Lewis, William, *d* London
"   Edward, *d* abroad
"   David, *d* Carmarthen
"   Joseph, *d* London
Leigh, George, of Halifax
Lennox, Gilbert, *d* Glasgow
Lewis, John, *d* Wilts 1811
Legood, Harriet, *o'wise* Harrap
Leman, Clement, *d* Bristol 1810
Lewis, George, of London 1775
Lewis, William, *o'wise* Penfold
Lee, George, civil engineer
Leadbeater, Sarah, Yorkshire, *d* 1865
Leslie, Hugh, London
Le Frank, James, Norfolk, *d* 1864
Leman, Abraham, of America
Lewis, Mary, Lambeth 1850
Lee, Edward C., mariner, *d* abroad
Lennon, James, *d* London 1861
Lenton, Thomas, *d* Kent 1860
Leslie, Robert, London, merchant
Leaver, Miss, of Bath
Leslie Family, Scotch
Ledger, Sarah, formerly Davies
Lees, Sarah, Gloucestershire, *d* 1838
Lean, John Harvey, of London 1816
Levitt, Lewis, of London 1834

NEXT OF KIN. 43

Lee, William, of Scotland
Le Pennell, Eliza, *dau.* of Chas.
Lee, Thomas, porter 1836
Leigh, William
Lempriere, George, of Rotherham
Leeke, John, of Grosvenor-place
Leabury, John, of Yorkshire, *d* 1853
Leake, Wm., of Wimbledon, Surrey
" Thos., of Handsworth, Staff'rd
Leather, Henry } uncles of Elizab'th
" James } Banks
Leathart, Rebecca, Islington, *d* 1835
Ledger, John, of Chelsea
Lee, John S., *d* London 1841
" James, seaman Navy
" Nebuchadnezzar, of India 1800
" Peter, seaman M S
" Thomas, of Plymouth, *d* abroad
" Dr. Thomas, married Miss Bray
" Thomas, *d* in America
Lefhew, Capt. Hy., G. Legion, *d* 1827
Leftwich, Susannah, of London
Legge, Eliza'hW. Teignmouth, *d* 1843
Leggett, William G., master-mariner, *d* abroad
Leggatt, Anne } sisters to John L.,
" Jane } the grandfather
" Mary } of Mary Mullen
" Susan }
Leighton, James, seaman, *d* 1841
" Frances, servant, *d* 1840
" Mary, of Glasgow, 1793
" Mary, *alias* Morton
" Sarah, *o'wise* Cook, 1812
Leith, George, *d* abroad 1862
Leman, Sir Wm., of Hertford, *d* 1701
Lennot, Alexander
" Mary
Leo, Capt. Daniel, *d* Bath 1803
Leonard, John, quartermaster
Lepine, Francis, native of France
" Maria, *d* Westminster
Laporte, Anthy., of London, 1760-80
Lernoult, Rev. Francis, *d* 1806
Lessine, Francis, of France
Lester, Mary, of Essex
Leven, George } relatives of Ann L.,
" James } servant in London
" Wm. } 1765
Lever, Mary A., *d* Camberwell 1864
Leavington, Jermh., of Brompton *d* 1843
Levy, Benjamin, of London, 1690
Leybourn, Ann, of Yorkshire, *d* 1822
Lewis, Benjamin, of Salisbury
" Lieut. Col. Charles, *d* 1852

Lewis, Cath., of Woolwich 1836
" Elias, of Bath
" George, *d* abroad, 1862
" Hugh, *d* London, 1813
" James, seaman, *d* 1844
" James, of Chester
" Jane, *d* abroad 1844
" Jane
' John, seaman Navy
" Rev. Richard, of Sussex, *d* 1783
" Samuel, *d* London 1858
" Samuel, *d* in India
" Lieut. Col. Wm., *d* abroad 1817
" William, seaman, *d* 1841
Leworth, William, of Clerkenwell
Lines, Elizabeth, of Suffolk
Lilley, Abraham, of Chelsea
Lightfoot, William, law agent
Litherland, James, seaman
Lightfoot, Elizabeth, *frmly* Smith
Linsey, Thomas, *d* Norfolk
Lister, James, *d* Calcutta
Lincoln, Edmund, *d* abroad
Little, Sarah, of Hungerford
Lindo, Alexander, of London 1810
Lillie, James R., of Aberdeen
Little, John S., *d* Surrey, 1868
Lindsey, John, Aberdare, *d* 1867
Lindsey, John, of Lincolnshire
Lindwart, Percy, *d* Ireland 1867
Livingston, Andrew, of Glasgow
Lithgoe, William, waiter
Lind, Edward
" Francis
" George
Littlepage, Mary, *frmly* Bramley
Liliey, Elizabeth, *w* London, *d* 1845
Liveley, William H., of Clerkenwell
Lisner, Elzbth., *o'wise* Dressler 1820
Lisabe, Francis B., *d* Cork 1866
Liart, Samuel, of Cornwall 1800
Lightfoot, J. G. R., *d* abroad 1863
Lilley, John, of Taunton
Linaker, Thomas, farmer, Leicester
Lindfield, Mrs. S., of Walworth
Lindbergh, M. H., *o'wise* McDonald
Lindley, Hester, *w*, Kensington
Lindsay, Lieut. Col. Adam, *d* 1812
" John H., of London
" Henry, *d* in India
" Thomas, jeweller, Bristol
Ling, Thomas, *d* Greenwich 1847
" Fina, Great Yarmouth, *d* 1858
Lington, Maria, *frmly* Nixon
Linton, Sarah, of Denton, Sussex
Lisner, Joseph, tailor, London, 1808

Litchfield Ann } of Mansfield,
" Frances } Notts, 1790
" Col. John
Little, Elizabeth, *d* Southwark
Lithgow, William, of Edinburgh 1798
Linwood, Wm., of Sproatley, York
Livermoor, Thomas, *d* at Durham
Lloyd, William, *d* 1869
" Thomas
" Richard, *d* Westminster
" Thomas, *d* Cardigan 1815
Lluellyn, Rev. R., *d* Sanderton 1770
Lloyd, John, of Kensington 1830
" Selina S. *dau.* of John
" Amelia M. *o'wise* Tarbuck
" Mrs. Ann, of London 1814
" Cath., of Birmingham
" Celia, *d* London 1824
" David, attorney, Brecknock
" Lucy M., *dau.* of John
" Lieut. Col. Richard, *d* abroad 1813
" William, tailor, London 1848
Lorne, Alexander, of Scotland
Loney, William, *d* Middlesex
Low, Thomas, *d* America
Lord, Aaron, *d* Gloucestershire 1795
Lowe, Sarah, *d* Middlesex 1869
Loft, Mary, *dau.* of William
Lowden, John, *d* Middlesex
Longley, H. F., of Camberwell
Long, William, *d* London 1868
Lovell, Benjamin Charles
Lockead, Isabella, *o'wise* Paul
" William, carpenter
Long, Joseph, of Wilts
Lovell, Elzbth., *d* Gloucestershire 1830
Lord, Thomas D., of Devon 1824
Loft, William, of Southwark
Lowrie, Robert, of Leith
Lomas, James, of London
Lockyer, Henry F., general, *d* 1860
Lockwood, John H., London 1847
Lonsdale, E., *d* abroad, 1862
Lockyer, Joseph
Louner, Charles, living 1795
Lowe, Elizabeth, *frm'y* Hudson
Lowdey, Thomas, Cardiff, mariner
Lockwood, Catherine, Middlesex
Lowe, Robert, of Scotland
Low, Margaret, of Fermanagh
Long, Joanna, Wamborough
Lopdell, Honor, Reading 1800
Lorrimer, Charles, living 1795
Lothian, Walter, of Edinburgh 1796
" Janet, *o'wise* Wilkie

Lott, Johanna, *d* abroad 1837
Louth, James, seaman, *d* 1831
" Rev. Robert
Love, Rev. David, of Essex, *d* 1828
Loveridge, Lieut. J. E., *d* in India
Loving, John, of Middlesex 1731
Low, Robert, seaman M S
Lowe, John, carpenter, Westminster
" Maria S., Lincolnshire *d* 1835
" Mary H., *d* London
Lowdell, George, of Surrey, *d* 1827
Louden, D., Esq., *d* abroad
Lowry, Robert A., *d* London 1842
Loan, Mary, *m* T. Huxley
" Meliora, *frmly* Shetterden
Loat, Henry, of Wrexham, N. Wales
Lockett, James, *d* London 1841
" John, clothier, London
" John, servant, *d* 1860
Lockey, George F., of London 1823
Lockhart, Stephen, of Scotland 1799
Lockyer, Henrietta, of Chelsea
Logan, Daniel, *d* abroad 1857
" Margaretta, *o'wise* Robertson
London, William, *d* London 1860
Long, Catharine, *d* Wilts 1814
" Lieut. Col. John, *d* abroad
" Joshua, of London 1795
" William, merchant, London
Lonsdale, F. L., of Kingston, Surrey
Loombe, Sir John, *d* 1817
Lyton, John R., *d* Herts
Luff, John, *d* Hants 1797
Lupton, Thomas } of Leeds
" George H. }
Ludlow, John, of London
Luxford, Ann Georgianna
Luyken, Joseph H. M., *d* 1832
Lundie, Henry, merchant, *d* 1855
Lucas, Fred'k J., went abroad 1859
Lyll, William, left Edinburgh 1840
Lyons, Mrs., of Mayo, Ireland
Lynall, Mary, *m* R. Tagg 1772
Lushington, C. A., of London 1839
Lyon, Anthony, of Wandsworth
Lysons, Robert, of Boston
Lynch, William, of Kennington 1814
Lubbock, Joseph, painter, London
Lucas, Sarah, London, *d* 1848
" Mary, *o'wise* Pollard
" Wm., pawnbroker, London
Luce, Hester, of Gloucestershire
Luck, Mary, servant, *d* 1833
" Thomas, *d* in London
Lucking, Thomas
" Margaret

Lucock, Jane, of Ockley, Surrey
Ludlum, Henry, *d* abroad 1857
Ludwig, Ann, *frmly* Doyle
Luer, Mr. apothecary
Luff, John, mariner
Luke, Dugald, of Glasgow, *d* 1784
Lumbruggen, Rev. Henry, *d* abroad
Lumley, Jane, *o'wise* Lascelles
" Mary, " Parkinson
" Sarah, " Abrams
" Elzbth., " Coates
" Ann " Steward
Lumsden, J. F., attorney, London
Lunnon, Thomas, of Bucks, *d* 1841
Luscombe, Matthew, of Devonshire
Lynch, Richard, *d* London, 1843
" John, seaman M S
Lyne, Edward, native of Malmsbury
" Maria, of Moatlands, Berks
" Edward ⎫ uncles of S. Lyne
" Joseph ⎬ Stephens, of Roe-
" Richard ⎨ hampton, Surrey,
" William ⎭ who died 1860
Lyon, Peter, of London, *d* 1788
Lysaght, Margaret, of Dublin
Lytcott, Philip, merchant, *d* abroad
Lythell, Edward, printer, Cambridge
" Ann, sister to Edward
" Thos. of Richmond, Surrey

M

McCallum, John, *d* London 1869
McLacklan, James, of Lincolnshire
McNeil, Neil, of Glasgow, *d* 1747-9
McGuire, William, *d* London
McPherson, Duncan, *d* abroad 1851
McCarthy, Phœbe, of Middlesex 1821
McLims, John, of Lambeth 1858
McKenzie, Mary, of Edinburgh
McKellar, Mr., of Ceylon, 1845
McCormick, John, *d* Surrey 1866
McCann, John, *d* Longford 1867
McIntosh, Duncan, of Perth, *d* 1838
McConnell, Margaret. *dau.* of James
McCarthy, Joseph, of Killarney
McKenna, Bridget, Liverpool, *d* 1865
McKenzie, Angus, *d* America 1867
McNeilance, Mary Ann, of Ireland
McMurtrie, Andrew, of Ayrshire
" David, *d* America 1860
McAdam, Marian, of Canada 1839
McIntosh, Duncan, of America 1813
McDouall, John
McDonald, Jemima, living 1800
" George, *d* Stafford 1865

M'Adam, James, of Scotland, *d* abrd
M'Alpine, Jno., mariner, *d* abrd 1859
" Lieut. R., *d* in India
" Lieut. Rich'd, *d* in France
" Lieut. Robert, *d* 1826
M'Allister, Rich'd A., Sydney 1831
M'Arthur, James
M'Auliffe, Denis, seaman M S
M'Bain, Mrs. Mary, *d* abroad 1847
M'Barrett, Capt. G. G.
M'Caan, Francis, of Ireland, *d* 1845
M'Callum, Gilbert, seaman M S
M'Carthy, A. F. T., R N, *d* 1840
M'Clellan, Robt. surgeon, Hampstead
M'Cogan, Samuel, clerk
M'Coomb, James, seaman Navy
M'Cormack, Maurice, coachman
M'Coy, —, surgeon, *d* 1862
M'Cluer, John, *d* abroad 1796
M'Cray, Dennis, *d* Surrey 1815
M'Cullock, John, coachman, *d* 1857
" Rev. Robert, of Dairsee
M'Cullam, Alex., of Greenock 1842
M'Cune, Robert
M'Dermott, Phil., *d* Westminster 1862
M'Donald, Alex., *d* Middlesex 1839
" Elzbth, *d* at Reading 1820
" James, *d* abroad 1822
" John, seaman Navy
" John, surgeon RN, *d* 1824
M'Dougall, Lieut. Alex., *d* 1825
" Robert, seaman Navy
M'Dowell, Elzbth, Buckingham 1760
" Michael, *d* abroad 1856
M'Egan, W. B. surgeon, *d* abroad
M'Eiver, Jane, Greenwich, *d* 1835
M'Farlane, Major Alex., *d* abrd 1807
M'Farson, John, seaman M S
M'Gonnell, Patrick, *d* in America
M'Grath, Major Eugene, *d* abroad
M'Gregor, Agnes, *o'wise* Hunter
" Rev. Alex., of Perth, *d* 1835
" Elzbth, *d* in Glasgow 1864
" William, of Glasgow 1840
M'Halee, John C., tailor, New York
M'Intyre, —, Army Surgeon
" Robert, of Scotland
" Isablla. of Dumbartonshire
M'Kay, John, seaman Navy *d* 1812
" Wm. P., *d* in America 1861
M'Kenzie, Patrick, army surgeon
" Samuel, seaman Navy
M'Key, Robert, *d* abroad 1833
M'Kidd, Alexander, Liverpool
M'Laran, Margaret, *d* 1863
M'Laughten, Archbld, merchant 1800

M'Lean, Hugh, of Jamaica, d 1843
" John, seaman 1850
" Robert, seaman, d abroad
M'Leod, Jane, d London 1846
" John, seaman M S
" Margaret } of London
" William }
" William, of Banff, d 1842
M'Mellan, Margt., Islington, d 1840
M'Millan, Thos., E I C S, d 1811
M'Mullon, Thos., gardener, d 1831
M'Nabb, Thos., d abroad 1818
M'Nair, —, of London 1812
M'Neah, Elzbth., frmly Ladd, d 1852
M'Neal, Robert, brother to Thomas
M'Neill, Malcolm, d 1860-1
M'Pherson, Patience, d Islington 1830
" William, seaman M S
M'Quire, James, mariner, d 1807
M'Whirter, Hugh, of Bleachfield 1799
M'Whirter, J. P.
M'Williams, Thos., of Scotland, d abd
" Williams, seaman Navy
May, John, of London
Mawson, Margaret, o'wise Robson
" John, of Twickenham
Macolla, John, of Nova Scotia
Mackenzie, Alex., of London 1830
Martin, Thomas } relatives of
" John } Mary Fish-
" Mary Elzbth. } burn
" Robert }
Macdonald, Colonel Alexander
" Sir John
" James Bonassey
Martin, Robert, of London 1814
Macfarlane, Elizabeth, d abroad
Madden, Patrick, of Middlesex 1840
Maddocks, William, d Kent 1835
Martin, Richard, d Essex 1846
" Anne, o'wise Nunn
Marshall James, d Scotland 1850
Martin, John, d abroad 1867
" Elizabeth, frmly Lavis
Mason, Richard, d Surrey
Matson, Henry, merchant
Marston, Job } of Worcester-
" Christopher } shire, 1700
" John }
Matthews, Catherine, d London
Marriott, Samuel, d Middlesex
Mayhew, Mary, d Sussex
Mallory, John, d London
Martindale, John, d Liverpool
Mapperly, Elizabeth, d Bath
Macaile, Matthew, d Africa

Matthews, Margaret, of Canterbury
Malcolm, John, d London
Martin, William, d London
Mallett, Lucy, d Paris 1795
Massoth, Vincent, d Russia 1798
Mason, Ann, d London
Maddock, Robert, d Witney 1829
Majendie, Andrew, d abroad 1782
Mare, John, d Wilts 1805
Martin, Sarah, d Oxfordshire
Matthews, Joseph, of Hants
Mayne, Phillip, of Berkshire
Mackay, Alexander, d Australia
Marr, Peter, of Edinburgh
Maris, John } of Norfolk
" Maria }
Madeline, Prudence } left Paw for
" Rosalie } Dublin 1838
Malinson, Richard, Newcastle 1860
Mackay, Thomas, of Clapham
Mason Elizabeth, frmly Bourne
Macdowell, Hay, d India 1865
Macfarlane, William, Bayswater 1851
Matthew, John, London 1760
Massey, Gilbert, Bethnal Green
March, William, son of Abel
Macknair, James, went abroad 1828
Martin, John, Isle of Sheppey
Mackall, Daniel, d Chelsea 1861
Major, John T. W., musician
Mayne, John, of Ilfracombe
Matherwick, James } natives of Som-
" John } erset
Mahoney, John, of Waterford
Martin, Ann, frmly Gray
Macarthy, Dennis, d 1865
Mason, Teresa, Camberwell Road
Masters, Elizabeth, Australia
Mackness, William C., of Bedford
Maynard, Thomas, London 1821
Mason, John, seaman M S
Matis, Andrew, seaman M S
Mayo, John, of Bayford
Matthews, James } relatives of
" Samuel } Isaac
Maskell, Daniel, of Tattersal, d 1867
Matthews, Isaac, d London 1864
Marshall, John, d Yorkshire 1867
Matthews, D., d abroad 1867
Mallock, John, of Glasgow 1854
Martin, William, Durham, d 1867
Madgwick, Mary A., Middlesex
Maltwood, Susannah, London 1813
Mann, William, of Kent, d 1865
Manning, Thomas, d Kent 1865
Maclean, John S., d abroad 1865

Maysey, Richard, of Rutland, d 1797
Marsh, Mary A., servant 1862
Macabe, Christopher, d Ham 1846
Macauley, General, d abroad 1817
" George W., underwriter
)Macclarey, Sarah, *frmly* Eales 1778
Macdonald, Angus, living 1794
" John, of Swepstone 1855
" Maria H., of France
" Peter, d London 1770
Macdougall, Geo., brother to Dugald
Macdowell, Elizabeth, of Bucks
Mace, Philip, mariner, of Yarmouth
Macey, William, d in London
Macfae, John, native of Ireland
Macgillioray, David, of Scotland, d 1820
Macintosh, Edward, d abroad 1805
Machin, Mary A., of Shrewsbury
Mack, Ann, Littlehampton, d 1843
" Mary, Fitzroy Square
Mackay, Alex., of Sunderland N B
" Angus, merchant, London
" James, of Skirray, d 1790
" Bessy ⎫
" Elizabeth ⎬ daughters of
" Jane ⎭ James
" Lieut. Robert S., d abroad
Mackenzie, Dugald, d abroad 1857
" Colin, d abroad 1858
" Capt. Alex'der W. Army
" John Ford, living 1798
" Capt. Thomas A., d 1856
Mackerell, Capt. Timothy, d abroad
Mackey, Thomas, mariner, d 1809
" Mary, London
Mackinron, Capt. D. W., d 1857-8
Mackintosh, F. M., d 1775
Mackley, Ann, of Kent
Macleod, Lieut. Allan, d abroad
Macnair, James, of Glasgow, d abd
Macnamara, Thomas, d abroad
Macpherson, Francis, d London
" Lieut. Col., d 1814
Macqueen, Capt. Donald, d abd 1826
Macquire, William, d abroad 1822
Maddox, Henry, of Hampshire, d 1840
Madgwick, Mary A., London
Mahoney, John, R N, d 1823
Main, Andrew, master-mariner
Maize, James, of London, 1800-20
Major, Jonathan W., d in Kent 1842
Mahan, Elizabeth, Walworth, d 1843
Mallett, Wm., labourer, Oxford
Mallalieu, Ben., of Yorkshire, d 1845
Mallough, Jer., of New York, d 1823

Malone, Patrick, of Alloa, N B
Maltzan, Baroness de, *frmly* Crawf'd
Mankin, John, mariner
Mann, Joseph, of Liverpool
" William, seaman Navy
" Colonel G., of Quebec, 1800
Manners, Rich'd., left England 1815
Manners, —, killed at Waterloo
Mannon, Edward, of London 1828
Manning, Lewis, of Chelsea
Manowick, George, seaman M S
Mansell, Elzbth. Brentford, d 1844
Manley, John, of London, d 1743
Mansfield, Wm., master R N, d 1812
Mansell, Ann D., of Lewes, Sussex
" Mary, Lambeth, d 1827
Manks, William, d in America
Mansfield, Thomas, seaman Navy
March, Berrington, d 1842
Marchand, John P., d London 1808
March, Sarah, *frmly* Jones
Markam, Mrs. Ann, of Cambridge
" Edward
" Mary Frances
" Jacques ⎫ children of Ed-
' William ⎭ ward and Mary
Markell, Sarah, of Newington
Marland, Martin, living 1775
Marrett, Philip T., d in India
Mace, Charles, of London 1812
Mackenzie, Murdoch, of London 1805
Mackintosh, John, of London 1810
Malcolm, Samuel, of London 1812
March, Thomas, of London 1830
Marks, John, of London 1844
Marshall, William, of Bermondsey
Martin, Adam, of London 1811
" Francis P., of London 1820
" James, of Enfield 1812
" Thomas, of London 1820
Mathews, James H., Middlesex 1837
Maunder, Samuel, of London 1836
Maynard, Thomas, of London 1821
Matthews, Joseph H., d 1849
Maciejowski, Stanislaus, d London 1868
Manning, William, of Lambeth
Maddison, Robert, d abroad 1777
Magnay, Christopher J., of London
Marriott, Martha, of Northampton
" Mrs. W., of Jamaica
Marsden, Thomas, of London 1810
Marshall, James, d Edinburgh 1829
" James B., of Dumfernline
" Jane, Newport Pagnell

GENERAL INDEX.

Marshall, John, H E I C S
" Mary, *o'wise* Turner, 1773
" Samuel, of Kennington
" William, of Islington
" William, of Scotland
" Mary, wife of W. Sheoch
" W. C., builder, Portsea
" W. C., gardener, Portsea
" Thomas, of Bloomsbury
" Daniel ⎫ children of
" Elizabeth ⎬ Daniel, of
" Sarah ⎭ Bloomsbury
Martin, General Claude, *d* 1800
" David, living 1789
" Esther, *dau.* of John
" Emma ⎫
" George ⎬ of London
" George, coachman
" John, *d* in Mexico
" Mr., tailor, Soho
" Mary, *frmly* Benoist
" Robert, of Chelsea
" Sarah, of London
" Thomas, *d* abroad 1800
" Thomas, seaman Navy
" Thenes, mariner
" William, *d* Kingsland
" William, seaman Navy
" —, *d* abroad 1862
Mason, Ann, Hadley, *d* 1829
Maslin, Sarah, *frmly* Thorp
Mason, George ⎫ of Edinburgh
" James ⎬ 1800
Massey, Charles, *d* abroad 1798
" Mary, Essex, *d* 1798
Massie, James, of Lancashire, *d* 1834
" Thomas, of Cheshire
" William, surgeon, 1778
Matthews, Mary, native of Kent
" Mary, *d* 1832
" Jas., of Monmouth, *d* 1811
Matthas, Hannah, *d* 1864
Mate, William L., of Dover
Mather, James, *d* in India
" William, *d* Brixton 1830
Matchell, Wm., of Surrey, *d* 1811
Maurice, Elizabeth A., London, *d* 1864
Maw, Abdy C., *d* abroad 1842
Mawhood, Richd., of Wakefield 1790
Maxwell, James, merchant, *d* abroad
Maxwell, James, seaman Navy
May, John, seaman Navy
" William, sergeant Army
" Wm., brother to Margt. Palmer
" Wm., *d* Birmingham 1760
Mayer, Michael E., *d* abroad

Mayer, John C., of Ireland, *d* 1801
Mayhew, Cath., *d* Bath 1830
Mayne, Terry G., *d* abroad 1802
" James, *d* in Dorset 1849
Mayo, Joseph B., of Hereford, *d* 1675
" Mary, *dau.* of James, *d* 1864
Mahan, Richard, *d* West Indies
Masters, Charles, of London 1843
Maslin, Edward
May, Maria, servant 1842
Macindoe, William, of Kincardine
Malony, Patrick, *d* Liverpool 1868
Matfield Family
Matfield, Erick, *d* abroad 1813
Mackay, Martin, *d* in India
Macgilliardie, Anne, seamstress
Matthew, Emily Jane
Meginnis, Elizabeth, *o'wise* David
Metcalf, John
Mendel, Samuel, of Mincing Lane
Meredith, William, *d* Middlesex
" Elizabeth, *d* Wrexham
Meyrick, James, *d* Westminster
Meyer, John Baptist, *d* London
Mercardo, Solomon, *d* London
Menforte, Manuel M., merchant
Mears, William M., *d* Liverpool
Menzies, Edward, of Perthshire
Meik, Margaret L., *o'wise* Macarthy
Mercer, E. G., of Camberwell 1866
Metize, Mr., of Soho
Mends, Jane, Plymouth, *d* 1867
Mealey, William, of London 1810
" William, Brighton 1840
Meggott, Eliza, Scotland, *d* 1857
Meyer, Nathan M., living 1796
Meanley, Jeremiah, Liverpool, *d* 1863
Meares, George
" Hannah, *frmly* Gardener
" Elzbth., niece of T. Wainman
Meadows, Thos., bro. to Ellen Gore
Meddowcroft, Wm., of Cheshire *d* 1835
" Mary, *o'wise* Stanley
Medlicott, John, Commander R N
Meek, Elizabeth, York, *d* 1861
Mee, Mary, Worcester, *d* 1810
Meggison, Robert, *d* abroad 1808
Meiklejohn, Ed., mariner, *d* abroad
Mell, William, *d* Shrewsbury 1831
Melvin, Alexander, *d* abroad 1813
Menzie, Joseph, seaman Navy
Mercer, Israel, of Lancashire, *d* 1828
Meredith, Louisa, of London, 1796
" Mary, *dau.* of Louis
" John, of London
Merredith, Catherine, of Shropshire

Merrick, Mrs., of Essex
Merry, Ann, *d* London
" Ann, *o'wise* Hibble, *d* 1833
Merryman, L., mariner, *d* 1810
Mervin, Fran., of Rotherhithe, *d* 1807
Metcalf, Edward, of London
Meynott, Samuel, of London
Mill, William, went to America
Miller, Henry, of London 1816
Mitchell, Jane, of Stepney
" Georgiana, living 1810
Millar, Pauncefort, *d* Jamaica
Miles, Richard } *d* in London
" John }
Miller, Charles, *d* Gloucestershire
Mitchell, Robert, *d* Guildford
Miller, James, *d* Carlisle 1791
Mills, Mary, of Wilts
Mitchell, C., *o'wise* Elder
Miller, James }
" William } brothers and sister
" Jane }
Mingay, John, of East India House
Mitchell, Samuel, Dorset, *d* 1864
Minor, George S. } of Somers Town
" Andrew R. } 1850
Mitchell, James Harrington
Mills, Thomas, *d* New Zealand 1862
Millet, John, *d* in America
Mitchell, Thos. B., of Adelaide 1848
Mitchels, Anna, native of Hanover
Mills, George, of London 1833
Miller, Alexander, of London 1840
" James, of London 1835
Mitchell, E. C., of London 1836
Milner, Joseph, of London 1810
Mitchell, Strasburg, London 1812
Minshull, George R., of London
Mill, Nicholas P., serg't of marines
Miller, Mr., of Long Acre
Mitchelson, John R., seaman R N
Millward, Thomas N., of Jamaica
Millward Family, of Jamaica
Mitchell, William L., of Calcutta
Michener, Richard, of Eaton, Bucks
Middleton, Mary, *o'wise* Healey
" Lord, *d* 1835
" John, of Somers Town
" Elzbt. of Kensington 1802
Midling, Joseph, of Surrey
Milburn, Capt. Reginald, *d* abroad
Mild, John, of Ashford and London
Miley, John, seaman M S
Mill, George, of Fifeshire, *d* 1841
Millard, John, of London, 1807
Miles, John, of Chesham

Miles, Thomas, mariner, *d* abroad
" Edward } related to
" John } Jefferson Miles,
" William } living in
" Elizabeth } London, 1800
" Francis }
" Elizabeth, *o'wise* Harris
Miller, Andrew, seaman M S
" Charles, mariner, *d* 1846
" Daniel, native of Prussia
" Elizabeth, of Kingston 1804
" Francis, of Westminster
" Jacob, merchant, Edinburgh
" James, of Edinburgh 1800
" James, merchant 1811
" John, of London 1806
" John, of Edinburgh
" John, of Woolwich, *d* 1811
" John, native of Jersey
" Margaret, *o'wise* Martin
" Mary, of Newington, Surrey
" Nathan, son of James
" Thomas, of London 1700
Mills, Charles E., *d* in India
" Ephraim, seaman, Navy
" John, of London
" Major, of Teddington
" William, painter, Walworth
Millington, Mary A., London
Milgreave, Margaret, of Cheshire
Milnes, Mary, of Liverpool
Mingay, John, of Edinburgh, *d* 1861
Minster, Thomas, *d* abroad 1850-1
Missett, Mary, Lambeth, *d* 1842
Mitchell, Elzbth. of Chatham, *d* abrd
" John, *d* London 1827
" Margaret, *d* at Stratford
" Robert, of Bristol, *d* 1812
Morrish, John, of Hoxton
Modley, Matilda Louisa
Moore, Mary, wife of W. H. M—
Morson, Thomas
Mounier, Maria, *o'wise* Skinner
Morris, Charlotte
Montgomery, Count Hugh de, *d* 1868
Morland, Michael, of Redgate
Mole, Christopher, *d* London
Monke, William, *d* 1775
Morrell, Henry, *d* Staffordshire
Morris, Ann, *o'wise* Hasser
Morrice, John, *d* Herts
Moss, James, *d* Manchester
Morrell, Richard, *d* Birmingham
Mottram, Ann, *d* Stockport, 1793
" Peter, *d* Stockport
Morley, Elzbth., *d* Westminster 1796

Morris, Valentine, *d* West Indies
Moody, Mary, *d* Southampton 1823
Morrison, Ellen, *d* in Australia
Morel, Elizabeth, London, *d* 1866
Monday, William, of Lichfield
    oss, Evelina, Dover 1856
Morrison, Catherine, London 1856
Moss, Sophia, *frmly* Grange
Morris, Sarah, *d* in Middlesex
Morgan, William, seaman, M S
Moss, Alfred W., of Wandsworth
Moran, J., *d* at sea 1867
Moore, Eliza, *o'wise* Swainson
" Rev. David Brown
Morris, Robert, *d* in Middlesex 1825
Morgan, Elzbth., Cheltenham, *d* 1864
Morris, J., *d* abroad 1864
Moore, G., of Derry, *d* 1863
Morgan, Louisa
Morris, Mary, Reigate, *d* 1867
Moreham, John, London 1800
Mobbs, Aaron, *d* in Essex
" Elizabeth } of Cripplegate,
" Sarah } London
" John, of Islington, *d* 1791
" Joseph, of Southwark 1790
Moffett, Jameson, merchant
Moffatt, Sophia F., of Devonshire
" G., *d* abroad 1862
Mole, Rev. James, of Worcestershire
Molineaux, Arabella, Tooting
Mollison, John, of London
Moir, Lieut. James, *d* abroad
Moncrief, Capt. H. A., *d* abroad
Monday, Sophia S., Kennington, 1836
Monger, Ann, Battersea
Monk, Catharine, Brompton
Monkhouse, John, *d* Southwark 1830
" Rev. John, *d* Hantz 1828
" Thos., of the Isle of Man
Monson, Sarah, of Westminster
" Hon. T. G. B., *d* 1841
Montgomery, Lieut. A., *d* 1807
Moorhouse, John, of Chelsea 1823
More, Alexander, of London 1832
Morrison, John, of London 1812
Monro, Isabella, *d* Peebles 1867
More, Mary, *frmly* Bailey
Moore, George, *d* Chelsea 1867
Moss, George, left Cornwall 1865
Morgan, Jane, *frmly* Williams
Moate, Joseph, of Whitechapel 1842
Molineux, William, of London 1835
Morgue, Fulcrand
Morgan, John, of London 1818
Moseley, John, of Whitechapel 1826

Montgomery, William, of Carlow
Moody, Robert S.
" Jane, *frmly* Sims, *d* 1834
" Isaac, of Corsham, Wilts
" Ann, *d* in London
Moore, Charles, seaman M S
" Dinah, London 1830
" Eleanor, *d* at Chelsea
" Henry S., surgeon, *d* 1850
" Hester, *frmly* Young
" James, of London 1810
" Rev. J. J., *d* abroad 1845
" John, servant
" Capt. M., R N
" Thomas, mariner, *d* abroad
" Lieut-Col. W., *d* 1848
More, Francis A., *d* London 1845
Morehead, Thomas D. W., *d* abroad
Morehen, John
" Richard } of London 1824
" Ann, *o'wise* Archer
" Elizabeth, *o'wise* Tuck
" Martha, *o'wise* Fuller
" Mary, *o'wise* Bury
Moreton, Mary, of Glasgow
" Rev. R. J., *d* Essex 1826
" Robt., *d* Birmingham 1802
" Joseph, of Derby, *d* abroad
Mordaunt, Montague, of London
Morgan, John, of Scotland
" James, of Shropshire
" Stephen, of Shropshire
Moriarty, Phillis, *d* 1858
Morley, Joseph, of Radford
" James, of Painswick
Morrall, Johanna } children of Wm.
" Mary } Morrall or Mor-
" Sarah } roll, of Portsm'th
Morrell, Jane, Uxbridge, *d* 1830
Morris, Charlotte, New York 1840
" Charles, of Lambeth 1759
" Mrs. Elizabeth, *d* in America
" John, seaman, *d* 1837
" Lieut. Peter, *d* abroad 1848
" Peter, seaman, *d* 1854
" Susan, cook, Brighton
" Thomas, of London 1700
" Thos., of Montgomery 1767
Morrison, ——, surgeon Army
" Eliza, Brighton, 1849
" Dr. J. B. N., of Brighton
" Morris, *d* at Chelsea
Morroll, Mary, *frmly* Gray
Morse, Major Charles, *d* 1855–6
Morton, Francis, of Middlesex
" Catherine E., *d* London 1852

NEXT OF KIN. 51

Mortlock, Jno. W., *d* Cambridge 1833
" W Cambridge, *d* 1828
Mosman, John, of London, *d* 1807
" Mary, wife of John
" Mary, *dau.* of John
" William, of Newcastle 1796
Moss, Elizabeth, *d* at Kircudbright
" Capt. John, *d* abroad
" Sarah, of Doncaster
Mossum, Mary, of Kilkenny
Motley, Mary, Hereford, *d* 1861
Mott, Mary, *frmly* Christmas
Mottram, Robert, *d* Birmingham
Moulton, Wm., *d* Newcastle 1772
Mountford, Capt. Francis, *d* abroad
" C., seaman M S, *d* 1829
Moyce, John, tailor, Kingsland
Moyse, Shadrach, of Scotland 1812
Munro, Hector Edwin
Murrell, William, *d* London 1700
Munday, Stephen, *d* London
Murphy, Robert, *d* Ireland 1785
Muir, George, *d* London
Mudford, Nixon, of Shoreditch
Mumford, Joseph, of Westminster
Munden, Edmund
Muston, Charlotte M., *frmly* Nowell
Munk, James, *d* Poole 1866
Murray, Robert, London 1834
Munday, Jane, *o'wise* Tiley, *d* 1855
Mulcock, George C., seaman
Murrell, William, of Middlesex
Murphy, John J., *d* London 1866
Munsell, Hannah, London
Murch, Miss Aurelia
Munday, Elizabeth, Cheshire *d* 1865
Murray, Robert A., *d* 1858
Much, John, of Berkshire 1800
Muhle, B. G., of London 1798
Mullagan, Thomas, seaman Navy
Munro, James, *d* abroad 1862
" Robert, *d* London 1768
Munt, Henry, Lieut-Col., *d* abroad
Mupstone, James, master-mariner
Murray, Thomas, of Edinburgh 1796
" Ursula, *frmly* Baker
Murrell, Judith, of Peckham
Murphy, William, *d* at sea 1860
" Thomas, *d* abroad 1857
Muse, William
Musgrave, Simon, of Haltwistle
Myers, Daniel C., *d* abroad 1860
Mylburn, Catherine, Stepney, 1786
Myles, Samuel, sergeant, *d* abroad

N

Naunton, William, of Suffolk
Naldi, Joseph, *d* abroad
Nash, James, of London 1805
Nabb, John, *d* Preston 1794
Nailor, Elizabeth, of Mawley, Salop
Naish, G., *d* abroad 1863
Nash, Rev. J. W., *d* abroad
Nattes, Mr. } of Hammersmith
" Mrs. } 1815
Nattis, Ensign J. W., *d* abroad
Naughton, Michael, of Ireland
Nelson, Hugh, *d* Penrith
Newport, John, *d* Herts
Nevy, John, of Devonshire
Neethorpe, Edward, of London
Nelson, Barbara Jacoba
Nerestant, Charles E., *d* 1868-9
Newton, Wm., of Westminster 1825
Neal, Robert Joseph
Nector, Ursula, *d* 1814
Neilson, Archibald, of London 1821
Newman, Henry, of London 1816
Newbery, Maria, housekeeper
Newsham, Isabella
Newbury, Thomas, of London
" Charles, of London
" Ann, wife of Charles
Nevit, James, mariner
Nevill, Barbara, of Salford
Newman, Henry, of Hampshire
Nesbit, Henry, solicitor
Neville, William, *d* London 1824
" Jessica, Bucks, *d* 1862
Newbegin, Elzbth, *frmly* Hutchinson
Newberry, Harriett, *frmly* Goodman
Neal, Robert, *d* in Australia
" Mary, of Liverpool
Neale, James, transported 1845
" Wm., of Marylebone, *d* 1829
" Elizabeth } of Isleworth,
" John } Surrey
Neane, Robert, *d* abroad 1851-2
Nee, Edward, married J. Palmer
Nee, Joseph } child'n of Edward
" Catharine }
Nedham, Samuel, *d* abroad 1835
Negus, Charles, *d* London 1812
Neild, Lieut. Fred. J., *d* abroad 1838
Nelmes, John, of Pentonville
Nelson, Alexander, seaman *d* 1841
" George, *d* India 1806
" George, *d* India 1857
" John, seaman, *d* 1824
" Lieut. John, *d* abroad 1807

Nelson, Peter, seaman, *d* 1806
" Robert, tailor, London
Nesbitt, John, underwriter
Nevay, James, left Scotland 1752
Nevill, James, seaman M S
Nevin, William, servant
Newbegin, William, *d* abroad 1862
Newcomb, Ann, *d* London 1807
Newenham, S. A. *frmly* Waring
Newell, Wm., farmer, Goring, *d* 1830
Newland, Lieut. George, *d* abroad
Newman, George, of Wapping
Newton, Isaac, of Manchester
" J., Army surgeon
" James, *d* London 1799
Nichol, Anthony, *d* Lichfield
Nicholls, Francis, *d* Newcastle
Nightingale, Miles, *d* London
Nicholson, Jeremiah, Berks
Nightingale, John, *d* Surrey
Nisbet, Robert, *d* Jamaica
Nicholas, Peter, of Hants
Nixon, Ann, servant 1859
Nield, Frederick J., *d* 1838
Nicol, John, of Marylebone
Nilman, William M., America 1843
Nicholson, Elizabeth, of London 1860
Nicks, Thomas J., of Clerkenwell
Nichol, Colin, merchant, Glasgow
Nicholas, John, *d* Shropshire 1843
Nicholls, Jacob, of Kensington
" James, *d* Marylebone 1857
" John, seaman, *d* 1807
" Lieut. Charles, *d* 1814
" Mary, of Norfolk
" William, of Poplar
" William, seaman, *d* 1809
Nicholson, Charles, seaman, *d* 1841
" Mrs. Eliz., of London 1821
Nicol, Mary, *otherwise* Warren
" Susan, *otherwise* Smith
Nicolay, Capt. Thos. F., *d* abrd 1853
Nicoll Family, of Bedfordshire
" Wm., of Bedfordshire, *d* 1726
" William, of Herts, *d* 1746
" Samuel, of Herts, *d* 1758
Nickson, Elizabeth, London
Niele, J., drum-major 89th Regt.
Nielson, Niel, seaman M S
" Jane, *d* abroad 1808
" Adam, brother to Jane
Nievan, H. D., *d* in India
Nisbett, Amelia, *otherwise* Morut
" Josiah, of West Indies
Nixon, John, *d* at Pimlico
" Maria, of Lancashire, *d* 1827

North, Thomas, of Sussex
Norman, Elizabeth, *d* Westminster
Norman, Edward, *d* Middlesex
Norrys, Anne ⎱ daughters of
" Margaret ⎰ Edward
Norman, Mrs., of Marylebone 1818
Norton, Thomas Francis
Noble, George, *d* abroad 1828
Noble, Thomas, *d* India
Nowell, Charlotte M., *o'wise* Muston
Norton, Ensign G. E. B., *d* abrd 1841
Norris, Miss
Norton, William, son of James
Nott, John, son of William
Norton, Mr., hosier, Strand
Noble, Mr., brother of George
Nolan, John M., surgeon
Norris, Thomas, Southwark 1847
Noddle, Ellen, of Westmoreland
Noble, William, of London, *d* abroad
Noddings, Robert, of Ely, *d* 1835
Nokes, Major James
Noon, Matthew, seaman, *d* 1819
Noone, Rebecca, of Finsbury, *d* 1815
Nordin, Thomas, *d* London 1830
Norman, John, *d* Kennington
Norris, J. B., coachbuilder, India
" Self, of London, 1750-60
North, Mary, Acton, *d* 1859
" Rev. Nathan'l, of Winchester
" Joseph, seaman M S
Norton, Eleanor D.
" Samuel, seaman M S
" W., son of James, 1824
Nowell, Alex., of Marylebone, 1835
" Philip, of Bath
Nowland, Mary, *d* Yarmouth 1849
" John, seaman, *d* 1810
Nutin, John, of London 1798
Nudd, Eliza S., *frmly* Gaskin
Nunn, Anne, *frmly* Martin
" William ⎱ children of John
" Martha ⎰
Nugent, John, of Lambeth

O

O'Brien, Francis, *d* abroad
O'Farris, Charles, *d* abroad
O'Keef, Hugh M., *d* Middlesex
O'Halloran, W. A., left England 1852
O'Byrne, James
" Anna Maria
" Marse Agnes
O'Brien, James, *d* in Africa

NEXT OF KIN. 53

O'Brien, John, *d* abroad 1859
O'Hara, Henry, *d* London 1804
O'Hebir, Charles, of Ireland, *d* abd
O'Lawlor, Major John, *d* 1824
O'Mahoney, Jeremiah
O'Neill, Major Thomas, *d* 1832
O'Reilly, Hugh, *d* abroad
O'Reilley, Rev. S., *d* abroad 1844
O'Shaughnessy, Capt. Peter
Oakham, James, *d* Surrey 1862
Oakham, Hannah, *o'wise* Cole
Odell, Islep, *d* Middlesex 1864
Oacks, Mary, *dau.* of Benjamin, 1770
Oakes, Elizabeth, *frmly* Gray
Odall, Elizabeth, *o' wise* Webb
Odell, Major John, *d* 1833
Ody, Ann, Malmsbury, *d* 1852
Ogden, John, of Manchester, 1793
Ogilby, Catherine, *frmly* Miller
Ogilvie, David, uncle to J. F. Marsh
Oldfield, Joseph, of King's Lynn
Oldham, Samuel, *d* abroad 1778
Oliphant, James, *d* Scotland 1791
" James B., of Gask, N B
Olliver, Elizabeth, *w*, London
" George, seaman
" Ensign James D., *d* abroad
" Jane, Dorsetshire
" Thomas, of Liverpool
" Col. Wm. C., *d* abroad 1835
Olson, Michael, seaman M S
Olton, Juliana, *frmly* Starkey
Older, James, of London, 1839
Olrod, Jane, Sarah
Opie, John, *d* London 1807
Ord, Captain Edward H., *d* 1860-1
" William C., *d* India
Otway, Elizabeth, *d* Middlesex
Ommanney, William, *d* Hants
Orford, Robert, *d* Middlesex
Osborn, Elizabeth, of Greenwich
Osborne, Mary, *frmly* Owens
Ormond, John, of Kilkenny
Orsborn, Charles, labourer, Norfolk
Osborn, Charles, of Woolwich, 1835
Osebrook, William, of Lincolnshire
Osmond, Ann, *w*, of Herts, *d* 1814
Ouiseau, Harriet, *d* Newington
Oulton, Richard, of Cheshire
Over, Ann, of London
Overton, William, of Kenilworth
Owen, Ann, of Anglesea
" Cath., married J. Smith 1705
" Elizabeth, of Anglesea
" James, of Whitechapel
" James, seaman Navy

Owen, Janet, Twickenham, *d* 1858
" M., sergeant, *d* abroad
" Owen, tailor, London
" Owen, executor to M. Jones
Oysten, Henry, mariner, *d* 1832
Overall, Elizabeth, *d* London

P

Palmer, Jane, of Ramsey
Packer, Mary, *d* Bristol
Palmer, Joseph, *d* Middlesex
Page, Robert, *d* Bucks
" William, *d* 1792
Parry, Love, of Carmarthen
Pamphlet, John
Parham, —, a gardener
Payne Family
Partington, Sarah, Lancashire
Partridge, Samuel Henry
Packham, Ann, of Brighton
Parish, Robert, *d* London 1860
Paul, Isabella, widow
Parker, John, *d* Hants 1824
Parnham, George, of Sussex
Patterson, W. R., of Preston Pans
Parham, Charles, *d* Sussex 1864
Packwood, John, civil engineer
Page, Ann
Parkinson, Hannah, *frmly* Hassell
Parker, Mrs., *dau.* of Thos. Vincent
Palmer, Hannah, *frmly* Oakman
Paterson, Margaret, *frmly* Rae
Pake, Ann, *o'wise* Staples
Parker, Samuel, *d* abroad 1858
Page, Peter, Captain, *d* Surrey
Palmer, Charles, mariner, *d* 1865
Parrott, Mesech, servant
Parsons, Mary A., Pimlico 1864
Patterson, George, of Dorsetshire
Parker, Arthur, of Exmouth
Payne, Hannah, of Piccadilly 1820
Pauncefort, Robert, barrister
Pascoe, Richard, seaman M S
Paruther, Frederick, son of John
Parker, Mrs. E. P. W., Regent's Park
Palmer, William, of London 1838
Parker, John, of London
Page, Richard, of London 1836
Park, John, of London 1828
Partridge, Ann, of Wapping 1817
Payne, Hannah, of Piccadilly 1818
Parker, Charles G., of Chelmsford
Palfreman, George ⎱ of Manchester
" J.A.J. ⎰
Parker, Mrs., maiden name Vincent

Passmore, James, of London
Paul, Dr., Bishop of Oxford 1663
Pattersen, Jacob, of Norway
Patulla Family
Pace, Ann, *d* at Woodburn
Padman, Mrs. wife of Isaac
Page, George, mariner, *d* 1809
" Samuel, of London, *d* 1836
" William, M., of Yorkshire
Paine, John, *d* in Surrey
" John, of London, *d* 1839
Palmer, Bartholomew, of London, *d* 1798
Palmer, John, seaman Navy
" John, son of Samuel
" Job, *frmly* of China
" Martha, of Kent
" Matthew, of Stoke, Bucks
Parker, James, seaman, *d* 1812
" John, mariner
" Mary } of Clare Market,
" Thomas } London, 1781
" Thomas, of Rochampton
Parkin, Jane, *o'wise* Arthurs
Parkinson, Sarah, *frmly* Lumley
" James, living 1810
Parks, Catharine, of Brighton
Parrott, Margaret, *w* of John
Parry, Ann, of Anglesea
" Elizabeth, *w* London
" George, of Poplar
" Kitty, *d* Anglesea 1820
" Mary, *frmly* Oakes
" Rev. Owen } of Anglesea.
" William }
" George ⎫
" Richard ⎬ brothers & sisters
" Thomas ⎬ living 1770-80
" William ⎭
" Ann ⎫
" Harriet ⎬ descendants of
" Lucy ⎬ W.
" Mary ⎭
Parsons, Edward, of Southend, Essex
Parson, Sarah, London, *d* 1815
Partridge, Joseph, of London
Pash, George, *d* abroad 1862
Pashley, Charles W., *d* London 1851
Patch, William, of Finsbury, 1840
Paterson, James, *d* Leith, 1831
Paton, James, of Perth, 1810
" Joseph, of London, 1804
Patrick, Adam, of Chelsea
" Charles, of Scotland, *d* abd
" Ann, wife of John
" Thos., engineer, Liverpool

Patten, Rev. Thomas, of Berks, 1790
" Robert, nephew of Thomas
" Thos., grandfather of Thos.
" Thomas S., *d* India 1780
Patterson, Alexander, *d* at Fulham
" Charles, *d* abroad 1825
" James, seaman Navy
" James, seaman M S
" Lieut. James, R N
" John, seaman Navy
" Rebecca, of Finsbury
" Thomas, seaman, *d* 1846
" Thos., of Preston *d* abd
" Robert, seaman Navy
" Wm., of London, 1804
Payne, James, of Hereford, *d* 1814
" Philip, of Gloucestershire
" Philip of Essex, *d* 1829
Pepwell, Jane, wife of Thomas
Peachey, Mary, *d* London
Peachey, Gracchus, of Sussex
Peck, Thomas }
" John } of Boston, America.
" Ann }
Pennell, William, of Horncastle
Pescod, William, Winchester, *d* 1760
Petre, Nathaniel G., *d* London
Peppin, Joseph, of Northamptonshire
Perchard, Peter, of London, 1800
Pearson, Matthew, of Dublin
Pettitt, John, *d* Salford 1836
Peche, Chas. D, of Southampton, 1824
Penoyer, William, *d* London
Pelissier, Elizabeth, *d* abroad 1839
Peplow, Jas. R., Bethnal Green, 1840
Pearce, George, went abroad 1852
" Eliza, *frmly* Collins
Percival, James, *d* Norfolk 1831
" Charles, *d* Paris 1842
Pedder, Robert, of Brighton
" Frederick Hoffman
Pease, Joseph, of Liverpool
Penny, Elizabeth, *o'wise* Glazier
Pease, William, of Yorkshire
Perryman, Mary A., Chippenham 1841
Pearson, Thomas, *d* Essex 1864
" William, of London, 1828
Perigal, John, of London 1816
Perkins, John, of London, 1846
" Joseph, of London 1811
Peters, James, of Littlehampton 1836
Percy Family, of Bucks 1500
Peters, Robert, of Scotland
Peacock, John, Yorkshire, *d* 1866
Pearce, Ann, *frmly* Hearn
Pearson, Juliana, London 1832

Percy, James } living 1763
" Anthony }
Pennell, Eliza Le, *dau.* of Charles
Pennefather, Major K., *d* abroad
Peffers, David, of Haddingtonshire
Petrie, William, *d* abroad 1848
Percy, Elizabeth, *frmly* Parish
Petty, Henrietta
Perry, James, of Waldingfield
Peerless, James, builder, Bromley
Penruddoche, Thomas, *d* Hants 1867
Peaveridge, Antony, seaman M S
Peach, Sarah, *o'wise* Skegg
Peacock, Thomas
" William
" Mary, *d* Homerton 1832
Pearce, Thomas, of Westminster
" Ann } of Bath and Isling-
" John } ton 1800
Pearl, Ann, of Newfoundland
Pearice, Capt. Edward, *d* 1838
Pearse, Ann A., *d* at Bristol
Pearson, Robert, of Devonshire
" Robert, seaman, *d* 1815
" Sarah, *frmly* Sweetman
" Thomas, baker, London
Peasgood, Susannah, *frmly* Dennis
Peart, Thomas, *d* Lambeth 1861
Peat, William, of Derbyshire
Perry, Nathaniel, *d* London 1847
" Sarah, *o'wise* Brown
" William, of London
Perryman, — of Berkshire
Pescod, Sarah, Alverstoke, *d* 1820
Pester, Elizabeth, living 1800
Peters, Thomas, tailor, Mortlake
" John, butcher, Bristol
" Simon, seaman Navy
" Peter, seaman M S
Peterson, Charles, seaman, *d* 1844
Peto, Sarah, *d* in Surrey 1829
" William, of Surrey, *d* 1835
" Joseph
" Mary A.
Petril, William, *d* India, 1848
Peyton, John W., *d* in S. America
Peck, Capt. Thomas, *d* 1777
" Christian, wife of Thomas
" Hannah, of Northumberland
Pedder, Edward, farmer, Kent
Peddle, Rev. John, of Somerset
Pedley, Francis, *d* abroad
Peg, Cornet William, 25th Dragoons
Pelipier, Elizabeth, *d* abroad 1839
Pemberton, Harriett, West Indies
" James, of Liverpool 1823

Penaire, Elizabeth, *frmly* Beale
Pendrill, George
" Humphrey
" John
" Richard
" William
Pendry, Jacob, of Warfield, Berks
" Elizabeth, servant
Penfold, Henry, seaman M S
Penman, Fanny, of Workington
Penn, Thomas, grocer, Hackney
Pennell, Lowell, of London 1810
" Jane, *frmly* Voughton
Peuny, John, seaman Navy
" Stephen } sons of Thomas, of
" Thomas } Somerset 1780
Percival, Joseph, of Southwark
Perdine, Jas., of Kensington *d* 1827
Perkins, Elizabeth, of Cambridge
Perochon, John E., *d* London 1826
Perrett, R., of London 1800
Perriman, Deborah, of Somerset
Phillips, John, *m* A. Slade
" Judith, of Ireland
" William, of Middlesex
Phillipson, Richard, of London
Phipps, John, of London
" John, of West Indies
Phelps, Caroline, living 1855
Phillips, George, *d* Surrey 1865
Philpot, William
" Elizabeth
Phillips, S. E., *frmly* Whildon
Phelps, Thomas, *d* abroad 1867
Phillips, Charles, surgeon, 1822
" Nathaniel T. Somerset
" John, of Cornhill 1815
Phelan, Edward, of Ireland, *d* abroad
Phillipan, William, seaman Navy
Phillips, Catharine, *d* Croydon 1828
" Elizabeth C, of London
" George, of London
" Robert, of Kirkaldy 1796
" William, of Kent
" Whinifred, of Wilts
Philpot, Charlotte C., of Lambeth
Phipps, Mary, *o'wise* Price
Pickmere, Amelia, *d* Lancashire
Pickney, Saintloe, of Nottingham
Pilkington, Eglington, of Yorkshire
Pilman, John, *d* London
Pickney, James, *d* Yorkshire 1751
Pickett, John, *d* Middlesex
Pipping, John, *d* Bristol 1776
" Thomas, *d* Bristol 1786
" William, *d* Bristol 1789

Piggott, George, of Southwark
Pike, Elizabeth, *d* Bath 1869
Pimpton, Ann, *d* Scotland 1869
Pickard, Martha, *o'wise* Freeman
Pierce, Robert, *d* Surrey 1867
Pitt, James, *d* Gloucestershire 1830
Pitchers, William, *d* Surrey 1865
Pitkin, Richard, of Shoreditch
Pike, Susannah, of the Strand
Pierce, George, left England 1852
Piercey, Whyley, of Leicestershire
Pinfold, William L., went abrd 1820
Pistell, Charles B., Notts, *d* 1846
Pickernell, Jeremiah, of Hants
Pill, George, London 1838
Pickthall, William, *d* London 1865
Piercey, Richard, living 1750-80
Pink, Martha ⎫
" Richard ⎬ formerly living in
" Elizabeth ⎬ the Edgware Road,
" Jane ⎬ London
" Sophia ⎭
Pilgrim, Thomas, of Islington 1852
Pinhorn, John, of Isle of Wight
Piercey, Miss, *dau.* of Edward 1854
Pickam, Mary, Brompton, *d* 1825
Pickbourn, James, *d* in America
Pickett, Elizabeth, Clapton, *d* 1848
" Francis, of Rotherhithe 1790
" John, bank clerk
" Elizabeth, sister to John
Pickering, Elizabeth, *o'wise* Horton
Pickersgill, William, *d* London 1858
Pierce, Thomas, of Wilts, *d* 1829
" Mary, *frmly* Shillock
Pierie, John, of London 1776
" Major William, *d* abroad 1812
" Margaret, sister to John
Piers, John, seaman M S
Pike, Mary, London, *d* 1820
Pilbrow, Thos. of Bethnal Green 1849
Pilkington, James, of London
" Wm. of Marylebone, *d* 1828
" Joseph, of Ireland 1844
Pinkston, Rebecca, Islington, *d* 1848
Pinto, Francisco, J.G. *d* in S. America
Piper, John, of London, *d* 1826
" G. sergeant, *d* in Jamaica
Pitcairn, Lieut. Alex. *d* abroad 1825
Pitches, William, of Norwich, *d* 1810
Pitter, John, of Stockbridge, Hants
Pollock, Robert, engineer
Pool, Jonathan, of Cheshire
Poole, Abraham, *d* Windermere 1860
Polchampton, —, *d* London 1772
Poole, Jane, of Somers Town

Pope, John, *d* Newark
Porter, Nathaniel, of London
Pope, James, *d* Madeira
Polkinghorne, Michael, of Cornwall
Powell, Price, of Hereford
" John, of Bristol
" Ann, *d* Middlesex
" Joshua, *d* Surrey 1793
Porter, Penelope, *d* Lichfield
Poole, Samuel, of Gloucester
Poole, T., *d* at sea, 1856
Pook, John, of Golden Square
Pounsberry, E., *d* abroad 1865
Pope, Thomas, Kenilworth, *d* 1831
" Mary, Kenilworth, *d* 1864
Polglaze, Henry, *d* Kensington 1844
Powis, John, of Brixton
Pope, Margaret, Middlesex, *d* 1867
Porris, Mary, *b* London 1759
Porteous, Charles, *frmly* of Hants
Poole, Vernon, *d* Leamington 1867
Porter, Henry, of London 1812
Pollard, William, of London 1812
Potter, Samuel, of London 1830
Porch, Sarah, *frmly* Howell
Polley, Ralph, of Essex, *d* 1831
" Susan, wife of Ralph
Porrett, William, *d* abroad 1867
Porter, Catherine, living 1815
Powell, William H., *d* Middlesex 1865
" George, seaman, *d* 1812
" John, born about 1760
" Jn. D. of Staffordshire, *d* 1822
" John, seaman Navy
" Joseph, of Birmingham
" Margaret, of Middlesex 1814
" Mary, *frmly* Moffatt
" Richard, tailor, London 1767
Power, Ann, Whitechapel, *d* 1834
" Susannah, of Bloomsb'y, *d* 1843
Pontiguy, Henry, merchant, London
Pocock, Jane, of Chelsea and Hants
" John, of Paddington, *d* 1831
Polchet, Louisa, *d* at Sandhurst
Pollard, Edmund, of London 1786
Polstern, Elizabeth, *o'wise* Wilson
Pool, Catharine, of Marylebone, *d* 1853
Poole, John, of London, *d* 1836
" John, son of Hugh, of Somerset
Pooley, Elzbth., London, *d* 1855
Pope, Edward, *d* Bayswater 1815-20
Popham, Stephen P., R N, *d* 1842
Porter, Mary, Islington, *d* 1856
" William, *d* at Pimlico
Porteous, Alexander, of Perth 1810
Porsons, Theodore, *d* abroad 1856

NEXT OF KIN. 57

Pott, John, *d* London 1848
Potter, W. H., *d* abroad 1800
Pountney, Benjamin, *d* London 1832
Poulton, Robert, farmer, Essex
Powell, Ann, London, *d* 1833
" Catharine, of Herefordshire
" Ensign C. J., *d* abroad
" Evan, of Brecon
" Frances, of Bermondsey 1767
Playle, Mary, *o'wise* Chapman
Plowden Family, of Norfolk
Plunkett, John, *d* abroad
" James F., *d* London 1862
Place, Daniel, private 67th Foot
Plomer, Edward, solicitor 1822
Plumber, Eugenie, Brompton 1863
Plumbe, Catherine, of Leicestershire
Plant, Catherine *frmly* Barnett
Prathernon, George, living 1800
Present, Christopher, R., of Suffolk
Price, James, *d* Surrey 1869
" David, of Warminster 1826
Preston, Rev. Thomas
Proctor, James, engineer
Prowde, Francis, of Somerset
Pretyman, Elizabeth, *d* Kent 1780
Pritty, William, *d* India
Price, Mary A., *frmly* Sampson
Proven, John, *d* in Australia
Price, Edward T. J.
Pryor, George, of Edgeware Road 1826
Price, Catherine, *b* 1792
Probert, James C., mariner 1865
Pritchard, Esther, *d* Birmingham
Proctor, Thomas
" George ⎫
" John ⎪ nephews and
" Christopher ⎬ nieces of the
" Isabella ⎪ Rev. Christopher Preston,
" William ⎪ of Atherstone,
" Mary ⎭ *d* 1783
" Richard
Preston, C., Warwick, *d* 1783
" Thomas
Price, Charlotte, London, *d* 1863
Pratt, Edward, seaman M S
" Grace, Yorkshire, *d* 1813
Preddy, William, Southwark
Prentice, John L., of London 1813
Preston, Louisa, London, *d* 1842
" Sarah, *d* America 1806
Prevost, William, *d* America 1826
Price, Anna M., *o'wise* Betts
" Edward ⎫ of Wales, *d* in Lon-
" John ⎬ don 1807-18
" John, seaman, *d* 1836

Price, Harriet, Wolverhampton 1854
" Rebecca, *frmly* Haddock
" Rees, of Cardigan, *d* 1827
" Thos. B., of Staffordshire, *d* 1836
" William A., *d* in India
" Wm. Yeoman of the Guard 1826
Primrose, James, of Fifeshire, 1800
Prince, Daniel, seaman, *d* 1814
" Edward ⎱ of Park Terrace,
" Margaret ⎰ Kensington
" Catherine, of Chelsea, *d* abroad
Prior, Sarah, Westminster 1785
" John, *d* abroad 1820
Pritchard, Maria, Cheshire
" Sarah, of Newington
" William, of Southwark
Prince, Z. G., *d* London 1855
Protheroe, James L., *d* in India
Prouse, Elizabeth, Isle of Wight 1836
Proudfoot, James, of Perth 1810
Prouting, Elizabeth, Bermondsey 1823
Pruday, John, of Northampton
Pryer, Elizabeth, *o'wise* Honeymoon
Pullen, William, *d* Jamaica
" Robert, of London
Pulford, Sarah, *o'wise* Avis
Purkis, Henry J., *d* Middlesex 1865
Pugh, Sarah, *d* Kent 1867
Purkis, Emma, *dau.* of John
Purcell, Eleanor, Brompton, *d* 1857
" John, brother of Eleanor
" George, brother of John
Punshon, Mary, Newcastle-on-Tyne
Putnam, James, *d* Middlesex
Purvis, Richard, seaman Navy
Puttock, James, of Kent, *d* 1840
Purton, Hannah, of Somerset
Pyke, Mary, of London
Pym, Capt. Barton, *d* abroad
Pugh, Mary, Rotherhithe
" William, seaman, *d* 1851
Pullen, John, surgeon, Bath, 1838
Pulteney, Charles S., surgeon, 1780
" George A., *d* 1793
" Daniel, *d* 1811
Purchas, John, London
Purches, Sarah, of Lambeth
Purdon, Margaret, *frmly* Sweeney
Purser, J., *d* in India
Purvis, J. E., Army surgeon

Q

Quinn, James, of Liverpool
Quanborough, Edward, of Liverpool
Quanbrough, George, *d* abroad 1860

GENERAL INDEX.

Quick, Martha, *dau.* of James
Quin, James S., mariner, *d* abroad
Quinton, Ann, *frmly* Shepherd
Quist, C. A., *d* Woolwich 1821

R

Rapp, Christopher C., *d* London 1854
" Augustus F., *d* London 1858
Raines, John S., of London, 1820
Randall, Nicholas, of Bedford
Raille, Elizabeth, *d* Jamaica
Rayner, William, of Worcestershire
Ramsden, Richard, *d* Herts, 1850
Raynor, Charlotte, of Layton
Ramsay, Isabella, Hampstead 1840
Rathbone, John E., of Staffordshire
Ray, Matilda, Croydon
Ralph, James, of Marylebone
Rae, Margaret, *o'wise* Paterson
Raymer, William, *d* abroad 1856
Randall, William
Ramsey, Ellen, of Manchester
Ralph, James, mariner R N
Rankin, Janet, Dumbarton
Randes, Grace, *frmly* Wood
Rattenbury, Ann, of Melbourne
Ramsay, Robert, of London, 1840
Ramsbottom, Richard, of London
Ramshaw, James, of London
" William, of London
Rance, Sarah, of Guildford
Rathbone, Ewd. J. of Wolverhampton
Razer, James, of London, 1742
Rae, David, master-mariner, *d* 1822
Radford, Henry, seaman 1819
Rain, Charles, of Durham, *d* 1826
Rainsden, John, of London, 1697
Rainsford, Ensign Marcus, *d* 1817
Raley, Elizabeth, *frmly* Fulbrook
Ramsay, Thos., master-mariner, 1807
" Peter, master R N, *d* 1804
Ramsey, James, of Perth, 1810
Ramshire, Robert, of London, 1750
Rankin, Charles, of London
Randall, Joseph, of Dublin, 1821
Rankine, Charles, surgeon, Scotland
Ranson, Mary, of Westminster, 1790
Raphael, Alexander, of Venice
Rawlence, Marmaduke, *d* 1795
Rawling, John, of Kensington
Rawlins, Anthony H., *d* abroad
Rawlinson, Thomas, *d* abroad 1856
" Mat., of Cheshire, *d* 1816
" Richard, of London, 1752

Rawson, Hannah, Yorkshire
Rayner, Elizabeth, *o'wise* Mahon
" Mary, *frmly* Adams, 1796
Reynolds, Edward, *d* London
Read, James, *d* London
Reeve, Mary, *d* Middlesex
Reynolds, John, of Gloucestershire
Redwyn, Mary *frmly* Hayward
Remhold, Julius, of London, 1843
Reatley, —, *d* abroad, 1869
Read, William, *d* Dorsetshire
Reeve, Elizabeth F., Bath, 1800
" Mary, Somerset, *d* 1866
Remberry, Gerhard A., *d* Leeds 1864
Redding, J., *d* abroad 1864
Read, Joanna, niece of Mrs. Payne
Reardon, Frederick, of Dublin
Reed, Elizabeth ⎫ nieces of
" Mary ⎭ Mary Rushton
Reynolds, John, of Mile-End
Remington, Richard, *alias* Rivers
" Thomas, of Manchester
Rennald, Alexander, London 1765
Redacleave, John
Reynolds, Caroline, *frmly* Barber
Reubridge Family ⎫ of Cripplegate
" Joseph ⎭ 1780
Reynolds, John ⎫ of Kentish Town
" Matilda ⎭ 1854
Renny, James II., of London 1830
Reilly, John, of London 1828
Read, Rev. Richard, of Barkstone
Renwick, James, of London 1867
Rennett, Hugh P., *d* Paris 1868
Read, George, seaman Norfolk
" John, victualler London
" Lieut. Jno. V. C., R N, *d* 1858
" Samuel, of Willenhall, Stafford
" William, of Staffordshire
Reader, Susannah, *s*, *d* Surrey 1860
Reavins, Francis, clerk Chelsea
Redford, Sarah, *w*, Teddington, *d* 1838
Redmond, Capt. Thomas
Redwood, Capt., 5th Dragoons
Reed, Charlotte, *s*, *d* London
" Thomas, *d* Rotherhithe
Reeks, Sarah, *w*, New York
Reeve, George, *d* London 1790
" Thomas, of Suffolk, *d* 1840
Reeves, Elizabeth, Surrey, *d* 1777
" Elizabeth ⎫ children of
" Francis K. ⎬ Francis, of
" John ⎬ Lambeth, who
" William ⎭ died 1787
" John, of London

Reeves, John ⎫ of Hampshire,
"   Mary ⎭   d 1846
"   Thomas, of London
"   William, of London, d 1804
Reid, James, d London 1827
"   Margaret, frmly Miller
Remmell, Dr. John, d abd 1820
Remond, Catharine Reading, d 1814
Renfrew, James, seaman, d 1819
Renshaw, Wm., of Manchester
Reynolds, Ann, of Sydenham 1824
"   John, paymast. Army 1802
"   Admiral John, 1784
"   Mary, d Somerset 1856
"   Wm., of Stourbridge
Rhodes, John, of Newington
"   Capt., d abroad 1864
"   George, of London 1828
"   Mary, of Camfield, Leeds
"   Rev. James Armitage
"   Ann, of Camfield, Leeds
"   John William
Richards, Major R. W., d abroad
Rice, William, of Monmouth 1830
Riley, Stephen D., d India
"   William
Richards, Anna M., of Surrey 1825
Richardson, James, d Bristol
Richard, Susannah, d abroad
Richardson, John, d Kent
Riley, Hugh, of Liverpool
Richards, John, of Westminster
Ritchie, William, of Edinburgh
Risdon, John, d Middlesex 1865
Richardson, Wm., of Cockermouth
Richardson, John T
Richards, Thomas, of London 1850
"   Charles, of Walham Green
Ripon, Sackville, of Westmoreland
Rice, Margaret, Paris, d 1794
"   Sarah, frmly Onions
"   John P., d abroad 1859
"   Mary, d abroad 1859
Rich, James, of Somerset
Richards, John, planter W. I., 1862
"   Charlotte, dau. of John
Richardson, Humphrey
"   Ann, Marylebone
"   Frederick, seaman Navy
"   John, of Durham, d 1803
"   Lieut. Saml., R M, d 1861
"   Wm., d America 1824
"   J., of Westminster 1767
Rider, Sarah, Worcestershire
"   James, seaman Navy
Ridley, Matthew, d America 1805

Riches, John, builder, Birmingham
Rigg, Mary, married J. Rooke, 1810
"   Hannah, o'wise Worrall
Riley, Elizabeth, of Essex
Riordon, Thomas, d abroad
Riorteau, Jane, o'wise Anderson
Rise, Aaron, of Somerset 1829
Risdale, John, d abroad 1862
Ritchie, John, of Perth 1810
Riter, John, seaman, d 1841
Roebuck, Thomas, d London
Rogers, Theophilos ⎫
"   Robert   ⎬ of Northampt'n
"   Timothy   ⎭
"   Richard, of America 1754
Robinson, Henry, of Yorkshire
"   Ann, d Liverpool
Robins, Elizabeth, d Middlesex
Rogers, John N., d London
Robinson, Ann, d Middlesex
Rotherham, Mary, d Middlesex 1741
"   Ann, o'wise Wyatt
Rolfe, William, d Suffolk
Roswell, William, of Sussex
Rowed, Mary Ann, frmly Anderson
Robinson, Thomas, went to America
Rowles, Lieut. Henry
Robinson, James, d Yorkshire 1869
Robertson, Duncan, d Middlesex
Roach, John, seaman, d 1821
"   Hannah, of Marylebone
Robbins, Mary, Dublin, d 1858
Roberts, Alice, London, d 1841
"   Ann, frmly Knight, d 1775
Rowles, Stephen, of Huntingdon
Rowlinson, Elzbth., Langarotte 1835
Rowte, John, d at Chelsea
Royley, T., draper, London 1656
Royle, Henry, d Manchester 1860
Royston, Alice, frmly Gilbert
Rozier, Elizabeth, of Rotherhithe
Rosalie, left Paris for Dublin 1838
Robertson, George J., of Dumfries
Robinson, George, of Dover 1817
Rogers, John   ⎫ of Mile End,
"   Hannah   ⎭   Middlesex
Ross, Jane Mrs., of Perthshire
Rockey, James, of Blackrock
Robertson, Elzbth., Dundee, d 1866
Roffey, Sarah, London 1760-80
Roberts, Ann, frmly Ensley
Rogers, Arthur ⎫
"   George   ⎬ of Dean-street, Soho
"   Sarah   ⎭
Robertson, Bower R., d Pembroke 1851

Rosenbohn, Johanna, d London 1862
Robinson, William, of Liverpool
Rowland, Robert, of Bristol 1838
Rogers, James, of Holt, Hants
Rowbottom, Mark, of Matlock
Rogers, Anne, *frmly* Hollins
" John, d Middlesex 1865
Ronaldson, Wm., d Surrey 1865
Ronaldson, Wm., d London
Robinson, H. B., *frmly* Ross
Robins, John, of London
Rose, Joseph, auctioneer 1840
Rodmell, Sarah, Sussex
Robson, Wm. D., d Salford 1867
Robertson, Alex. ⎱ of Limehouse
" James ⎰ 1820
Rochfort, F., of London 1840
Roscow, Robt. of London 1820
Ross, Colin, of London 1812
Rordansy, Henry, of London 1815
Robinson, Samuel, of London
Rowcroft, Thomas, of London
Robertson, John, of Glasgow, d 1832
Robinson, Joseph
" Rebecca, Essex, d 1866
" Raseley ⎫
" John ⎪ brothers and
" Alfred ⎬ sister of
" Wm. ⎪ Rebecca
" Mary ⎭
Rome, Mary, *frmly* Robinson
Ronaldson, Wm., d Middlesex 1867
Robertson, Sophia G., of Canada
Roberts, Dorothy, *frmly* Williams
Robinson, Mrs. Heaton B.
Roberts, Ann J., *frmly* Burrows
" Lieut. Christopher, R N
" Capt. Christopher T., Army
" Ed. E., paymaster R N, 1863
" Edward, native of Wales
" Frances, of Marylebone
" John, solicitor, London
" Owen, cook, M S
" William, of Sheffield
Robertson, John, of Plewlands 1797
" John, mariner, d 1812
" Capt. John, d abd 1805
" James, of Patrick
Robinson, Elzbth., Berwick, d 1820
" Frank, seaman, d 1841
" James, seaman, d 1828
" John, seaman, d 1851
" John, d London 1845
" Richard, butcher, M S
" Richard, of Dublin
" Sarah, Hackney

Robinson, Susannah, of N. Thursley
" Commander T., d abroad
" Thomas, d in India 1806
" William, d in India
Robson, Joseph, of Stepney
Roby, James, of Westminster, d 1822
Rockard, A. C. R., of Berwick, d 1859
Rockett, Dudley, of York, d 1803
Roe, James, solicitor, London
" Mary, *o'wise* Doyle
" Samuel, army surgeon
Roebuck, John J., of West Indies
Rofe, Rebecca W., d Walworth 1819
Roffey, Janet, Wimbledon, d 1823
Rogers, Mary, of Camden Town
Rollinson, Nancy, *o'wise* Sugars
Rooke, Mary, *frmly* Rigg, 1810
Rooney, Malachy, d abroad 1849
Roote, Timothy, of London, 1776
Rose, Robert, of Bucks, d 1810
" Mary, *frmly* Derby
" Lieut. John R., d 1815
Rosenburgh, Andrew, seaman
Ross, Major Alexander, d 1828
" Maria A., d abroad 1847
" Peter, of Edinburgh, d 1863
Roward, William, d Edinburgh
Rowe, Abraham, d in Cornwall
" Capt. Benjamin, d 1819
" Thomas, seaman, d 1814
" Thomas
" William, d abroad 1863
Rowcroft, Eliza, Whitechapel 1843
Rowland, David, of Denbigh, d 1848
Rowlatt, Thomas, sergeant, d 1794
Russell, Richard
" Margaret
" Edward, of Middlesex
Rudpath, John, of Clapton
Russell, Alice, d Herts
Ruddach, Thomas, d 1798
Russell, Ann, *o'wise* Bryant
" Edward, Bristol, d 1864
" Sarah, *frmly* Staples
" Richard ⎫
" Mary ⎬ children of
" Sarah ⎭ Sarah Russell
" John, d Aldershot 1866
Ryder, Job, of Cheltenham
" Job Henry, of Bethnal Green
Ryan, Michael, d abroad 1864
Rudland, Francis, of Bath
Rudsdett, John, d at Corby 1851
Ruffle, Elizabeth, milliner, London
Rugely, Susan, of Patten
Rumley, John, mariner, d 1820

NEXT OF KIN. 61

Rumbold, J. G., surg'n, *d* abroad 1821
Rushbrook, Mary, of Rotherhithe
Rushworth, Benjamin } of London
" William } 1805
Russell, C., *d* in India 1815
" Edward, of Surrey
" Sir R. G., of Bucks
" Thomas, sergeant, *d* abroad
Rutherford, Jane, *d* London
" Mary, of Scotland
Rutledge, Capt., of India, 1789
Rutter, Susannah, London, *d* 1843
Ryan, Colonel Charles, *d* London
Ryley, Samuel, of London 1743

S

Sander, Mrs. of St. John's Wood
Savage, Sarah, servant
Sayer, Lydia, *o'wise* Wade
Sainthill, Samuel
Sardeson, Elizabeth, of Alverton
Salter, Humphrey, *d* London
Say, John, of Norfolk
Savage, James, *d* London 1784
Saxton, John, of Bolton, *d* 1838
Sankey, Sarah A., Chatham 1865
Salmon, Rachael B., Hackney, *d* 1862
" Ann } of Brentford,
" Elizabeth } Essex
Saunders, Sarah, of Herts, *d* 1838
Santer, Elizabeth, *frmly* Bradley
Sadler, Captain James, *d* abroad
Sanderson, Robert, Stromness 1796
Saunders Family, living 1716
Sansom, Paul, of Harwich
Saunders, James }
" John } of Kensington
" Frederick }
Sawer, William }
" Elizabeth }
" Charlotte { children of John
" Sarah { & Mary Sawyer
" Hannah }
" Lucy }
" William, *d* London 1811
Salter, Sarah, Mile End 1846
Salmon, Robert, son of John
Sawkell, John, of Durham
Savage, William, linen draper
" Mary Hannah
Salt, Sarah, of Finsbury
Savage, John, of London
· Sadler, Richard, merchant, *d* abroad
Sage, Mr., of India 1787

Saggers, Ann } descendants of W.
" John }
" John } nephews of Ann
" William } and John
Saise, Mary, Hereford, *d* 1806
Salmon, Sarah, niece of Mrs. Irish
" John, of Sunderland 1805
Salmond, James, of Yorkshire, *d* 1859
Salter, Lieut. John, R N
Sampson, John, servant
Sanders, Thomas C., of London 1800
" Joseph, of Langley, Herts
Sanderson, Ann, of Edinburgh 1855
" Elizabeth, *d* Cumberland
" John, of Westmoreland
" Nicholas, of Whitehaven
Sanderson, William, of London
Sanford, William, of the R N
Sandison, Robert, of Scotland 1796
Sandys, Samuel, of Bristol 1780
Saunders, Charles, *d* abroad 1862
" Henry, native of Exeter
" Lieut. T., *d* abroad 1805
" Joseph, of Oxford, *d* 1836
" Walter M., of Kent 1800
Savill, Joseph, of Essex
Saville, Benjamin
Savage, William, of London 1809
Savory, Francis, of Surrey 1780
Sawyer, Robert, gardener, Dorset
Sawkins, Mrs. Mary, of Chelsea
Sayer, George, surgeon, London
" John, of Cambridge 1720
Scarville, Jeremiah, *d* Sussex
Scotnay, Bryant, *d* Middlesex
Schleinzer, Joseph M., *d* London
Scott, Sarah, *d* Westminster
Scanlan, John J., *d* Middlesex 1869
Schofield, Mary, *d* 1869
Scriven, John Hampden
Sclater, Thomas, of Denmark
Scott, John, *d* Liverpool 1869
" William H., *d* 1868
Scaife, William } seamen
" John C. }
Scruby, Susan, *o'wise* Polley
Scott, Thomas, of Madrid 1835
Scaife, Jane, of Westmoreland
Scales, Ann, *o'wise* Le Costa
School, John, ship carpenter 1826
Schovell, Noal, of New York
Schory, Capt. Michael, *d* abroad
Schram, Mary, London, *d* 1818
Scorah, Ann, *dau.* of William
Scolay, Robert, seaman, *d* 1823
Scott, Archibald, purser R N 1796

Scott, Elizabeth, *d* London 1812
" Hannah, *d* in India
" Isabella, *d* London 1856
" James, seaman, *d* 1814
" John, *d* Westminster 1815
" John, of Glasgow, *d* abroad
" John R. D. D., of Westminster
" Joseph, of Durham, *d* 1833
" Robert, seaman Navy
" Sarah, *o'wise* Butler
" Thomas, *d* London 1841
Scouler, Lieut. James B., *d* abroad
Scougall, John, Leith 1800
Scroggs, Richard, of Worcestershire
Scrambler, John, of Southwark
Scudmore, Ann } of London
" William } *d* 1775
Seager, Eliza, wife of Henry
Seymour, James, living 1843
Seaborn, Thomas, of Middlesex
Seymour, Jane, of Berkshire
Selby, Thomas J., *d* Bucks
Seymour, Elizabeth, *d* Middlesex
Search, James, left England 1860
Sewell, Frederick, of Stockwell
Seaman, George, of London 1815
Seel, Charles M., went abroad 1852
Seymour, Mrs. of Berkeley Square 1852
Seftley, Charles, of Berkeley Square 1820
Seabrook, Elizabeth, of Plumstead
Seagrave, Thomas, seaman, *d* 1845
Seaman, James, of Swansea, *d* 1825
" Mary, *o'wise* Holmes
Searles, Susanh., Paddington, *d* 1806
Searle, Francis, of London 1818
Sedden, Elizab'h } daughters of John
" Esther } of Manchester
Selby, Ann J., *d* Plymouth 1862
" Clarke, living 1760
Settle, John, merchant, York
Sewards, Robert, of Melbourne
Sewell, John G., of Norfolk
" Mary, of London
" William, of Lambeth
Seyer, Capt. R. T., *d* abroad 1833
Seymour, Lieut. Robert, *d* abroad
Shakeshaft, John }
" Ann } of Ewell, Surrey
" Richard, surgeon 1790
" Susannah, *o'wise* Foley
Shepperd, Thomas, of London
Shuttlewood, Thos., *d* Falmouth 1753
Sherman, Elizabeth }
" Ezekiel } of Colchester

Short, Grace, *d* Devonshire
Shady, Peter M., *d* Bristol
Shanks, Fitzroy, of Sydney
Sharpe, Valentine, of Wisbeach
Sheppard, William, of Clapham
Shaw, Jane, *d* Kent 1868
Sherwood, Hannah, *o'wise* Colbach
Sharpe, Thomas
Sheldon Family
Shute, Stephen, *d* Devon 1824
Shackleton, William, *d* York 1800
Shepherd, Conolly, left Liverp'l 1859
Shackleton, John, of Lancashire
Shepherd, Wm., of Kent Road 1847
Shaw, John, of Coldstream 1800
Shargood, Martha, Islington 1865
Sheldon, James, *m* C. Smart
Shaw, Duncan, of Southwark 1830
" William } sons of A. Shaw, of
" Andrew } Canada
Shepherd, Thomas
Shaw, Mary, *frmly* Hassell
Shepherd, Sarah, *dau.* of James
Shirley, Samuel, of London 1830
Shield, J. R., of Cray's Court 1862
Shippore Family
Shaw, James D., Newcastle *d* 1865
" Mary, *o'wise* Creak
Sherville, John James, of London
Shakeshaft, Chas., *d* Brompton 1843
Shapton, G., of Plymouth
Shakespear, Arthur, of London 1800
Shard, Frances M., of Devon
Sharpe, Edward, of Lincoln, *d* 1840
Sharples, John, of Lancashire
Shave, John T., of Calcutta
Shaw, Agnes, *o'wise* Donaldson
" Capt. A., West India Regiment
" Hector, *d* in India
" John J., seaman
" Thomas, of America 1783
" William, of Scotland
Shearman, Robert, of Chelsea
Sheffield, Elizbth., *d* Longhead 1765
Sheldon, William
Shelmerdine, Daniel, of Lancashire
Shepherd, Elizabeth, *d* Surrey
" John, seaman
" Kesiah, of Essex
" Lieut. H., *d* abroad 1824
" Susannah, *o'wise* Hedges
" William, seaman 1820
" William, of London 1700
Shephard, Samuel, of Stratford 1760
Sherratt, Charles, of London 1770
Sherlock, Amelia, London 1819

Sherston, Capt. Hugh W.
Shetterden, Thos. ⎱ died early in the
" Elzbh. ⎰ last century
" Meliora, *o'wise* Loan
" Dorothy *o'wise* Smith
" Elizabeth *o'wise* Clarke
Shields, John T., *d* London 1835
Shilham, Thomas, living 1790
Shipley, Lieut. George L., *d* 1822
Shipmore, Elzbth., sist. to D. Hatfield
Shore, John, sergeant-major
Short, Alice, *d* 1784
" Cath., Market Harborough
" Capt. William, of Somerset
Shubrick, Richard ⎱ of America, *d*
" Sarah ⎰ 1760-90
Simpson, Thomas, son of Walter
Silver, Mrs., of Pimlico
Sibbald, Alexander, *d* Glasgow
" Mary, *o'wise* Brown
Sierra, Moses, *d* London
Singleton, James, of Kendal
Sidbury, John, of Devon
Simson, Nathan, *d* London
Simson, Dysie, widow
Simmington, Eleanor, of Scotland
Simpson, Thomas, *d* Middlesex
" Andrew, *d* Scotland
Sidden, Samuel, of Rochester
" Jane, *o'wise* Butler
Singleton, Maria
Simpson, William G., *d* abroad
" George, mariner, *d* 1777
Sidden, Elizabeth, London 1775
Sidebotham, —, London 1774
" John, *d* abroad 1854
Silcock, Benjamin, of London
Silver, Ann, London 1838
Silvester, Ann, sister to E. Box
" Thomas, of Bristol
Sime, Henry, *d* abroad 1836
" Walter, of Aberdeen 1797
Simeon, David, *d* abroad
Simeons, —, *d* abroad
Simes, John, of Islington 1765
Simkins, Thomas, of Islington
Simmons, John, *d* about 1790
" Thomas, of Lincoln
Simpkin, John, of Norfolk 1857
Simpson, Aitken M., *d* 1861
" Lieut. Andrew, *d* 1816
" Elzbth., of Woodorling 1825
" Edward, seaman
" John, of Leicester, *d* 1841
" Sarah, *o'wise* Leake
" W. E., of Edinburgh 1793

Simple, Robert, of Edinburgh 1796
Sims, Jane, *o'wise* Moody 1834
Simson, Thomas, mariner
Sipp, Joseph, master-mariner
Sinclair, George, seaman
Singer, Hannah, *d* London 1808
Skerrett, Ann, *o'wise* Wyer
Skinner, Joseph, of Devonport
Skelding, Jane, *o'wise* Scaife
Skelton, William, went abroad
Skymer, Margaret, widow
Skinner, Mr., of Camden Town
" Sarah, *dau.* of Robert
Skae, David, of Edinburgh 1798
Skeen, Richard M., of Kennington
Skeene, —, army surgeon
Skelton, Belona, *d* 1849
" John, of Dublin
Skerry, Elizabeth, Birmingham
Skinner, Barbara, *frmly* Opie 1770
Slade, Amelia, *o'wise* Phillips
" John, *d* London
Slight, Samuel, clerk
Slade Family
Skeff, S., *d* abroad 1860
Slaughter, W. P. N., *d* London 1865
Sloane, Mary, sister of William
Slumbers, Caroline, London
Sloane, William, London
Sleap, Elizabeth ⎱ children of
" Ann M. ⎰ John
Slater, Joseph, mariner, *d* 1800
Slator, George, of London
Sloat, John, *d* Bermondsey 1855
Sloe, Mary, *d* Surrey 1863
Smith, Andrew, *d* Southampton
" Peter, *d* Suffolk
" Ann, *d* London
" Matthew, *d* Norfolk
Smithes, Voyce, *d* Surrey
Smith, Elizabeth, *o'wise* Lightfoot
" Thomas, *d* London, 1767
Smyth, Ann, *d* Surrey 1774
Smith, Dorothy, of Surrey
Smithies, Charles, *d* Surrey
Smith Family, of Gloucestershire
" John, *d* Oxfordshire
" Thomas, *d* London 1776
" William, *d* Middlesex
" Mary, *d* Middlesex 1795
" Thomas, of Worcestershire
" Thomas, watchmaker
" John, mariner
" James, W., *d* London 1845
" Susannah, *dau.* of Charles
" Jane, *o'wise* Hurst

Smith, Mary, of London 1842
Smart, John, of Middlesex 1820
Smith, Henry Harwood
" Robert, *d* America 1867
" Mary, of Islington
" Hervey, living 1765
" John, of R. Navy 1831
Smythies, Thomas, of Liverpool
Smith, Ann, of Seven Dials 1815
" Sarah, *frmly* Hudson
" Michael John, of Jamaica
Smithson, Caroline, Yorkshire 1865
Smith, Hannah, Warwick
" Martha, Sheffield, *d* 1865
" J. T. B., *d* Middlesex 1864
" Alexander S., Liverpool, *d* 1865
" John, of Sussex, *d* 1862
" George, Aberdeen, *d* 1866
Smither, Samuel } children of Caro-
" Caroline } line
Smith, George, of Nottingham
" Edmund, Melbourne, *d* 1852
" Alexander, of Glassingal
" Dorothy, *frmly* Churchill
" Eliza, *frmly* Ellis, *d* 1858
" Elizabeth, *o'wise* Wilkie
" Robert, of Pittenween, N B
" Barbara, *frmly* Gauden
Smout, John, *o'wise* J. Evans
Small, Elizabeth
" William, of Chobham
Smith, Frances, of Maidstone 1815
" Wm., of Gower Street 1810
Smyth, Constantine J., Dublin 1848
Smith, Richard, of Piccadilly 1830
Smallbones, John, *d* Paddington
Smallman, Solomon, of India
Small, Henry, seaman, *d* 1822
" William, *d* in Herts 1823
Smart, William, of Horsham
Smeaton, Catharine, *frmly* Coventry
Smith, Abel, of Worcester, *d* 1846
" Ann, London, *d* 1843
" Ann M., *o'wise* Summers
" David, of London, *d* 1811
" Dorothy, *frmly* Shetterden
" E., draper, Birmingham
" Edward, of London
" Edward, seaman, *d* 1814
" Elizabeth, sister to Thomas
" Eliza, of Leicestershire
" Francis, *o'wise* Wellard
" Francis, seaman, *d* 1822
" George, seaman, *d* 1850
" George, of London 1805
" George, seaman, *d* 1818

Smith, George, yeoman, Bath
" Gerard, of London 1770
" Henry, of Suffolk 1829
" Henry L., of Greenwich
" James, yeoman, Lettendy
" James, of Bilston, *d* 1862
" James, of, Tenterden, *d* 182?
" Capt. James, *d* 1828
" James, of Macclesfield, *d* 1843
" Jane, *frmly* Payne
" John, seaman, *d* 1846
" John, of Manchester, *d* abrd
" John, mariner, *d* 1836
" John, of Buntingford, *d* 1811
" John, *m* Catharine Owen
" John, seaman, *d* 1819
" John, of Aberdeen 1800
" John, *d* Islington 1824
" John, of Glasgow 1810
" John, of Lettendy, N B
" Joseph, *d* Lambeth
" Mary, Leamington 1853
" Mary, *frmly* Hill, *d* 1831
" Phillip, *d* London 1813
" Robert, of Bermondsey 1789
" Robert, seaman, *d* 1818
" Samuel, brother of John
" Sarah, Litchfield
" Sarah, *frmly* Bellas, *d* 1841
" Susan, *frmly* Nicoll
" Thomas, baker, London
" Thomas, seaman, *d* 1814
" Thomas, master-mariner
" William, E., cf London
" William, seaman, *d* 1821
" William, of Deptford 1817
" William, *d* at Andover
" Lieut. W., *d* in India
" Capt. Llewellyn, *d* 1848
Smithson, Wm., of London 1774
Smyth, Lieut. Arthur, *d* 1837
Smyth, James, of London
Snell, John, *d* Suffolk 1775
Snelson, Frances, of London
Snell, Anna M., of Bideford 1838
Snodgrass, Thomas, *d* London 1794
Snow, William, *d* Middlesex 1815
Soulby, Mary
Soper, James, of Brighton
Sowdon, William, went abroad
Soare, William H., *d* Chelsea 1867
Southby, George, of Southwark
South, Mary, *frmly* Bailey
Southwark Bridge Shareholders
Solomon, Myer, of Westminster
Sommers, William

NEXT OF KIN. 65

Sommers, Letitia, wife of William
Sooley, John, nephew of Elzbth. S.
Southbrook, Sophia, of London
Sovereign, John, seaman
Sowden, Ann, *frmly* Oakes
Sparkes, James, *o'wise* Watts
Spyr, James, of London
Spiers, Ebenezer, son of James
Sparrow, Robert, of Norfolk
Spray, Adryan, of Sussex
Speed, Charles, of Kent
Sparks, William, *d* Middlesex
Spencer, William G., *d* Bristol
Spackman, Rachael, of Huntingdon
Spencer, Sarah, of Derbyshire
Spencer, Eleanor, *d* Surrey 1814
Spalding, Charles, of Lambeth
Spanger, J. D., *d* Kent 1868
Sprake, Stephen B., of Dorset
Spencer, Sarah, *d* Surrey
Spiller, William, of Belfast
Spence, Ann, living 1800
  " Hannah, went abroad 1851
Spencer, Mary, *frmly* Sparrow
Sparrow, Major George, *d* abroad
  " George W., of Kensington
Spencer, Major Robert, *d* abroad
Sparks, Ruth W., *o'wise* Large, *d* 1861
Sparke, William, London 1760
Spiller, Susan, of Belfast
Squire, Dorothy, *d* 1819
Spackman, John, of London
Sparke, Andrew K., *d* in India
Sparrock, Richard, seaman
Sparrow, Frances, London, *d* 1847
Sparvell, Sarah, of Berkshire
Speller, Elizabeth, *frmly* Yeates
Spencer, Adam } of London 1780
  " Ann }
  " Elizabeth, *d* Australia 1833
  " Elizabeth, *d* America
  " Helen A., Notts, *d* 1863
  " Jane, *o'wise* Bown
  " John, master-mariner 1826
  " Mary, Surrey
  " Capt. Robert, *d* India
  " Thomas W. G., of London
  " Wm., of Camden Town 1838
Spiers, Colonel Alexander, *d* 1847
Spooner, Major, *d* Chelsea 1848
Spottiswoode, Wm. } of Glenfernal,
  " James } 1796
Spriley, Thomas, seaman, *d* 1818
Spyers, Elizabeth, *d* Wandsworth 1820
Squire, Harriett, of Bethnal Green

Stuart, Mary, *d* London 1772
Stephens, John, *d* Barnstaple
Stirzaker, Thomas, *d* Yorkshire
Stone, John, *d* America
Stroud, Richard, *d* Surrey
Stanhope, Charlotte, *d* Nottingham
Stone, Francis, *d* London
Staples, Archibald, *d* India
Stirpin, John A., *d* Denham
Strongfellow, William, *d* London
Staines, Jeffry, *d* Essex
Stephens, W. F. D., *d* Middlesex
Stopford, C. J. B., *d* Bath 1870
Stewart, Charles, *d* Yorkshire 1869
Studd, William
  " Theophilus
Stone, Eliza Martha
Stewart, Donald, of Scotland
  " Bella
  " Henry, living 1820
Stevens, Edward } legatees of C.
  " Frances } Carter
  " Jane }
Stares, Elizabeth, *frmly* Williams
St. John, Baroness Susannah L.
Stafford, William, of Lewes, Sussex
Stark, Wm., of Shoreditch, *d* 1824
Starling, Lieut. Colonel P.
Stephens, Joel, of London, *d* 1765
Stewart, Capt. Charles, R N, *d* 1814
Stinton, Joseph, of Hereford, *d* 1821
Strong, John, of Islington
  " Thomas, publican, Brompton
Story, Sarah, *w*, Nottingham, *d* 1819
Stowe, George, of Berkshire, *d* 1863
Stafford, John, living 1640
  " Family, Leicestershire
Stower, Mary A., Australia 1853
Stafford Family, Yorkshire
Stevens, George, servant
  " Frederick S., *d* Rutland
Stephenson, Robert, of Hull
Stern, Edward, of London
Strudwick, Hannah, *frmly* Bottom
Stevens, John, *d* London 1802
Steadman, Anne, *frmly* Greening
Strudwick, Sarah, *frmly* Lamb
Stapp, Sarah } formerly residing in
  " Mary } Malta
Strange, R., *d* in Australia
Stuart, James P. } of Ireland, *d* in
  " Priscilla } America
Stetson, Samuel, *d* in America
Stephenson, George, Northumberland 1861
Stibbert, Giles, *d* Bath 1859

Stockley, Mary, *dau.* of John
Stewart, Ann, Bath, *d* 1861
Stevens, Edmund P., of London 1847
Stone, George, of Islington 1844
Staples, John, Riverhead, *d* 1810
" Ann, *frmly* Peake
Sturkey, Edwin, of Montgomery
Stone, E. J. R. ⎱ grandchildren of
" S. R. ⎰ Edward Russell
Strong, Mary, of Millbank 1858-9
Stephens, Sophia, Hackney 1855
Stabbs, J., *d* abroad 1864
Stockwell, John, of London 1810
Stanhope, Maria Elizabeth, of London 1820
Stedman, Chas. H., of London 1850
Stephens, Augustus, of St. Ives 1830
Stevens, John, of Harrow 1830
Stuckbury, Charles, of London 1815
Stowell, Esther, *frmly* of Southampton
Stares, John, of Broxford, *d* 1865
Stael, Ann, *frmly* Addington
Stevens, Elizabeth, *o'wise* Bicknell
Stapleton, J. M., *frmly* of Dublin
St. Catharine's Dock Estate
Stockell, Robert, of Westminster
Stackhouse, Elzbth, *o'wise* King
" Thomas, born 1776
Stafford, Geo. T., born London 1801
Stag, Capt. David D., *d* 1860-1
Staines, Sarah, Lambeth 1828
Stains, Thomas, mariner
Stalker, Alice ⎱
" Daniel ⎱ of Dublin and
" Isab'lla ⎰ Shrewsbury
" Jane ⎰ 1820
" John ⎰
Stallion, William, of Bucks
Standowick, Rev. J., *d* Norwich 1802
Stanfield, Thos., of Middlesex, *d* 1825
Stanford, Elizabeth, *frmly* Story
Stangroom, Christopher
Stanton, Daniel, of Bristol
Staunton, W. G., army surgeon
Stay, Betty, *frm'y* Hayward
" Janet, Wimbledon
Steady, John, of Lambeth, *d* 1833
Steedman, James, of Glasgow
Steel, Henry, of Egham
" Robert, of S. Shields
Steele, Ann, Arundell
Steeple, William, *d* abroad 1854
Steer, Elizabeth, of Isleworth 1770
Steers, Thomas, *d* Marylebone 1847
Stehelin, Capt. C. B., *d* 1827

Stein, Andrew ⎱ distillers 1814
" Charles ⎰
Steinorth, Ellen, of Southwark
Steir, John, seaman, *d* 1837
Stent, Rebecca, *d* Middlesex 1832
Stephani, J. L., of London 1812
Stephens, Dorothy, *frmly* Melling
" James, seaman, *d* 1818
" James, victualler, London
" Mary, *o'wise* Hunt
" Phillis, Middlesex
" Richard, of Ripley, *d* 1845
" Samuel, *d* Marylebone
" Thomas, *d* Hackney 1783
Stephenson, Nathaniel ⎱ of Paisley
" Thomas ⎰ 1814
" Susannah, Hampstead
Stevens, Eleanor, Kent, *d* 1838
Stevenson, Alex. of Scotland, *d* 1778
" Pat'k, of Edinburgh 1798
" Capt. S. T., *d* India 1816
Steward, Ann, *frmly* Lumley
" James, seaman, *d* 1819
" Charles, *d* London 1835
Stewart, Alex., of Glasgow 1810
" Archibald, native of Perth
" Henry, seaman, *d* 1848
" James, living 1804
" James, sergeant, *d* abroad
" James, mariner, *d* 1841
" John, seaman, *d* 1863
" John ⎱ sons of Andrew,
" Robert ⎰ of Stirling
" Isabella, of Edinburgh
" Kenneth, B., *d* 1820
" Robert, of Linlithgow
" Thomas, of Bedford
" Margaret, of Lanark 1794
Stock, Rebecca, Essex
Stockton, John, of Yorkshire
Stockwell, John G., of Bermondsey
" Thomas, seaman, *d* 1822
Stoddart, John, *d* Poplar 1821
Stokes, John, of Clerkenwell
" Wm., of Marylebone 1780
Stokoe, Lieut-Col. J. C., *d* abroad
Stone, Elzbth., Cheltenham, *d* 1860
" John R., of Barnes
" Richard, of Blandford
Stoneson, William, seaman, *d* 1820
Storrs, Ann, Chesterfield, *d* 1863
Story, Eleanor ⎱
" Elizabeth ⎰ living in 1846
" George L. ⎰
" John ⎰
Stowick, Louisa, of London

Stowes, John, seaman, *d* 1822
Strahan, James, planter, W. Indies
Strange, George, of Worcester
Straton, Isabella, of Edinburgh
Stratford, John, *d* Southwark 1840
Street, John, tailor, London
" Thomas, Chelsea pensioner
Strefford, Chrstr. of Whitechapel 1817
Strivens, Stephen, of Ramsgate
Strong, Elizabeth, *frmly* Hadkinson
Stroud, Samuel, *d* Dublin 183)
Stunt, Thomas W., mariner, *d* 1824
Stubbs, John, *d* London 1818
" Charles, of Dorset
" John ⎫ brothers and sister
" Robert ⎬ of Elizabeth Ives,
" Mary ⎭ of Shropshire
" George ⎫
" John ⎬ nephews of Elizabeth Ives
" Robert ⎭
Stuart, Robert, merchant, 1820
" Alexander, of Glasgow 1810
Sturrock, Ensign H., *d* abroad
Sturt, John, *d* Sussex 1815
Styler, George, seaman, *d* 1818
Styles, Thos., master-mariner, *d* 1860
Swete, Benjamin, *d* London
Swan, George C., *d* York 1788
Swallow, Robert, *d* Rotherham
Sugden, Charlotte, *d* Ipswich
Sullivan, J. F., *d* abroad 1863
Sutherland, James, R Navy, *d* 1814
Sutcliff, Edwin, of Whitechapel
Summerland, Mrs., Gravesend 1862
Swain, Bonner, formerly in the Navy
Swainson, Eliza, *frmly* Moore
Symons, Sophia, *frmly* Cheeseman
Surrell, Harriett, London 1867
Summers, Daniel, Woodford, *d* 1865
Swallow, Rev. W. H., *d* 1867
Swan, Henry, of Esher
Sweet, Samuel W., of London
Syfret, Stephen, of London
Symonds, Eliza
" Matilda ⎬ of Brighton
" Joseph ⎭
Sudon, Chas. L., 60th Regt. of Foot
Sugars, Nancy, sister to Robert
Sugrue, Charles, *d* abroad 1816
Suker, William, *d* Bobbington 1800
Sullivan, John, seaman 1822
Summers, Ann, of Harpenden
" James H., *d* abroad 1810
Surrey, Charlotte, *frmly* Fullwood
Surtees, A. A., of Camden Town
Suter, Rev. Thomas H., *d* 1861

Sutton, F. M., of Notts, *d* 1826
Swaddell, Maria, *frmly* Cope
Swaisland, George, seaman, *d* 1864
Swanson, John, seaman
Swayne, Lieut. John B.
Sweeny, Margaret, of Plymouth
" John, seaman M S
Sweetapple, John, of London 1690
Swindle, John, wine merchant
Swindall, Ann, *d* Lambeth 1845
Swift, Vincent, *d* London 1820
Swinarton, Richard, *d* London 1858
Syfret, Charlotte, of Kennington
Symondson, Anne
" Catharine
" Frances E.
Symons, Lieut. John, *d* abroad 1835
Swann, Anna, of London
Symkin, Sarah, *o'wise* Darrell
Sykes, Thomas, of Yorkshire

T

Taylor, Janet, *dau.* of Peter
Tagg, Abraham, of Derbyshire
" Elizabeth, *w*, *d* 1846
Taylor, Robert, of London 1838
Tann, Charles, *d* Sydney 1848
Taylor, Thomas, of Cheshire
" Milborne, *d* Bristol
" Elizabeth, *d* Middlesex
" John, *d* Surrey 1707
Tancred, Christopher, of Yorkshire
Taylor, William, *d* London
" Jonathan, of Lyme Regis
Tawney, Sarah, *o'wise* Darwent
Talbot, Thomas, *d* Hereford 1787
Tanner, Nicholas, *d* Surrey
Taylor, Mary, *d* Middlesex
Tate, Edmund, *d* Middlesex 1829
Taylor, Mary A., *d* London 1864
Talbot, Joshua, of Leicester
Tabor, J. S., *d* abroad 1849
Taitt, Chas. W. W., of Bathurst 1853
Tait, Capt. Alexander, *d* Edinburgh
Taylor, Joseph, of Edinburgh
" Gabriel, *b* 1782
" John, of Lincolnshire, *d* 1861
" Ann, *d* 1861
Talbot, James, of Windsor 1850
Tagg, Richard, of Staffordshire 1772
" Mary, *frmly* Lynall 1772
Taylor, John, of London 1815
" Peter, of Scotland
Tapner, John, of Woolwich

68   GENERAL INDEX.

Tapner, Elizabeth ⎱ daughters of
"   Catherine ⎰   John
Tarrald, Gabriel, mariner, d 1777
Taffe, Mathew, seaman
Talbot, Lieut-Colonel
"   Sarah, Guildford 1862
Tallentire, Thomas, d London 1816
Tannatt, Edward, of Montgomery
Tanner, George, of Essex
Tapp, William, d London 1848
Tappin, Mary, of Warwickshire
Tarbuck, James, of Lancashire
Target, Thomas, d London
Tasker, Edward, d abroad 1858
Tasman, Elizabeth, London
Tate, Admiral George
Tatem, Henry, seaman, d 1811
Taylerson, Ann, Sunderland
"   Margaret, Durham
Taylor, Ann, Gloucester 1855
"   Anthony, d India
"   Charles, of Devon
"   Elzabth., of Manchester 1857
"   Harriet, London 1847
"   John, of West Bromwich
"   John S., of London
"   John W., seaman 1823
"   Mary, d in. of Charles
"   Mary A., Somerset 1843
"   Thomas, mariner, d 1843
"   William, of Walthamstow
"   William, d abroad 1856
"   William, of Louth, Lincoln
Tempest, George, d abroad
Teague, Adam
"   Joel
Teagles, John Charles, of London
Teall, Jane, wife of Timothy
"   Mary, d Lancashire 1864
Teasdale, Mary, Wetherby
"   Marmaduke, d 1795
Teaster, John, seaman, d 1824
Tedford, Honoria, d in India
Terry, Martha, of Mortlake
"   Rebecca, o'wise Beech
Tether, Thomas, d London 1846
Thomas, John E.
Thornly, Rebecca, o'wise Cooper
Thompson, Mr., d London 1835
Thibault, Joseph E.
Thomson, Robert, of Glasgow
Thorowgood, Wm., d London
Thompson, John, d 1715
Thomson, Thomas, d abd 1750
Thomas, Theophilus, of Glamorgan
"   Samuel S., d abd 1797

Thirkill, Christopher, of Durham
Thomson, Thos. S., d Glasgow 1860
Thornaby, Daniel, of Manchester
Thompson, James, son of Rev. E.
Thomas, Sarah
Thompson, Samuel, of Belfast
Thurgood, Wm., London 1820
Thomson, James, of Scotland
"   Alexander G.
Thomas, George, seaman
"   Charles, chymist
Thompson, Ovid, Liverpool 1839
Thomson, David, mason, Greenock
Thomas, Wm., of London
Thorn, Mary, o'wise Jennings 1865
Thielthorpe, Wm., of Kensington
Thompson, John T., d abroad 1857
"   Dr. W., army surgeon
           1820
"   Wm., of London 1830
"   Alderman
"   Wm., d London 1777
Thornton, Thomas, of Greenwich
Thomas, Mary, servant 1847
Thomson, Ann, of Yorkshire
"   Helen, of Edinburgh
"   John, master-mariner
"   Capt. John, of S. Shields
"   Marmaduke, d 1846
"   Thomas, of Brixton
"   William, of London
"   William, of Kensington
Thorne, Charles J., of London
"   James, seaman, d 1834
Thornton, Capt. James, d abroad
"   Susan, of Totness
Thornycroft, Ann, Chester 1831
Thorpe, Charles J., of London
"   Jane, London 1800
Thacker, J. S., mariner, d abroad
Thackstone, Rebecca, w, Portsea
Thomas, Henry, seaman, d 1821
"   James, seaman Navy
"   John, seaman, d 1839
"   John, seaman, d 1821
"   John, brother of M. Cumley
"   John, d Liverpool 1820
"   Joseph, seaman, d 1818
"   Philip, of Pembroke
"   Robert, d London 1820
"   Sarah, Norwich, d 1842
Thomason, Wm., d in India
Thomlinson, John, d London
"   Jane, d York 1817
Thompson, Allan, merchant 1808
"   Charles, seaman, d 1822

NEXT OF KIN. 69

Thompson, Elizabeth, Kennington
" Elzbth. A., *o'wise* Otway
" Euphemia, *d* abd 1828
" James, seaman M S
" John, seaman M S
" John, seaman, *d* 1814
" John, *frmly* in the Army
" John, *d* Edinburgh
" John T., gunner 1828
" Mary, Pimlico 1854
" Richard, of Dover
" Robert, paymaster Army
" Lieut. W. R., *d* abd. 1818
" Capt. Wm., *d* abd 1828
" William, seaman M S
" William, of London
Tibbenham, John, *d* Suffolk
Tillyard, Mary Ann
Tibbs, Wm., *d* abroad 1864
Tickel, Mary
Tickel, Jane
Tipper, Joseph, of Deal
Tillottson, John, of Wapping 1845
Timson, George, of London 1834
Timbrell, W. H., of Lewisham
Tierney, Robert, *d* London
Tilly, Joseph, of London 1788
Tindale, Rev. Geo., of Yorkshire
Tisdale, Lieut. Harmer, *d* 1825
" John, *d* America 1805
Todd, Henry J., of London 1843
Toulmin, Samuel, *d* London 1809
Todd, W. W., *d* Herefordshire
Tomkiss, Edward, *d* Shrewsbury
Toogood, John, *d* Dorset 1852
" Elzbth., *d* Dorset 1868
Townsend, Septimus, *b* at Durbridge
Tole, Samuel, of Beeston, Notts
Todd, Arch'd, Knightsbridge 1849
" John, mariner
Tooth, Griffith, of Uttoxeter, *d* 1861
Tomson, Sarah, Kent, *d* 1865
Townshend, Cattarn, of Leicestersh'e
Toms, Rev. William
Tobin, Ann, *d* at Lisbon
" Eleanor, of Kilkenny
Tod, Francis, of London 1778
Todd, Jacob, seaman, *d* 1826
" John, *d* London
Toderingham, Thomas, *d* abroad
Tollett, Maria, *o'wise* Clifford
Tolson, Eleanor, Westminster 1786
" Mary, Bloomsbury 1786
Tomalin, Obadiah, of London 1816
Tomlinson, Geo., of Norfolk 1802
Tompkins, Paul, of London

Toombs, John, of Gloucester 1822
Toomer, John, of Somerset
Tooth, James, *d* Rugely 1842
Towers, James, of London
Townley, Ann, Norfolk 1825
" Rev. Geo., living 1774
" Robert
' George
" Rev. William, *d* Kent
Townsend, Margaret, *d* Sheffield 1815
Trinder, Jane, *d* Middlesex
" Thomas, of Gloucestershire
Tracey, Robert, of Gloucestershire
Trafford, Richard, *d* Liverpool
Trinder, Thomas, of Oxfordshire
Tranter, James, of Gloucestershire
Trotter, Charles, of Calcutta
Trenwith, Rebecca, *d* Cornwall 1796
Troup, James, *d* London 1867
Trimble, William, *d* 1828
Truster, Edward, *d* 1848
Trimnell, Mrs., *alias* Wilcox
Truslove, Henry, *d* Birmingham 1840
Trist, Richard, *d* Brighton 1867
Trent, Ann, Llanegward, *d* 1866
Treston, Edward, *d* India 1849
Tranter, Philip, Warwick, *d* 1862
Treatt, Edwin O S.
" George B.
Tryon, Samuel
Tracey, James, *d* Marylebone 1818
Trapp, Samuel, of Birmingham
Travist, Wm., *d* Lambeth 1843
Trenery, Wm., of London 1850
Trinby, George, of London
Trinks, Charles, *d* 1782-4
Trivett, Wm., of London
Trott, Matthew, *d* Upwell 1827
Trotter, W. C., *d* Australia 1855
Trow, Ann, London, *d* 1828
Tucker, Catharine, *frmly* Redman
Tulley, Thomas, of Brighton
" Charles, of Clayton
Turner, Charlotte, of Stockwell
" John, *d* Essex
Tuck, Adam, *d* Wiltshire
Tutet, Mark Cephas, *d* London
Turney, George, of Acton
Tucker, Nathaniel B., *d* 1857
Turner, Mary, *d* Kent
" Ann, *d* Dawsley 1835
Tucker, Allan, of Yorkshire
" Capt. N. B., *d* 1857
Tulford, Maria, London, *d* 1817
Tullaterton, Margaret, of Kilkenny
Tumber, Joel, S. H., of Manchester

GENERAL INDEX.

Turnbull, Andrew, seaman, *d* 1822
" Thomas, seaman, *d* 1813
" Henry, of Scotland, *d* 1806
" William, *d* at Hackney
Turner, Adam, *d* Sunderland
" Betty, *o'wise* Wilkins
" Elizabeth, *o'wise* Cullum
" Elizabeth, Homerton 1854
" Henry, *d* in Kent
" James, *d* Suffolk 1847
" James, seaman, *d* 1814
" John, clerk, *d* aged 86
" John, *d* West Indies
" Mary, *frmly* Marshall
" Robert, of Sunderland
" John, *d* Marylebone 1842
" Richard, seaman, *d* 1821
" Sarah, *d* Surrey 1829
" Thomas P., *d* 1812
" Frederick, of Bloomsb'y 1838
" Thomas, of London 1820
" Robert, seaman, *d* 1868
" John Price, of Exeter
" Robert Drysdale
Turnor, Exuperious, of Bucks
Turnidge, Martha, Essex
Turkington, James, surgeon R N
Turwell, Bates F., of Cambridge
Turpin, James, of Lambeth 1832
Turlington, Ann, of Reading
Tyler, William, of Walthamstow
Tyssen, Francis J., *d* Middlesex

U

Underhill, Richard, *d* Lincoln 1815
Underwood, John, *d* Middlesex
Urquhart, Jane, living 1800
Underdown, Elizabeth, Derby
" Elzbth. L., *frmly* Howe
Underwood, Sophia, of Somerset
" Thos., of Chipping Barnet
Unwin, James W., *d* Derby 1846
Umfreville, Sarah, *frmly* Conyers

V

Vandome, Ed. L., *d* Wilts 1858
Vaughan, Maurice, master-mariner
Varey, Wm., son of Col. Jas. 1792
Varndell Family, of Berkshire
Varney, Harriet, London, *d* 1852
Vasper, John, seaman, *d* 1832
" Capt. J. H. A., *d* 1851
Vauspall, Francis C., *d* 1822-3

Vaux, John, of Clerkenwell
Verdenhulm, Elizabeth, living 1805
Vernon, Thomas, *d* London 1838
Vevers, Sarah, *frmly* Dick 1806
Vincent, Jane, of Brighton
Vaughan, Chrysogen, *d* 1798
Vickerman, Hannah, *w*, *d* 1865
Vosper, Capt. H. A., *d* 1850-1
Vallantine, William
Vivers, Sarah
Van de Wall, Phillip
Vaughan, Fanny, *w*, living 1860
Vance, Hugh, of London 1810
Vanderburgh, Joseph, of Middlesex
Vint, Martha Elizbth., *w*, Essex, *d* 1867
Voice, Anna Maria
" John
Vokins, Robert
Voysey, Thomas James
Vincent, Riches, of King's Lynn
" Richard, of Guildford
Vine, Thomas, carpenter, *d* 1784
Viney, Charles, *d* Surrey, 1756
" W. W., of Bucks and London
Vintner, William, grocer, London
Virtue, Capt., marines, 1849
Vivers, —, *d* in Australia
Vizac, Mrs. M., *d* India 1804
Vogel, John W., of London 1805
Votes, George, seaman 1820
Voughton, Jane, *o'wise* Bennett
Vernon, Thomas, living 1757
Vollum, Mary, native of France

W

Walkley, Harriett A.
Ward, Thomas, of Warwickshire
Waller, Sarah, *d* Kent 1869
Waterman, William, builder
Waterman, Jane, of Camden Town
Walker, Cecil S. Taylor
Watts, James, *o'wise* Sparkes
Waters, Edward, of Monmouth 1725
Watson, W. H., of Maida Vale
Waterall, Elizabeth, *o'wise* Tagg
Watts, John, *d* America 1841
" Ann, *o'wise* Desormeux
Watson, James, of Carlisle
Waring, John, *d* London
Warham, Winnifred, *d* Middlesex
Waterman, John, *d* Middlesex
Warren, Elizabeth } of London
" John }
Waller, Richd., of the Isle of Wight
Waddell, Thomas, *d* Perth

Wainman, Thomas, of Notts
Walford, Elizabeth, *d* London
Walker, John, *d* Middlesex 1806
Waring, Eliza, of Oxfordshire
Watkins, Daniel J., *d* London 1808
Warren, Thomas, of London 1840
Watts, Walter, of London 1841
Walker, James, of Wapping 1810
Wall, Joseph, of Greenwich 1810
Warren, Thomas, of Canonbury 1846
" Thomas M., of London 1845
Wantry, Gabriel F. of Edinburgh 1780
Ward, Eliza, *frmly* Wood
Wall, Mary Ann, London 1832
Wantress Family
Wate, Eliza S., *w* of Mr. Wate
Wade, Alfred, of Oxford Street
Watchorn, Ann
Washbrooke, Hen., *d* Ludbrooke 1865
Warne, Mr., of Holborn
Waterworth, William, of Blackburn
Waddington, H. C., *d* abroad 1842
" Mary, Salop 1831
Wade, George, of Wakefield
" Benjamin, carpenter
" Peter, *d* in India
Wadley, John, drummer, 48th Regt.
Wain, John, of London 1810
Waine, James, of Northampton 1788
Waite, Sarah, Bermondsey 1857
Wake, Jane, *frmly* Hayward
Wakeford, Walter, of Somerset
Walcott, Elisha, of Canada 1811
Wales, Hannah, *o'wise* Warne
" Hannah, *b* 1768
Walham, Mary, of Clifton
Walcott, Edward, of London
Walker, Peter, of Fifeshire 1797
" Ann, of Lindfield
" David, uncle of Jane
" Ensign George, *d* India
" George, of Leeds
" Ensign Henry, *d* abd 1842
" James, of London 1800
" James, exor. to A. Anderson
" Jane, Aberdeen
" Janet, native of Scotland
" John, *d* London 1811
" John, *d* Southwark 1812
" John, of Homerton
" Mary, of Marylebone
" Mary, *frmly* Covert
" Samuel, of Manchester 1850
" Stiers, seaman M S
" Thomas, seaman M S
" William, *d* Yorkshire 1846

Wall, George ⎫
" John ⎬ brothers, living 1820
" Samuel ⎭
" Stephen, living 1790
" Stephen ⎫ brothers, died about
" John ⎭ 1768
Walker, Joseph, left England 1830
Watson, Alexander G., of Cheshunt
Walker, Wm. J., *d* Deptford 1860
Waskett, Elizabeth
Walker, M., of Whitehaven
" James, *d* before 1815
Wardrop, Thomas J. ⎫
" Andrew
" James ⎬ nephews and
" Margaret ⎬ nieces of Hen-
" Margaret ⎭ ry Lundie
" Mary
" Catherine
Waite, John, Marylebone, *d* 1829
Wait, Stephen ⎫ brothers of John
" Thomas ⎭
Warren, Joseph, of Gloucestershire
Watts, Ann
Watt, James, *d* 1864
Watts, Anna M., *frmly* Glaine
Watkins, Ann E., of London
Waterhouse, Stephen, living 1770
Waller, Martin, of Southwark 1855
Waddington, H. C., *d* abroad 1842
Warner, James C., *d* 1850-1
Walker, Frank, of North Carolina
" Alexander, of Australia
Waldron, Catherine, servant
Watson, William, *m* M. Palmer
" John, of Manchester
Wasey, Oliver, footman 1850
Watkins, Towel, *d* Middlesex 1863
Warren, Thomas, of Islington 1850
Walmsley, William, of Bath
Walter, Rev. Daniel, of Sussex
Watson, E. W., of Tottenham-court-rd
Watson, Elizabeth, *d* in Lambeth
" George, seaman, d 1823
" John, *d* Durham 1814
" John, of London 1764
" John, of Oxford
" Mary, of Lincolnshire
" Peter, *d* London
" Richard, living 1797
" Richard, *d* Yorkshire 1817
" Thomas, *d* abroad 1810-12
" Thomas, of Edinburgh 1796
" Thomas, *d* Watford 1800
" William, *d* Liverpool 1847
" William, captain, *d* America

72   GENERAL INDEX.

Watts, Ann, Worcestershire
" Robert, Lieut. R N
" Samuel, *d* Westminster
" William, of Thorpe 1766
Wall, Charles .
" George ⎫ children of
" James ⎬ Stephen, and
" John ⎭ living 1790
" Samuel
" Benjamin ⎫
" Charles ⎬ child'n of Charles,
" John ⎬ and living 1790
" William ⎭
" Mary, London, 1787
" James, son of Mary, *d* 1794
" James, *d* London 1803
Wallace, Mr., *d* abroad 1863
Walland, William, *d* Surrey 1780
Waller, Elizabeth, Berkshire
" John, *d* London 1811
Wallis, Elizabeth, Bath, *d* 1847
" Thomas, of Wallingford
" W. H., major, *d* abroad 1820
Walpole, Elizabeth, *d* Cheshunt 1841
Walsh, Andrew, *d* London 1828
Walser, John, seaman, *d* 1822
Walter, Wm. J., *d* Deptford 1860
Ward, Ann, *frmly* Collins
" George, seaman, *d* 1817
" John, of Derby 1788
" John, *d* China 1857
" Mary, living 1777
" Sarah, of Finsbury
" Sarah, of Hull
" Sarah Mrs., of Bucks
" Sophia, Hitchin, *d* 1856
" Thomas, seaman
Warden, Charles, of London 1798
" Chas., master-mariner 1825
Warne, Hannah, *d* 1845
Warner, Jonathan
" James C., Lieut. 1860
" George, *d* Surrey 1850
" John, of Stratford 1783
Warrall, John, of Marylebone 1806
Warren, Mary, *frmly* Nicol
" Sir P., V.-Admiral
" Robert, seaman, *d* 1813
" Michael, of Cork
" Samson, *d* 1816
Waterhouse, F. M., of Eastbourne
Waterman, D. Mrs., of Middlesex
Waters, Edmund ⎱ of Marylebone
" Morgan ⎰ 1802
Watkins, J. G. R., *d* abroad 1810
" Richard, *d* London 1833

Watkins, Samuel, of London
" William, of Hoxton 1823
" William C., of Kennington
Watson, Alex., *d* Middlesex 1807
Webb, John, of Wilts, *d* 1740-50
Webb, Marmaduke A., *d* Middlesex
Westrup, George, of Whitechapel
Webley, Walter, of Monmouth 1737
Welsh, Thomas, went abroad
Welsford, William, of Devon
Webb, Clarissa Julia, of Paris
Wells, Daniel, of Sussex
West, Charles M., *d* India 1838
Weels, John, of Hartlepool
Wells, Sarah, of Gloucestershire
Wedgwood, John, of Staffordshire
Wennington, Charlotte, Pelsall 1845
Westfold, Thomas, *d* abroad 1826
Welsh, Robert, of Harwich
" Lady Hester, *d* Eltham 1826
West, Capt. J. E., of Swansea
" Thomas, London, surgeon
Weeks, J. M., Bristol, *d* 1865
Webb, William, of Somerset
West, Elizabeth, Stratford-le-Bow
Weston, William ⎱ children of James
" Ann ⎰ and Mary Weston
Westlake, Henry George, of Essex
Weatherall, Captain, of Australia
West, John, butler
" Joseph, of Shoreditch 1840
Webster, George, *d* Canada 1865
" Sarah, *w*, Canada 1867
Weatherhead, Thos. of Wokingham
Westerby, Dinah, *frmly* Stopford
West New Jersey Society
Webb, Ensign Henry, *d* 1777
Wells, Jonah S., of Islington
West, Charlotte, *d* Surrey 1840
" Edward, of London 1694
" Francis, seaman, *d* 1823
" Frances ⎱ of London
" John ⎰
" Henry ⎱ of Feltham,
" John ⎬ Middlesex
" Nicholas ⎭
" Morris, of Edinburgh, 1800
Weston, Elizabeth, *d* Wilts 1819
" James, of Sherborne
" Robert H., of Birmingham
Westall, William, army surgeon
Westmoreland, W.
Welsh, John, seaman, *d* 1811
" William, seaman M S
Welter, J. F., *d* abroad 1862
Werrett, Sarah, Bermondsey

Wescott, John, } of London d 1790
" Hannah
West, — surgeon 4th Regt. Foot
Wear, Thomas, d in India
Wearland, William, of Surrey, d 1770
Webb, Ann, dau. of Edward
" Elizabeth Mrs., of London
" Elizabeth, frmly Odall
" John, d India 1802
" John seaman, d 1822
" John, S., mariner, Portsea
" John, seaman Navy
" James, d Greenwich
" Maria, o'wise Knox
" William, seaman Navy
" William, of India, 1817
Webster, Thomas, of Orkney
Wedlake, Priscilla, P. of Middlesex
Weekly, Edward, of Kent, 1725
Weir, George, d London 1829
" William, of Edinburgh
Weight, Theophilus, mariner
Weldon, Sarah, of London 1810
" Sarah, of Halifax
" William, d Yorkshire 1838
Wellard, William, of Kent
Welles, John, of London 1805
Wellman, William, d London 1803
Wells, Elizabeth, Wanborough
" Elizabeth } of Mitcham,
" Hannah } Surrey
" Peter
" Gideon, d Gainsborough 1810
" Sarah, Gloucestershire
White, Thomas and his wife
Whiffin, George, of Calais 1812
Wharmby, John, Cheshire, d 1864
White, James, of London 1810
Wheatley, Charles, of Hammersmith
Whitehead, George, of Kendall
Whitewell Elizabeth, schoolmistress
Wheelhouse, George, of Kent, d 1864
Whyte, John, of Toronto
Wheable, Ann C. Walworth, d 1865
White, J., d abroad 1863
Whitbrook, Charles } went to
" Ann } America
White, Christopher
" Harvey
Whiteway, Thos. B. d Cornwall 1868
White, Nathaniel, d Middlesex 1783
" Robert
" Mary, o'wise Banks
" Martha, o'wise Elland
Whitworth, John Harry
Whately, Thomas, d Herts 1867

Whitely, Mary Ann
Whiteford, Francis, of Louth
Whittney, William, d abroad
White, Frances, frmly Wyndham
Whittaker, William, d London
White, James, d Surrey 1794
Whitaker, John, of Norwich
Wheeler, William, d India
White, William, d Surrey
" William, d abroad 1799
" John, d Surrey
" William, ship steward
Whildon Family
Whistler, Charles, of Odiham
Whildon, Susannah E., London 1780
" Elizabeth } of London,
" Sarah } 1780
Whitfield, Amelia, frmly Smart
White, G. F., of London 1842
Whitaker, Joseph, of London 1845
White, John, of Dundalk
Wheeler, John G., d abroad 1867
White, William }
" Mary } living in Yorkshire
" Hannah }
Wilkinson, George, of London 1823
Whare, Ann, o'wise Thomson
Wheatley, John, of Darlington
Wheeler, Elizabeth, frmly Rice
Wheeler, Thos. L., d London 1792
Whillan, Alice A., of Margate
Whitaker, —., of Sligo
" Joseph, of Bloomsbury
" Mary, frmly Brook
" Steph., d Marylebone 1734
White, Ann, d London 1860
" Elizabeth, frmly Fullwood
" Francis, of London 1791
" Francis, ensign, d 1825
" Hannah, frmly Moore
" John, master-mariner, d 1806
" John, d Yorkshire 1837
" John, of London 1805
" John, of Canada 1796
" John, gunner Navy 1821
" John, of Mitcham
" Mary, of Norfolk 1818
" Mary, Pimlico, d 1823
" Michael, d Bucks 1839
" Robert, d London
" Rosetta, d London 1831
" Thomas, Captain, d 1819
" Thomas, seaman, d 1818
" W. R., army surgeon
" William, steward Navy
Whitehead, John, seaman

GENERAL INDEX.

Whitehead, Robert, of Scotland, 1796
Whitelaw, Wm., *d* Kennington 1861
Whitfield, Joana L., *d* abroad 1837
Whiting, Margaret, of Somerset
" Anthony, *d* Kent 1841
Whyte, J., of Bermondsey 1796
Wilson, Timothy, *d* Surrey
Wightwick, James, *d* Tunstall
Wingfield, Timothy, *d* Amersham
Williams, John, of Tenby
Willsbee, Sarah, *o'wise* Campbell
Withers, Samuel, *d* Kent 1755
Wilson, Joseph, *d* London
Wilson, Ann, *dau.* of Joseph
Wilson, Joseph, of Scotland
Wilkins, Samuel, *d* Surrey
Williams, Sarah, of Ipswich
Wilkins, John, of Yorkshire
Wilson, Hugh, of Ayr
Williams, Sarah, *d* London
" William, *d* America
" Edward, of Chipston
" Edward, *d* London
" Lydia, *o'wise* Sayer
Wiggins, Charles, of London
William, William, of Devon 1730
Winterbottom, John F., *d* Berks 1868
Willis, Catherine A., *d* Bath 1864
Williams, Sophia, of Witney
Wigman, Watt, of Surrey
William, Benjamin
William, John, of London 1828
Wilby, Charlotte, of Suffolk
Wilby, Simon, *d* Suffolk 1861
Williamson, Mary, Rosa A.
Winter, Noel
" Conyers
Wise, John, *d* Berks 1851
Wilkinson, Joseph, *d* Surrey
Williams, William, son of Thomas
Willmott, Ann, *frmly* Harris
Williams William, of London
Williamson, J. F., *d* London 1828
Willis, Thomas, *d* Surrey 1790
" Mary A., of Yorkshire
Wingrove, William, *d* Surrey
Wiston, John, *d* Hants 1831
Williams, Ann, *d* Jersey
Wickers, Thomas, of Lincoln 1775
Williams, Joseph, of Oxfordshire
Willcock, Thomas, of Exeter
Wiggins, Joseph, of Brighton 1850
Willcox, Julia, *o'wise* Trimnell
Williams, George, seaman M S
Wistow, John, of Southampton
Wilson, Rickenson, of Cumberland

Wilkinson, Herbert, of America
Wilson, William Dicker
Wildman, Mary, *frmly* Cheesman
Williams, David
Wilkinson, Joseph B., went abrd 1852
" Ann, *w* of William
Winter, William, of New Cross
Wilson, William W., of Bowness
Witham, Alice A., Kent, *d* 1856
Wiginton, Mary A., of Hackney 1823
Wilson, J., *d* abroad
Williams, Lieut., *d* China 1864
" Maria } of London
" Mary } 1832
Wiseman, William } living 1750
" Elizabeth }
Williams, Ann, Brixton, *d* 1865
Willett, Christian, Greenwich *d* 1858
Williams, Mary, *o'wise* Jones
Wilkinson, Jonathan, London
Winder, Elizabeth, *frmly* Rowes
Wise, Reginald A., son of Mary
Willis, Mary A., Yorkshire, *d* 1862
Willard, Richard, Sussex, *d* 1862
Winch, William, of Wimbledon
Wilks, Mary, *d* Worcestershire, 1862
Williams, William, *d* abroad 1860
Williamson, Thomas, of Marylebone
Winn, John, *d* in Devon 1860
Winsor, Eliza, of Regent's Park
Wilson, John C., formerly of Calcutta
Williams, William, *d* Middlesex 1865
Wilson, John } of Edinburgh
" Elizabeth }
Williams, Jane, *d* abroad
Wilkinson, Catherine, *d* 1866
Williams, John, *d* Westminster 1832
Wilson, John, of Stafford
" John, of Scotland
Wilkinson, John, of London 1812
Wilson, Christopher } ironmongers,
" Edmond } London 1820
" Thomas }
" John E., Southwark 1810
Williamson, James, of Lambeth 1810
Winwood, Catherine
Williams, Elizabeth, Hereford, *d* 1868
Wilson, John, of Canada
" Archibald, mariner
Williams, Thomas, of Tottenham
Williams, Mary, living 1815
Wiltshire, George }
" Robert }
" George } of Clapham
" Frederick }
Wilcocks, Sarah, of Staines

Wild, John, of London
Wilder, James, seaman
Wildey, Thomas, d in America
Wilkie, James, d London 1795
" Patrick, Lieut., d 1828
Wilkins, Betsey, Hants
" Martha, of Marylebone
" Thomas, of Pentonville 1844
Wilkinson, B. C., Lieut., d 1823
" John, Ensign, d 1830
" James, d abroad 1840
" Susan'h, of Northampton
Wilks, Francis, of London 1740
Willett, Rickett, of Cardiff, d 1827
Williams, A., d in London
" Ann, Marylebone
" Ann, Tottenham 1840
" Charles, seaman 1824
" David, d in Australia
" David, seaman, d 1842
" Elizabeth, d London
" Elizabeth, d Bristol 1848
" George, seaman
" Henry, seaman, d 1822
" Henry, alias Rogers
" J. H. T., master-mariner
" James, d 1820
" J. H., mariner, d abrd 1833
" John H., d Ipswich 1850
" John, d London 1818
" John, seaman, d 1837
" John A. S., d abroad 1812
" John, seaman, Navy
" Lieut., d China 1864
" Mary, dau. of Capt. W.
" Mary, frmly Keasure
" Mary, living 1800
" Mary, Bristol, d 1806
" Thomas, seaman
" Thomas, of Cardiff
" Thomas, of Liverpool
" William, of London 1800
" William, seaman
Williamson, Ann, Worthing 1842
" Dorothy, d London 1780
Willimore, Harriett, frmly Wheeler
Willis, Sarah, of London
" Henry, of London 1705
" William, d Glasgow 1858
Willmott, H., Thornton, d 1820
" Hannah, of Yorkshire
" Arthur M., d abroad
Willson, Elizabeth P., w of Thomas
Wills, Thomas ⎱ of Herts, d at the
" Sarah ⎰ Cape of Good Hope
Wilson, Alexander, d in Paris

Wilson, Emma, Ventnor, d 1859
" Henry, mariner, d 1834
" Ida E., frmly Gainsford
Wilson, Isaac, ship carpenter 1816
" James, E I C S, d abroad
" James, d Southwark 1813
" James, of Monmouth, d 1817
" Jas.J.Dr.,d Manchester 1865
" James, seaman, d 1827
" James, seaman, d 1851
" John, master R N, d 1827
" John, quartermaster Army
" John, d London
" John, of Suffolk
" John C., of Mansfield, d 1828
" Jonas, seaman M S
" Joseph, attorney, d 1820
" Lawrence S., d in India
" Maria, o'wise Campbell
" Mary, Brentford, d 1833
" Margaret, of London
" Nathaniel, of Glasgow,d 1822
" Parnell, Brompton
" Robert ⎱ merchants, Lond'n
" Thos. ⎰
" Thomas, of Stourbridge
" Thomas, seaman, d 1822
" Thomas, captain
" Thomas, m E. Polstern
" Thos., executor to T. Patten
" Thomas, Esq.
" T., d abroad 1863
" William, of Surrey, d 1794
" William, of London
" Alexander ⎫
" John ⎪
" Robert ⎬ children of
" Thomas ⎪ Robert & Maria
" Samuel ⎪ Wilson, all
" Elizabeth ⎪ living in 1775
" Jane ⎪
" Maria ⎭
Wilton, William H., d 1847
Wingrove, Elizabeth, frmly Roach
Winkles, Peter, of Bloomsbury
Winter, Samuel, of America 1781
" Ann ⎫
" Benjamin ⎬ living in 1775
" Thomas ⎭
Wise, Sarah, d 1829
Wiseman, James, d London 1861
Wiseheart, John, writer, Glasgow
Wissett, John, Lieut-Colonel
Witchurch, Sarah, dau. of James
Withy, Mary, London, d 1841
Witmill, Joseph, of Crowmarsh

GENERAL INDEX.

Wichells, Henry, *d* London 1848
Wolfe, James W. M.
" Janet, *o'wise* Mills 1776
Wotton, Martha
Wood, John, son of George
Woodford, Ann Eliza, *d* Bath
Wood, Georgiana R., *d* Herts 1857
Wormal, Israel, *d* London 1737
Wolley, Margaret, of Worcestershire
Woodruff, Daniel, *d* Middlesex
Wood, John, of London
Wood, Charles E., *d* abroad 1798
Woodhead, Anthony, of Edinburgh
Worth, Jacob W., *d* London
Wood, Clement, of Lincoln 1755-9
Wood, Grace, *o'wise* Randes
" John Samuel, of Norwich
Worgan, John, living 1790
Wood, Henry, of Newington 1820
Woodrow, Robert, of Norfolk
" Lewis, J., *d* London 1860
Wollaston, Mr., lost at sea, 1852-3
Wood, Hicklington, native of Ripon
" James, of Glasgow
" Matthias, of Barnsley
" William, of Reigate 1800
Woods, Joseph S., went abroad 1840
Worsley, Ephraim, Middlesex
Wookey, Charles, of 16th Regt.
Wood, Eliza, *dau.* of Thomas
Woodroff, Thos., brother of Stephen
Woolley, John, of Stockwell
Wolff, Ernest, of London 1838
Wood, Charles, of London 1850
" Humphrey, of London 1812
" Thomas, of London 1845
Wolgar, William, schoolmaster
" Ellen, wife of William
Wolley, Charles S., *d* in America
Wood, Ann, of Soho 1762
" Ann, *frmly* Ling
" Elizabeth, London 1827
" Eliza, *d* Hampstead
" Charles, of Lincolnshire, *d* 1819
" Isaac, of Lincoln, *d* 1849
" Henry, of Australia 1820
" James, merchant, *d* abroad
" John, native of Wakefield
" John, *d* Bath 1780
" John, seaman, *d* 1818
" Mary, *o'wise* Day
" Matthew, *d* abroad 1863
" Robert, *d* London 1842
" Samuel, of Clerkenwell
" William, labourer
" William, seaman, *d* 1814

Wood, William, clerk, *d* 1828
Woodham, W., *d* London 1838
Woodhouse, Elizabeth, *frmly* Bond
Woodman, John Slater
Woodcock, John, *d* Surrey 1828
Woodward, Jane, of Rottingdean
" Mary A.J., *d* Portsmouth
" Thos., married M. Hayes
Wooldridge, Frank, Lieut. R N
Wooley, Thomas, of Bloomsbury
Woolfe, William, of Surrey
Woolley, Wm. Dr., *d* India
Woollard, Thomas, of Colchester
Woolnough, Mary, *d* Yarmouth
Woolridge, Benjn., of Surrey, 1724
Woods, Ann, of Bungay
Wordie, Cath , Cheltenham 1837
Wordsworth, Elzbth., Reading 1847
Worlidge, Edward, *d* 1840
Worth, Robert, *d* in London
Worthington, James, *d* London
Worral, Henry, of Manchester
" Hannah, *frmly* Rigg
" Mary, *o'wise* Rooke
Wolfe, Robert, *d* abroad 1864
Wrench, Edward, *d* Cheshire
Wright, John W., *d* Northampton 1867
" John, *d* Cheshire 1868
" William, *d* Lincolnshire 1848
" Wm., of Hackney-road 1815
" John, of London 1742
" Margaret, of Aberdeen
" Peter, *d* London
" W. H., *d* London 1840
" Thomas } brothers of
" Barnard } Elzbth. Flatters
" Robert }
" Louisa, of Greenwich
" Geo. T., of Birmingham 1820
" Francis, *d* Lambeth 1866
" George, of Lincolnshire
Wraith, Robert, *d* Stournmouth 1811
Wraughton, N. Capt., *d* 1851
Wrentmore, Ann, *d* Devon 1831
Wright, Cath., *d* Dundee
" Elizabeth, of Aldley
" Francis, *d* Lambeth 1856
" Geo. S. of Birmingham 1820
" Hannah, Lambeth, *d* 1828
" John L., of Brechin, N B
" L. Capt., of Chatham 1718
" Lucy, Middlesex, *d* 1795
Wynne, Grace, of Ruthin
Wynn, Benjamin, *d* Yorkshire
Wyer, Ann, *frmly* Skerrett
Wyatt, C. P., of Ghent, 1850

Wylds, Michael, *b* Jersey 1764
Wylde, John, of Bolton
Wynard, Richard L. *d* Middlesex 1826
Wyse, Edmund, of London 1780
Wheelwright, Hannah, *d* Hoxton

Y

Yardley, John, *d* Suffolk 1827
Yare, Ann P., London, *d* 1813
Yarnold, Cath., Surrey, *d* 1858
Yates, Thomas } of Maidenhead
" Mary }
" William
Yate, Ellen, of Hillington 1851
Yeaman, Margt. S., of Perthshire
Yeo, Samuel R., *o'wise* Jowett
Yeoman, Thomas, Rev., of Stoke
Yeomans, Sarah, *o'wise* Bostock
York, William, *d* Middlesex
Young, Sarah, *frmly* Elmes
" Elizabeth, *d* Cardiff
Youlden, John C., of Camden Town
Young, Richard, of Edinburgh
" F.J., married Miss McDonald
Young, Jeffrey M., of Norfolk
Youle, Ann

Yorke, Sir Joseph
Young, Thomas, of Battersea
" Thomas, of Rosetta, W B
" James } of Dundee,
" David } mariners
Youd, Mary, *w*, Hampstead 1821
Youl, Robert, master-mariner
Young, Anna, Rochester, *d* 1859
" Edward, *d* Bristol 1855
" George, *d* India
" George, *d* Yorkshire 1849
" Hester, *o'wise* Moore
" James, of Camden Town
" James, *d* abroad 1806
" James, *d* 1825
" James, of Edinburgh 1796
" John, *d* Isle of Wight
" Peter, ship carpenter
" William, sailmaker, *d* 1840
" William, of Edinburgh 1796
Yule, Andrew, *d* abroad 1850
Yuill, William, of London

Z

Zornlen, Eleanor, of Camberwell
Zimmerman, F. C., of London 1815

INDEX TO CHANCERY ADVERTISEMENTS.

THE HEIRS-AT-LAW, NEXT OF KIN, AND RELATIVES OF THE FOLLOWING PERSONS HAVE BEEN ADVERTISED FOR BY THE COURT OF CHANCERY SINCE THE YEAR 1700.

A

Abbott, James, *d* Westminster 1791
Abel, James, *d* Hampstead 1817
Abondio, Margaret, *d* Lambeth 1840
Abraham, George, *d* London 1834
Ackers, James, *d* Lancashire 1824
Acton, John, of Burslem, *d* 1853
Acworth, Ball B., *d* 1818
Adams, Elbth., Shrewsbury, *d* 1789
" John, of Newport, Salop
" John, *d* Westminster 1832
" Tabitha, *frmly* Spencer
Adamthwaite, J. Rev., *d* Warwick
Adkin, William, *d* Suffolk 1813
Adnam Roder, *d* Fulham 1823
Ainsworth, David, *d* Lancashire 1824
" Thos., *d* Lancashire 1848
Aisley, Stephen, *d* Surrey 1805
Alder, Ann, of Portsmouth, *d* abroad
Aldred, John, *d* France 1839
Aldren, Mary, Lancaster, *d* 1835
Alexander, Catherine, *frmly* Elkin
Allen, Ann, *d* in Herts
" George, of Essex, *d* 1841
" John, of Isleworth, *d* 1825
" John, *d* London 1799
" Key, surgeon, Chesham
" Thomas, *o'wise* Bradford
" William, *d* Southwark 1833
Allison, Esther, Yorkshire 1829
" Jane, Durham, *d* 1836
Amies, John, *b* 1766, *d* 1815
Amy, Ann, Cornwall 1790-9
Anderson, Ann, Windsor, *d* 1835
" Andrew, major, *d* 1824
" Joshua, *d* Carlisle 1846
" William, surgeon, *d* 1763
Andrews, Eleanor, *frmly* Elkins
" John, of Hants, *d* 1814

Andrews, John, of Devon, *d* 1762
" Thos. of Manchester, *d* 1843
Andrus, George, of Kent, *d* 1847
Annison, W. G., *d* London 1795
Antt, Bridget T., *o'wise* Profit
Applebee, John, of Essex, 1825
Appleby, William, *d* Southwark 1810
Arbourin, Charles, of London, *d* 1856
" James, *d* London 1821
Arden, S., *d* Wolverhampton
Arman, Sarah, of Wilts
Armfield, Eliza A., Falmouth
Armistead, Arthur, *d* Cheshire 1857
Armstrong, Anna J., Bristol 1816
" Eliza, Bristol, *d* 1818
Arnold, John, of Cardington
" Richard, of Norfolk, *d* 1818
Arnot, David G., of Oxon, *d* 1842
Arthur, Boyle, of Bath, *d* 1844
" Maria, Bath, *d* 1851
" Robert, of London, *d* 1815
Arundell, Richard, *d* Cornwall 1832
" W. B., of Kensington, *d* 1827
Ashbee, Thomas, of Kent, *d* 1831
Ashcroft, Elizabeth, *frmly* Arnold
Ashton, James, *d* Marylebone 1803
" John, of Cheshire, *d* 1846
Aspland, Elizabeth, Ipswich, *d* 1852
Asprey, Alice, *o'wise* Bradford
" Bedwin, *o'wise* Bradford
Athorpe, Mary, *frmly* Smith
Atkins, John, *d* Stockwell 1786
Atkinson, Mary, *d* Lancashire 1847
" Mary A., *d* Lincoln 1854
Attwell, Thomas, *d* Marylebone 1831
Austin, Robert, of Kent, *d* 1832
Austwick, Joseph, *d* Devon 1838
Autrobus, Philip, *d* Cheshire 1830
Avarn, John, *d* Surrey 1809
Aveis, Judith, *o'wise* Phillips
Avery, David, *d* London 1775-6

Avery, Thomas, *d* Faversham 1799
Ayes, Ralph, *d* Essex 1818
Ayres, James, of Froome
Ayscough, Ann, Hants, *d* 1828

B

Baas, Joachim G., *d* London 1767
Backhouse, John, *d* Yorkshire 1796
" Thomas, of Bucks, *d* 1800
Bacon, John, of Durham, *d* 1752
Bacon, John, *d* Northumberland 1739
" William, *d* Durham 1748
Baile, George, *d* Carmarthen 1851
Bailey, Benjamin, of London, *d* 1840
" Hannah, *d* Marylebone 1808
" Henry, of London, *d* 1774
" Jeremiah, *d* Wilts 1841
" John, *d* Wilts 1840
" Thomas, *d* Wilts 1835
Bailie, Elbth., *d* Bath 1831
Baiston, Robert, *d* Billingham 1845
Bagley, John, *d* Yorkshire 1812
Baker, H. E. R., Capt., *d* 1820
" John, *d* London 1811
" John, of Essex 1790
" John, *d* Essex 1836
" Joseph, *d* Stafford 1840
" Susannah, *frmly* Phillips
" Thomas, *d* Stockwell 1814
" Thomas E., *d* Wilts 1813
" William, of Bidford, 1786
" William, *d* Surrey 1814
" William B., *d* Turkey 1856
Baldwin, Charles, *d* Manchester 1801
" John, *d* Lancashire, 1819
Ballenden, James, *d* London 1841
Balshaw, Mary, *frmly* Higson
Bampton, Ann, *frmly* Reeves
Banks, Ann, *o'wise* Halliday
" Moses, *d* Brentford 1824
" Paul Sir, *d* Cork 1788
Bannister, Jas. D, *d* Westminster 1840
" William, *d* Yorkshire 1849
Barber, Charles, of Calcutta, *d* 1799
" Daniel, of Moulton, *d* 1826
" Isaac, of Rochester, *d* 1831
Barfield, Mary, Colchester, *d* 1834
Barker, Ann, Yorkshire, *d* 1773
" Sarah, of Kent, *d* 1808
Barley, William, *d* March 1810
Barnes, Diana, Gloucestershire
" Jno. K., *d* Worcestershire 1844
Baron, Cath., Lancashire, *d* 1861
" Thomas, *d* Lancashire, 1846
Barr, Martha, Surrey, *d* 1854

Barrett, James, of Ledbury, *d* 1841
" John, of London, *d* 1796
" Robert, of Norfolk, *d* 1820
Barrington, Paul, *d* Westminster 1765
Barrow, John P., of Somerset
Bartholomew, R. J. *d* Plymouth 1845
Bartlett, Elbth., *d* Middlesex 1845
" Henry W., *d* Lambeth 1828
" Samuel, *d* Wimborne 1820
Barton, Richard, *d* Surrey 1822
" Thomas, *d* Manchester 1822
" Thomas, *d* Shrewsbury 1791
" William, *d* Froome 1804
Basden, Samuel T., *d* 1859
Basire, James, *d* London 1812
Baskett, Wm., indigo planter, *d* 1831
Basnett, James, *d* Lancashire 1832
Bateman, H. W., of Woodstock, *d* 1823
" Ann, *d* 1833
" Ann, *d* 1834
Bates, Abraham. *d* Devon, 1833
" William, *d* Enfield 1788
Batson, James, *d* Worcester 1820
" Ann, *w* of James, *d* 1839
Batley, Ellen, *d* Yorkshire 1820
" Mary, Manchester, *d* 1837
Bawtree, Mary, Hants, *d* 1844
Baxter, James, master-mariner, *d* 1801
Bayley, Thomas, of Kent, *d* 1743
" Hannah, Surrey, *d* 1796
Baylies, Robert, *d* Worcester 1842
Baylis, Elbth. *d* Worcestershire 1828
" Henry, master-mariner, *d* 1831
Bayly, Lucy, *frmly* Oakes
" Zachary, *d* Jamaica 1769
Beales, Sarah, Cambridge, *d* 1840
Bean, Frances E., *o'wise* King
Beard, John, *d* Twickenham 1813
" Thomas F., *d* Kensington 1847
Beardsell, George, *d* Yorkshire 1705
Beart, Charles, *d* Suffolk 1780
Beasley, Richard, of Abingdon 1775
Beauchamp, Finetta, Kent, *d* 1782
Beavis, Elbth., Devon, *d* 1800
" Peter, *d* Surrey 1803
Beavitt, George, *d* London 1799
Beckett, Amelia, of Berks, *d* 1847
" John, of Berks, *d* 1846
Beckwith, H. B., *d* York 1834
Beet, Rebecca, of Northampton
" Richard, of Wedington
Belcher, Robert, *d* Doncaster 1827
Beldam, John, *d* Cambridge 1832
Belin, Elzbth., wife of Peter, *d* 1784
Bell, Elzbth. M., Kensington, *d* 1851
" James, *d* Battersea 1814

Bell, Mary, *d* Middlesex 1854
" Sarah, *frmly* Luff
" Stephen, *d* Falmouth 1815
" William, *d* Dumfries 1832
Bellinger, Walter, *d* London 1780
Benacock, Joseph, of London
" Esther, *w* of Joseph
Bengough, Henry, solicitor, *d* 1818
Benjamin, Moses, *d* London 1827
Bennett, William, *d* Shropshire 1855
" William, of Derby, *d* 1860
Benwicke, James, of Cornwall
" Joseph, of Devon
Benson, John, *d* Westminster 1827
Bentall, Elizabeth, Surrey, *d* 1814
Bently, Thomas, *d* Notts 1818
Benton, Sarah, Essex, *d* 1834
Benwell, Peter S., *d* Surrey 1848
Berresford, John, of Wilts 1780
Berington, John, *d* abroad 1852
Bermes, Sarah, *d* Westminster 1845
Berrey, Charles J., *d* Paris 1803
Berrington, John, *d* London 1780
Berryhill, Samuel, *d* London 1824
Bertie, Pereggine Honble, *d* 1790
Best, William, *d* Essex 1823
Betts, Anna M., *frmly* Prince
Betty, Andrew, *d* London 1817
Beynon, Thomas, *d* Herts 1778
" Thomas, *d* 1833
Biddles, James, *d* London 1834
" John } brothers of James
" Thomas } who *d* in London
" William } 1834
Biggs, Gilbert, *d* in Hants
" Thomas, of Kent
Bilham, John, *d* Norfolk 1854
Billers, Joanna, Bristol, *d* 1769
Billingsley, Hannah, *d* 1780
Binches, Henry, *d* London 1834
Bingham, John, of Somerset
" William, *d* London 1811
Birch, Charles D., Calcutta 1837
" John B., *d* India 1829
" John R., *d* Woodford 1855
Bird, Jane, Durham, *d* 1835
" Richard, *d* India 1842
" Sarah, of Worcester
Birkett, Henry, *d* Australia 1854
Birley, Hugh H., *d* Lancashire 1845
Bishop, John, *d* Bucks 1813
" John, of Southwark
" William, of Middlesex 1830
Bitten, Robert, *d* London 1808
Blackhall, George, *d* 1709
Blackmore, John, *d* Marylebone 1827

Blackford, Robt. P., *d* Osborne 1790
Blagrove, Fredk., *d* Petersham 1817
Blake, Thomas, *d* London 1833
" William, of Chelsea, *d* 1838
Blakelock, Sarah, *frmly* Clough
Bland, Thomas, *d* Isleworth 1816
Bleakey, Robert, *d* Pentonville 1850
Bleaze, Thomas, *d* Manchester 1809
Bludworth, Augusta, Hants, *d* 1803
Boag, William, surgeon, *d* abrd 1806
Bockett, Louisa A., *d* Surrey 1858
Bogg, Robert W., *d* Hoxton 1835
Boileau, S. B. General, *d* 1860
Bold, Ebenezer, of Wigan
Bolt, Richard, of Oxford, *d* 1817
Bolton, David, *d* Gloucestershire 1814
" Mason Colonel, *d* 1718
Bomford, Thomas, *d* Brenock 1844
Bond, Ann, London, *d* 1800
" John, of Somerset, *d* 1835
" Phillis, Gorhambury, *d* 1853
Boncock, Joseph, *d* Islington 1825
Bonnes, Elizabeth C., Kent, *d* 1830
Bonnor, James, *d* India 1824
Bonsom, Thomas, *d* Lincoln 1830
Bonus, James, *d* London 1834
Booth, Charles Sir, *d* Kent 1795
" James, *d* Kent 1830
" Mary, London, *d* 1796
" William, of Notts, *d* 1824
Boreham, Michael, *d* Feltham 1814
Borwick, Henry T., *d* Middlesex 1827
Bottomley, Joseph, *d* London 1794
Boughton, Wm., *d* Worcester 1831
Bourn, Aaron, of Wolverhptn, *d* 1794
Bowden, Thomas, of London 1796
Bower, Catherine
Bowers, Mary A. niece of E. Longuisty
Bowis, Peter, *d* Essex 1830
Bowles, John, *d* Berks 1798
Bowring, Benj., *d* Dorchester 1837
Boyes, Thomas, *d* Yorkshire 1838
Brabbin, Betty, wife of Samuel
Bradby, Daniel, *d* India 1805
Braddon, Elbth., Marylebone, *d* 1823
" Mary, Canterbury, *d* 1834
Brade, Eleanor, *frmly* Kidd
Bradford, Alice, *o'wise* Asprey
" Richard, *d* Surrey 1816
" Sarah, *o'wise* Bedwin
Bradley, John, *d* Somerset 1792
" Robert, *d* Lancashire
Bradshaw, Humphrey, of Westmst'r
" Peter, of Wigan, *d* 1857
Bragg, Robert, *d* Westminster 1777
Brailsford, Samuel, *d* Derby 1797

Braine, Honor, Bristol, *d* 1837
Brame, Benjamin, *d* Ipswich 1857
Brand, Rene, *d* Marylebone 1808
Brandon, Samuel, *d* Surrey 1818
" William, *d* London 1806
Bratley, John, of Cambridge 1798
Brazier, Mary M., Rye, *d* 1846
Bree, Elizabeth, Middlesex, *d* 1845
Brent, Frances, London, *d* 1739
Brett, Elizabeth, Adington, *d* 1813
Brien, Honor, Bristol, *d* 1837
Brigham, William, surgeon, *d* 1821
Bright, Mary, Oxford, *d* 1834
" Mary, Yeovil, *d* 1810
Brimble, Albert, *d* Southwark 1733
Brinley, Sarah, Swansea, *d* 1835
Brinton, William, *d* Portsea 1848
Broadly, Elizabeth, *o'wise* Kennett
Broadwood, Matthew, *d* London 1840
Brock, William, of Cheshire
Brockett, William, merchant, *d* 1807
Brodie, Alexander, *d* Surrey 1811
Bromley, Thomas, *d* Brighton 1827
Brooke, George, *d* Marylebone 1823
" T. of ChippingSodbury, *d* 1813
" Frances, " *d* 1832
Brookes, Francis, of Stafford, *d* 1836
" William Colonel, *d* 1834
Brooks, John, *d* Lambeth 1788
" Mary M., Surrey, *d* 1853
Brookland, Emma, of Netherbury
Broughton, Sarah, Gloucester
Brown, Catherine, *o'wise* Lambert
" Ed C., *d* Somerset 1817
" Eliza, *frm'y* Batchelor
" Frances A., *d* 1835
" George, of Strathavon, N B
" George G., *d* Bath 1842
" Henry W. ⎫ sons of Joseph,
" Joseph ⎭ *d* 1844-45
" Joseph, of Portsea, *d* 1840
" James, *d* London 1836
" John, of Blankly, Lincoln
" John, of Hereford, *d* 1806
" John B., *d* Torquay 1833
" Malcolm, *d* Wilts 1847
" Mary, Lincolnshire, *d* 1859
" Mary, Axholme, *d* 1822
" Mary, Holbeach, *d* 1850
" Robert A., Leicestershire 1824
" Robert, of Somerset
" Sarah, Islington, *d* 1830
" Stafford, *d* Wilts 1847
" Thomas, of Beds., *d* 1821
" Wade, *d* Monkton Farleigh 1851
Brown, William, *d* Stafford 1856
" William, *d* America 1811
" William, of Henley, *d* 1822
Browne, Elizabeth, *d* Kent 1817
" James E., *d* India 1813
Browning, James, *d* London 1861
Broxup, Zachariah, *d* Tottenham 1830
Bruton, Thos., *d* Staffordshire 1844
Brumby, Martin, of Notts
Bryant, Joseph, *d* Somerset 1799
" Mary, *d* Caldicot 1842
" Robert, *d* Middlesex, 1832
Brydges, James, of Harrow, *d* 1789
Buchanan, Peter, *d* London 1794
Buck, Margaret, *d* Lancashire 1830
" William, *d* Liverpool 1826
Buckeridge, M. D., Captain, *d* 1799
Buckle, Francis, *d* Peterborough 1823
" William, *d* " 1828
Buckley, Alice, of Yorkshire, *d* 1859
" H., Mrs., of Cheshire 1788
" William, of Chelsea
Budd, William, *d* Hants 1840
Budden, Robert, *d* Dorset 1811
Budge, Elizabeth, Kent, *d* 1775
Buffar, Pyke, of Greenwich 1770
Bunbury, W. H. Colonel, *d* 1833
Burcham, William, *d* Norfolk 1799
Burdekin, Joseph, *d* Yorkshire 1822
Burdon, Mary, Stockton, *d* 1821
Burgess, Daniel, *d* Liverpool 1840
" Richard, *d* Leicester 1754
Burke, Jane J., Bath, *d* 1802
Burnard, John, of Somerset
Burnett, William, of Hants 1843
Barridge, Thomas, of Tenterton
Burrows, Elizabeth, Liverpool, *d* 1835
Burton, Edward, *d* Bristol 1826
" Eliza M., *o'wise* Price
" Frances, Suffolk, *d* 1807
" Rachel, *o'wise* Chance
Burton, Peter, of Edmonton 1780
Bush, Charlotte, of Herts, *d* 1835
Buswell, Wm., *d* Abingdon 1629
Butter, Bernard, *d* Bath 1822
" Betty ⎫ brothers and sister
" Jacob ⎬ of Bernard,
" Joseph ⎭ of Bath
Butler, Ann, London, *d* 1826
" Robert, of Kilkenny, *d* 1788
" Samuel, *d* Middlesex 1837
" William, *d* Brentford 1858
By, Henry, of Sussex, *d* 1852
Byrne, James, *d* London 1815
" Maria, London, *d* 1826
Bythesea, Edmund, *d* Bath 1842

C

Callard, Sush., d Westminster 1857
Callow, Rebecca, North'ton, d 1826
" Rebecca, North'ton d 1823
Came, Barbara, Hoxton, d 1727
Cameron, Donald, d Caxton 1821
Campbell, Allen, Colonel, d 1794
" W. W., of Ireland, d 1858
Campion, Jane, London, d 1834
Cane, Dorothy, Chelsea d 1843
Canning, Richard, d Ipswich 1789
Capper, Ann, Sussex, d 1843
Caradine, Richard, d Kensington 1825
Carden, James, d London 1803
Cardinal Charles
Carlton, Elzbth., o'wise Powney
Carmichael, John, merchant d 1781
Carpenter, Ann, Sussex, d 1857
" James, d Wilts 1819
" George, General, d 1855
Carr, Jeremiah, d London 1775
Carroll, Robert, of Demarara, d 1805
Carruthers, John, d Berks 1857
Carter, Anna M., d Dorset 1844
" Henry, d Oxford 1843
" John, d Durham 1835
" Sybella, Kent, d 1835
Cartledge, Page, Lincoln
Cartlich, John, d Macclesfield 1836
Cartwright, Peter, d Liverpool 1811
" Isabella, dau. of Peter
Cass, John, d Herts 1813
Castle, Robert, d 1800
" Janet, wife of Robert, d 1792
" W. H., d Bermondsey 1858
Causton, Nathaniel, d London 1782
Cawston, Mary, Middlesex 1806
Cawthorn, Thomas, d Leeds 1839
Cawood, Sarah, Yorkshire, d 1848
Chad, George, Sir, Bart., d 1815
Chamberlain, Sarah, w, London
Chambers, George, d Middlesex 1836
" James, d Manchester 1847
" John, d Shepperton 1776
Chandler, Edward, d Lambeth 1740
" James H., d Kent, 1855
Chapman, Anth'y, d Middlesex 1772
" Joseph, d Yorkshire 1817
" Thomas, d 1795
" Thomas, d Yorkshire 1846
Charlton, Matthew, d Elsdon 1862
Charters, Thomas, d abroad 1847
Chatteris, William, d London 1819
Cheine, Margaret, w of Robert
Chidell, Eliza, of Emsworth

Chidley, Thomas, d London 1816
Child, John T., of Andover
Chilton, John, d Westminster 1799
Chitty, Mary, Hackney, 1790
Choat, Joseph, d Tichingfield 1828
Chodwick, Thomas, d Surrey 1854
Claer, James, d Surrey 1814
Clare, Ann, Salop, d 1823
Clark, Bradshaw, Capt. d 1819
" David, d Glo'cestershire 1830
" Daniel, d London 1820
" George, d London 1830
" Richard, d London 1796
" Robert T., of Surrey
" Sarah, Bristol, d 1804
Clarke, Ann, Bucks d 1810
" John, d Leamgt'n Priors 1855
" John, of London 1780
" John, of Cambridge, d 1748
" John, d Warwickshire 1814
" Jos. A., d Cumberland 1849
" William, d Northampton 1814
Clarkson, Isabella, o'wise McKenzie
Claremont, Gabriel
Clay, Margt., d Tynemouth 1845
" Martha, Essex d 1803
" Wm., d Herts 1813
Claydon, John, d Cambridge 1834
Clegg, John, of Lincolnshire
Cleghorn, Robert, d London 1824
Clemence, Chris., d Cornwall 1850
Clement, Henry, of Chichester
" John, of Darlington 1799
Clements, Mary, frmly French
" Mich'l H., of Lincolnshire
Clerk, William L., of Kent
Cleathing, John, d 1841
Cleverly, Richard, d London 1833
Clex, Maria, Manchester, d 1850
Cliffe, Robert, d Lincoln 1792
Clobery, John B.H., d Cornwall 1805
Clough, Sarah, o'wise Gledill
Clubley, George, d Scarborough 1837
Clues, Sarah, Middlesex d 1838
Cobb, William, d Yorkshire 1810
Cochrane, John, d Middlesex 1835
" Margt. D., Mid'lesx, d 1834
" Peter, of Renfrew, d 1831
Cockoll, Wm., d Kensington 1733
Cocker, John R., d London 1834
Cocking, Selina, d Marylebone 1836
Codd, John, d Lincolnshire 1836
Codrington, Thos. S., d Wilts 1839
Coe, William, d Suffolk 1778
Coffin, Isaac Sir, d 1839
Coghlan, Andrew, Colonel, d 1837

Cohen, Gabriel, d Surrey 1839
Cole, Ann, frmly Strong
"   James, d Chelsea 1793
"   John, of Kent, d 1803
Collier, Wm., d Knightsbridge 1835
Collin, Elbth. O, Durham, d 1846
Collingwood, A. L., Bath, d 1856
Collins, Ann, o'wise Ward
"   John, d Dunthorpe 1856
"   Robert, of London
"   Sophia, Surrey, d 1815
"   William, Rev., of Sutton
Collis, Cath., Herts, d 1814
Colt, James, Rev., d Leominster 1832
Coltman, Thos., d Lincoln 1826
Colewell, John, d Cornwall 1817
Comely, Wm., of Somerset, d 1818
Coney, Margt., o'wise Abondio
Connett, Eleanor, Devon, d 1816
Consett, C. C., d Surrey 1852
"   Peter, d Yorkshire 1839
Constable, W.H.M., d Yorkshire 1797
Cook, Hannah, of Woburn 1738
"   Jane, Cheltenham, d 1852
"   John P., d London 1831
"   Thos., d Gloucester 1850
Cooke, Charles, d Hereford 1840
"   Edward, d Haversham
"   John, d Lincoln 1854
"   Hannah   } of
"   Matthew   } Gloucestershire
Cooper, Ann, o'wise Davis, d 1830
"   Ann, Wolverhampton, d 1775
"   Cooper, Edward, d Surrey
"   Frances, Leicester, d 1818
"   John, d Suffolk 1819
Cope, Edward, d Cheltenham 1849
"   James, of Staffordshire
Coppinger, Jane, d 1723
Corbett, Michael, d Gloucester 1830
Corfield, John, d Worcestershire 1825
Corpe, Thomas, of Herts, d 1847
Corrall, Ann, Bath, d 1832
Cotterell, Charles, of Essex, d 1807
Cotton, Mary, Herts, d 1838
Coulton, Margt., Essex, d 1819
Coulston, Elbth., of Westminster
"   Frances, London, 1780
Councel, Mary, d Somerset 1841
Courtney, Jane W., d 1847
Coutts, Alexander, d London 1804
Coventry, Thomas, d London 1798
Coward, Leonard, d Bath 1798
Cowleshaw, John, d Shardlow 1838
Cowling, L. L. S., d France 1830
Cox, Charles, of Kent, d 1822

Cox, Elizabeth, Turnham Green
Coyle, John, d Sydney 1846
Conway, J. C., d Flint 1836
Cracroft, Robt., d Monmouth 1832
Cragie, John, Colonel, d 1840
Craigill, Wm., d Orthwaite 1846
Cramer, Sarah, o'wise Procter
Cramp, John, of Sussex, d 1854
Crane, John, d Birmingham 1857
"   H. S., d Essex 1848
Crapp, Thomas, d Devonport 1829
Crayle, James   } living
"   William   } 1750-90
Creasy, James, d London 1816
Cresey, William, of Terrington
Cresswell, Ann, Mrs., of Sussex
Crew, Louisa, Islington, d 1808
Cribb, Henry, d Marylebone 1843
Crichton, Benjamin T., d Kent 1855
Cripps, John D., d Bristol 1847
Crispe, Edward, of Kent, d 1823
"   William, of Kent, d 1808
Croft, Mary, o'wise Laud
Crofts, Jane, d Middlesex 1849
Crombie, James, d Surrey 1798
"   Alexander } brother and
"   Jane   } sisters of Jas.
"   Margaret   } of Deptford
Crompton, Sarah, Marylebone
Crosbie, Jno. T. master-mariner d 1838
Crosley, Samuel, d London 1845
Crosse, John, of Bradford, d 1816
Crossland, Thomas, d Chelsea 1776
Crookes, Jonathan, d York 1778
Crouch, Charles, d Tottenham 1830
"   James, d Somerset 1835
"   Mary, Andover, d 1832
Crow, John, d Liverpool 1841
Crowhurst, Elbth., Chelsea d 1833
"   William, d Chelsea 1831
Croxton, Thomas, d Portsmouth 1826
Crumbleholme, Geo., d America 1820
Crump, William, of Worcester
Crussell, John, d Chelmsford 1852
Cruwys, Bridget, London, d 1794
"   Dorothy, London, d 1757
Cullen, Murty, of Essex, d 1807
Culling, Isaac, d Kennington 1808
"   James, d Kennington 1823
Cumming, Edw'd, d Lancashire 1844
Cunningham, Jerh. d Yorkshire 1843
Currie, Eliza, frmly Hubbald
Curtis, John, d Bristol 1822
"   Susannah, d 1832
Cushen, Edward } of
"   Mary   } Southampton

Custance, James, of Sutton, Cambshr
Cuthell, John, d London 1828

D

Dalrymple, G. H., Lieut. 91st Regt.
Dalton, Thomas Rev., d Essex 1829
Dance, William, d Middlesex 1811
Danger, Elizabeth, Oxford d 1854
Dare, John W., d India 1838
Darjeant, James, of Essex, d 1810
Darke, Elizabeth, Exeter d 1859
Darker, William, of Notts, d 1824
Darley, Frances, d Bristol 1816
Darrell, Sarah, Cornwall, d 1795
Davenport, C. Rev., of Yorkshire
Davidson, Mungo, of Scotland, d 1774
" Alex. ⎫ sons of Mungo,
" John ⎬ who d Amer'a 1774
" Sarah, of Isle of Ely, d 1846
" Sarah, of Kent, d 1846
Davies, Ann, Islington, d 1832
" Jane, Gloucester
" Jenny, Worthing, d 1820
" John, of Carmarthen
" John, of Telgartte, d 1819
" Meredith, of Telgartte, d 1818
" Robert, d London 1810
" Sarah, Coventry, d 1832
" William, d London 1827
Davis, Abraham, d Gloucester 1804
" Henry, of Oxford
" Jenny, Islington
" John C., d abroad 1807
" Richard, d Shadwell 1811
" Susanunh, Swansea d 1833
" William, of London
Davison, Wm., of N. Shields, d 1809
Dawe, James, d Middlesex 1829
Dawson, Harriett, d Kenningt'n 1858
" Sarah, Stafford d 1834
Day, Charles, of Edgeware, d 1836
" Frank, of Madras, d 1800
" James, d Rochester 1844
" John, d Kent 1832
" Mary H., d Isle of Wight
" Samuel, d Southwark 1832
Dean, Thomas, of London, d abd 1806
" Thomas, d Middlesex 1819
" William, d Camberwell 1784
Death, John R., of Kent, d 1835
Debney, Thomas, d London 1841
De Blanchy, Ann, Bath d 1853
Decafour, Mary, Canterbury d 1835
Dela Motte, Peter, d Weymouth 1814
Delves, Hugh, of Wavretree d 1844

Denn, William, of Bloomsbury
Dennis, Sarah, Lambeth d 1835
Dennson, Samuel, d London 1776
Dent, Ann, of Yorkshire
Dent, Joseph, d London 1773
Denton, Elizabeth, d Durham 1773
Devaynes, John, d London
Devereux, John, d France 1838
Deverill, John, d Bucks 1837
Dewar, Caroline
" Caroline L.
Dewell, Thomas, d Gosport 1825
Dick, Alex., of Southwark d 1803
" Ann, o'wise Norris, d 1822
" James, d London 1806
" Sarah, o,wise Vevars, d 1806
" William, d Windsor 1800
Dickin, Stephen, d Shrewsbury 1843
Dickon, Thomas, d Yorkshire 1827
Dike, Elizabeth, Gloucester d 1856
Dimsdale, Ann, Hereford, d 1832
Dixon, James, of Lancaster
Dobson, Margaret, Durham d 1808
" Sophia, of London 1787
Dod, Ann, Middlesex d 1843
" Thomas, of Edgbaston
Dodd, Wm., d Northumberland 1809
Dodwell, W , d Lincolnshire 1824
Donville, Christopher, of Bath d 1859
Dorsdell, Rich'd, d Scarborough 1800
Dott, James, of Scotland d 1843
Doubleday, Robert, d London 1809
Douglas, H. N. Colonel, d 1849
" John, d 1814
" William, of Preston d 1859
Dowding, Peter, of Shire Hampton
Dowling, John, d London 1807
Downer, Susan, d London 1816
Drakely, John, d Worcester 1810
Draper, Robert, of London
Druce, Robert A., d Middlesex 1829
Dudding, John, of Yorkshire
Dudley, Mary A., Wednesbury
Duffield, Job, d Islington 1850
Dufty, John, Major d 1810
Dugdale, Henry G., d Worcester 1840
Duncalf, Mary, Adlington d 1842
Duncan, Helen, o'wise Stevenson
Dunlop, Conyers, d London 1799
Dunn, Ann, Islington d 1829
" John, d Berks 1842
" Richard M., of Derby, d 1829
" William, of London, d 1801
Durbin, Alice, Long Ashton d 1834
" Henry, d Bristol 1798
Duval, William, Captain, d 1807

CHANCERY ADVERTISEMENTS. 85

Dyke, Joseph, *d* Wolverhamp'n 1815
Dykes, Phillip, of Suffolk
" Susan, of Suffolk *d* 1821

E

Eades, John, *d* Staffordshire 1835
Earlesman, Richard, *d* Wilts 1831
Eastaff, William, *d* Bedford 1859
Eastland, Elzbth. S., Surrey *d* 1832
Eaton, George, *d* Pimlico 1828
" Harriett, Hampstead *d* 1857
" Robert, *d* Staffordshire 1855
" Sush. M., *d* Peckham 1853
" William, *d* Middlesex 1828
Edden, Thomas, *d* Worcester 1811
Eden, Robert J., *d* Windleston 1844
Edes, John, of Chipping Morton
" William, *d* Edmonton 1777
Edgar, Mary A., Ipswich, *d* 1835
Edkins, George, *d* London 1821
Edmonds, Charles, *d* London 1847
Edmonson, William, of Leeds *d* 1816
Edward, Margaret, Ludlow, *d* 1816
Edwards, Ann, Gloucester, *d* 1834
" Cath., Marylebone, *d* 1816
" Charles, *d* Middlesex
" Edward, Colonel, *d* 1836
" Elizabeth, *frmly* Yew
" Grace, *frmly* Ogle
" Iron, of Herts, *d* 1814
" John, of Beds, *d* 1840
" John, of Chester, *d* 1854
" Price C., of Somers't, *d* 1855
Egerton, Thomas, *d* London 1830
Eglington, Richard, *d* Norwich 1827
Eldridge, Thomas, of Essex, *d* 1851
Elgin, Ann, Yorkshire, *d* 1822
Elkin, Catharine, *o'wise* Alexander
" Priscilla, *o'wise* Hume
" Rose, " Kopman
" Sarah, " Lewin
Elkins, Elzbth., " Yew, *d* 1819
Ellerker, John, of Lancaster
Elliott, Mary S., Brighton
" Sush., *d* Norfolk 1841
" William, of Essex, *d* 1801
Ellis, Charles, of Dalston, *d* 1845
" Ellis, of Denbigh, *d* 1818
" John, *d* Middlesex, 1849
" Mary, Cork, *d* 1850
" Richard, of Cheshire, *d* 1851
" Thomas, of Sussex, *d* 1829
Ellison, Ralph, *d* Yorkshire 1805
Elly, Richard, *d* Gloucester 1755
Elms, Richard, *d* Wisborough 1804

Elmsley, Peter, *d* Oxford 1825
Elmslie, James, *d* Surrey 1833
Elrington, Thomas, of Aston
Elson, Joseph, *d* Ramsgate 1827
Elston, Joseph C., of Laleham, *d* 1833
Elton, William, Colonel *d* 1847
Ennis, Edward M., Captain, *d* 1843
Ernest, Peter, *d* Middlesex 1845
Erule, Constantia, of Wilts
Essery, Mary, Cornwall, *d* 1830
Evans, Alice, Hoxton, *d* 1823
" Edward, *d* Hoxton
" Elzbth., Bristol, *d* 1851
" Mary A., *d* London 1855
" Samuel, *d* Marylebone 1835
" Sarah, Pembroke, *d* 1831
" Sarah, Bristol, *d* 1817
Evanson, Eleanor, Bath, *d* 1800
Evelyn, Mary, *frmly* Turton, *d* 1817
Everett, Ann, *frmly* Tolson, *d* 1834
Evers, Mary, *frmly* Lawkins
Everson, Cath., Suffolk, *d* 1825
Exton, George, *d* London 1749
" Mary, Herts, *d* 1799
" Mary N., Herts, *d* 1799
Eyre, James, *d* Sheffield 1818

F

Fackerell, Edward, *d* London 1780
Fairbrain, James, *d* Cumberland 1835
Fairbank, Thomas, of Yorkshire
Falkner, Richard, of Northampton
Falls, Sophia, *frmly* Orme
Fardell, David, *d* Wisbeach 1838
Farm, William, *d* London 1812
Farmor, George, of Holbeach
Farnham, Sush. S., of Grantham
" Wm., *d* Launceston, 1802
Farr, John, of Ormskirk, *d* 1764
" Susan, *o'wise* Dykes
Farraine, Joyce, Norwich, *d* 1824
Farquhar, John, *d* Wilts, 1826
Farthing, Robert, *d* Norfolk 1792
Faverson, John, of Kent, *d* 1844
Fawcett, Ann, Yorkshire, *d* 1856
" Charlotte, *w* of Sir Wm.
Fawnt, George, of Leicestershire
Fearns, Louisa, Westmoreland, *d* 1849
Featherby, Sush., Lincoln, *d* 1846
Fell, Agnes, of Lancashire, *d* 1824
Felton, Wm., *d* Berks 1821
Fenner, Zachariah, of Surrey
Fenton, John, *d* America 1799
Fenwick, Cath., Reyton, *d* 1838
Ferguson, Elzbth., *frmly* Amis

Ferguson, George, *d* Cumberland 1821
" Wm. Lieut., *d* 1800
Field, Joshua, *d* Yorkshire 1809
Fielder, John, *d* Lymington 1793
Fildes, Jonathan, *d* Rochdale 1840
Finch, Robt., *d* Rome, 1830
" Thomas, *d* Sussex 1820
Fisher, Ellen, *frmly* Balshaw
" John, of Whitehaven
" Sarah, *frmly* Dean
Fiske, Wm., of Norfolk, *d* 1826
Fitzgerald, Edward, *d* Africa 1833
" Keane, of Herts, *d* 1831
Fitzmaurice, Hon., London 1785
Fleet, Elzbth., Deal, *d* 1820
Fleming, Wm., *d* London 1837
Fleming, Wm., of Lancashire
Fletcher, Geo., *d* Notts 1845
" James, *d* Suffolk 1841
" James, *d* Lancashire 1836
" Martha, London, *d* 1804
" Mary A., Middlesex, *d* 1859
" Paul, *d* Yorkshire 1829
" Thomas, *d* London 1797
Flesher, Thos., *d* Blakesley 1797
Flitcroft, Henry, of Hamstead 1790
Fly, Henry, of Willesden, *d* 1833
Forbes, Cath., Poplar, *d* 1820
" George J., *d* 1836
" Nathaniel, General, *d* 1851
Ford, William, *d* Dagenham 1825
Fordyce, James, *d* Bath, 1796
Forster, Wm., of Norfolk, *d* 1820
Forty, Daniel, E., *d* London, 1841
Forwald, Wm., *d* Middlesex 1848
Foster, Daniel G., *d* London 1835
" Elzbth., Sherborne 1827
" Francis, *d* abroad 1843
Fothergill, Anthony, Dr. *d* 1813
Fountaine, Mary, Chigwell, *d* 1804
Fowden, William, Captain
Fowler, Clara S., *d* Southampton 1856
" John, of Surrey, *d* 1786
Fox, Charles, Bermondsey 1823
" John, *d* Yorkshire, 1811
" John, *d* Westminster 1821
" John, of Kent, *d* 1828
" Sarah, Kent, *d* 1849
Francis, Maria P., Derby, *d* 1858
Franklin, John, *d* Sussex 1767
Fraser, James, *d* Westminster 1818
" James, of Ipswich
Frazer, Simon, of Scotland, *d* 1819
Freeman, James, of Durham
" John, *d* Enfield 1817
" Joseph, *d* Leicester 1824

Freeman, Robert, *d* Norfolk 1865
" Robert H., *d* Norwich 1847
French, Mary, of Dorset, *d* 1839
Friend, Daniel, master-mariner
" John, of Kent, *d* 1834
Frith, Mary, Kensington, *d* 1821
Frost, John, of Suffolk, *d* 1845
" Wm., of Essex, *d* 1814
Fry, John, of Marylebone, *d* 1812
" Thomas, of Kent, *d* 1810
Fullwood, Charles, of Luton, *d* 1832
" John, *d* Surrey
" Thomas, *d* Herts
Funnell, Thomas, *d* Kent 1812
Fyson, Samuel, of Brighton, *d* 1849
Flinn, John, Lieut., *d* 1810

G

Galbraith, Peter, *d* India 1815
Gale, Robert, *d* London 1816
Galloway, John, *d* Berks 1818
Gannon, P., *d* India
Gardiner, Thos., *d* Middlesex 1832
Gardner, Robert, *d* Kent 1856
Gardon, Wm., *d* Lancashire 1847
Garland, Theodora, Norwich, *d* 1843
Garner, Nicholas, *d* Nassau 1802
Garnett, John, Right Rev., 1700
Garrett, James, *d* Norfolk 1807
" John, *d* Devon
Garrod, John, of Hants, *d* 1774
Gaskin, Samuel, mariner, *d* 1821
Gates, Elbth., Brighton
Gayfere Thos., *d* Derbyshire 1815
Gearle, James, *d* Hants 1810
Gedney, John, *d* Yorkshire 1815
Gent, John, *d* Finsbury 1847
George, John F., *d* London 1836
" Hannah, Somerset
Germaine, Rachael, Manchester
Gibbon, Edward, of Marylebone
" Richard, of Marylebone
Gibson, John, *d* Manchester 1841
" Letitia, Croydon *d* 1831
Gilbert, John, of Whitechapel
Gilchrist, John B., *d* Edinburgh 1841
Gilder, Robert, *d* Berks 1842
Giles, Robert, *d* 1824
" William } butcher,
" Mary } *d* 1821
Gill, William, *d* Yorkshire 1814
Gilpin, Mary
Gilson, Lawrence, *d* London 1811
Gingell, Wm., H., *d* Finsbury 1837
Gittings, Sarah, Norwich

Glover, Elbth., Hampton 1813
" Joshua, d Hampton 1783
Glyn, John, d Bath 1836
Glynn, Wm., d Swansea 1839
Godolphus, Wm., d Westminster 1781
Godwyn, Daniel, of Westminster
Going, Susannah, of Essex
Goldborough, Robert ⎫ of America
" Sarah ⎭ 1770-1800
Goldsmith, John d Gt. Marlow 1803
Gonge, William, of Hammersmith
Goodall, John, d Derbyshire 1848
Goode, Eliza, of Southwark
" Edward, d Cambridge 1815
" John, d Hereford 1820
Goodear, Mary, o'wise Batty
" John, d Lancashire 1832
Goodall, Wm., d London 1833
Goodlad, Elzbth., Marylebone
Goodwin, Henry, of Surrey 1810
Goodyear, Daniel, d Surrey 1770
Goodyer, Sarah, Surrey d 1809
" John, of Essex, d 1824
Gordon, Henry, d Somerset 1839
Goring, George F., d Surrey 1827
Gorsuch, Thos. T., d Westminster 1820
Gorton, John, d Lambeth 1837
Gosden, John, d Sussex 1829
Gosling, Matthew, of Mold, d 1841
" Thos. W., d Surrey 1843
Gostling, John, d Middlesex 1841
Gould, Mary W. d Wolverhampt'n 1841
" Richard, d Sussex 1848
Graham, Sush., frmly Davis
Gram, Andrew, of Norway, d 1803
Grant, Angus, Major, d 1810
" Alex., of Banffshire
" Elbth., Setton d 1778
" Wm., d 1794
Grantham, James, d Manchester
Graves, Frances C., d Bristol 1832
" George, d London 1839
" George, Captain
Gray, Francis D., d 1846
" Richard H., d Surrey 1844
" Simon, d London 1842
" Wm., d Russsia 1819
Green, Edward, d Berks 1824
" Joseph, d Alcester 1784
" Joshua, d Rawden 1799
" Robert, d Melburn 1791
" Richard, d Dorset 1819
" Thomas, d Paddington 1843
Greenall, Wm., d Lancashire 1841
Greene, Elbth., Norwich, d 1803
Greet, Thos. Y., d Kent 1829

Gregory, Gregory, of Lincolnshire
" John, d Watford 1840
" John, of Shoreditch 1808
" Mary, d at Hornsey
Gregson, Ann, d London 1815
Grice, James, d Warrington 1837
Grier, Thos., d Deptford 1797
Griffin, John, d Wokingham 1790
Griffin, Mrs. of Woburn 1790
Griffith, John, d Sussex
" Joseph, d Cudworth 1814
Griffiths, Edward, d Bristol 1826
" Elizh., sister to M. Crumley
" Mary, Herts, d 1815
" Phillip, of Merthyr Tydvil
" Thos., d Woolwich 1823
" Vaughan, d London 1832
Grigg, Mary, Bloomsbury
Grimwood, John N., d Essex 1829
Grisbrook, Wm., d Lambeth 1808
Groome, William, of Arundel, d 1838
Grundy, Henry W., d Kent 1859
" John, d Lancashire 1829
Gudgeon, Thos., d Middlesex 1819
Guest, William, of Salop
Gurney, Mary, Dover, d 1843
Gurr, Elizabeth, o'wise West
Guthrie, Edward, d Stafford 1815
" Simon D., d Middlesex 1848
Gwalter, Hugh, d London 1806
Gwennass, Thomas, d Middlesex
Gwinnett, Emilia, of Glamorgan
" Button, d Wolverhampton
" Ann, d Wolverham'n 1781
Gwilt, William, d India 1804
Gwynn, John, of Westminster

H

Haddock, Martha, Chelsea
Hadley, Joseph, d Stafford 1842
Haigh, Charles, d Doncaster 1831
" Hannah, Calcutta
Halden, Elizabeth, Herts, 1822
Hale, Charles, of Devon, d 1795
" William, of Herts, d 1816
Halke, Elizabeth, Plymouth, d 1820
Halkes, Ed. T. D., d Chatham 1823
Hall, Charles A., Devon 1795
" James, d Monmouth 184–
" Thomas, d Pimlico 1838
" Thomas, d London 1786
" Sarah, Loudon, d 1813
" Charles ⎫ brothers of Thomas
" Peter ⎬ of London, who
" William ⎭ d 1786

Hall, William, *d* London 1852
Hallett, Ann, London, *d* 1817
Hallgate, Sarah, of Market Drayton
" James, of ditto, *d* 1820
Hallward, John, *d* Alcester 1765
Hames, Sarah, Surrey, *d* 1837
Hamborough, Maria, *d* 1816
Hamilton, Mary, Chichester
" Rob't, of Manchester 1800
" Thomas, of Brighton
Hammond, George, *d* Yorkshire 1767
" Martin, *d* India 1795
" Susan, of Sussex
" Thomas, *d* Cheshire 1852
Hampton, Chas. D., *d* Alborne Brook
" Joseph, *d* Lancashire 1827
Hanbury, William, *d* 1790
Hancock, John, *d* Stepney 1797
" Thomas, *d* Chelsea 1811
Handley, Michael, *d* Lincoln 1835
Hankin, Elizab'h, *d* Westminster 1788
Hanson, Edward, *d* Hackney 1803
Hany, Charles, *d* Devon 1833
Hapgood, Jane, *frmly* Luff
Haram, Ann, Surrey, *d* 1855
Harby, Sarah, Cambridge, *d* 1799
Harborne, Richard, *d* Aston 1840
Harcourt, W. B., *d* Berks 1847
Harden, John, *d* London 1791
Harding, Francis, *d* London 1777
" John, *d* Gloucester 1851
" John, *d* Culworth, 1826
" John, of Hindon, Wilts
" Wm., *d* Westmoreland 1845
" Sarah, *o'wise* Hallgate
Hardman, Elizab'h, *d* Wakefield 1764
Hardwick, Wm., *d* Manchester 1799
Hare, Charles J., *d* Herts, 1842
Hargrave, Timothy, *d* Brentford 1793
Hargraves, Alice, *d* Lancashire 1843
Harker, Henry, purser R N, *d* 1805
Harle, Ralph, *d* Newcastle 1746
Harley, Sarah, Cambridge, *d* 1799
Harman, Henry, *d* Worcester 1817
Harper, John, *d* Burton Latimer 1800
" Samuel, *d* Worcester 1832
Harris, Charles, *d* Lambeth 1854
" Dorothy, Devon, *d* 1833
" George, *d* London 1796
" John, *d* Hereford 1829
" Robert, *d* London 1838
" Thomas, of Devon, *d* 1836
" William, *d* Marylebone 1831
" William, *d* Westminster 1807
Harrison, Anna L., Stafford, *d* 1837
" Elizabeth, *d* Yorkshire 1818

Harrison, John, *d* Leeds 1856
" Grace, sister of John
" John, of Cumberland
" John R., *d* Middlesex 1844
" Isaac ⎫ brothers of
" John ⎬ Thomas, of Cam-
" Joseph ⎭ bridge
" Thomas, *d* Cambridge 1767
" Thos., *d* Paddington 1843
" Thomas, of Bucks
" William G., *d* Jamaica 1825
Harriss, Joseph, *d* Surrey 1835
Harriman, Joseph, of Perth, *d* 1847
Hart, Anthony, Sir, *d* 1831
" Louisa, *d* Clifton 1849
" Moses, *d* London 1756
" Napthali, *d* Islington 1828
" Robert C., *d* Shrewsbury 1818
" Sush. S., Shrewsbury
Hartley, John, *d* Kent 1833
" Hen. A., *d* Southamp'n 1850
" Wm. J., *d* Cheltenham 1846
Hartshorn, Jonathan, of Bilston
Hartwell, John, *d* Litchfield 1799
Harvey, Peter, *d* Cornwall 1817
Harwood, George, *d* Norfolk 1845
Hasted, John, *d* India 1823
" Francis, *d* India 1844
Haswell, Robert, *d* London 1841
Hatfield, Elizab'h, *frmly* Horn, *d* 1815
Hatrell, Sarah, *frmly* Cole
Hauptman, Fred'k, *d* London 1856
Haven, W. G., *d* abroad 1809
Haweirs, Jennet P., *frmly* Orton
Hawke, Hickory, *d* London 1832
Hawkins, Nicholas, of Isleworth
" Richard, servant, *d* 1845
Hay, Eliza J. M., *d* Walworth 1843
" Herbert, of Glyndborne
Hayes, Ann T., Kensington, *d* 1804
Hayman, James, *d* London 1833
Haynes, Eliza'h, Twickenham, *d* 1848
" David, of Essex, *d* 1843
" John, Major, *d* 1822
" Sarah, Southwark, *d* 1811
Hayton, John, *d* Yorkshire 1809
Hayward, Mary, Somerset, *d* 1851
" Thos., Lieut. R N, *d* 1795
Hazle, William, *d* Bristol 1770
" Judith, Bristol, *d* 1796
Head, Mary, Southwark
Heathcote, William, *d* Hants 1844
Heaton, James, *d* Lancashire 1848
Hebb, William, *d* Lincolnshire 1838
Heeks, Anker, of Middlesex
Heginbotham, Joseph, of Staleybr'ge

Heginbotham, Mary, Stafford *d* 1828
Hele, Charles S. S., of Middlesex
" Robert S., of Waltham, Essex
Henderson, Gabriel, mariner
Heney, Mary, Bristol
Henney, John, *d* Stafford 1825
Henniker, Jacob, Major, *d* 1843
Henshaw, Robert, *d* Exeter 1781
·Heny, Hugh, *d* London 1768
Hepburn, David, Colonel, *d* 1851
Heron Jane } aunts of Sarah Mor-
Herriott, Mary } gan, of London
Hervies, Robert, Colonel, *d* 1832
Heslop, Mary, Norfolk, *d* 1844
Hester, John, Egham, *d* 1839
Hevingham, Ann, *d* 1842
Hewett, Betty, *d* Pemberton 1832
" Edward, *d* London 1794
Hewlett, Jane, *d* London 1829
" John, *d* Norfolk 1844
Hibbard, John, of Wilts, *d* 1817
" Richard, uncle of John
Hichens, James, *d* Cornwall 1821
Hickinbotham, Jos., *d* London 1842
Hickman, Ann, Newnham, *d* 1799
Hicks, John, *d* Walthamstow 1856
" Mary A., *d* Hants 1830
Higgins, Bernard, Lieut. *d* 1801
" Ed. B., Major, *d* 1828
" John, of Bucks, *d* 1813
" Bartholomew, do. *d* 1817
Higginson, Nancy, *frmly* Melling
Higson, Frances, *d* Lancashire 1812
Hilder, Cath., Essex, *d* 1843
Hill, Charles D., of Bristol
" Charles, Colonel, *d* 1819
" John, Derby, *d* 1857
" Noah, son of Rev. N. Hill
" Rowland, Rev., *d* 1833
" Samuel, *d* Surrey 1806
" Sarah, Kensington, *d* 1795
" Thomas, *d* Surbiton 1839
" Thomas, *d* London 1790
" William, *d* Bath 1807
Hills, John, drum-major, *d* 1828
Hinde, John J., *d* Essex
" Mary A., Clapton, *d* 1856
Hindly, Letitia
Hine, John B., *d* Devon 1859
Hines, Richard, *d* Essex 1814
" Steward, *d* Essex 1814
Hinkley, James S., *d* London 1832
Hinves, William, *d* Marylebone 1832
Hippins, Elizab'th., Lambeth, *d* 1850
Hippuff, Charles, *d* London 1815
Hitchcock, R. J., *d* London 1846

Hitchcock, Wm., *d* Wilts 1820
Hitchman, Thos., *d* Soho 1827
Hobbs, Joseph, *d* Marylebone 1838
Hoddinot, Wm. *d* Edgbaston 1849
Hodge, Wm. R., *d* Liverpool 1811
Hodges, Sarah F., Middlesex, *d* 1851
Hodson, John, *d* Liverpool 1815
" Mary, *frmly* Southam
Hogg, Thomas, *d* Devon 1835
Holbeche, Thos., *d* Worcester 1811
Holder, John, *d* Hereford 1850
Holditch, Hannett, of King's Lynn
Holdsworth, Christopher, of Leeds
Holland, John, *d* Northampton 1793
Holliday, Thos. master-mariner, *d* 1789
Hollis, George, *d* Porchester 1797
Holloway, Ann, *frmly* Wrentmore
" John B., *d* Bloxham 1840
Hollows, Matthias, *d* Rochdale 1853
Holmes, Robert, *d* London 1823
" Robert, *d* Islington 1815
" Samuel, *d* Dublin 1826
" Samuel, *d* India 1855
Hood, Dorothy, Stepney
Hook, Elizabeth, *d* 1777
" Matthew, *d* Gloucester 1759
" Thomas B., of Bedford
Hooks, Robert, *d* London 1784
Hooper, John, *d* Brixton 1850
" Jonathan, *d* Somerset 1756
Hope, Susannah, Bath, *d* 1824
Hopton, Frances, Gloucester, *d* 1738
Horborne, Thos., *d* Warwick 1844
Horne, Charles, of Kent, *d* 1837
" William, *d* Poplar 1853
Horrell, Samuel, of Gloucester
Horrocks, William, *d* Nottingale 1854
Horspool, James, of Notts
Horton, Joshua T., of Yorkshire
Hoskins, Jeremiah } of Bromley
" Thomas } Kent.
" Richard, nephew of John
Hough, Henry, *d* Jamaica 1800
Houghton, Elizabeth, London
" Thomas, *d* Liverpool 1844
Houlston, Mary, Lambeth, *d* 1829
Houston, Elizabeth, Dublin, *d* 1833
Houstoun, Robert R., *d* Beds 1829
Howard, Charlotte R., Pinner, *d* 1854
" Dorothy C. wife of Rev. R. H.
" Daniel, *d* Essex 1849
" George F., *d* Surrey 1858
" Henry, *d* London 1818
" John, *d* Surrey 1816
" William, *d* Fulham 1802

Howcroft, James, of Lancashire
Howell, David, *d* Carmarthen 1788
" Samuel, of Bristol 1750
Hoy, John, *d* Marylebone 1804
Hucey, Rebecca, *frmly* Southam
Hucks, Robert, of Herts *d* 1814
Hubbard, William, *d* Russia
Hudson, Israel J., *d* Bristol 1812
" Richard, *d* Essex 1840
" William, *d* Middlesex 1820
Hughes, Elbth., Anglesea, *d* 1839
" John, of Pimlico, *d* 1820
Hulkes, E. S. D., *d* Kent 1823
Humby, Isabella, London, *d* 1843
Hummerston, James, *d* London 1810
Humpage, Elbth., *d* Bristol 1832
Hunt, Frances C., *o'wise* Graves
" Henry, of Pimlico, *d* 1847
" Samuel, *d* abroad 1824
Hunter, Benjamin, of Deptford
" John, Captain, *d* 1791
" Lucy, Manchester, *d* 1855
Hurst, Elbth, *o'wise* Theodore, *d* 1856
" Elizabeth, Camberwell, *d* 1826
" John, *d* London 1809
Hutchings, John, *d* London 1765
Hutchinson, Anthony, *d* Lincoln 1796
" Elbth. *d* Kensington 1858
" Isaac, *d* Brixton 1830
" Mary A. wife of Samuel
" Richard, brthr. to James
Hutton, Ellen, Lincoln, *d* 1806
Huxham, Robert, *d* Plymouth 1840
Hyatt, Sarah, Brompton, *d* 1821
Hyde, George, *d* abroad 1827
" Humphrey, of Kent, *d* 1718
" Robert, of Ardwick, *d* 1783
" Thomas, of Cheshire 1790
" William, *d* abroad 1787
Hymans, Hyman, *d* London 1842

I

Inge, Edward, of Coventry
" Edward, of Willenhall 1834
" John R., of Scarborough
Innes, William, *d* London 1794
Irel, George, *d* London 1846
Irving, William, *d* London 1835
Irwin, Eyles, of Clifton
Ives, Elizabeth, *frmly* Stubbs
" James, *d* Newington 1815

J

Jacob, John, *d* Middlesex 1807
Jackson, Decimus, of Southwark
" Ed. master-mariner, *d* 1829
" Ellen, Bath, *d* 1837
" Henry, *d* London 1822
" Isaac, *d* Lancashire 1858
" Jeremiah, *d* 1836
" John, of Hampton, *d* 1825
" Robert, *d* Wokington 1826
" Sarah, Westminster, *d* 1852
" Wm., *d* Staffordshire 1823
Jaffray, Thomas, *d* Jamaica
James, Elbth. S., *d* Hillingdon 1857
" Herbert B., *d* Jamaica 1840
" John H., *d* Jamaica 1835
" Mary, *d* America 1793
Jarratt, Grace, Sussex
Jarrett, John, of Kent, *d* 1861
Jeffreys, John, *d* Chiswick 1836
Jellis, Martha, Essex, *d* 1855
" William, brother to Martha
Jenkins, Lewis, *d* Glamorgan 1827
" S. Mrs., *d* Glamorgan 1821
" Thomas, *d* Canterbury 1803
Jenks, George, *d* Islington 1815
Jenkyns, Richard E.
Jennings, William, *d* Dorset 1854
Jermyn, Stephen, *d* Fulham 1796
Jernegan, George, *d* London 1815
Jessop, Richard, *d* Halifax 1835
Jobson, Abraham, *d* Cambridge 1830
Johnson, Charles, *d* Essex 1823
" Edward, of Middlesex
" William, *d* Surrey 1812
" William, *d* Yorkshire 1842
Jones, Ann, *d* Marylebone
" C. W. J., *d* Devon 1846
' Cornelius, *d* Salop 1817
" George, *d* Kent 1803
" Humphrey S., *d* 1827
" James, *d* London 1822
" John, *d* Marylebone 1844
" Mary, Wandsworth 1852
" Randle, *d* London 1817
" Richard, *d* Cardigan 1785
" Robert, *d* London 1808
" Rowland, *d* Carnarvon 1856
" Sarah, Lancashire, *d* 1839
" Thomas, of Denbigh, *d* 1820
" Thos., of Shrewsbury, *d* 1839
" William, of Denbigh, *d* 1849
" William, of Denbigh, *d* 1830
" William, of Denbigh
" William, *d* Carmarthen 1804

CHANCERY ADVERTISEMENTS. 91

Jones, William, of Brecon, d 1849
" William, of Hants, d 1853
" William, d London 1831
Jordaine, John, d London 1772
Jordis, Ann, Lambeth
Joy, Eleanor, Hants, d 1729
Joyce, Hester, d Paddington 1777
Juggins, Thomas, d Kent 1801

Knight, Elzbth., of Lambeth, d 1851
" Squire, d Southwark 1808
Knowler, George, d Canterbury 1802
Knowles, Thos., d Liverpool 1812
Knox, Kath., frmly Melling
Kopman, Rose, frmly Elkin
Kranen, Mary, Surrey, d 1791
Kynaston, Ann, d Chelsea 1795

K

Kane, Thomas, d Brentford 1846
Kannen, Matthew, surgeon, d 1823
Kay, Quinton, d London 1807
" William, of Yorkshire
Kaye, John, d Essex 1826
Keddell, Mary, Lancashire, d 1859
Keedwell, James, d Somerset 1840
Keegan, James, d London 1820
Keek, Anthony, d London 1736
Kempson, Lenda, Handsworth, d 1851
Kendall, William, d London 1816
" William, d Exeter 1832
Kenderdine, John, d Stafford 1828
Kennedy, Dorothy, d Devon 1848
Kennett, Elizabeth, o'wise Bradley
" Joseph, d Folkstone 1789
" James, son of Joseph, d 1833
" Wm., brother to Joseph
Kennimore, Mary, London, d 1837
Kentish, John, d Marylebone 1822
Kenworthy, Chas., d Somerset 1824
Kelly, William, of North Shields
Kerkshaw, Sarah, Rochdale, d 1844
Kernan, Patrick, d Dublin 1858
Kershaw, John, d Lancashire 1778
Kevern, William, d Devon 1798
Kewney, Joseph, of Notts, d 1840
Kidd, Cuthbert
" John, of Liverpool, d 1835
Kiddell, Ann, d Sidmouth 1847
Kidney, Christian, Bayswater, d 1826
Kilpatrick, John, d London 1840
Kindall, William, d London 1816
Kinlock, William, d India 1812
King, Frances E., frmly Bean
" Henry, d London 1819
" Mary, Warblington, d 1793
Kipping, Elizabeth, of Kent
Kirkham, Elizabeth, of Hertford
Kittermaster, John, of Surrey
Kleinert, S. G., d Highgate 1809
" Elzbth., " 1811
Knibb, Geo. d Newport Pagnell 1826
Knill, Jeremiah, d Chelsea 1837
Knight, David, d Norfolk 1844

L

Lacam, Benjamin, d London 1813
Lacey, Ann, Mrs., d London 1832
Lacon, John, d London 1797
Laidly, James, d London 1811
Lamb, Esther, Gloucester, d 1787
Lambe, Thomas, d London 1808
" Joseph, son of Thos., d 1809
" Maria D., dau. of Thos., d 1807
" Harriett " d 1810
Lambert, C., d Hemingford Gray 1844
" Henry, d Colewell 1814
" Mary, Clifton, d 1820
" Richard, d Surrey 1839
Lander, James, d Falmouth 1842
Landon, John, d Hackney, 1795
Lang, Thomas P., Major, d 1838
Langdon, Sush. H., wife of Thomas
Langley, William, d Glasgow 1830
Langton, Diana, Lincoln
Langtry, Elizabeth, frmly Reeves
Lanaway, John, d Glo'stershire 1831
Largent, Sush., Rochester, d 1835
La Rose, Louisa, London, d 1803
Laud, Mary, o'wise Croft, d 1853
Law, Alxr., of N B, d Devon 1840
" Thomas, d Southwark 1787
Lawrence, John, d America 1814
" John, of Worcester
" Joseph, of Warwickshire
Lea, Thomas, d Brompton 1854
Leach, John, d Wallington 1791
Leah, Henry, d Yorkshire 1846
Leake, Thomas, d London 1762
" William, of Wimbledon
Leat, Samuel, of Devon d 1817
Leathart, Thomas, d Islington 1832
Le Brethon, I.J.P., d Tottenham 1831
Lee, Ann, London 1847
" Maria T., Durham, 1851
Leggart, Samuel, d Norwich 1794
Le Hunt, Richard, d Pembroke 1831
Lernoult, Francis, Rev.
Le Saeur, Ann, frmly Ivie
Lestourgeon, George, d abroad 1855
Levey, Solomon, of London, d 1833

Lewin, Sarah, *frmly* Elkin
Lewington, George, *d* Hants, 1837
Lewis, Benjamin, *d* Salisbury 1826
" Charles, *d* Jamaica 1826
" David, *d* London 1810
" Elbth., *frmly* Lloyd
" Griffith, *d* Montgomery 1787
" John, *d* abroad 1819
" Thomas, *d* Montgomery 1818
" Richard, of Sussex, 1801
" William, of Carmarthen
Lighton, John H., *d* Kilkenny 1848
Lill, John, *d* London
Ling, Finia, Great Yarmouth, *d* 1858
Lissett, Jane, Oxford, *d* 1800
Lister, Elbth., *firmly* Kidd
Littler, Ralph, of London, *d* 1802
Lithgow, Hector, *d* India 1785
" Hugh } sons of Hector
" John
Lloyd, Cath., of Denbigh, *d* 1845
" John, *d* Norfolk 1848
" Edward ⎫
" Elbth. ⎬ brothers & sisters
" Francis ⎪ of the
" Jane ⎭ Rev. J. Lloyd
" Jane, London, *d* 1833
" Richard H., *d* Merioneth 1823
Llwyd, Alicia G. J., Glamorgan
Lock, William, of Berks, *d* 1852
Lockey, George, of London, *d* abd
Loft, George, of Suffolk, *d* 1843
Lomax, Jane, *d* Richmond 1827
Long, Cath., *d* Wilts 1814
" Mary, London, *d* 1849
" R. J., Lieut., *d* abroad 1840
Longhurst, James, *d* Stafford 1852
Lord, John, *d* Rochdale 1828
Losh, Elbth., Carlisle, *d* 1816
Loveday, William, *d* London 1827
Lovelace, John, of Devon, *d* 1803
Lovell, Mary J., of Somerset, *d* 1826
Lowdey, Thomas, *d* Cardiff 1835
Lowe, John, *d* Westminster 1815
Lowe, S. Mrs. ⎫ of Cheshire,
Lowndes, A. Mrs. ⎭ 1788
Lowther, Agnes, Lancaster, *d* 1810
Lucas, John, *d* Carmarthen 1773
Ludlow, John, *d* Surrey 1830
Luff, James, *o'wise* Hapgood
" Mary, " Grove
" Sarah, " Bell
Lullin, Ann H. *d* abroad 1858
Lungely, Henry, *d* Suffolk 1803
Lusby, Henry, *d* Essex 1830
Luscombe, M. H. S. Right Rev., *d* 1848

Lynal, Mary, *d* London 1799
Lyne, Mary, Berks, *d* 1853
Lyon, John, of Dover, *d* 1817
Lyse, Telno, *d* Worcester 1814
Lyttleton, Thomas, *d* Essex 1799

M

McCann, Magalen, *d* 1822
McCollough, Edward, *d* Cheshire 1836
McDougle, John, *d* London
McEiver, Jane, *frmly* Stewart
McEvoy, James, of Ireland, *d* 1795
McIver, John, of Hornaway, *d* 1820
McKinnell, John, of Manchester
McNabb, John, merchant, *d* 1802
McNicoll, Robert, mariner, *d* 1824
McPhail, James, *d* Surrey 1828
Macallaster, James, *d* abroad 1807
Macdonald, Alxr. Major, *d* 1824
" Elbth., *d* Reading 1820
Machason, Robert, *d* Egham 1800
Machathe, Alexr., of Salop
Machen, Mary, London, *d* 1807
Mackaness, Edward, of Birmingham
Mackare, Ann, Kent, 1803
Mackenzie, Alexr., *d* Southall 1793
" Donald, *d* abroad 1806
" James, *d* London
" Murdoch, son of James
Mackie, John, *d* Surrey 1839
Mackilwain, Ezekiel, *d* Hants 1803
Mackinnon, Chas., *d* Middlesex 1833
Mackintosh, Mary, Scotland
" Shaw, *d* about 1770
" Lachlan, *d* 1773
" Winwood, married 1710
" Mary, *o'wise* Reade, *d* 1713
" Helen, *o'wise* Thomson
Maclean, Roderick, Major, *d* 1836
" Sarah, Dame, *d* 1845
Macklewraith, Ann, *d* 1806
Macklow, Thos., *d* Birmingham 1837
Macphail, Mary, London, *d* 1790
Macpherson, Kenneth, Gen., *d* 1814
" Robert, Major, *d* 1823
Macquiston, Elbth. M., *d* 1822
Maddelbranch, S. M., *o'wise* Bermes
Maddock, Peter, *d* Cheshire 1825
" Sarah, wife of Peter
Maden, Edward, *d* Sheffield 1827
Mahon, Thomas, Rev., *d* 1780
Mahoney, Dennis, Colonel, *d* 1813
Malbon, Samuel, *d* Oxford 1791
Maldon, George, Rev., of Dublin
Mallam, Richard, *d* Berks 1846

Maltwood, James, of Rye
" Susn., d 1813
Mander, Jane, Truro, d 1812
Manistre, John Rev., d Notts 1809
Mann, Joseph, of Liverpool
Manning, John, d Northampton 1853
Manowick, Elbth. M., Bath, d 1790
Manson, Margaret, London, d 1849
Marchall, James, d London
Marcham, Thomas, of Bucks, d 1698
Margets, John, d Hants 1842
Marples, Thomas, d Derby 1803
Marsden, Sarah, Cheltenham 1829
Marsh, Adrian, of Datchett
" John, of Middlesex
" John F., d New York 1828
" Mary, Middlesex, d 1732
" William, of Bray
Marshall, Charles, d Sheffield 1817
" Elbth., d Kent 1830
" Robert, d Jamaica 1820
" Thomas, d Kent, 1837
" Timothy, d Streatley 1802
Marson, William, d Worksop 1835
Martin, Claude, General, d 1800
" Mary, Westminster, d 1765
" Robert, d Hants 1831
" Thomas, surgeon 1812
Martyn, Jane, *frmly* Wells 1730
Martyn, Samuel, of Devon b 1742
Marwood, J. B. S., d Somerset 1811
Mason, C. J., d Yorkshire 1834
" John, d Lambeth 1772
" John B., of Notts, d 1809
Matchwick, James, of Farnham
Mathias, Richd., d Pembroke 1833
Matrin, Amand, d Wessingford 1854
Matterson, Edward, of York d 1810
Matthews, Sarah, London d 1780
" Mary, sister to Sarah
Mattingley, Wm., d Surrey 1818
Maul, Samuel D., d Gloucester 1832
Maude, William, d Africa 1813
Mawby, Nathan, d Shepperton 1790
May, George, d Westminster 1857
Mayall, Abner, d Lancashire 1846
Maynard, Thos., d Croydon 1842
Maze, James, d London 1804
Meager, William, d Surrey 1825
Meckleson, Fredk., d London 1805
Meddowcroft, Edmund, of Chester
" Wm., solicitor d 1835
Meek, Henry, master-mariner, d 1827
Melland, Stephen, of Derby, d 1810
Melling, Edward, son of James
Mellis, James, d India 1843

Melton, William, d London 1832
Mendham, William, d Islington 1812
Mercer, James, d London 1765
Merricks, Elbth., d Sussex 1817
Messenger, John, d Marylebone 1786
" Jos., d Cumberland 1828
Metcalf, Elbth., Newington, d 1832
" Thos., d Bloomsbury 1750
" William, of Southwark
Metcalfe, Thomas, d abroad 1750
Meulh, William, d Taunton 1790
Meymott, Samuel, d London 1832
Meggett, Aitken, d London 1855
Michell, Peter F., d London 1818
Middleton, Ann F., Pimlico d 1823
Miles, Elbth., *frmly* How, d 1828
" James C., d Cheltenham 1849
" John, d Salisbury 1854
Milbourne, R. S. d Cumberland 1822
Mildrell, Benjn., d Middlesex 1816
Mill, Joseph, of Wilts, d 1857
Millard, Martha, Somerset d 1785
Miller, Charles, of Oxford
" Francis, d Westminster 1788
" Mary, Devon d 1804
" Mary, Surrey d 1817
" John, Rev.
Mills, Ann, Chipping Barnett 1799
" Hugh, of London, d 1788-9
" Thomas, d Wilts 1838
Milne, John
" Robert
" Thos., d Notts 1833
Milner, James, d London 1830
Milward, John, d Finsbury 1830
Minns, Ann, of Kent, d 1799
Minshull, John, d Swansea 1827
Minskip, Hannah, of Doncaster
Mister, Edw. S., d Carmarthen 1840
Mitchell, Bartlett, jeweller, London
" Mary, o'wise Houghton
" Robert, d Bristol 1812
" Thos., d Yorkshire 1814
" W. B., London
Mitford, Robert, d Paris 1836
Mockett, John, of Deal, d 1854
Moffatt, Thomas, d America 1819
" Mary, of d 1826
Moline, Deborah, Hillingdon, d 1842
Mollard, Sarah, *frmly* Castle, d 1775
Monkhouse, John, d Hants 1828
Monro, Jane, Whitehaven, d 1833
Montague, Ann C., *frmly* Wood
Moodie, Sarah, d Bath 1813
Moody, Isaac, of Coreham, Wilts
Moor, Mary, d Yorkshire 1829

Moor, Samuel, d London 1823
Moore, Catherine M., Exeter d 1846
" Ann, Derby, d 1821
" Edward, d Salisbury 1812
" Eleanor, of Edinburgh, d 1834
" James, d Middlesex 1817
" Jeremiah, d Carlisle 1818
" Thomas, d Plymouth 1798
Moores, Wm. L., of London, d 1839
Mordaunt, John, of Beds, d 1737
" John, of Bedford, d 1770
" Robt., of Heyth'rpe, d 1824
Morgan, David, d Montgomery 1801
" Evan, mast-mariner, d 1853
" James, of Ludlow
" James M., d Chepstow 1818
" Josiah, d India 1806
" Margaret, w of John
" Morgan, mast-mariner 1850
" Rachael, Monmouth, d 1854
" Richard, d Cardigan 1855
" Sarah, London, d 1780
" Thomas, Bristol
" Thomas, d Pembroke 1785
Morice, Lewis, d Cardigan 1852
Morley, John, of Surrey, d 1836
Morrillion, John, of Lincoln, d 1804
" Abraham, bro. of John
Morris, John, d Kent 1837
" Margt., Beaumaris, d 1805
" Sarah, Little Marlow, d 1857
" Thomas, d Hants 1835
" William, of Brecon, d 1846
Morrison, John R., d China 1843
" John, of Banffshire d 1835
" Sarah, d Norwich 1827
Morse, Elizabeth, Kent, d 1773
Moses, Henry, d Lancashire 1832
" Thomas, d Jamaica 1813
Moss, Mary, Cheltenham, d 1854
" Philip, d Suffolk 1842
Mortimer, Richard, of Middlesex
Morton, Thomas, of Yorkshire
Mountain, Sush., Norfolk, d 1824
Mowbray, Charlotte, Louth, d 1858
" Joseph, of London
Muir, Col. G., d London
Mulcaster, John, d Northumberland
Mullen, Jane, of Hants, d 1845
Mullings, Joseph, of Surrey, d 1827
Munro, Anna, of Oxford, d 1827
" James, d 1801
Murgairoyd, Hannah, York
Murray, John, d Middlesex 1854
Musgrave, Matthew, of London 1765
Myers, Arthur, of Surrey 1766

Myers, Rev. Timothy, d 1845

N

Nabb, John, d Preston 1794
Nash, Catherine, frmly Reeves
" Richard, d Ludlow 1815
Nasmith, James, d Cambridge 1808
Naylor, Abraham, d Yorkshire 1850
Neal, Thomas R., d Lincoln 1848
Neave, Joseph, d Lincolnshire 1838
Needham, L., of Derbyshire, d 1792
Needs, Ann, d Exeter 1812
" Charles, d Exeter 1836
Nelthorpe, Elizabeth, Suffolk, d 1801
Netherwood, Ann, London, d 1783
" George, d Jamaica
Newbold, Joseph, d Lancashire 1839
Newbury, Honor, d Kilburn 1848
" John, d Dulwich 1815
Newcombe, Ann, London, d 1806
Newman, Charles, d India 1782
" Henry, of Bristol, d 1787
" Thomas, d Surrey 1840
Newth, Mark, d Malmesbury 1808
Newton, James, d London 1830
" John, d Durham 1818
Nevill, William, d London 1824
Nicholas, Edward, d Wilts 1828
Nicholls, E. S., Brixton, d 1832
" Nicholas, d Yorkshire 1774
Nicol, Col. James, d 1831
" Emma, dau. of James, d 1832
Nicolson, John, d Carlisle 1795
Nippard, William, d Wilts 1844
Noble, Frederick, d Surrey 1847
Noddings, Robt., d Cambridge 1835
Nollekins, Joseph, d London 1823
Norman, Ann, o'wise Kynaston 1795
" Daniel, d Lancashire 1849
" Richard, d Westminst'r 1826
Norris, William, d Wilts 1828
Norton, James, d London 1809
" Jeremiah, of Essex
" Sarah, wife of Jeremiah
" Thomas G., d Boston 1831
Nowell, Phillip, d Bath 1851
Nowland, Richard, d India 1802
" Henrietta, d India 1805
Noyes, Sarah, Middlesex, d 1842
Nunn, Mrs. Elizabeth, d Essex 1790

O

O'Hara, Henry, d London 1804
Oakes, Betsy, spinster

Oakes, Lucy, o'wise Bayley, d 1823
Oakley, Ann, of Herts
" Richard, d Gloucester 1832
Oddie, John, d Yorkshire 1822
Ogle, George, d Berks 1828
Ogilvie, Henry, d London 1820
Older, James, d Surrey 1814
" Sarah, Kent
Oldham, Samuel, d India 1788
Oldman, William, d Middlesex 1851
Oliveira, Dominick, d London 1830
Oliver, Sarah, Newcastle, d 1799
Olliver, Harriett, Suffolk, d 1834
" Jane, cousin of T. Wainmar
" Sarah L., Teignmouth
Ollyer, Alice, Wilts, d 1811
Opie, John, d Marylebone 1807
Orbell, Samuel, d Essex 1782
Orme, Mary, d 1856
Orr, William, d Islington 1844
Osbaldiston, John, d Lancashire 1822
Osborn, Edward, of Berks, d 1808
" John, of Berks, d 1770
" Elbth. ⎫ children of John,
" James ⎬ of Berkshire
" Ann ⎪
" Charles ⎫ children of Edw.
" Edward ⎬ of Berkshire,
" Obed ⎪ who d 1808
" Thomas ⎭
" Mary, of Sussex
Osborne, John, of Wilts, d 1821   826
" John W., d Worcester 1
" Nathaniel, of Gloucestersh.
Osgoode, William, d London 1824
Ostell, Thomas, d London 1841
Otter, John, d West Chickerell 1813
Oven, John, d 1794
Owers, William, d Lambeth 1844
Oxley, Joshua, d Rotherhithe 1796

P

Page, Ann, Clerkenwell, d 1821
" Richard, d London 1824
" Sophia, d Norfolk 1838
Paget, Charles, d London 1799
Palmer, Herbert, of Kent
" John, d Cambridge 1834
" John, d Shrewsbury 1823
" John, d Norfolk 1805
" Mary, of Wokingham
Pargeter, Henry, d Hants 1846
Parker, Charles, d London 1785
" E. C., d Essex 1841
" Henry, d abroad 1842

Parker, Robert, d Rochester 1837
" William, of Notts, d 1825
Parken, Henrietta E., d Bayswater
" Sarah C., d Cheltenham 1839
Parlby, Thomas, d Devon 1798
Parnell, John, of Wicklow
Parr, Andrew
" Sally, wife of Andrew, 1822
Parrott, John, d Surrey 1832
Parry, John, d London 1824
" John, d Cardigan 1819
Parson, William, d Surrey 1799
Parsons, William, of Finchley, d 1829
" Daniel, d Worcester 1820
Partis, Fletcher, d Bath 1820
Partridge, Ann, d 1822
Passey, William, d Hereford 1805
Patson, Mary, frmly Kempson
Pate, Elizabeth, London, d 1808
Patterson, Chpr., d Bowness 1852
Patnam, James, d London
Patrickson, Hugh, d Cumberland 1858
" Isabella, " 1854
Patterson, Alexander, d Hoxton 1812
" James, of Perthshire
Payler, Col. James, d 1854
Peach, Col. Charles, d 1837
" Samuel, d Warwick 1832
Peake, Ann, d Aston 1844
Pearce, Richard, d Leicester 1814
" Robert, d Devon 1839
" Sarah, d Lambeth 1789
" William, of Westminster
Pearkes, Mary, London, d 1826
Pearson, Hannah, Falsgrave, d 1836
" Thomas, d London 1792
" William, d Southwark 1811
Peasgood, Sus., Wapping, d 1839
Peche, John, of Hampshire
Peckford, Posthumous, of London
Pedlingham, John P., d London 1842
Pell, James, d Norfolk 1811
Pendrill, Richard
" William
" George
" John
" Humphrey
Penford, Alice, Leicester
Penn, Thomas, d Surrey 1837
Pennell, Mary, Lincoln 1803
Penny, Alex., brother to Blake P—
Penrice, Thomas, d Swansea 1846
Penton, George, of London
Perchard, Hellier, of London
Percival, Isaac, of Stockport
Percivall, William, d Liverpool 1854

Perks, William, *d* Somerset 1825
Perrin, Ann, *d* Marlborough 1821
Peritt, Paul, *d* Wilts 1824
Perry, William, *d* Oxford 1830
Perryman, Edward, *d* Middlesex 1847
Pershouse, W. B., *d* Stafford 1843
Peto, Henry, of Surrey, *d* 1830
Peters, Thomas, of Mortlake, *d* 1837
Petrie, Col. Alexander, *d* 1844
Pettingall, G. H., *d* Salop 1838
Phillips, Elizabeth E., Westminster
" Evan, *d* Monmouth 1803
" George, mariner, *d* 1818
" George, *d* abroad 1806
" George, *d* Jamaica 1814
" John, of Cumberland
" John, of Royston, *d* 1826
" Mary, of Nova Scotia
" Mary, *d* France 1842
" Richard, *d* Oxford 1858
" William, *d* Derbyshire 1863
" William, of Surrey, *d* 1833
Phillipson, R. B. B., *d* Bath 1825
Phipps, Elizabeth, Gloucester
Pickering, William, *d* Yorkshire 1835
Pickrell, James, *d* Surrey 1847
Pierce, John H., *d* Axminster 1818
" Frederick, *d* 1825
" Thomas, of Wilts, *d* 1829
" Hannah, Wilts, *d* 1834
Pieschel, C. A. G., *d* Loudon 1821
Piggott, Francis, *d* Berks 1784
" Thomas, of Bucks
Pigot, Caroline, *d* abroad 1850
Pilbrow, Thomas, of Middlesex
Pinard, Eleanor
Pinnell, Archibald, *d* Berks 1829
Pitman, Elizabeth, *d* Devon 1824
Pittman, Joseph, *d* Lambeth 1814
Plews, Edward, of Derby, *d* 1833
Plowden, Henry C., *d* Hants 1821
Plumb, Joseph,*d* Worcestershire 1857
Plumbe, John
" Thomas
Pocock, Isaac, of London
Pollard, Joseph, *d* Leicester 1854
Pollitt, Robert, of Atterton
Porter, Alex. S., *d* Worcester 1850
" Rachel, *d* Kent 1856
Portis, Mary, Brighton, *d* 1835
Postlethwaite, Elbth., *d* Sussex 1834
Potts, Thomas, *d* London 1811
Poulson, William, of Leicester
" John } brothers to Jos. of
" Thomas } Leicester
Poulton, Elizabeth, Monmouthshire

Pounds, Robert, of Middlesex
Pountney, Mary, *d* Soho 1825
Powell, Catharine, Hampton Bishop
" Benjamin, *d* Brecon 1819
" D. F., *d* Tottenham 1848
" John, carpenter, London
" John, *d* Radnor, 1844
" Mary, Middlesex, *d* 1813
" Peggy, *o'wise* Kipping, *d* 1800
" Penelope, Glo'ster, *d* 1793
Power, Francis R., *d* Jamaica 1815
Powney, Elbth., wife of John, *d* 1837
Pratt, Edward, *d* London 1831
" Thomas B., of London
Prentice, William, *d* Surrey 1826
Preston, Ann, *o'wise* Needs, *d* 1812
" John, *d* Yorkshire 1814
Prevost, William, *d* London 1836
Price, David, *d* London 1840
" Mary, Carmarthen, *d* 1819
" Richard, *d* Chelsea 1834
" William, *d* Brecon 1835
Pridden, Ann, Chelsea, *d* 1847
" John, *d* Caddington 1825
Priddie, William, *d* West Indies
Pring, Joseph, *d* London 1815
Pritchard, Admiral John, *d* 1776
" Samuel, mariner, *d* 1812
Proctor, Sarah, *frmly* Cramer
Protheroe, John, of Clifton
Proudman, Elzbth., London, *d* 1854
Prouting, William, *d* London 1794
Pryce, Elizabeth, *d* Trylydden 1851
Puckler, Thomasaine, *d* 1824
Pughe, Elizabeth P., Herts, *d* 1832
" Price, *d* London 1815
Pulley, Henry, of Kent 1719
Pulteney, Charles, of Somerset
Putnam, James, *d* Middlesex
Pye, George, *d* Middlesex 1828
Pyke, Mary, Westminster, *d* 1823
Pynn, Lady Cecilia C., *d* 1849
Pyort, Robert Thomas, of Kent 1804

Q

Quarterman, George, *d* Kent 1846
Quelch, Elizabeth, Reading, *d* 1843
Quick, Thomas C., *d* Kent 1810
Quinton, Cornelius R., *d* 1838
Quirk, Mary, Toxteth-park, *d* 1845

R

Rabson, Richard, *d* Kensington 1784
Radcliffe, William S.

CHANCERY ADVERTISEMENTS. 97

Radford, Chas., *d* Birmingham 1829
Rainey, Thomas, *d* West Indies 1811
Rainsford, John, *d* Oxford 1839
Ramforth, Sarah, *frmly* Tatnall
Ramsbotham, Jas., *d* Liverpool 1827
Ramsden, Dyson, of Yorkshire
" John, *d* Middlesex 1826
Rance, Thos. F., *d* Middlesex 1843
Randall, Moses, *d* Gloucester 1781
Ranford, Ann, Shadwell, *d* 1784
Rawlins, Dudson, of Abingdon
" Joseph, *d* America 1784
Rawlinson, Geo., *d* Marylebone 1796
Ray, Sarah, Shadwell, *d* 1784
" W. C., *d* Boreham 1845
Raye, William, *d* Weldon 1828
Raybould, Geo., of Worcestershire
Redfern, John, *d* Stockport 1830
Reece, Edward, *d* Middlesex 1820
Reed, Chambers, *d* Cumberland 1820
Rees, Thomas, *d* Islington 1854
" William, *d* Monmouth 1807
Reeve, John C., *d* Bloomsbury 1835
Reeves, Christopher, *d* Surrey 1786
Reid, Anne, Middlesex, *d* 1811
Reilly, Hugh, *d* Middlesex 1854
" Thomas, *d* Stepney 1808
Remnant, Stephen, of Woolwich
Rennell, James, *d* London 1830
Renner, Ed., *d* Northumberland 1858
Rexworthy, Charles, *d* Somerset 1824
Reynolds, Ann, Surrey, *d* 1819
" Rev. M., *d* Suffolk 1797
" Robert F., *d* Essex 1846
" Stephen, *d* Essex 1775
Rhodes, Robert, of Reading, *d* 1853
" Mary, wife of Robert
Rice, James, *d* Putney 1859
Rich, Ann, Bristol, *d* 1778
" James, *d* Somerset 1815
Richard, James, *d* London 1806
" Joseph, *d* abroad 1823
Richards, Ann, of Cardigan
" Eliza, Bloomsbury, *d* 1839
" Francis W. *d* Somerset 1821
" Jane, *frmly* Lloyd
" Jane, of Lambeth
" John, *d* Guernsey 1828
" John, *d* Middlesex 1837
" Mary, of Lambeth
" Samuel, *d* Risley 1824
Richardson, Elbth., Cumberland
" John, *d* Norfolk 1848
" William, *d* Surrey 1843
Richards, Geo., *d* Middlesex 1831
Ride, William, of Westminster 1780

Rider, Edmund, living 1812
" Mark
" Ralph
Rigby, Ann, *d* Middlesex 1811
Ring, Richard, *d* Hants 1850
Rippett, Thomas, *d* Coventry 1800
" Mary, *d* Coventry 1802
Rippon, John, *d* Westmoreland
Rishton, Emor, *d* Yorkshire 1777
" Emor, jun., Yorkshire,1806
Risdon, Henry, of Devon
Roberts, Elliott R., *d* Bristol 1847
" Elbth., Middlesex, *d* 1843
" Frances, Middlesex
" James, *d* Denton 1845
" Lucretia, Newport, *d* 1824
" Richard, *d* Hackney 1842
" Robert, *d* Liverpool 1794
" Rowland, *d* Islington 1849
" Sarah, Surrey
Robertson, Benjamin, *d* Surrey 1800
Robins, Thomas, *d* London 1816
Robinson, Anthony, *d* London 1827
" Daniel, yeoman, *d* 1806
" Admiral Mark, *d* 1834
" Thomas, *d* Taunton 1801
" White, Jamaica 1806
" W.L.B. *d* Marylebone 1843
Rochford, Martha, *frmly* Strong
Rock, Thomas, of Surrey, *d* 1811
Rockwell, M. R., *d* Tottenham 1813
Rodgers, George, *d* London 1825
Roe, James, *d* Kensington 1853
Roebuck, Benjamin, of London
" Benj., *d* Yorkshire 1791
Rose, Rebecca W., Surrey, *d* 1819
Rogers, Aurelia, Penzance. *d* 1833
" John, *d* London 1831
' Samuel, *d* Westminster 1741
" William } relatives of
" Simon } Samuel
Rooke, John S., *d* Finsbury 1825
Roper, Jane, *d* Whitehaven 1790
Rose, Lewis, *d* Berks 1853
" James } of Isleworth
" Sarah }
Ross, George O. *d* Enfield 1825
Rothwell, Ralph, *d* Lancashire 1795
" Elzbth., Lancashire 1806
Rowe, Emilia A., Cork, *d* 1829
" John } sons of Joseph,
" Jacob } of Devon,
" W. S. } living 1750
Rowland, William, *d* Oxford 1835
Royds, Ann, Rochdale, *d* 1789
Royle, Samuel, *d* Lancashire 1820

Royle, William, *d* America
Roylance, John, *d* Cheshire 1812
Ruddy, Thomas, *d* Surrey 1850
Ruffin, Thomas, of London
Rumbold, Thomas ⎫ sons of Thomas,
" William ⎭ of London
Russ, John, *d* Berks 1825
Russell, Mary S., of London 1780
" Richard, *d* Surrey 1784
Rutter, Catherine, of Doncaster
Ryley, Catherine, of Carshalton
Rymsdyke, John V., *d* London

S

Sadler, William, *d* Lancashire 1789
" Robert, *d* Wilts 1839
Sainsbury, Charles, *d* London 1843
Salisbury, Martha, *d* Middlesex 1855
" Stephen, *d* Kent 1807
Salmon, John, *d* Bath 1809
" Robert, *d* Hexham 1786
Salt, Thomas, *d* Warwick 1833
Sampson, Ann, Marylebone *d* 1833
Sanderson, Elizabeth, Cumberland
" Jackson, *d* Birkley 1852
" Nicholas, surgeon *d* 1816
Sandford, Thos., *d* Somerset 1851
Sands, John, *d* 1802
Sandys, Mary, Middlesex 1811
Saner, Jacob, of London
Sargeant, George, *d* Middlesex 1844
" Samuel, *d* Rothwell 1832
Saunders, William, *d* Surrey 1776
Saunt, Mary, *o'wise* Gardener
Sause, Richard, *d* London
Savage, Wm., *d* Wolverhampton 1822
Savill, Joseph, *d* Essex 1823
Savignac, Alice, Middlesex 1805
Savory, Henry, of Hampstead 1822
Saward, William, *d* Essex 1840
Sawkins, Mary, Chelsea, *d* 1830
Saxton, William, *d* Brentford 1850
Sayer, Charles, *d* Sussex 1843
" Sarah, *d* Paddington 1850
Scarman, Ann, Chelsea *d* 1829
Scarpelain, John M.
Scholey, Martha, *d* Yorkshire 1828
Schuppe, Sarah, Essex *d* 1798
Stott, Betty, Rochdale *d* 1821
Scott, Major David, *d* India
" Elizabeth, of Cumberland
" Edmund, *d* Herts 1829
" James, *d* Marylebone 1833
" Joseph, *d* Durham 1833
" Walter, brother to David

Scouler, James B., *d* 1812
Scourfield, W. H., *d* Pembroke 1843
Seagrave, John, *d* London 1776
" Robert, *d* Notts 1790
Seaman, Amy, Chester *d* 1798
" Ann, Chester *d* 1829
Sergison, Ann, Sussex *d* 1806
Senhouse, Louisa W., Surrey, *d* 1845
Settle, John, *d* Yorkshire 1857
Seaward, Elbth., Marylebone, *d* 1820
" Robert, *d* Yorkshire 1854
Shaker, John, *d* Cramlington 1841
Shanks, John, purser R N, *d* 1817
" William, of Scotland, *d* 1825
Shapton, Gawen, *d* Devonport 1855
Sharp, Benjamin, *d* Romsey 1840
" Henry
Sharples, William, *d* Hindley 1841
Shaw, Christopher, *d* Chelsea 1770
" John, *d* Tottenham 1800
" Major Robert, *d* 1812
" William, *d* Liverpool 1841
Sheffield, Elbth., *d* Cumberland 1765
Shefford, William, *d* Marylebone 1791
Sheldon, Benj., *d* Leicestershire 1832
" Elbth., London, *d* 1829
Shelton, Col. John, *d* 1845
Shepherd, Alice, Yorkshire, *d* 1808
" John, of Gosport
" William, *d* India
Sheppy, William, *d* Totteridge 1835
Sherburne, John, *d* Hereford 1832
Sherrard, Joseph, *d* 1835
Shields, John T., of London 1794
Shirley, Henry, *d* London 1812
Shore, Lydia, Derbyshire, *d* 1839
Showell, Joseph, *d* Bedworth 1796
Shuttleworth, Fredk., *d* Notts 1823
Short, Charles, *d* India 1785
Shrapnell, William, *d* Bath 1848
Shuter, John, *d* Middlesex 1847
Silcock, Benj. B., of Yorkshire
Sim, James, *d* Bloomsbury 1833
" John, of Scotland, *d* 1824
" Robert, grandfather of John
Simpson, Capt. John, *d* 1849
Simson, Nathan, of London
Sims, Adam, *d* Kent 1817
Sims, Thomas, of Denton
Skelton, Belona, Middlesex, *d* 1849
" Jonathan, *d* Newcastle 1786
Skey, Mary, Wilts, *d* 1825
Skiff, Moses, *d* Middlesex 1819
Skinner, Barbara, Tottenham, *d* 1770
Slade, Mary, *o'wise* French, *d* 1839
" Sus. *frmly* Gilkinet, *d* 1841

Slater, Philip, *d* Middlesex 1808
" Thomas C. *d* Yorkshire 1831
Slatter, John, *d* London 1832
Sloan, David, *d* abroad 1829
" Stephen, *d* London 1823
Smallwood, Thomas, *d* Cheshire 1775
Smart, Elizabeth, of Durham
" John, *d* Sussex 1835
" Samuel, *d* Bristol 1849
Smith, Ann, *d* Lambeth, 1847
" Ann E. Middlesex, *d* 1847
" Benj. *d* Sheerness 1852
" Betty Shropshire, *d* 1829
" Charles, *d* London 1833
" David, Dundee
" Edward, *d* Stourport 1821
" Edward, *d* London 1790
" Eleanor, Brompton, *d* 1845
" Elizabeth, Brighton, *d* 1834
" Frances, Hoxton
" George, *d* India 1790
" Hannah, Newcastle, *d* 1858
" James, builder, Ramsgate
" John, *d* Warwickshire 1847
" John, surgeon, *d* India 1807
" John, *d* London 1792
" John, *d* Liverpool 1817
" Gen. Joseph, *d* 1790
" Mary, Gloucester, *d* 1831
" Mary, *d* Leamington 1858
" Mary, Berrick-Salem, *d* 1818
" Mary, Bristol, *d* 1734-6
" Richard, of Oxford
" Richard, of Worcestershire
" Robert, of Dundee, *d* 1795
" Sarah, *d* Cockermouth 1817
" Thomas, *d* Westminster 1812
" Thomas, *d* Coventry 1831
" Thomas, brother to Joseph
" William, *d* Birmingham 1841
" William, *d* Middlesex 1843
" William, *d* Shrewsbury 1828
" William, *d* Newcastle 1795
" William C., of Leicestershire
Smyth, George E., *d* Middlesex
Smythies, Thomas, of Liverpool
Snare, Robert, *d* Reading 1838
Snoll, Thomas, *d* Portsmouth 1786
Snepp, John, of Sussex, *d* 1857
Snibson, Ann, *o'wise* Moore
" Sarah, *o'wise* Morris, *d* 1857
Soper, William, *d* Surrey 1839
Sorel, Louisa, Enfield, *d* 1847
Sotheby, Capt. G. H., *d* 1838
Southam, John, *d* Bucks 1808
" Joyce, *d* 1849

Southam, Henry ⎫
" John ⎬ sons of John,
" Thomas ⎭ of Bucks,
" William ⎭ yeoman, *d* 1808
" S. L. S., *o'wise* Young
" Mary " Hodgson
" Rebecca " Hucey
Southby, Charles, *d* Berks 1834
Southerne, Ann, Bath, *d* 1832
Southgate, Wm., *d* Southwark 1807
Southmeade, Charlotte, Exeter
Sowerby, Robert, of Kent, *d* 1830
" William, of Kent, *d* 1817
Sparke, Richard, *d* Suffolk 1816
Sparkes, John, *d* London 1804
Sparks George, *d* Sidmouth 1824
Sparrow, Martha, of Ealing 1783
Spearman, Thos. R. purser, R N
Spencer, Elizabeth, *d* London 1784
" John, *d* London 1806
" John, *d* India 1766
Spicer, Mary, *o'wise* Kennett
Spilling, Thomas, *d* Norfolk 1829
Splidt, Philip, of London
Spooner, Thomas, *d* London 1839
" William, *d* Surrey 1836
Springhall, Godfrey, *d* London 1785
" James E.*d*Middlesex 1823
Spurstone, Rev.Dr.W.*d*Hackney1666
Squire, Thomas, *d* Folkestone 1810
Stagg, Lucinda, Kent, *d* 1833
Stains, William, *d* Canterbury 1827
Stalker, Alice, Stafford, *d* 1814
Stamp, James, of London
Stanley, Mary, *frmly* Meddowcroft
" Mary, *d* Lancashire 1833
Stark, William, *d* London 1824
Starkey, Henry, *d* Westminster
Starkie, Elbth., London, *d* 1780
Steady, John, *alias* Swain, *d* 1832
Stedman, Ellen, Middlesex, *d* 1855
Steele, William, *d* Shropshire 1807
Stevens, Ann, *w* of James, *d* 1834
" Elbth., *o'wise* Coles 1760
" Frederick, *d* Rutland 1833
" James, *d* London 1831
" Joel, *d* London 1765
" Lewis, *d* Exeter 1795
Stephenson, David, *d* 1807
" Hugh, *d* Lambeth 1821
" Robert, *d* Middlesex 1819
" William, *d* Beverley 1829
Sterne, Richard, *d* Beverley 1791
Stevens, Dorah, Liverpool, *d* 1815
" William, *d* Coventry 1800
Stevenson, Ann, of Hammersmith

Stevenson, Helen, *frmly* Duncan
" Mary, Islington 1801
Stieball, Bernard, *d* Frankfort 1830
Stewart, Dorothy C., York, *d* 1858
" Robert R., *d* Chelsea 1833
Steward, Mary, of Norwich
Steygould, Margt., Islington, *d* 1833
Stockdale, Jer., of London, *d* 1823
Stocker, Elbth. *o'wise* Aspland, *d* 1852
Stocking, Henry, *d* Norwich 1826
Stockton, John, of Nawton, York
" John, Kirckdale
Stobbs, Jane, London
Stokes, Hugh, of Pembroke, *d* 1822
Stone, Catharine, London
" Capt. Chas., *d* 1831
Stones, Thos., of Swettenham, *d* 1822
Storke, Thos., of Suffolk, *d* 1760
Story, Sarah, *frmly* Poole
Stow, Elbth. *o'wise* Miles, *d* 1828
St. Leger, Frances, Deal, *d* 1820
Stracey, Frances, of Herts, *d* 1857
Strachan, James, of Scotland, *d* 1810
Straffon, or } of Durham, *d* 1846
Straughton }
Strahan, Sir John, of Hammersmith
Strailer, Thomas, of Surrey, *d* 1798
Stratford, Francis, P. of London, *d* 1841
Stratton, Rebecca, Chelsea
Strode, Nathaniel, of Bristol, *d* 1794
" Jane, wife of Nathaniel, *d* 1805
" Jane, dau. of Nathaniel, *d* 1813
Strong, Hugh, *d* Wilts 1829
Stuart, Capt. Chas., R N, *d* 1814
Styles, Henry T., of London, *d* 1835
Sullivan, Daniel, of Cork, *d* 1843
Summers, Richard, of Somerset, *d* 1830
" William, of Hereford, *d* 1779
Sunderland, John, of Halifax, *d* 1820
Supple, Robert, of Clifton, *d* 1847
Surrey, Charlotte, *d* in Herts
Sutcliffe, John, of Lancashire, *d* 1845
" William, of Bath, *d* 1852
" Clara, Bath, *d* 1833
Sutherland, Charles, of Wilts, *d* 1839
Sutton, John, of Staffordshire
Sutton, Thos. of Lincolnshire, *d* 1845
" William, *d* Southwark 1820
Swain, Jenny, Stockport, *d* 1839
" Joseph, *d* Yorkshire 1831
Swainston, Isabella, London 1810
Swan, Jeremiah, of Sussex, *d* 1828
" William, of London, *d* 1831
Swarbreck, Jno. of Wokingham 1790
Sweetland, Edw. S., *d* 1809
Swelling, Rowling, of Kent, *d* 1843

Swindell, John, of London, *d* 1831
Swithenback, Eli, of Leeds, *d* 1840

T

Talbot, Francis, of Derbyshire, *d* 1850
" Thomas, *d* in Wilts 1843
Tallentire, Thomas, *d* London 1816
Tannatt, Elizabeth, *o'wise* Deacon
Tapper, Jane, of Sussex
Tarboton, Sarah, Bradford, *d* 1791
Tarbuck, James, of Lancashire, *d* 1831
" James, of Lancashire, *d* 1828
" Jas., son of Jas. of Prescott
" Jonathan, of Lancashire
Tarleton, Margaret, Liverpool 1780
Tarr, Susan, *o'wise* Dykes, *d* 1821
Tate, William, *d* Pentonville 1827
Tayleure, William, of London, *d* 1766
Taylor, Ann, sister of Thos., of Bath
" Ann, Everton, *d* 1839
" Ann, London, *d* 1800
" Charles, of Devon, *d* 1766
" Frances, Louth, *d* 1856
" Frances, of Surrey, *d* 1840
" Jacob } broth'rs of Thomas,
" James } of Bath
" James, *d* Manchester 1812
" John, *d* Durham 1798
" John, of Islington, *d* 1846
" John, of Tamworth
" John, of Wiggington
" Mary, legatee of A. Jobson
" Matthew, *d* Wilts 1814
" Randall, of Derby, *d* 1839
" Sarah R., *o'wise* Walker
" Sophia, of Rotherhithe, *d* 1831
" Susan, Limehouse, *d* 1818
" Thomas, of Surrey, *d* 1840
" Thomas, *d* Surrey 1808
" Wm., of Birmingham, *d* 1841
" Wm., of Middlesex, *d* 1837
" William, *d* Greenwich 1801
" William, *d* Oxford 1806
Teague, Thos. of Birmingham, *d* 1847
Telford, Thomas, of Dumfries, *d* 1834
Templar, Dudley, of Marylebone, *d* 1795
Tempest, S. P., Worcester, *d* 1821
Tennant, David, of Swansea, *d* 1839
Terrill, Anna, London, *d* 1803
Territt, William, of Suffolk, *d* 1836
Terry, Henry, of Southwark
" William, of Camberwell
Thayers, Ann, of Eckington, *d* 1847

Thedwall, Francis, of Folkstone, d 1847
Thelwall, Hannah, Lincoln, d 1800
Theodore, Elbth., o'wise Hurst, d 1856
Thirkhill, Thomas, d Bristol 1818
Thomas, Benjamin, of London, d 1821
" Francis L., d Middlesex 1849
" George, of Tenbury, d 1826
" George, d Essex 1806
" Harriett L., d London 1834
" John, of Cardigan, d 1819-20
" John, d Liverpool 1828
" Robert, d 1806
" William, of Worcestershire
Thomlinson, John G., d Durham 1807
Thompson, A. S. J. F., d Paris 1835
" Betty, Middlesex, d 1833
" John, d London 1829
" John, d Newcastle 1818
" Margt., Middlesex, d 1834
" Thos. of Yorkshire, d 1819
" Wm., of Stowe, Scotland
" William, of Hants, d 1829
" William, living 1700
Thomson, James, purser, d 1851
" Ann, Kent, d 1819
Thorne, Richard, d Amsterdam 1822
Tiffin, John, of Tottenham, d 1828
Tilley, Sarah, of Middlesex
Timson, Martha, Kent 1849
Tippell, William, d Suffolk 1797
Tifford, Sarah, d 1843
Todd, Henry, d Northampton, 1809
" Jane, Herts, d 1817
" William, d Middlesex 1849
Tolson, Henry, d Bridekirk 1724
Toms, Frances, Somerset 1828
Topham, Newhall, d London 1806
Toulmin, William, d London, 1805
Towell, Samuel, d London 1812
Towers, Elzbth., Lancashire, d 1825
Townsend, Margt., Sheffield, d 1815
Tranter, William, d Marylebone 1822
Trathen, John, of Devon, d 1829
Travers, Richard, of Dorset, d 1813
Treacher, Mary, frmly Vincent
Trenwith, Henry, relative of Rebecca
" Rebecca, d Cornwall 1790
Tripp, Henry, d Tunbridge 1831
Troutback, Samuel, d India
Truman, Elizabeth, d 1834
Truscott, Ann, Middlesex
Truss, John, d Pimlico 1815
Tubbey, Thomas, d Surrey 1845
Tucker, Ingram, d Kent 1851
" John, of Pembroke, d 1791
" John, of Wilts, d 1812

Tuder, Matthew, d India 1794
Turnbull, Henry, d Norfolk 1806
" Mary, frmly Musgrave
Turner, Elzbth., Marylebone, d 1845
" John, d London 1842
" Capt. John, d 1801
" Joseph M. W., d London 1851
" Sally, d Spelsbury 1819
" Sarah, d Kent 1833
" Sarah, frmly Tyce
" Walford, d 1849
Turnock, Elizabeth, Stafford, d 1832
Turst, Salone, London, d 1805
Tutin, Edward, of Notts, d 1784
Tutte, James, d Sussex 1824
Twiss, Gen. William, d 1827
Tyler, William, of Bristol

U

Underwood, John, of Homerton
" William, d London 1830
Unwin, Rowland, d Sussex 1837
Ure, Elizabeth, frmly Stoddard

V

Van Hacchen, Alexander, d London
Vaughan, Cath., d Gloucester 1832
" John, d India 1842
Vaux, Edward, of London
Veal, John, of Wilts, d 1805
Vellers, Robert, d Worcester 1815
Venn, Ann, Gloucester, d 1790
Vernon, Dorothy, Gloucester, d 1775
" Lydia, Bath, d 1789
Veriar, James, d London 1795
Vezey, John, of Notts, d 1819
Vicars, Richard, d Lincolnshire 1841
Vicq, Col. John, d 1832
Villebois, Frances E., d 1852

W

Waby, Edward, of Herts, d 1809
Waddell, Joseph, of Berwick
" William, d Berwick 1807
Wade, John, d Middlesex 1818
" Martha, o'wise Wildon
Walch, Elbth., Middlesex, d 1849
Walcott, Edmund, d London 1667
" Thomas L., of Gloucester

Wainwright, Thomas, *d* 1770
Waite, John, *d* Marylebone 1829
" James ⎫
" Thomas ⎬ brothers of John,
" Stephen ⎭ of Marylebone
" William
Waldron, Daniel, *d* Surrey 1806
Walford, Isaac, *d* Halstead 1849
Walker, Ann, Somerset, *d* 1801
" Eliza, *o'wise* Chidell, *d* 1843
" George, *d* Middlesex 1842
" John, *d* Homerton 1770
" John, *d* Kent 1805
" John, *d* Southwark 1802
" Elizabeth, of Lincolnshire
" Henry, *d* Middlesex 1830
" Lavender, *d* Kent 1829
" Mary A. *d* Staffordshire 1827
" Prudence, Oxford, *d* 1852
Wall, Edward, of Kilkenny, *d* 1819
" John, *d* Derbyshire 1769
" Robert, of Bermondsey, 1790
Wallace, John, *d* Paddington 1814
Waller, Elizabeth, of Lincolnshire
" George, *d* London 1842
" James, *d* Sussex 1811
Wallis, James, *d* London 1759
" Edward ⎫ brothers and
" John ⎬ sister of James,
" Sarah ⎭ of London
" John, *d* Pimlico 1808
" John, *d* Newcastle 1839
Walton, John, *d* Cumberland 1818
" John, *d* London 1794
" Thomas, of Chester, *d* 1757
Walker, Mary A. *o'wise* Hicks, *d* 1830
" Mary A. wife of David, *d* 1831
Wake, William, *d* Bermondsey 1847
Warburton, George, *d* Bow 1778
" Joseph, *d* Lambeth 1817
Ward, Chas., of Chipping Wycombe
" George, of London
" Henry, *d* Exmouth 1848
" John A., *d* abroad
" Robert, *d* Norwich 1836
" Robert, *d* Darlington 1790
" Sarah, London, *d* 1819
" Sir Thomas, *d* 1788
Wardle, James, *d* India 1832
" James, of Stafford, *d* 1828
" James, of Stafford, *d* 1831
Waring, Sarah, *o'wise* Newenham
" Ann, Surrey, *d* 1842
Warre, John, of Dublin 1780
Warren, Elizabeth C., Norfolk
Warwick, Thomas, *d* London 1813

Warren, Edw., *d* Northampton 1820
Waterhouse, Jno. *d* Birmingham 1776
Watermouth, Frances, Liverpool
Waters, William, of Surrey, *d* 1841
Watkins, Henry, *d* Westminster 1834
" H. A., *d* Southwell 1832
" John, *d* Lancashire 1821
" John, *d* Lancashire 1759
" Margt. A., of Notts, *d* 1832
" Mary, *d* London 1810
" Richard, *d* Worcester
" Thomas, *d* Middlesex 1830
" William, *d* Kent 1808
Watson, Ann, Yorkshire
" George, *d* Suffolk 1827
" Henry, of Suffolk
" Jane, Durham, *d* 1838
" Richard, *d* London 1808
" William, *d* Lincolnshire 1813
Watts, Ann, Worcestershire, *d* 1859
" Rev. Clement
" George, *d* Norfolk 1789
" John, *d* Pimlico 1849
" Robert, of London 1790
Webb, Ann, *d* Bristol 1841
" Elizabeth, *frmly* Odall
" Elizabeth, Cheshire, *d* 1828
" Elizabeth, Oxford, *d* 1792
" Job, of Birmingham
" John, *d* London 1788
" Thomas, *d* Sherborne 1808
Webber, Ann, *d* Gloucestershire 1834
" Thomas, of Surrey
Weekes, Elizabeth B., *frmly* Dixon
Wegg, William, *d* Norfolk 1827
Weighway, Edward, *d* Salop 1826
Welch, Elizabeth, Bath, *d* 1843
Weldon, William, *d* Yorkshire 1838
Weller, Edward, *d* Marylebone 1819
" James, *d* Surrey 1832
" Richard, *d* Lambeth 1807
Welles, William, Worcester
Wellis, Sam'l, of Chipping Wycombe
Wells, John, of Hartlepool
Wellstood, John, *d* Liverpool 1848
Welsford, Mary, of Brighton
Weppler, Elizabeth B., Kent, *d* 1820
West, Elizabeth, *frmly* Gurr, *d* 1822
Westbeech, John, *d* Ramsgate 1813
Westbrook, John, *d* Heston 1829
Westerman, Sarah, *frmly* Pennington
Weston, George, *d* Islington 1805
" Thomas, *d* Enfield 1816
Wetherell, Thomas, *d* Middlesex 1814
Whadcott, James, of Surrey
Wharton, Sarah, *o'wise* Maddock

Wharton, Thomas, of Shropshire
" Thomas, of Birmingham
Whealley, Hugh, *d* Stafford 1835
" John, *d* Harlington 1855
Wheatley, Richard ⎫ uncles of John
" Samuel ⎭ Adams
Wheedall, Alice
" John
Wheeler, Henry, *d* Lancashire 1830
" Thomas, *d* Wilts 1830
" Ann ⎫
" James ⎪ sister & brothers
" John ⎬ of Thomas,
" Peter ⎪ of Manton, Wilts,
" Rich'd ⎪ yeoman
" Wm. ⎭
Whincopp, William, *d* Suffolk 1808
Whitaker, Robert, uncle of J. Kinsey
" Elizabeth, wife of Robert
" Eliz'h, of Tunbridge Wells
" William, *d* Higher Bencliffe
White, Amelia, Islington, *d* 1823
" Elizabeth, *d* Southgate
" John, *d* Westminster 1851
" Mary, King's Lynn, *d* 1811
" Sarah, Wolverhampton
" Samuel, *d* Cambridge 1793
" Col. Thomas
" William, *d* Jamaica 1799
" William, *d* Keswick 1811
Whitehead, Thomas, of Essex
" Thomas, of Poplar
Whiteman, Henry, *d* Cambridge 1816
Whitcomb, Thomas, *d* Worcester 1827
Whitfield, Rev. George, *d* 1832
" John, of Dulwich
" William, *d* London 1849
Whiting, John, *d* London 1801
" Margaret, *o'wise* Hayward
" Wm., legatee of A. Jobson
Whitridge, Steph., *d* Cumberland 1846
Whittaker, Elizabeth, *d* Kent 1848
" John, of Jamaica
" William, of London
Whittell, Sarah, Hornsey, *d* 1838
Whittingham, James, of Derby
Whitton, Edward, *d* Bucks 1774
Whorwood, Ann J.
Whyte, Alexander, *d* London 1832
Wickham, Robert, *d* Fulham 1832
Wilden, Joseph, *d* Shropshire 1828
Wildon, John, *d* London 1794
" Martha, *frmly* Stone, *d* 1809
Wilebore, Isaac, *d* Upwell 1788
Wilkins, Ann, Bedminster 1780
" John, *d* Marylebone 1832

Wilkins, John, *d* Wilts 1730
" Julia, *d* Wilts 1730
" Mary, *frmly* Field, *d* 1839
Wilkinson, Alex., *d* Cambridge 1819
" Ann, of Derby, *d* 1827
" Henry, *d* Wentworth 1768
" Henry, *d* Middlesex 1791
" John, *d* Pimlico 1833
" John, *d* London 1823
" Joseph, *d* Yorkshire 1773
" Thomas, *d* Darfield 1765
" Wm., *d* Yorkshire 1766
Williams, Ann, Tottenham
" Anthony, *d* Surrey 1810
" Charles, *d* India
" David, *d* Glamorgan 1827
" David, *d* Carmarthen 1819
" Edwd., of Monmouthshire
" Edward, *d* Mold 1827
" Elizabeth, Pimlico, *d* 1839
" John, *d* Wales 1797
" John, Cardigan
" John, *d* Brompton 1833
" John, *d* Monmouth 1821
" John, *d* Worcester 1843
" John, *d* Cardigan 1806
" John, *d* Middlesex 1774
" Lieut. John, *d* 1837
" John J., *d* Merioneth 1842
" John A. S., of Bristol
" Mary, Bristol, *d* 1806
" Mary, *d* Westminster 1845
" Margaret, Oswestry, *d* 1812
" Margaret, *o'wise* Morgan
" Rachael of Wales, *d* 1797
" Samuel, *d* Middlesex 1833
" Thomas, of Worcester
" Thomas, Cardigan
Williamson, J., *d* London 1828
" Maria A., Chelsea, *d* 1854
" Richard, *d* Suffolk 1832
" S. T., of Lincolnshire
" William, *d* Cheshire, 1816
Willats, Thomas, *d* London 1831
Willis, Arthur, *d* London 1857
" John, of London
Wilmore, Edward, *d* London 1858
Wilson, Anthony, *d* Bristol 1824
" Charles, *d* London 1846
" Elizabeth, London, *d* 1854
" Elizab'h, Nottingham, *d* 1793
" Elizab'h W., Finsbury, *d* 1851
" James A., *d* 1806 ⎫ of
" James, *d* 1805 ⎭ Kendal
" Joseph, *d* Middlesex 1820
" Mary, Worcester

Wilson, William, of Harrow
" William, *d* Launton 1826
Wimpey, William, *d* Devon 1814
Windsor, Elizabeth, of Ringwood
Windson, C. K., Taunton, *d* 1835
Wingfield, Eliza, *frmly* Julian
Wingrave, Matthew, *d* Herts 1849
Winkworth, Sarah, widow
Winter, John, *d* Acton 1843
Winterbottam, John, *d* 1838
" Joseph, of Yorkshire
Wintle, Sarah, Glo'stershire, *d* 1841
Wisdome, Thomas, of Herts, *d* 1801
Wiseman, Wm., *d* Middlesex 1842
Witham, William, *d* Yorkshire 1851
Withering, William, *d* Somerset 1832
Withers, Henry, *d* Wrexford 1806
" Joseph, *d* Kent 1755
Withnall, Thomas, *d* Hants 1826
Wivell, Abraham, *d* Middlesex 1827
Wood, Abraham, *d* Lancashire 1830
" Eleanor, living 1810
" George, *d* Stoke-upon-Trent
Woodcock, Elizabeth, Cheltenham
Woodhouse, John, *d* Leominster 1820
" Mary, Leominster 1842
Woodroff, William, *d* Notts 1843
Woodward, Hannah, Lancashire
Woodyatt, Ann, *frmly* Jones |
" John, of Marylebone
Woolaston, Richard, *d* Salop 1845
Woolaway, Agnes, Herts, *d* 1855
Wooley, Sarah, Stockport, *d* 1806
Woolfe, William, *d* Surrey 1828
Woolmer, Elizabeth, *frmly* Hubbard
Wordie, Catherine, Jamaica
Wornell, Alexander, *d* Surrey 1832
Worallow, John, *d* Wolverhampton

Worship, James, *d* Norwich 1792
Worth, Jacob W., *d* London 1838
Worthington, Jonathan
Wreight, Henry, of Kent, *d* 1840
Wrench, Peter E., *d* Norfolk 1778
Wright, Ann B., Clifton, *d* 1830
" Barbara, London *d* 1829
" Francis, *d* Chelsea 1817
" Jane, London, *d* 1772
" John, *d* Cheshire 1831
" Mary A., Oxford, *d* 1842
" Peter, *d* London 1843
" Thomas, *d* 1770-80
Wroth, Henry, *d* Islington 1729
" Mary, *o'wise* Fowke, *d* 1763
Wyatt, Daniel, *d* Glo'stershire 1783
 Henry, *d* Glo'stershire 1847
" Martha, *fmly* Hawkins, *d* 1858
" Thomas, of Salisbury
Wyche, Mary, Sussex, *d* 1810
Wynne, Edward, *d* London 1807
" George, *d* Surrey 1834
" Margaret R., *d* Berks 1844
" Robert, of Kensington

Y

Yates, Elizabeth
" Sally, *frmly* Greenwood
" William, *d* Lancashire 1813
Yeomans, Rev. John, *d* 1823
Yerbury, Richard, *d* London
Yew, Samuel, *d* Wilts 1757
Young, Mary, Lincolnshire, *d* 1837
" Mary P., Surrey, *d* 1834
" S. L. S., *o'wise* Hanshaw
Younghusband, William, of London

INDEX TO LEGATEES AND PERSONS ADVERTISED FOR.

LEGATEES AND PERSONS WHO HAVE BEEN ADVERTISED FOR SINCE THE YEAR 1800.

A

Abbott, George, jun., of Mark Lane
Abraham, Elizabeth, *o'wise* Torry
Abrams, Mary, *frmly* Lumly
Adams, Thomas J., appraiser
" James
" Christian
" William ⎫ legatees of
" Mary ⎬ John Truss, of
" Caroline ⎭ Pimlico
" John, of Newport
" Peter, of Devonshire
" Harriett, spinster
" Ann, *frmly* Curl
" Miss, milliner
" Geo., son of Geo. and Mary
Adcock, Henry, civil engineer
Adlar, William
Addenbrooke, B. B., of London
Aird, Donald, schoolmaster
Ainsworth, Thos., of Loughborough
Aitkin, Mary A., of Soho
Aitkins, Ann E. ⎫
" John ⎬ children of Ann,
" Peter ⎬ of London
" William ⎭
Ager, Joseph, of Suffolk
Aland, Robert O., of Soho
Aldons Thomas, of Colchester
Albeth, Rebecca, of Denbighshire
Alden, Elizabeth, *frmly* Harding
Alderson, Fanny, governess, 1856
Aldridge, Hugh W., seaman
" Flora
" James, seaman

Alfrey, George ⎫ sons of George,
" Joseph ⎭ tide-waiter
Allan, Mary C., *dau.* of William
" Susannah S., of Norfolk
" Alexander, of Montrose, N B
" John, of Montrose, N B
Allen, Mrs. Elizabeth
" Thomas, went abroad
" Sarah, *dau.* of Henry, of Bucks
" Mary, servant
" William A., of Kensington
Allender, James, engineer, &c.
Allers, William ⎫ relatives of
" Henry ⎬ William Pinchback
" John ⎭ of Camberwell
Alsopp, William, of Leicestershire
Alsop, John, of London 1816
" William, son of Robert
Ambrose, Elbth. B., *dau.* of Thomas
Anderson, John, of Gottenburgh
" John, of Aberdeen
" Frederick W., seaman
" William, broker, London
" Alfred, of New York, 1832
" John, of London
" Jos., of Cambridgeshire
Andrews, mariner, of Fulham
" William, of Deptford
" George, of Basingstoke
" Joseph, of Dublin
" Jane
" Wm., carver and gilder
" Wm., of Clerkenwell, 1821
Anglis, William, of Coventry
Annesley, Robert M., of London
Anthony, John

(105)

Anstee, John ⎫ of Buckinghamshire
" Sarah ⎭
Apperley, Charles O., Esq.
Appleby, Wm., left Liverpool 1850
Applebee, James, of Westminster
Armstrong, Robert, of Finsbury
"   John, of Newport, Salop
"   Mr., of London, 1818
"   Sarah, of Ryal, Lincoln
"   Daniel, of 70th Rgt.
Armitage, Frederick ⎫ of Mile End
" Francis ⎭ London 1849
Armit, John L., of Farnham
Armsby, Col. ⎫ of East Barnet
" Mrs. ⎭
Arnon, Elizabeth
Arnold, John, of Bedfordshire
"   Charlotte P., lady's-maid
'   Richard, mariner, Poplar
"   Mary Ann
Arthur, Robert, of Whitwell, Derby
Ash, Robert, went to Africa
" Francis, of Blackfriars
Aspinall, Peter, mariner
Aston, Thos., vet. surgeon, Madras
Ashley, James ⎫ cousins to James,
" Elbth. ⎭ of Herts.
Ashkettle, Mary, of London
Ashworth, John, brthr. to Margaret
Ashby, Samuel
Ashworth, James, broker
Aston, John G., of Birmingham
Atchison, Anna M. F., of Chelsea
Atcheson, Robt. S., *frmly* of London
Atkin, Dr., of Edinburgh
Atkins, Geo., son of Ann, of London
"   John, of Somerset
"   Jane, wife of T. Jones
"   Charles, went abroad
"   Philip
"   William, seaman
"   Mrs. Mary A., of Eton
Atkinson, Mr. J. Wray
"   Catharine, wife of Rich.
"   James, son of Robert
"   William, of Dublin
"   John William, chymist
Attree, W. H., surgeon
Austin, Robert, of London
"   Thos.,neph.of Sophia Brown
Aubert, Dorothy ⎫
"   Olympia ⎬ legatees of
"   Harriett ⎬ Baroness
"   Alexander ⎬ Susannah L.
"   Anthony ⎭ St. John
Avis, Thomas, painter

Ayliffe, William, son of John
Aylesbury, Mary, children of
Ayton, Elzbth., married Mr. Malmsbury 1841
Ayliffe, Alfred, nephew of Samuel
Ayrton, Edward, of Kent

B

Bacon, Richard, of Birmingham 1857
Bailey, John, father of Emma, who died 1843
" Elbth., native of Marlboro'
" Martha
" John
" Maria, *frmly* Haines
" Frederick, of Tooting
Baillie, Peter, native of Paisley
"   John ⎫ sons of John, of
"   William ⎭ Edinburgh
Bainbrigge, William A.
Baines, William, of Yorkshire
Baird, William, of Lochend
Baker, Henry, footman
"   John, son of Jane
"   George & Son, tailors
"   Mary R., *frmly* of Charlton
"   Charles ⎫ legatees of
"   Elbth. ⎭ James Trowbridge
"   John, shoemaker, of Henley
"   Thomas, seaman
"   Henry, of Colchester
"   James, seaman, of Poplar
"   Elizabeth, w of Joseph, R N
"   Samuel ⎫ legatees of
"   Richard ⎭ J. Twentyman
"   George, ironmonger
"   Frederick, mariner
"   John, of Norfolk
"   Ann, niece of Sam. Crouch
"   James, of Oxford
"   Thomas, of Cripplegate
"   Henry, ship-carpenter
Balmont, Wm., solicitor, Somerset
Balderson, James
Balsdon, William, tailor
Balderson, Hannah
Balshaw, Mary, *frmly* Higson
Baldock, Mrs., of Canterbury
Ball, Thomas, of South Australia
" Edward, of Gravesend
" Thos. ⎫ related to John Hope,
" John ⎭ of Devizes
Ballard, Mrs., *o'wise* Benson
Ball, Richard, of Gaunton

Ballantine, Agnes } cousins of Jane Crookhill, of
" Janet } Manchester
Balls, Elizabeth, of Suffolk
Bank, John, of Edinburgh
Banks, Charles, of Kent
Bannister, Clementina, of Norwich
" Edward
Banks, John, shoemaker, Suffolk
Barber, Caroline, *o'wise* Reynolds
Barclay, John, of Scotland
Barby, Edwin V., seaman
Barfoot, Samuel, nephew to Robert
Barlow, Mr., of Beaumont Street
Barker, Mr., of Cheshunt, 1818
" Mr. } of New Square,
" Miss } Minories
" Mary, of Elston
" Sarah } daughters of
" Ann } Sarah Burns
" Thomas B., of Hull
Barber, W. H., solicitor
Barlow, Sarah, of Hull
" Sarah, of Brighton
" Francis, of Bedford-square
Barford, John Richard
Barnard, Charles } of Sussex
" Richard }
Barnes, David, corporal 16th Regt.
" William, of Edgeware-road
" Alice, *dau.* of William
" Eleanor
Barnes Family
" Robert, of Bermondsey 1856
Barnett, Sarah, housekeeper
" John L., of London
" John G., of London
Barnes, Wm., of Woking
Bardsley, William, of Nottingham
Baron Family
Barr, Sophia C. } nephew and niece of
" Chas. G. } H. Barr, of Suffolk
" Hugh, of Paisley N B
Barratt, Elizabeth Jane
Barrett, Samuel, of London
Barrow, John P., of Somerset
Barry, Augustus, of 14th or 16th Reg
" Mrs. Elizabeth
" Jacobus } descendants of W.
" Elizabeth } Beauchamp
" Mary, *frmly* Grimes
" Henry, Esq.
Barter, Mary } daughter of Henry B.
" Jane } of Dorset
Barton, Mary, daughter of James
Bartlett, Rosamond

Bartlett William, of Weymouth
" Elizabeth, niece of J. Cullen
Barton, Esther, cousin of T. Craven
Baskell, Mrs. Juana, of London
Batson, John, son of Alice
Bateman, Diana
Batley, Mary, *o'wise* Gordon
Baltham, James, solicitor's clerk
Bate, James, servant
Baton, D., native of Scotland
Bathies, William, native of Dublin
Bateman, James, solicitor
Bathe, Anne, of Drayton
Baxter, Alexander, of Lancashire
" Mary, *o'wise* Timmons
Bawdon, John, attorney, Somerset
Baynes, Mary, *o'wise* Shanley
Bayley, Mary, servant
Baylee, Henry H., of Limerick
Baynton, Sarah, legatee of J. Truss
Baynes, Robert, of Bishop's Stortford
Badkin, Richard, enlisted 1825
Beazley, Thomas
Beagley, Helen, of Oxford Street
Beesley, James, of Turville Bucks
Bellamy, George L.
Benson, Wm., of Liverpool
Beecham, William, of Dover
Bell, William, of Brompton 1844
" W. H., seaman
" E. Mr., ship surgeon
" John, of Northamptonshire
" William G., commission agent
" James, went to Sydney 1853
" James, of Ripon
" Christopher, son of Thomas
" Joseph Copeland
Besley, James, son of Thomas
Beaumont, Edward, of London
Beamish, Francis, seaman
Bellamy, John, *frmly* of Derby
Beasley, Alfred
Beaumont, Sarah, *frmly* Scott
Beyer, Mary, *dau.* of Charles
Bennett, Martin
" Elizabeth
" John }
" Elizabeth } legatees of Ann
" Sarah } Bennett,
" Mary } of Norwich
" Thomas }
" David H., of Notts
" James, son of Andrew
" John, left London 1841
" Rebecca, of Leicestershire
Berriman, George

108 LEGATEES

Beard, Charles, carpenter
Berrey, Sarah, *dau.* of G. Anderson
" James ⎱ of Idle, near
" Thomas ⎰ Bradford
Beltman, Vincent
Bernard, Hewitt
Beck, William, groom
Beaumont, Francis, of Liverpool 1837
Beck, Isaac, of Birmingham
Bear, Mary, legatee of M. Portis
Beard, Thomas
" Lieut. John, H E I C S
Beard, Abel, mariner
Belk, George, of Yorkshire
" Hannah, sister to Wm.
Bealson, Mrs. Mary, living 1811
Benjamin, John
Beaumont, Thomas, of Shropshire
Beale, Fanny J., spinster
Bevie, John W., of Cheltenham
Benedick, Maria, of Regent Circus
Bently, Edward, of Runwell
Bellamy, Elizabeth, of Yorkshire
Beeson, Thomas, of Leicester
Bennedy, Mark
Beeching, James
Berridge, Thomas, farmer 1861
Best, William, of Louth, Lincoln
" Sarah, sister of William
Bigot, Miss H., teacher of drawing
Bissett, Ann, *frmly* Wheeler
Binns, William, of Sheffield
Biggs, Ann ⎱ legatees of
" Bryant ⎰ James Trowbridge
Bishop, Thomas C., of Berks
" Hannah ⎱ sisters of Thos., of
" Elbth. ⎰ Manchester
Billingham, Robert, of Scarboro'
Birmingham, Lieut. John W., Army
Birley, Sarah A., of Australia
Birkenshaw, Nathaniel C., of Oxford
Bickerstaff, Richard, son of John
Bingley, Catharine, *frmly* Milner
Bisney, Sarah, *dau.* of William
Bilding, Sarah, *o'wise* Lewis
Bignell, George, of Tunbridge Wells
Bishop, Mary, servant
Bickersteth, David, of Scotland
Bird, William, son of Susannah
" William ⎱ of Devonshire
" Bridget ⎰
" Mr., of Mortlake, Surrey
Bishop, Robert W., of London
Birch, William, went abroad 1800
Bishop, John O., of Bushey
Blunden, Susanna, of Surrey

Blakely, Robert, of Belfast
Blackall, Charles, of Berkshire
Black, James L., of Edinburgh
Bloy, Louisa, of Marylebone
Blackbone, John H. P., of Essex
Black, Margaret, *frmly* Coventry
Blyth, Lloyd
Blackbourne, T.
Blanchard, Elizabeth
Blomely, Thomas, of Gateshead 1840
Blain, William, of Galloway
Bland, Richard
Blair, Richard, son of Alexander
Blunt, Jane, servant to J. Stockdale
Blake, John, brother to Mary
Blackburn, Joshua, of Huddersfield
Bown, John, native of Notts
Boast, William, left Yorkshire 1858
Booth, Elizabeth, nurse
Bodgers, Mr., banker of Ludlow
Bowness, G. H., son of Rev. Dr. B—.
Bostock, Peter, of Cheshire
Box, John, proctor, Doctors' Commons
Bond, Joseph, of London
Bowren, Amelia, daughter of Jessie
Bosser, Rev. William, late of Durham
Bonner, Emily, servant
Bothwell, William, of Halifax
Bousfield, Richard P., of London
Booth, William Henry
Bowles, Lydia, of Essex
Booth, Jas. R. ⎱ grandchil. of Jere'h,
" Elbth. ⎰ of Croydon
Boulton, Chas. ⎱ nephews and niece
" Wm. ⎰ of Henry B—, of
" Margt. ⎰ Piccadilly
Bothamley, Emma, servant
Boyton, Michael, of Dover
Boyd, William, son of Cathcart
Bowman, Joseph, of Cumberland
Boys, Mary S., *frmly* Preston
Boniton, Francis, sen.
Boulton, Robert, merchant 1835
Bonny, James, of Lancashire
Bodley, George, of East Sheen
Bockett, John W., of Bloomsbury
Bowker, —, Family
Bowman, Joseph, of Penrith
Boydell, Thomas, of Shropshire
Boyd, William, sadler, &c.
Booth James, servant
Bradley, James, of Leicester
Bray, James, valet
Braithwaite, Samuel, brother to Robt.
Bradbury, William ⎱ of Staffordshire
" Thomas ⎰

ADVERTISEMENTS. 109

Braden, Sarah, sister to James
Bradley, James, grandson of Walter
Brady, Matthew, of Bermondsey 1834
Braden, Sarah, of Bucks
Bray, Philip, native of Winchelsea
Bramwell, Stephen ⎫ sons of Geo.
" George ⎬ of Pilsley,
" Thomas ⎭ Derbyshire.
Branscombe, Fred. went abroad 1856
Bradford, Louisa, widow
Bratt, Ann
Brett, Edw. W. ⎫ brothers, *frmly* in
" Wm. J. ⎭ or near London
Bretland Family, of London
Breton, Elial E., of London
Brennand, Benjamin, of Yorkshire
Brennan, Ann, of Romford
" Margaret, *frmly* Slinger
Brenan, Jeremiah ⎫ mariners, left
" John R. ⎬ Dublin 1837-40
" James ⎭
Brittain, Harriett, of Southwark
Bridgeland, Elizabeth, Hackney
Brittain, Susan, of Cambridgeshire
Brough, Mary ⎫ of Greenwich, Kent
" Ann ⎭
Brooks, John ⎫ of London 1810
" Elbth. ⎭
Brooke, Sarah A. *frmly* Harrison
Bromley, Andrew, of Whitechapel
Bromett, John W., of Jamaica 1820
Brodie, James, of Cambridge
Broom, Frances
Brough, W. P. of Laughterton
Brooks, Mr. Reuben
Broomley, Charles, of Corsham Wilts
Brock, Thos. ⎫ left home about 1850,
" Geo. ⎭ aged 5 and 3 years
Bromley, Jeremiah
" Benjamin
" Henry
Brookman, Susannah
Brotherton, John, of Warwick
Bromhead, Benjamin, son of John
Broad, Mary, *dau.* of Thomas
Brookfield, Ann, *frmly* of London
Brooks, Jane, Birmingham
Broad, Charles, gardener
Brown, John E. of Melbourne 1854
" Mrs. of Germany
" Mary Ann
" John, of Finchley
" David, brother to Lady Molesworth
" Sarah, of Sheffield
" Thomas, son of John

Brown, Thos., son of Thos. & Sarah
" Mary, of Suffolk
" John
" Ebenezer, left Leith 1809
" George, of Strathaven
" John, went abroad 1817
" Mary S. *frmly* Goode
" George, seaman
" John, native of Wilts
" Robt.,went to Australia 1858
" Samuel, of Derbyshire
" James ⎫ sons of Samuel, of
" John ⎭ Banwell
" Joseph, of London
" Edward, son of Anthony
" James ⎫ of London 1831
" George ⎭
" Robert, of London
" Agnes, *frmly* M'Whinnie
" Mary, *frmly* Hall
" John, of Manchester
Browne, Dr. James
Browning, Thomas, of Whitstable
Brownall, Robert C., of Stepney
Brownlows, Charles, of Oxford
Bryant, Joseph, went to Tasmania
Brunwin, Ann, of Essex
Bryant, Helen, of Stamford Hill
Brumby, Thomas, of Yorkshire
Burt, John, son of Jas. of Kingsland
Bullock, Peter, of Whitechapel
Butler, James
Burdett, James ⎫ brothers of Wm.,
" Phillip ⎭ of Middlesex
Butler, Mrs. Rosa
Bullen, William, hatter, London
Burns, John, son of Cornet B—
Burchett Family, of London
Burton, Wm. C. of Hyde Park
Buckmaster,William, of London 1824
Buchanan, Jane, niece of H. Lundie
Burnett, John W., of Jamaica 1820
Budd, Charles, left England 1836
Buxton, Miss, of Manchester
Butt, Mr. of London 1818
Burrows, Edward T. ⎫
" Dennis ⎬ children of
" Mary A. C. ⎬ Dennis,
" Eropa P. ⎬ who was
" Ann P. ⎬ married
" William P. ⎬ 1726
" John ⎭
Bush, George, native of Martinique
Burgess, Mr. James
Burns, Robert, *frmly* of Belfast
Burnes, Mrs. Sarah

LEGATEES

Burd, John, of Devonshire
Buckland, Thomas, tailor
Bullin, Penelope, of Spitalfields 1835
Burtt, John, coachman
Burdon, Sarah, *dau.* of Joseph
Button, Mary, of Woodchurch, Kent
Bull, Mrs., of Southampton
Butler, Mary
Burrows, Mrs., *w* of John
Burch, John, of Mersham, Kent
Buchanan, William, of London and Glasgow
Burt, Robert William, of Sussex
" James, of Sussex
Burnham, William, tailor
Burgess, James, clerk
Bufton, Ann, servant to J. Stockdale
Burgon, Mary } *daus.* of Joseph B—
" Hanh. } and nieces of H.
" Ann } Minskip
Busleman, Jane, of Kennington 1835
Burke, Mrs. D. of Ireland
Buxton, Jane, *dau.* of Mrs. Mortimore
Burnell, Ann, *frmly* Jenkins
Burke, Thomas } sons of Elizabeth
" Patrick } B—, of Dublin
Burnham, John D., of Yorkshire
Burt, John, of London 1835
Butler, H. H., of Clapham 1834
" Edward, of Cheltenham
Bull, William, brother to James
Butt, Elizabeth E. A., of Colne
Butler, Thos., of Soho and Australia
Butt, Miss, of Houghton, Hants
Bywell, Vincent, of Southwark, 1836
Byfield, Elbth. } children of
" Mary } James B—, of
" Hannah } Pentonville 1804
Bowman, John } sons of John,
" Joseph } of Sarking
Bourson, Anthony
Brunt, Isaac, of Exeter
Battams, Ann

C

Cahil, Patrick, of Scotland
Callard, Charles, went to Australia
Caldwell, Benjamin, ship engineer
Caink, Edward, of Oswestry
Callow, John, brother to Mary
Calder, William, mariner
Callow, John, baker, Worcestershire
Campbell, Douglas, seaman
" Mr. of New York
" Jean, of Argyleshire, N B

Campbell, Mary, of Montserrat
" C., servant to Lady Kerr
" Colin, of Dumbartonshire
" Constantia, *w* of Alex.
" Wellesley, of H E I C S
Cannock, Charles
Canny, Matthew F., born Ireland 1810
Carus, William, of Lancashire
Carpenter, James, brother to Daniel
" Thos., nephew to Daniel
Cardy, Mary, of Peckham
Carley, John, working jeweller
Carr, James T., surgeon, H E I C S
" George } of Newcastle-upon-
" Mary } tyne
Carter, Mary
" Eliza, of Bethnal-green
" F., of Middlesex Hospital 1832
" Alfred, of London 1837
" John, tanner
" Joshua } of London 1800
" Samuel }
Cartwright, Sarah, of Nottingham
" Matthew, of Philadelphia
Cartledge, Frederick, of Yorkshire
Carr, George, of Suffolk
Cary, Henry, of Piccadilly
Carson, Isabella, of Australia
Cass, Mary, of Yorkshire
Cassons, Ann, *o'wise* Kitchens
Cassidy, Geo. H., son of Alexander
Cartwright, John, of Warrington
Caltober, Martha, *frmly* Slight
Chamberlayne, R. John, waiter
Chambers, William C., seaman
" Samuel, of Dumfries
Charles, Richard } carpenters, sons
" Robert } of Richard C—,
" William } of Dublin
Charrison, Thomas, steward R N
Chapman, George, of Middlesex
" M. A., *frmly* Langhorne
" Thomas
Chapple, William, trunkmaker
Chadley, Sarah, of High Wycombe
Chaddock, William, of Cheshire
Chawnor, Mr., of Manchester
Chandlers, Fanny, of Suffolk
Chalmers, Robert K., of N B
Charles, Thomas, of Devon
Charters, James, of Ireland
Cheston, Rev. J. B., of Gloucester
Cherrey, Ann, *w* of John
Cheeseman, John } sons of John
" Chas. J. } of Deptford
Checkley, William, of Swansea

ADVERTISEMENTS. 111

Chinton, George, of Kensington
Child, Anthony, servant
" John A., of Romsey
Chilmain, Thos. } brother and sister
" Jane } to Frances
Cheeseman, Kate, *dau.* of W. Hughes
Choak, Charles, brother of Caroline
Christmas, John, of Ockham, Surrey
Chidcot, Sarah, of Bristol
Churchman, Mrs. Charlotte
Church, Thomas } children of
" Mary J. } George C—, of
" Jane J. } Northamptonsh'e
Chumley, Martha, of London 1819
Clark, James } children of
" Ann } Edward C—
" Mrs. Hannah
" Ann } of Stepney
" James }
" William, of Spitalfields
" Elizabeth, wife of Samuel
" George, builder
" Robert, of Stepney
" Catherine, wife of William
" John, of Yorkshire
Clarke, Mrs. Ann, of North Brixton
" Simon, Esq.
Clare, Ann, legatee of W. H. Vincent
Clayter, Mary, of Horsham, Sussex
" George } grandchildren of
" Matilda } Wm.,of Horsham
Clavering, William A.
Clayton, Edward, of Worcestershire
" David, of Lincolnshire
Clewer, John } sons of Mrs. C—,
" Edw. } who *d* Madras 1829
Cleveland, Sarah, of Kent
Clement, Richard, of Plumstead
Clifford, Charles F., of H E I C S
Clipson, William, of Westminster
Cobley, Elizabeth
Cobb, Ellen, native of Chichester
" Phœbe, of Kent
Cobson, George, of California
Cock, George, grocer, Plymouth
Cocker, Joseph, of Derby
Coe, George, of Acton, Suffolk
" Thos. Jno., went to Australia
Coglan, Elizabeth A.
Cole, Ann, of Lincolnshire
" Wm., servant to Lady Arden
Coles, Thomas J., of London
" George, of the Royal Artillery
" Ann, of Burley, Hants
" Sarah, *o'wise* Hawks
Collins, Edmund, clerk, Stockport

Collins, Wm., of Westergate, Sussex
" Omar, son of William
" Mr., of Berks and Oxon
Collier, James, 22nd Dragoons
Collard, Charles, of Chelsea
Collison, Charles, baker
Collett, Charles, servant
" Frederick, of Ipswich
Coleman, Harriett, servant
" Sarah A.
" Fanny
" Charles
Coles, Dan. neph.of LucyWhitworth
Colville, Josiah Henry
Cooper, George, of Preston
" George, of California 1856
" George, of Skelton
" James Henry
" Emma
" John, of Misterton, Notts
" Susannah, of Walworth
" Mrs., *w* of Dr. John
" Sarah, *frmly* Harrison
Cooler, Samuel
Cook, George, of Byfleet, Surrey
" Mr., of Swindon, Wilts
" William, of Northampton
" Jane, of Byfleet, Surrey
Cooke, Jane, of Shoreham
" Mrs. Mary
" C. J., of Regent's Park 1838
Corner, James, of Scotland
Cowper, — Family of, Dorset
Coombs, Alfred, solicitor
Cox, George, *alias* Oxford George
Corgan, Teresa, of Cheltenham
Cousens, J., tailor, London
Cox, James, servant to Mr. Curling
Cornish, W. B., of Exeter
" Benjamin
" Daniel
" William
" Charles
" Benjamin
" Mary
Cornish, Harry, of Deptford
Conolly, Valentine
Cowley, Stephen, of Warwickshire
Constable, Mrs. Elizabeth
Cox, Mary A.
" Jane
" Wm., nephew to Mrs. Flower
" Richard, of Hobart-town
" Maria S., Pimlico
" William M., schoolmaster
Coupland, Walter

LEGATEES

Coventry, Andrew } bro. & sisters
" Catharine } of Charles,
" Margaret } of Glasgow
" Elbth., legatee of J. Truss
Cotton, Sarah, legatee of B. St. John
Cotterell, Thomas, of Bloomsbury
" Sarah J.
" Phillis P.
Coy, John, druggist, of Royston
Compton, Mrs., of Camberwell
Constantine, Martha
Cornwall, Ann, of Dublin
Corson, Elizabeth, *o'wise* Ross
Cornelia, John B.
" James
" Mary
Constable, Joseph, of Manchester
Corney, Elizabeth, of Pentonville
Coulter, John, of Brandon
Coultart, W. R., architect
Coupland, Agnes, *o'wise* Whitbrook
Cowell, Mr., grocer, Richmond
Craynes, John, of Winchester 1841
Crawford, Elizabeth, of Shorne Kent
Crane, Thomas, of Chester
Crawford, Miss
" John, of Durham 1830
" Charles, seaman
" C. C., sister to H. Lundie
Crabtree, James, of Yorkshire
Craddock, Richard, son of Capt. C—
Creed, William, jun., tailor
Crew, Robert
Crease, E. M. H. married Ed. Turner
Crisp, William, of North America
Crick, Mrs., of London
Cross, Horatio, of the West Indies
Crossley, Mrs., *dau.* of J. M. King
Crowe, Wm., professor of language
Cross, David, footman 1840
Crook, James R., of Brixton
Croyle, Charles, of Dorset
Crout, James, of Lambeth
Crouch, William }
" John }
" Thomas } nephews of
" James } Samuel Crouch
" Edward }
" Stephen }
Crossland, Thomas, of Rotherham
Cross, Sarah, *o'wise* Marsden
Crooks, Rebecca, *frmly* Farley
Crowley, James, of Brandon
Curling, Thomas } sons of William
" William } of Shadwell
Curline, James

Currie, James, baker, Scotland
" George T., seaman N B
Curren, Michael, of Belfast
Curtis, John, of Ryall, Lincoln
Cuthbert, Rev. Dr. W., of Middlesex
Curtis, James, of Kent
Cubbin, Sarah, of Hants
Curtis, Dorothy, of Walworth 1850
Cutting, Sarah, daughter of John
Cundrie, Ellen }
" Mattie } sisters to Isabella
" Jane } C—, of Liverpool
" Wm., brother of Isabella
" Ann
" Mattie
" Christopher } nephews of
" William } Isabella
Curteis, George, of Norfolk
Curd, Frederick G., of Gravesend
Cunningham, Susannah, of Ireland
Cavell, Thomas, of Deal
Clifford, Susan } children of Thomas
" Maria } and Maria, of
" John } Walworth, Surrey

D

Dale, James, of Scarborough
" Sarah, of Baddingham
Dalton, Mrs., of Chelsea
" Sophia
Dallimore, Ann, *o'wise* Williams
Daniel, John S., of Lambeth
" Mr. S. of Bethnal Green 1851
Daubidon, Samuel, of Manchester
Daffs, Mrs. Eliza, of Yorkshire
Davies, Elb'th, daughter of William
" Alfred, *frmly* of Preston
" David, of Enfield
Davis, John, of Luton, Beds
" Henry, clerk
" Thomas, of Reading
" Joseph, native of Shropshire
" John William, of Cork
" Eliza, legatee of J. Clark
" Herbert, engraver
Davison, James, of Chelsea
" John, of Durham
Dawes, Elizabeth, servant
Davy, Thomas, joiner
Dawson, Thomas, of E I C S
" Mary, of Lancashire
" William, of London 1825
" Mary, of Westmoreland
Debell, John } natives of Corn-
" William } wall

ADVERTISEMENTS. 113

Dewer, John, of Dublin
Dew, Sarah } of Albany street,
" Mary } Regent's Park
Dell, Mary, daughter of Mary
Dent, Lydia, servant
Deards, William, of London
Devaux, Mrs. Maria
Dean, Mary, *frmly* Pendry
Dewell, Francis, of Suffolk
Dewe, Henry, left England 1844
De Granville, Edw'd, of Sunderland
Denny, Louisa, of Hampshire
Dennison, Mary, servant
Dennis, Edward, of Waltham Abbey
Digby, James, of Devonshire
Dibden, Stephen
Dickson, William B., of Shrewsbury
Ditchburn, Margaret, niece of John
Dixon, George, grocer, Coventry
Digby, John R. } chil. of William,
" Anne E. } of Sudbury
Dix, Sarah, *o'wise* Hurst
Dickinson, John, nephew to Elzb'th
Dickens, Elizabeth, *frmly* Thomson
Dix, Elizabeth, daughter of J. Plant
Dixon, George, builder, Marylebone
Dickson, Jane, servant
Dimbley, Sarah, went abroad
Dobbs, William L., ship's steward
Doherty, Elizabeth
Douglas, William, seaman
" Alexander, of Devon
" Eliza, of Soho 1820
" Thomas
" Mr.
" Gordon, went abroad 1847
Dobson, John, son of Richard
Donnell, Mary, *frmly* Marony
Dore, Joseph } sons of John D——
" Richard } of Notts
Dodd, James, of Lambeth
" David } legatees of H.
" John } Dodd
" Edmund
" Blanchy
" Rachael
Dodsworth, Thomas, of London 1837
Dowley, Thomas, farmer of Plaistow
Downie, John, of Lincoln College
Dossett, Edward D. S.
Doyle, Michael, footman 1812
Doone, Anne, of Romford, Essex
Dolman, William, of Boulogne
Downham, Joseph, of Basinstoke
Dolan, Sarah, sister to Maria C. D.
Draper, Thomas, son of Samuel

Drinkwater, Mary, *dau.* of Samuel
Drinkwater,—, nurse
Draper, William, seaman 1860
Drummond, Francis P., of Marylebone
Duke, Henry }
" William } chil. of Sarah D—.
" Mary }
Dugdale, Thomas
" John B.
Dunlop, James, of Russell-sq.
Duckett, Thomas, of Yorkshire
Dutton, Mary
Dunn, Harriet, daughter of Thomas
Dudgeon, Susannah, Leicester 1848
Duberly, Elizabeth, of London 1832
Dunstan, John, of London
Dunham, Samuel A., L.L.D.
Dunbar, John } chil. of William, of
" Sarah } Bloomsbury
Dunsdale, Henry, of London
Dychoff, Henry } sons of Sarah
" William } and William

E

Eade, Mary, *frm'y* Thrower
Eason, Charles, seaman
Easton, William, of Bermondsey
Eden, John, of Pimlico
Edmond, Robert, of Derby
Edwards, John, of Liverpool
" Wm., of Gloucestershire
East, Sam'l, of Mile-end, Middlesex
Egan, Terence C. J.
Elland, Richard
Eldridge, Fanny, servant
" James, of Spitalfields
" Henry, left England 1830
Elgin, Eliza, *frmly* Parsons
Elder, James, native of Scotland
Elkins, Francis, of Hanbury
Ellis, Hugh, brother to Mrs. Scott
" Joseph, J., of Worcester
" Robert } from
" Henry } Aberdare
" Joseph, went to Tasmania 1854
" Thomas, brother to Joseph
Emmins, George, son of Betsy
English, John } of
" Joseph } Whittlesey
" Emma, daughter of Robert
England, Ann S., London
Endacott, John, of Jersey
Erskine, Samuel H., of N B
Escott, Ann, of Dorsetshire

Estell, Regent H., seaman
Evans, —, of Kidderminster
" George ⎫ children of George
" Martha ⎬ of Lambeth
" Mrs., housekeeper
" George ⎫ father and
" Charles ⎬ brothers of
" Thomas ⎪ George, who died
" John ⎭ in Australia
" Mary ⎫ daughters of Mr. E—,
" Ann ⎭ of London
Eve, William H., went abroad 1851
Everett, Elizabeth, Romford
Emery, Mary, of Hoxton 1828
Eyles, Charlotte, *dau.* of Admiral E—

F

Farr, Alex. W., midshipman 1852
Fawcett, Elizabeth, of Whitby
Fairclough, Henry, of Sunderland
Fairweather, William, of Yorkshire
Fairclough, W. H., of London
Fallon, Margaret, wife of Henry
Facer, Charlotte ⎫ of Warwick
" Thomas ⎭
Fayle, William, of Ireland
Farquar, Mrs. Christian
Faulkner, James, of Lingfield, Surrey
Felton, Robert, of Salisbury
Fetwell, William, of Hayes
Fenton, James, of Lenton
Ferguson, John, of Exeter
" Samuel D., of Kennington
Fearnhead, Mr., of Cheshunt 1818
Ferris, Charles, of Kent
Feley, Maria, native of Galway
Feint, Gaspar, of Guernsey
Finlay, Archer, of America
Fidler, Isaac, of Islington
Field, Sarah, servant
" Henrietta, *dau.* of Frances A.
" Augusta
Fielder, Mr., brother to Joseph
Fitzgerald, Charles, of Limerick
Finch, Caroline, milliner
Fischer, George E., of Hanover
Firman, William
Firth, Mrs. Martha, of Idle
Findlay, John, shoemaker
Finlay, James, of Dalston
Flavell, Henry, of Warwickshire
Flemming, W. T., of Exeter
Fletcher, George, of Yorkshire
Flint, Leonard, of Yorkshire
" George, of Northumberland

Fletcher, David, clerk
" John ⎫
" James ⎬ children of
" Roger ⎪ Esther F. and
" Richard ⎪ nephews and
" Joseph ⎬ nieces of
" William ⎪ Hannah
" Jones ⎪ Minskip, of
" Elbth. ⎪ Doncaster
" Hannah ⎭
Floyd, Joseph, of Nuneaton
Ford, Benjamin, of Kew
Forbes, Mrs., of Kennington
Forman, Wm., of Walworth, Surrey
Fogg, Robert W., of Bedford-row
Folderoy, Thomas, of Shropshire
Foster, Mary
" Ann, of Stockton-on-Tees
" Jane, *dau.* of John
Forde, Arthur Brownlow
Forey, Lieut. Samuel
Foster, W. C., native of Kent
Forman, William, brother of John
Forster, George, of Norfolk
Forrest, William, of Norwood
Forsham, Elizabeth, of Liverpool
Foreman, Thos. serv't. to J.Stockwell
Foot, Berkely ⎫ sons of Matthew,
" Frederick ⎭ of Wicklow
Foster, James ⎫ sons of Thomas, of
" Henry ⎭ Thames Ditton.
Foy, Mrs.
Fowle, James, servant
Fox, Miss S., of Exmouth 1856
" Mrs. Jane, of Yorkshire
Fowler, Mary, servant 1828
Fox, Charles, of Wiltshire
Fraser, Jane, legatee of D.McPherson
Franklin, Mary, *w* of William
" Maria H.
Francis, Thomas, of Whilcot
" Phillip, of Kerry
" Elizabeth, *dau.* of Philip
" Jane, sister to Vincent
Frazier, Miss., *dau.* of Simon
Frazer, Archd. C., of West Indies
Fraser, —, Family
" James, of Limehouse
Freeman, Robert, of Norwich
" J., solicitor's clerk 1857
Freborn, Martha ⎫ sisters to Emma
" Caroline ⎭ Williams
Free, Mr., Accountant
French, James, of Limehouse
Frost, George, of Yorkshire
" Samuel, of Shoreditch

ADVERTISEMENTS.   115

Fryer, John ⎫ of Long Crendon,
"   William ⎭   Bucks
Furze, Mr., of London 1818
Funnell, Edward, courier
Frant, Joseph S., of Leeds

G

Gane, Ann, of Salisbury
Garland, Susan, servant
Gardner, William, servant
"   Richard, of Mincing-lane
"   Thomas, butcher, Tasmania
Gardiner, Charles ⎫ of St. Martin's-
"   Sarah   ⎭   lane, 1845
Garlic, Lawrence
"   Mary
Garnick, Wm., commercial traveller
Garton, John, of Pointon-Few
Gartside, James, of Oldham
Garrod, John, servant
Gaiger, George, of Sparsholt
Gaynor, Joseph, of Ireland
Gelder, William, brother to Mary
Geary, William, of Nuneaton
Gerrish, Rebecca, *dau.* of R. Lee
Gernon, James, of Dublin
George, John, of Worcestershire
Gibbs, Jennings, of Kent
"   William, of Canterbury
"   Cecilia, niece of F. Lippincott
"   John, of Bromley, Kent
"   Charles
Gibbins, Ann, *o'wise* O'Donnell
Gibson, Richard, of Lancaster
"   James
"   Alexander ⎫ children of
"   Christian ⎬ Thomas G.,
"   Helen   ⎨ of Potwood,
"   Thomas   ⎭ Peebleshire
"   Charlotte M., of Deptford
"   Fanny ⎫ daughters of John,
"   Ellen ⎭   of London
"   Nicholas, of North America
"   Sarah, *o'wise* Race
Gibbons, William, mariner, of N B
Gilpin, Richard, legatee of Mary G—
Gill, Frederick, of Devonshire
"   Ann, *dau.* of John
"   Thomas, solicitor
Gillett, Mary, of Wilts
Gillman, Charlotte, *o'wise* Solman
Gillam, Thomas, footman
Giles, John, servant
"   George, nephew of John
Glover, Henry S., of Brighton

Glover, William, of Reading
Glue, Sarah, servant
Goble, William, native of Kent
Goff, William, chemist
Godman, Christopher, solicitor
Godbee, James, of London
Golton, Olivia, of Stepney
Golding, William, of Cheapside 1839
Gollond, Maria
Gollshead, Mrs.
Gooch, Matthew
"   Ann
Goodson, William, nephew of Joseph
Goode, John ⎫
"   Henry   ⎬ nephews and
"   Susannah ⎨ nieces of
"   Ambrose ⎨ Edward G., of
"   Hannah   ⎨ Cambridge,
"   Henry   ⎨ who died
"   Samuel   ⎨ 1815
"   Mary S. ⎭
Goodall, Edward ⎫ hotel kpr. *frmly*
"   Caroline   ⎭ of Sheffield
Gordon, George, nephew of C. Goode
"   John H. ⎫ of Regent's Park
"   Mrs.   ⎭ 1840
"   Mrs. G., *frmly* Bushman
"   Miss Eleanor E.
"   George, naval officer
"   William, of Seymour Street
Gorringe, Thomas, of Kentish Town
Gove, George, of Bloomsbury
Gould, Edward
Gostelove, —, Family of, Dorset
Grace, Henry ⎫ descendants of the
"   Jane   ⎭ brothers and sisters
Grange, Joseph, of Hoxton
Graham, William, of Dundee police
"   Jane, *o'wise* Clark
"   Ann, *frmly* Ausdall
"   Susannah
Grant, Robert, surgeon, Kilkenny
Gray, Paul, of Yorkshire
"   David F., of West Indies
"   Allan, Esq.
"   Maria, servant 1852
"   Elijah ⎫ of March,
"   William ⎭   Cambridge
Graystone, Sarah, *frmly* Thurston
Graves, Dr. J. W., of Brompton
"   James, native of Woolwich
Green, Susan, of Lincolnshire
"   Hannah, servant to Lady Kerr
"   Emily, wife of Litchfield
"   Rebecca ⎫ of Ryall, Lincoln
"   Sarah   ⎭

116 LEGATEES

Green, William, of Brigham
Greening, Joseph H., of Chester
Greenwood, Henry, of Grantham
Greenfield, Isabella, *dau.* of Alexand'r
Greig, Philip H., son of Dr. G—
Gregory, Charles } of London
" William } 1847
" Richard B., surgeon
" Thomas, of Hanwell 1824
" Edward, carver, etc.
" Thomas R., son of Thomas
Grier, Robert, of Carlisle
" Margaret, *o'wise* Little
" Ann, *o'wise* Nisbett
Griffies, John } nephews of W.
" William } White, of Sutton
Griffin, James, farmer
Griffiths, Ann, niece of Mrs. Davis
" Henry C., of America 1854
Griggs, John B., of Diss, Norfolk
Grigge, Mrs. C., of Calcutta
Grisdale, Matthew, of Whitehaven
Groom, Richard, of London
Grosse, Joseph
Grocock, William H., son of Hannah
Grogan, Thomas, publican
Groome, Susannah E.
Grimshaw, William
Grubb, Mary, *frmly* Cooper
Grubin, Mrs., of Pimlico
Grubb, Thos., of Porchester
Gulley, James, of Gloucestershire
Gunston, Mary, of Kennington
" Emily } sisters to Letitia
" Harriet } Hart, of Dublin
Guthrie, William } of Worcester-
" Jane } shir.
Gunn, Edward, of Wivenhoe, Essex
Gunnis, Elizabeth, *dau.* of Edward
Guest, William V., of London 1851
Gwynne, Thomas T. } chil. of Thos.
" Mary Ann } of Shropshire
Giles, H., of Notting-hill

H

Hackett, William, of Oxford
Hague, Thomas)
" John } natives of Cornwall
" Lucy)
Haines, Elbth., niece of E. Lonquisty
Hall, John C., master-mariner
" James } nephew and niece of
" Elizabh. } George H., of York
" Eliza, Miss, of Grantham
" John

Hall, Mary Ann, of Bedfordshire
" Geo. sen., of Kingsland-road
" James } natives of Sussex
" William }
Halder, Mr., of London 1839
Hamblin, Maria
Hammond, Oliver, seaman, 1854
" Geo., brother of Richard
" Jas., of West Chillington
Hamilton, Mary Ann, servant
Hampton, Mary A., of Netherton
Hanson, John) children of
" Thomas } William, of Bow
" Elizabth }
" William } brothers of Jas.,
" George } of Lichfield
" Fanny, *dau.* of George
Hance, Henry
Hankins, Thomas, of Kenningt'n 1856
Hankin, Geo., nephew to C. Kendrick
Hancock, Fanny, of Devonport
Hanson, Mr. J., architect
Handover, Louisa, of Staines
Harbour, John) children of Sarah,
" Sarah } of Suffolk
Harding, Louisa, wife of Charles
Hares Matthew, of Tasmania 1846
Harden, Mr. Thomas
Harland, Edward, of South Molton st
Harding, Samuel, of Somerset
Harby, Philip, of Leicestershire
Harrington, Eudocia, *frmly* Shee
" Martha
" Thomas, of Nottingham
Harris, Charles R., carver, &c
" Charles)
" James } of Gloucestershire
" William)
" Sarah, of Hants
" Thomas, of Hackney
" John T., of Islington
Harrison, Sarah A., *o'wise* Brooke
" John, of London
" Emma, of Edinburgh
" Samuel, of Drury-lane
" Josiah, sen.)
" Josiah, jun. | of South-
" William } wark,
" Eliza Jane | Surrey
" Sarah)
" Charles, of Yorkshire
Hart, Mrs. Letitia } of Dublin
" Mr. Thomas } 1798
" Roach D., went to Australia
" Charles, native of Stafford
" Reuben, of Portsmouth

ADVERTISEMENTS. 117

Hart, Henry, of London
" James, of Barking
Harwood, John, son of George
Harriott, Robert Edward
Hastie, Hastie, of Alnwick
" Charles, of Calcutta
Hatching, Robert, of Manchester
Hawarden, Edward, of Somerset
Hawkins, Eliza, lived *frmly* in Hants
" Charles, of Kingston
" Thomas, son of Henry
" Family, of Herts
" Thomas } nephew & niece
" Ann } of E. Lonquisty
Hawson, Thomas, of H E I C S
Hawton, Joseph, of Sherrington
Hayden, William, of Camberwell
Hays, William, of Pimlico 1844
Hayward, W. C., of Bermuda
" James, of Poole
" John W. or children
" Phœbe, *o'wise* Boyes
" Jane, *o'wise* Wake
" Benj. } child. of Benj. T.
" Elbth. } H.—, of London
Hayes, Henry } chil. of Henry and
" Fredk. } Margaret H., of
" Louisa } London
Haynes, Benjamin
Hayley, George, of the Kent-road
" Mrs., of Brighton
Haywood, Charles, of Pentonville
Hayman, Edward, of Deal
Haynes, Sarah, native of Battersea
Hayes, Henry, of London
Hayton, Margaret
Haslock, William
Hazel, William, of Suffolk
Harvey, Robert, merchant 1800
Healey, Michael, of Southwark
" John, of Holborn
Heald, Patty } legatees of W. H.
Heath, Richard } Vincent
Heard —, Family
Hearne, Charles H., seaman
" Mrs. Algernon J.
Hebditch, John, of Limehouse
Hedge, Capt., of New York
Hellman, John, of Plymouth
Hellyer, Sarah, *o'wise* Watson
Hedges, David, of Farrington
Hemming, —, Family, of Berks
Henderson, James, of Liverpool
" George, brother to Eliz'h
" John, of London
" John, of Glasgow

Henderson, Francis E.
Henshaw, Ann, went to America
Henvill, Edward, son of Rev. P. H.—
Herbert, Tyrell, Esq., of Antigua
" Edward, of Australia
" George of Coleford 1844
" Thomas M., of Birmingham
Heslitt, Mrs. S., of Hounslow
Hewling, George, of Jersey
Hewson, Richard, of St. John's-wood
Hewett, John, of Lymington
" Mary } nephew and niece
" Joseph } of J. Osbaldston
Hewitt, Miss, of Somers-town 1852
Hewett, John } natives of Devon,
" William } went abroad
Hewlett, Emma, of Stepney
Heywood, Mary A., of Mayfair
Hesse, Mr. D. E., of Ludgate-hill
Hicks, Ann, *w* of Finsbury
Higgs, Charles, of Worthing
" Ann, of Oxfordshire
Higgins, Joshua, of Cheshire
Hickson, John B., of Derbyshire
Hildreth, William, of Newcastle
Hilliard, or Hillyard, attorney
Hill, Thomas, of Suffolk
" Allan, of Bedfordshire
" Thomas, of Derby
" Margaret, of Queen street
" Eliza, *w* of Thomas
" Esther, *o'wise* Plaskett
" Mary, of Newport Salop
Hills, W. S., of Lewisham, Kent
Hilton, Lieut. G. A.
Hinsley Fred.
Hindman, Harriett, of Suffolk
Hippisley, Captain, of Dorset
Hirst, Henry J., of Masbro'
Hoile, Isaac, corn merchant
Holmes, Clara
Holloway, —, servant to Lady Kerr
Hodgeman, Elizabeth
Hodgskin, Phœbe, of Bucks
Hodgson, Miles, of Rochdale
Holland, John, builder
Hodgkinson, Geo., of Aldersgate st.
Holloway, John, clerk
Hodgman, Alex'dr M., of Ramsgate
Hocken, Edward, commercial trav'r
Hockley, Leonora, servant
Hollins, Francis A.
Holt, Charlotte, *w* of George
Hoghen, Emma M. M. A., of Kent
Holdsworth, Abraham, of London
Hodson, Ann Elizabeth, of Hull

LEGATEES

Holmes, James, solicitor
Hoggar, William
" Mary
Hobbs, Thomas, seaman
Hodges, Samuel, of Euston-road
Hoad, Edmund, son of Thomas
Hodgkin, Charles, seaman
Holgate, Caroline, *daug.* of George
Holbrook, George, of Chester
Hodson, Stephen, tailor
Hoar, Eleanor, *o'wise* Clark
Holland, Isaac, of Wilts
Holdsworth, John H. of Bayswater
Holt, William J. of Grantham
Horah, Mrs. Sarah, *w* of Major H.
Horne, Mr., baker, Brixton
Horborne, Edward, of Solihull
Hope, John, of Edinburgh
Hopkinson, George } of
 " Isabella } Liverpool
Hoslee, John, of Sudbury 1820
Horton, Mary A., *o'wise* Hawkins
 " Henry, went abroad 1842
Houghton, Thomas, of Norfolk
Houston, Miss Innes
Hopkins, Elizabeth, *o'wise* Smith
How, Mr., of London 1818
Howard, George, of Yorkshire
 " Catherine, *frmly* Symons
 " Thomas, of Knutsford
 " Reuben, son of R. H.—
 " Wm., of Drury-lane 1832
 " Edward J., of Brompton
Howe, Baldwin W., of Kent
Howie, James, seaman 1853
Howell, Mary } of Pembroke-
 " William } shire
Howlan, Timothy, seaman London
Howes, William, native of Oxford
Howison, Archibald, of Falkirk, N B
Hoyle, James
Hopkins, Harriet, of Southwark
Horwood, John } of
 " Elzbth. } Aylesbury
Hoffman, Elbth. *dau.* of Capt. F. H—
Hughes, Chas. of 77th Regt. of Foot
Hudson, William } of
 " Mary } Nottingham
Husband, Arthur, of Fifeshire
Hutchinson, Edward, of Leith
Hunter, Robert, of Edinburgh
Hurst, Sarah, *o'wise* Dix
Hutton, Mrs. S., of Northumberland
Hunt, Ellen, of Shepherd's Bush
Hussman, Peter, seaman 1854?
Hutchinson, John, of Birkenshaw

Hughes, John T. } both in
 " Ellen } Australia
 " Sarah A., *o'wise* Birley
 " Ann, *o'wise* Jenkins
Hurst, George, of Kingston-on-Hull
Hunter, Ann
 " John, solicitor 1837
Hutton, Mrs. M., servant
Hutchinson, Betty, of Preston
Huntley, William, of Ecclescliffe
Hughes, Thomas, clerk 1840
Humphreys, Rebec., of Sittingbourne
Hunter, Henry, of London
 " Jane, of Nettleton-court
Hutchinson, Elbth., of London 1839
Hughes, Thomas W., of Islington
 " Eliza, *o'wise* Elgie
Hurst, Henry, of Yorkshire
Hughes, John, of Gloucester
Hurry, William, of Romford
Humphreys, Nathaniel, of Antigua
Hurt, Frederick, hosier, London
Hulond, Frederick, of Bath
Hughes, Ellen M., of Somerset
Hurst, Mrs. Emma, of Melbourne
Huson, T. or E., of Halford
Huggins, R., of Water lane 1850
Hutchinson, Thomas, servant
Huckin, Charles, brother to Henry
Hudson, George, of Yorkshire
 " Sarah, *o'wise* Smith
Hawkesley, John W., carpenter

I

Impleton, Thomas, of Hornsey
Ingall, Edward, of Gravesend 1842
Inge, Edward, of Coventry
 " John R., of Scarborough
Ingram, Adam, of Roxburgh
Innell, Mrs. Mary
Innes, Christiana, of Ross-shire
 " Geo. J. W. } legatees of W.
 " James } H. Vincent, Esq.
 " Louisa, of Ceylon
 " Robert D., of Canada
 " James L. }
 " John T. } of Mexico
 " Claude A. }
 " Lewis C., of Madras
Inskip, Louisa, of London 1854-6
Ireson, Elizabeth
Ironmonger, David, of America 1845
Irwin, Mr., of Hampstead
 " Selina, *dau.* of James

Isaacs, Mrs. Ann, of Whitechapel
Ivery, Ann, of Lambeth

J

Jackson, James, seaman, Poplar
" Mrs. Mary
" George ⎫ brother and sisters
" Ann ⎬ of John
" Sarah ⎭
Jack, Alex., native of Perthshire
Jacob, Abraham, seaman
" Charles, coachman
" Elizabeth S., of Pottern, Wilts
Jackson, Jno., heir-at-law of Sampson
James, Harriett, of Regent street
" John, of London 1805
" Amelia, servant
Jacobs, John ⎫ formerly of
" William ⎭ Chelsea
Jaffray, Thomas, of Dublin
Jagger, John ⎫ sons of John and
" Joseph ⎭ Mary
Jarvis, W. Henry, of Hanway street
Jardine David, of Plymouth
Jarratt, John, of Monmouthshire
Jayes, Elizabeth, of Southwark
Jefferey, Eliza, of London and Exeter
Jefferies, John, of Somerset
Jeffreys, Ann, wife of John
Jeffrey, William, of Rotherithe
Jeffries, Thos., of Romford, Essex
Jenkins, Ann, wife of Robert
" William, schoolmaster, R N
" William, of Australia
Jephcott, Thomas, of Willoughby
Jepson, Mrs., of Manchester
Johnson, John, steward
" Edward W., of the H E I C S
" Mary, of Worcester
" Geo., of 12th Regt. of Foot
" James, of Vauxhall
" Mrs. Ann, of Sussex
" William
" Elizabeth
" Sarah, legatee of Mr. Gilpin
" Joseph L., of Yorkshire
" Eliza ⎫ relatives of Miss
" Wm. R. ⎭ Leigh
" Eliza G. of Kennington 1859
" Harriett, of Notting-hill
" Sarah, daughter of Harriett
" Mrs. Elizabeth, of Edgeware road
" Dr. Edward
" Thomas, of Macclesfield
" Thomas, of Southwark 1838

Johnson, John, heir-at-law of Daniel
" Thomas B., son of Francis
Johnstone, Robert, of Finsbury
" C.J.C., left England 1844
Jones, John ⎫ of Clerkenwell
" William ⎭ 1830
" Fanny, servant
" Mrs., of Clerkenwell
" Edward, of London
" Thomas, of Clerkenwell 1832
" Benjamin, son of Henry
" Jane, of Fleet street
" Jane, *frmly* Castleman
" Eleanor, of Southwark 1824
" Margaret, *o'wise* Wilcox
" Mary A., legatee of Mrs. Cortisos
" William, of Iscoyed
" Fanny, of Kidderminster 1833
" James, of Warrington
" Arthur B., of Manchester
" George, of Notting-hill
" William, son of John
" Francis ⎫ cousins of Elbth.
" Harriett ⎭ Lawrence
" William S., of Bagshot
Jordon, James
Joslin, Mrs. Caroline, of Canada
Jowsey, Fanny
Joyce, Rev. Jeremiah
Jupe, Mary, of Mere, Wilts
Judson, Mrs., *w* of Thomas
Julian, Robert, of Beccles

K

Kay, Thomas, of Brookshaw
" B., Esq., of Sydney, 1853
" James, native of Scotland
Kaye, John, of Netherton
" John ⎫ clothdressers of
" William ⎬ Yorkshire
" Peter ⎭
Keate, George, legatee of Jno. Truss
Kearnes, John, traveller
Keene, Hannah, *frmly* Thurston
Keep, William, native of Welwyn
Keen, Mrs., of Stratford-place
" Alice, laundry-maid
Keegan, William, of Surrey 1812
Kelly, Ann, native of Kildare
" Samuel, seaman
Keeler, Vincent
" Richard
" George
Kelsey, Ruth

120 LEGATEES

Kemp, William, of Egham, Surrey
Kendall, John P., of Marylebone
Kendrick, James, of Edgeware road
Kenknight, William } of Cliffe, Kent
" Mary
Kennett, Henry, of Dover
Kennedy, Angus
Kenny, Edward
" Anna B.
Kerr, James, of London, 1844
Keymer, Charlotte E., of Suffolk
Kibbey, W., son of W. C. K—
Kilvington, John | legatees of Ann
" Ann | Orfeur
King, Mary Ann Chapman
" John, of Norfolk
" John, of Sudbury
" Jane, cousin of Mary Smith
" Elizabeth, of London
" Mary, of Somerset
" Mary, of Suffolk
" Thomas A., of Greenwich
" William, of Wiltshire
" Samuel, son of Serjeant K—
" Mary A., of Tasmania
Kingsbury, Phœbe, w, Marylebone
Kingsworth, W.M., nephew of Thos.
Kingsley, John, of Bedforshire
Kinsley, W. B. } sons of Wm. K—
" Edward
Kinsman, Robert J.
" Susan O. B.
Kirley, Mrs. Elizabeth
Kirksep, John
Kirby, John, left Plymouth 1833
Kitchin, James L., of Guernsey
" Ann, frmly Cassons
Kittrick, Thomas, of Brompton
Knight, Richard, of Cork
" John, servant
Knowles, John, of Isle of Wight
" Thomas, seaman
Knox, Mary, of Hoxton 1828

L

Labrum, Robert
" George
" Charles
Lacey, Mary A., frmly Sherwin
" Thomas, seaman
Lait, Matilda, of Gloucestershire
Lambert, William, son of James
" Rebecca, of Ramsgate
Lamb, Thomas, solicitor
" Charles

Lane, Sophia, niece of J. Wilson
Langworth, Robert, of Pentonville
Lanigan, Stephen
" Anne } daus. of Stephen
" Maria F. } of Brighton
Lane, Ann, frmly Walsam
" Penelope
Lake, John, purser 1814
Lavery, Catherine, of Brussels 1864
Lavington, Mrs., of Staines
Larrard, Charles, of Croydon
Lavis, Elizabeth, frmly Brown
Law, John, of New Zealand 1859
" Robert C., of Bristol
" Thomas, of Stoke Newington
Lawrence, John
" William } of Bethnal-
" Mary A. } green
" Sarah
Lawrey, Mary, of Kendal
Lawson, Agnes, wife of Dr. L—
Lawton, George, of Dorset
Laxton, Ann } daus. of Thomas
" Mary L—, of Everton
" Sarah } Beds.
Lay, Emma, of Southwark
Leake, Thomas
Leatherbarrow, Thos., of Manchester
Lea, Benjamin, of Alcester
Leake, John, left home 1858
Leairs Charles, J.M., of Birmingham
Lebbey, Agnes } servants
" Elizabeth
Ledicott, William, hatter 1840
Ledwick, William
" Evan } legatees of Vin-
" Martha } cent Francis, of
" Hannah } Camden-town
Ledger, John } children of Sarah
" Henry L—, of Here-
" Sarah } fordshire
Lee, Agnes, frmly Scott
" Isabella, of London 1852
" Charles D., of Bilston
" William, of Wandsworth
Leeks, James, of Suffolk
Leedham, George T., of Coventry
Legg, John } of Burford-bridge
" Sarah }
Legget, John, seaman
Leigh, Robert, seaman
" Family
Lennon, Patrick S., of Ireland
Leomain, William C., Esq.
Levick, Elizabeth, of Norfolk
" George, of Clayworth

ADVERTISEMENTS.   121

Lewis, W. A. D., of Basingstoke
" Hannah, servant
" William C., of Worcester
" Mary, aged 50
Letsom, George
Lewthwaite, John, son of Thomas
Leppard, Ann, sister to Edward
Leslie, W. W., native of Edinburgh
" Henry, master-mariner
Lethbridge, G., of Portsea
Lindsey, Charles, of Westminster
Livock, Sarah Ann, servant
Lightfoot, Trefina, *dau.* of John
Lingham, George A.
Little, John, of London
Lipscombe, Geo., M.D., of Southwark
Lipcombe, Charles, of Hants
Linay, William, of Orkney
Lindsay, John } of London 1843
" Mary }
Little, Margaret, of Lockerbie, N B
Lloyd, Richard, of Shrewsbury
" William, of Salt Lake City
" Joseph, of Worcestershire
Lockier, William, of Gloucestershire
Lockett, Mary D., wife of John
Lockwood, George, of Lincoln
Longlands, Alexander
Long, George, of Ramsgate
" Jane, *o'wise* Nettleford
Lore, Maria, of Vauxhall
Lourie, —, Family, of London
Loudon, —, Family
Lovett, John W., Madras Artillery
Lovatt, Thomas, of Manchester
" Mary, of Piccadilly
Lovejoy, Cassandra, *frmly* Burton
Lowe, Charles, of Stratford-on-Avon
" Mary A., *o'wise* Pike
Loxdall, William
Luce, Lawrence
Lucas, Harriett, of Portsea 1811
" Maria, of Finsbury
Luckhurst, Lucy
Luke, Dennis
Ludlam, George, of Leicester
Lyle, William, left Edinburgh 1840
Lyrick, Hannah, *frmly* Cooper
Lyon, Gordon, went to India 1820
Lyford, Richard, of Egham, Surrey
Lyons, Solomon, of Newport

M

McAlpine, John, seaman
McAffee, Joseph, of Tipperary

McClung, James, *frmly* of Ayr, N B
McCormack, Edward, tailor 1837
McColl, James II. } *frmly* of South
" Agnes } Shields, Dur-
" Jane } ham, late of
" Mary } Australia
McCullock, John, neph. of J. Thomson
McDonald, Donald, son of Alexander
McDougal, Joseph, Edinburgh
McDrummond, Mrs. of Brighton
McGowan, Robert, of Jamaica
McGaw, Peter, son of James
McGregor, Christian
" Margaret
McIntyre, Miss, of Liverpool
McKay, John, of Scotland, seaman
McKinlay, William, of 80th Regt.
McKeene, Maxwell
McKellar, James, of Glasgow
McKenzie, Isabella, *frmly* Clarkson
McLaren, Robert, nephew of James
McLaughton, Archibald, living 1800
McLeod, Mary, of Lambeth
" Gordon, went abroad 1363
" Angus, of Scotland
McMullon, Thomas, of Ludlow
McNair, —, of London 1812
McPherson, Jane, legatee of Duncan
McVane, William, of Ireland
Macdonald, B. R., seaman
" Daniel, son of James
Maclean, James, of Wicklow
Mackay, James, went to Australia
" Murdock, Mr.
" Geo. } sons of Angus M—
" James } of Islington
" Mary A. } *daus.* of Angus
" James }
Macaulay, Robert, plumber, Lincoln
Mackenzie, Lilias, *dau.* of Col. A. M—
Macgregor, Grieg, engineer, of N B
Macfarlane, Louisa, *dau.* of Andrew
Mackley, Mary, of Rotherhithe
Macquire, Alexander, of Drury-lane
Macey, George, of Ramsgate
Machell, Henry, of Yorkshire
Madden, Capt. Lewis, of R. Marines
Maddeford, Edward, of London 1832
Mainwaring, Chas. son of Admiral M.
Malone, Thomas, traveller
Mallyon, William B., of Ramsgate
Malyn, John, surgeon, Westminster
Mann, Thomas, mariner
" Robert, private, 10th Hussars
" James, of Edinburgh 1840
" William, of Cumberland

LEGATEES

Manning, Jacob L.
Maitland, John, of London
Manners, Thos., of West India Regt.
Maney, James
" George C.
Manvell, Jesse, native of Surrey
March, William, of Whetstone
Martin, Robert John, clerk
" Robert A., of Galway
" Anna M., of Westminster
" Louisa
" William, French cook
" John, of Dorsetshire
" Maria Ann
" Thomas J., from America
Marsh, John, of Chelmsford
" Ann, *frmly* Betts
Marshall, William, of Holland 1844
" Charles, of 72nd Regt.
" John, brother to William
" Henry, seaman
" Mr., tailor 1818
" Vine W.
Marriott, Joseph, of Coventry
Morley, William, painter
Markham, —, Family
Marsden, Sarah, *frmly* Cross
Marks, Mr., of Kent-road 1849
Martell, Marvina, of Paris
Marsh, Mary A., servant 1852
Massey, Harriett, of Green street
" Ann, *frmly* Riley
Mason, Sarah, of Bury St. Edmunds
" Mr., of London 1818
" Charlotte, servant
" Boulton, of London
Massey, Elizabeth, *frmly* Watson
Masson, John, merchant, London
Matthews, Charles ⎫ sons of John,
" Thomas ⎭ of Kent
" Martha, servant
" Henry
" George, baker 1834
" Robert, son of Edward
" Elizabeth, servant
Mathieson, John L., of Dumfries
Mathison, Farquhar
Maundrell, Thomas
Mauldon, Frederick, of Brixton
Maude, Mary A., of Camberwell
Maver, Mary, of Brixton
Mawor, William, of Boston, Lincoln
Mawle, Frederick ⎫ child. of Thomas
" Maria C. ⎬ and Martha, of
" Louisa A. ⎭ Chelsea
Mapham, Elizabeth, cook

Mayne, Mary ⎫
" Catherine ⎬ sisters of Philip
" Martha ⎭ M—, of Berks
Mealing, William, of Suffolk
Mead, Elizabeth, servant 1845
Measey, Mary A., *dau.* of Thomas
Mears, Thomas, of Shropshire
Manley, Benjamin ⎫
" Richard ⎬ ch. of Jeremiah
" Priscilla ⎬ M—, of Liverp'l
" Jane ⎭
Meade, Jno. R., of Dublin and London
Meachem, James, seaman
Medwell, Daniel
Medland, Henry, nephew of William
Mellish, Russell ⎫ railway guards
" William ⎭
Menzies, James
Meredith, Joseph, of Hereford 1823
Metcalfe, Henry B. ⎫
" B. W. A. ⎬ sons of Joseph
" Mary, *dau.* of John
Messinck, Elizabeth
Middleton, Mrs., of Blackheath
" Jane, of Gravesend
" Charles, seaman 1823
" Hannah
Michell, George ⎫
" Harriett ⎬ legatees of Mary
" Mary ⎭ Waller
Milne, John
" Stewart, of Dalston
Miller, James, of Clerkenwell
" Charles G., native of N B
" John, Rev.
" James, merchant 1811
" Mrs. Walter, of Highgate
" Boyde, of Castle-court
" John
" Charles
" Wm. ⎫ of Edinburgh, went to
" Philip ⎭ America 1841
" Maria J.
Mills, Charles M. ⎫ chil. of Charlotte
" Susan P. ⎭ E. Mills
" James, of Clerkenwell 1838
Millwood, Phœbe
Milsom, George P.
" Macleod
Minshull, Ellen, milliner 1845
Minet, Reb'ca, native of East Harling
Mitchborn, John, Blunham
Mitchell, John, of Yorkshire
" Mary Ann, servant
" John, of Newfoundland
" Miss Lois, of Stratford

ADVERTISEMENTS.   123

Mitchell, Samuel T. ⎫
"   Christiana ⎬ of Dorsetshire
"   Sarah   ⎭
"   Thos. B., of Adelaide 1849
Mohrink, John   ⎫
"   Joseph ⎬ sons of Thomas
"   George ⎭
Monk, Eliza, *dau.* of Rachel
"   William, of Wilts
Monicke, John T. ⎫
"   Ann   ⎬ bro. and sisters
"   Lucy ⎬ of John M—, of
"   Eliza ⎭ Clerkenwell
Montgomery, Rich'd, of Hampstead
Morgan, Louisa
"   James ⎫
"   Henry ⎬ seamen
"   David, of Brecon
"   Elizabeth ⎫
"   Charles   ⎬ of Hoxton
"   James, of Hereford
"   Philip, private 5th Reg. Foot
"   James, went to America
"   William, native of Portsea
"   Benjamin, of Holborn
Morgue, Fulcrand, of London
Morley, Jemima, servant
Morris, Ann, *dau.* of William
"   Caroline, sister to Valentine
"   Miss Ann, of Chelsea
"   W. W., of London
"   Mary A., born at Bletchington
"   William, brother of M. A—
"   Jane, of the *Blue Anchor* tav.
"   Lieut. Peter, R N
Morrison, Howard, in California
"   Janet, of Blantyre
"   Mary, *dau.* of Morris
"   Arthur D., clerk
Morrisette, Mrs.
"   Janetta J.
Morrow, John, son of Thomas
Morgan, Wm., brother to Capt. M—
Mortimer, Ellen, of St. John's-wood
Moriarty, Miss Elizabeth
Mordaunt, Mary, niece of John
Moor, William, coachman
Moore, Lieut. Henry, 41st Regt.
"   Benjamin, of Clerkenwell
"   Emma, of Hendon 1830
"   Agnes, of Nelson-square 1835
"   Ann, of High Wycombe
"   John, servant 1828
"   Philip, of Hants
"   Rich'd, legatee of Mrs. Turner
"   Ann, *frmly* Hearne

Moore, John, of Belfast
Moody, James, of Wellington, Salop
Mottram, Henry C., of Clerkenwell
Moseley, Mrs. ⎫ *w* & *dau.* of Richard
"   Ann   ⎭ of Shoreditch
Moget, James, of Harling
Moseley, Joseph, of Brighton
Mullen, Bridget, *o'wise* Crisham
Murray, Francis, son of Patrick
"   William, of Isle of Wight
Mullins, Elizabeth, *frmly* Norris
"   Mary, *dau.* of Ellen
Murrell, William, of Higham
Mullard, William, of Knighton
Mullen, John
Munton, Charles
Muldoon, Patrick, wine merchant
Murrell, Dinah, *w* 1840
Munro, William, of London 1840
Munday, Edwin H., of Chippenham
"   Mrs., of Dorsetshire
Muller, Mary
Murray, Margaret
Murphy, W. S., of North America

N

Naine, Mrs., of Gravesend
Nalder, Francis W., of Melksham
Nash, William, of Egham, Surrey
Naylor, Robert, of Leeds.
Neal, William ⎫ brothers of Robert,
"   John   ⎬ who died in
"   Jeremiah ⎭ Australia
Neate, Eliza, of Bristol
Needham, Jane, Somers-town
Nelson, Joseph, of Peckham-rye
Nepecker, Mrs.
Nettleship, Edward, chemist
Newman, John, of Coventry
"   Mrs., of Chelsea
"   Margaret
"   Hannah
Newnham, Barbara, *dau.* of John
Newton, James, shoemaker, Notts
"   Geo., joiner, Camden-town
"   H. C., of St. John's-wood
Nichols, Martha, of London 1819
"   Mary, of Norfolk
Nicholson, Ann, wife of James
"   Robert, of London
"   Thomas, of Walhampton
Nisbet, Ann, of Carlisle
Niven, John, of London 1829

124 LEGATEES

Nixon, William
" Ann, servant 1859
Noble, Mr., brother to George
" John, of "Lloyd's"
Noad, John, of Bath 1851
Noon, Maria, of Wimborne
Noonan, Mrs. E., of Dublin
Norris, Alexander, seaman
North, George, of Southampton 1836
Norton, Louisa
Nunn, Edmund ⎫ sons of George N-,
" George ⎬ Trinity Pilot,
" John ⎭ Aldeburgh

O

Oakley, Jane, of Hoxton
" Charles, of Whitechapel
O'Dwyer, William ⎫ born in France
" George ⎬ abt. 1790, went
" Richard ⎭ to America
Odell, John, or his sister
Odlum, Lieut. Abraham
Oliphant, Benjamin ⎫ natives of Shet-
" Gideon ⎭ land
Olliver, John, of Acton 1841
" James, of the Blockade service
Ollivant, Thomas, merchant, London
Onslow, E., of Calcutta 1850
Ogilvy, Lady, w of Sir William
O'Reilly, Patrick
Osbaldston, Adam, cousin of John
Orton, Private William, Artillery
Oriel, Henry, seaman
Osborn, George, married Miss Cook
" James ⎫ chil. of John O., of
" Elbth. ⎬ Tylehurst
" Ann ⎫
" Charles ⎬ chil. of Edward O.
" Edward ⎬ of Tylehurst,
" Obed. ⎬ who died 1808
" Thomas ⎭
Osborne, Lucinda C., frmly Humphrey
" Isabella
" Georgina
Outlaw, Thomas, of Northampton
Ovenden, Elbth., of Clerkenwell
Overman, Jacob, of Whitechapel
Owen, William, of Ridinghouse-lane
" Private John, 60th Rifles
" Harvey ⎫ children of Hugh
" Margaret ⎬
" David, son of Rev. Jeremiah
Orchard, Frederick, of Cheshire

P

Pacey, Barbara, native of Worcester
Page, Alfred, of Danbury, Essex
" Thomas E., clerk
" Samuel, mariner
Paine, Maria, of Vauxhall
" Jane, legatee of J. Stockdale
Palmer, Leonard G. ⎫
" Frederick W. ⎬ of Tasmania
" Mary Ann ⎭
" Henry, of Camden Town
" Mr. R., of Furnival's Inn
" Henry, of Clifton
" Matilda, of Banffshire
Parker, Benjamin ⎫ of Barley,
" Frederick ⎭ Hants
" Willmot, solicitor
" William, of London 1838
" Anthony, brother to Charles
" George W., of Bayswater
" William, mariner, R N
" Agnes, wife of Dr. Lawson
" Christopher M.
Parkinson, Robert
Parker, John, joiner, Glasgow
Parrock, Jane, native of Wales
Parry, Richard, mariner
" Richard, son of R. C. P—
" Richard, of Greenwich
Parsons, Mary Ann, of Pimlico, 1864
" Eliza, o'wise Elgie
" John, gasfitter, Marylebone
Passmore, William
Pascoe, James, of Plymouth
Patchett, Henry ⎫ went to America
" Sarah ⎭
Paterson, Alfred, of Lambeth
" Charles, of Stranraer
Patterson, William, of Dublin
" Thomas, of Edinburgh
" Thomas, of Alnwick
" N.H., seaman, Edinburgh
" William, clerk
" Thomas, gardener
" John, tailor
Patton, Mr., of Bridport
Paxton, Joseph, landing-waiter H MC
Payne, Maria
" Rebecca, servant, Pimlico
" Joseph, of Kingston, Surrey
" Walter, shoemaker, Glo'ster
Peacock, Eliza A., went to America
" Samuel, of Sheffield
" James, of Glasgow
Fearce, Jane E., of Hackney

ADVERTISEMENTS. 125

Pearson, Joseph, of Cumberland
" Charles, of Walworth
" James, went to Australia
" John
Pears, George, of London
Pelder, W.L., nephew of Sir John P—
Pelham, Mr.
Pemberton, Benjamin, of Walsall
" William, son of William
" William, son of Thomas
Penny, W. J. H., of Tasmania 1836
Penton, Thos., surgeon, Kennington
Pendrill, —, Family
Penny, Charles
Pepper, Sarah, of London
Peppin, William H., of Dulverton
Percival, Thomas } of Hereford
" Susan }
Perfect, Thomas, son of William
Perry, Elizabeth, wife of Thomas
Perryman, Peter, of ship "Regard"
Peto, Joseph } chil. of William, of
" Mary A. } Surrey
Petchel, William, of Lincolnshire
Peterkin, Alexander, of Edinburgh
Peters, Henry R., of Bristol
Phelan, Sarah, servant
Pheasey, Joseph, of Wolverhampton
Phibbs, Richard, of Bushey, Herts
Phillips, Charles J., of Herefordshire
" Nathaniel, of Marylebone
" Thomas, valet
" John, shipkeeper
" Jacob, carpenter
Phipps, Olivia, o'wise Dallas
Pilcher, Capt., of the merchant service
" Mrs., wife of Captain P—
Pilgrim, Elizabeth, o'wise Johnson
Pirie, George, of Rotherhithe
Pierce, James
" Jane
" John
" Elizabeth } children of
" Mary } William and
" Stephen } Sarah P.
" Thomas
" William
Pitt, George, of Twyford, Hants
Place, D. M. M. C. H. G.
Plant, John } of Derbyshire
" Mary }
Plaskett, Esther, w of William
Plasterer, William A., of Pentonville
Plumb, Mar
Potterton, Thomas, of America
Pollard, Edward, of Gould-square

Ponsford, James, of London
Porter, Ellen, o'wise Faby
Powell, John, of Dublin
Porter, Cath., legatee of John Truss
" John, son of Caleb
" John, of Bandon
" Mary, Mrs.
" Thomas, mariner
" Charlotte
Poulton, Robert, of Bedfordshire
" Mary, sister to Robert
Ponusberry, John, of Taunton
Postle, Henry, native of Norfolk
Prayer Family
Pratt, George, of Newman street
" John, legatee of M. Boreham
" Martha, of Barking
Pratten, Lieut. John } of Margate
" Themor }
Prevost, William
Price, Joseph, solicitor
" Stephen, grandson of S. Bishop
" David, surgeon 1822
" Francis, waiter, Gloucester
" Charles, of Hereford
" Phœbe, maiden name Francis
" Thomas, of Harley, Worcester
" Ann, niece of Samuel
Pridley, William, of Twickenham
Pritchett, Capt.
Pritchard, Jane, actress
" Isaac, of Deal
" James L., of London
Prior, Fanny, servant
" Mr., of Stockwell 1848
Prodgers, Mr., banker, Ludlow
Prosser, Rev. W., late of Durham
" Charles, of Monmouthshire
Pruson, Charles } of Walthamstow
" Sarah }
Pratt, John, native of Sussex
Pryde, James, of Dundee, N B
Purkis, Charles, left Kent 1821
Pugh, Mrs. Edward
Puddifoot, William Charles
Punchard, Mrs. Elizabeth
Purse, George, native of Lyndhurst
Putland, Edward, auctioneer
Puffy, Mrs. Mary, of Hackney
Pugh, William, footman
Pyke, John, of Liverpool
Percy, Mrs., frmly Parish
Perry, James, of Waldringfield

Q

Quincey, John, of Ryal, Lincoln
Quinton, Ann, *frmly* Shepherd
Quick, John, seaman, son of Richard

R

Radclyffe, John
Radford, William, of Bristol
Race, Sarah, *frmly* Gibson
Rapley, James, of Hampshire
Ramsden, Joseph
" Richard, servant
Ravenscroft, Charles } of Jersey
" Sarah }
" Valentine
" Louisa
Rawlings, John, butcher, Newgate
Ray, William, of Edenbridge, Kent
Rayner, Robert S.
" Alfred H.
Read, Richard, brother to Penelope
" William, of Wiltshire
" Charles, grandson of John
" Ezekiel, went to America
Rees, George, surgeon
Reese, William, husband of Jane
Reeves, Elizabeth, of America
Reid, David, of Dumfries
" Daniel, J. of Wolverhampton
" James, legatee of T. Griffith
" William, brother to Walter
Reilly, William A. of Dublin
Renshaw, Ann E. } legatees of
" Jas. R. } Ellen Stedman
Renwick, Thomas, son of David
Reynolds, Catherine, *frmly* Broom
" Francis, of the Strand 1856
" Kitty, of Camberwell
" Francis, of Islington
Rhodes, William, nephew of T. Toole
" Samuel } nephews of
" Richard } Mary Budd
Rhynd, William, seaman
Rich, Mrs., *dau* of Mrs. Whitfield
Richards, John, solicitor
" Catherine, of Bloomsbury
" Richard, of Exeter
" Joel, of West Cowes
" Thomas, of Gloucestershire
" Robert, of Shropshire
Richardson, Thos., left Bucks 1845-6
" John, of Swanbourne
" Samuel, of Kensington

Richardson, William, son of Robert
" Alexander, of Edgeware
" Catherine } lived at
" Robert } Duckett
" Charlotte } 1811
" Mrs. M. of Hackney
" C. S. of Tunbridge
Richbell, Ann, *frmly* Thrower
Riches, Selina, *frmly* Clifford
Rickard, Henry, of Doncaster
Rickcord, John George
Riddock, James, native of Scotland
Rigg, George } of Stokenchurch,
" Eliza } Oxford
Riley, Ann, *o'wise* Massey
Riseburgh, —, Family
Ritchie, Miss, schoolmistress 1854
Riseborough, Robert, mariner
Robert, Miss E., of Camden-town 1854
Roberts, John, of Dublin
" R. J. purser, R N
" John, publican, Hamstead
Robertson, Elizabeth } of London
" Catherine }
" Thomas, of Bloomsbury
" Robert, seaman, Aberdeen
" David, gardener, N B
Robathan, William, son of Ann
Robinson, Joan, of Yorkshire
" John, *frmly* of Kendall
" James, convict in 1830
" Private George, 96th Regt.
" James, brother to Sarah
" Henry, seaman
" William, of Berks
" Frances, niece of John
Robins, Mr. E. T., of London
Robson, Charles, of Boston
Rodgers, Captain John, of Falmouth
Roe, George J., of Tipperary
Rogers, George
" Charles, brother to Henry
" Miss } of Kensington
" Miss Mary } 1816
" Isaac, of London
Rogerson, Mary A., of Manchester
Rolt, Edward C., tutor
Rolls, John, son of Captain R.
Rose, Elizabeth
Ross, William C., of Quebec
" Matilda, of Clapham-road
" William, carpenter, Brentford
" Elizabeth, *frmyl* Corson
" Hugh, of Laing, Sutherland
Root, Charles } of Essex
" Thomas }

ADVERTISEMENTS. 127

Rotheroe, Elizabeth ⎫ sisters
" Winifred ⎭ of Henry
Rotton, Benjamin, of Gloucester
Rowe, Thomas
Rowley, William, went abroad 1790
Rowland, Robert, of Bristol 1838
Ruddock, Hannah, *dau.* of Ann
Ruding, Mrs., of Barnes 1845
Rudland, Robert, of Suffolk
Ruddock, Philip ⎫ of Lopham,
" Joseph ⎭ Suffolk
Rugely, Ann
" Elizabeth
" Frances
" Henry ⎬ brothers and sisters
" Matthew
" Rowland
" Susan
" William
Rulton, Mary, of London 1825
Russell, Ann
" Ann, of Leaham, Kent
Rutherford, George, of Trinidad
Rutledge, Sarah H., *w,* Brighton
Rycroft, Elizabeth, of Yorkshire
Ryves, Miss Jane W.

S

Sabey, Richard, of Ashwell, Herts
Sadler, Elizabeth ⎫ grandchil. of
" Susannah T. ⎭ Sam. Thrower
Saiman, James, gardener 1856-7
Sainsbury, John, of Maida-hill 1861
Salmon, Thomas, of Tasmania
" John
Sanford, James, of London 1825
Sanderson, William, of Wooton, Beds
Sandom, Alice, of South Sea
Salmon, Susannah, of Yorkshire
Sampson, George, of Folkestone
Sarsfield, Patrick, son of Simon
Saunders, Joseph
Savage, John W., son of Capt. J. S.
Scadding, Henry, son of Henry
Scaife, John ⎫ seamen
" William ⎭
Scanlan, Nicholas, sadler, of Ireland
" Jane, wife of Nicholas
Scotes, Elizabeth, *dau.* of Joseph
Scott, Agnes, *o'wise* Lee
" John, brother of Walter
" Paulina, of Edinburgh
" Thomas, son of William
" James, of Beauchamp, N B
" James, servant

Scott, Eleanor, native of Cumberland
" Sarah, *o'wise* Beaumont
" Elizabeth, servant
" John, solicitor's clerk 1835
" Frances M., of Southwark
" James, clerk
Scully, Mr.
Seaton Clara, *o'wise* Wilson
Searle, Hannah, *frmly* Goode
Sextie, John, son of Robert
Sexly, John S., of Dorsetshire
Sedgeley, Hannah F., of Finsbury
Seymour, James, of Canada 1843
" Edward, of London 1808
" Thomas, seaman 1810
Seyton, Elbth., niece of Valentine Morris
Shaw, Ellen, servant
Sharp, Ann, servant 1826
Shaw, Henry, draper
" James, of Ireland
" Mr. William, traveller
Shand, Adam, of Aberdeen
Shanley, Mary, *o'wise* Baynes
Sharp, John F., of Walworth 1846
" John, butcher, Warwick
Sharples, Elizabeth, of Marylebone
Shea, or Shaw, Thomas
Shearn, George, tailor
Sheffield, Elizabeth, of Hampstead
" Charles, of Kingsland
Shelley, William, of London
Sheldon, William, *o'wise* Sherradon
" William, of Stevenage
Shepherd, Thomas, solicitor's clerk
" Robert, of Marylebone
" Henry
" William, glover
Sherwin, Eleanor, of Whitehaven 1856
Sherratt, Dorothy, *dau.* of John
" Samuel, of Macclesfield
Sherrard, —, Family
Sherlock, Sarah Ann
Shipley, Elizabeth
Shiridge, James, cousin of Richard
Shoosmith, George ⎫ of Chichester
" Ellen ⎭
Showbridge, John K., Isle of Man
Shore, George, of Soho
Sibson, James, of Berkeley-square
Sigel, Charles George
Silvester, Ann
Silver, John
Simmons, John, of Wolverhampton
Simons, William, of Cheltenham
Simkins, Charles

Simpson, Elizabeth, of Chelsea
" Ellen, of Chelsea
" Frederick, schoolmaster
" Mrs. Elizabeth
" Thomas, butcher
" John, of Shipborne, Kent
Singer, Luke, son of Hannah
Sims John, of Hackney
" ary, sister to Catherine
" Mr., butler
Singleton, Elbth., of Lincolnshire
Skidmore, John, of Stockwith 1821
Skitter, Stephen H., son of Elizabeth
Skarden, James, of Devonshire
Slater, Joseph, of Stafford
" Charles Henry
" John A., of Ilford, Essex
Sleep, John, of Bath
Slight, Martha, *o'wise* Caltober
Slinger, Margaret ⎫
" Richard ⎬ chil. of Richd. S—
" Stephen ⎭ of Kirby Lonsdale
" Tempest
Small, Thomas, brother to Henry
Smallwood, Mrs. L., of Edgeware-road
Small, Rebecca, of Sittingbourne 1843
Smith, Anthony, H. of Southwark 1833
" Charles, of London 1814
" Charles G., of Oxford
" Elizabeth, Swallowfield
" Edgefield
" Elizabeth, *frmly* Richardson
" Frederick D., mariner
" George, of Southwark 1840
" George, of Aldgate
" George, of Stanton
" Joseph S, of Lincolnshire
" John F., of Stamford street
" James, coachman 1840
" James, of Leith
" Joseph, of Bermuda
" John, of Clapham-road 1850
" John, of Manchester 1838
" Jonathan, brother of Sarah
" John, of London 1807
" John, of Lambeth
" John, *o'wise* J. S. Thompson
" James, livery-stable keeper
" James, of Gateshead 1840
" Janet, of Perth 1837
" John, of Newark-upon-Trent
" Henry, of Blackburn
" Mary, wife of Samuel
" Mrs. wife of Thos. S., seaman
" Mr., of Kingsland-road
" Matilda, cousin of Mary

Smith, Richard, native of Great Stukly
" Richard J., broker
" Richard, of Hants
" Richard
" Rachel, of Camberwell
" Richard, of London 1814
" Samuel, living 1800
" Sarah, of Lincolnshire
" Sarah, *frmly* Hudson
" William
Smithers, John, carpenter
Smythies, Thomas, of Liverpool
Smyth, Martha, of Brompton 1847
Smoult, William, of Newcastle
Snowden, William
Snow, Jeremiah, of Ratcliffe
Somerville, John, of Glasgow
Southern, John, of Durham
Sollom, Ann, of Bermondsey
Soames, Robert, seaman, 1860
Solley, John, of Kent
Somerville, John, of Cumberland
Speirs, Richard, seaman
Spencer, Richard F., of Westminster
" Joseph ⎫ sons of James S—,
" John ⎬ who died 1821
" William ⎫ chil. of William,
" Mary ⎭ of Camden Town
" Mary, sister to Major Sparrow
" Charles, driving master 1821
" Anna M., wife of Charles
" Ann, native of Tottenham
Sparrow, Sarah, of London 1829
Spadie, Charlotte, *dau.* of John
Spiney, John, legatee of Lydia Ward
Spooner, George, of Southwark
Spry, Thomas
Squires, Eliza, of Essex
Stanmore, William, of Berks 1843
Stagol John ⎫
" Jonathan ⎬
" Maria ⎬ chil. of John S—
" Fanny ⎬
" Patty ⎭
Stack, Rose, of Hemel Hempstead
Stapley, Ann, married a gardener
Staples, Ann, of Whitechapel
Stainer, Thomas, of Hull and Louth
Stacey, Thomas, servant
Staples, Charles, *alias* Simmons
Stallion, Henry, tailor, Oxford street
Stevenson, Robert, went abroad 1821
Steel, Mary A., Oxford
Stephhenson, F., of Westminster
Stephens, Alfred, chemist
Steel, Robert L., of Edinburgh

ADVERTISEMENTS.

Stein, Andrew } distillers
"   Charles   } 1814
Stephenson, John A., of London 1794
Stewart, James, legatee of G. Ealand
Stevens, Mary A., of Whitechapel
Stent, Mary, sister to R. Poulton
Stewart, Catherine, of Aberdeen
"   Ann, *dau.* of Catherine
Stephens, James A., of Hendon
"   Henry   } chil. of Henry,
"   Hannah } of Glo'stershire
Stewart, Rev. Henry, of Greenwich
"   Thomas, native of Farnham
Steed, John, civil engineer
Stephen, Thomas, seaman
Steele, Forbes, wife of Charles
Stewart, Mr. Butler
Stirling, Ellen, of London 1845
Stilwell, Richard, of Edmonton
Stenton, Harriet, *w*, United States
Stivens, Sarah, *dau.* of James
Stone, Charles, from Bombay
"   Richard, of Blandford
Stock, Henry, of Woodford
Stone Family
Stonhill, Fred., of Leighton Buzzard
Stockham, Mary A., *o'wise* Wiggins
Stopforth, Richard, of Liverpool 1842
Stockley, Harriett } children of
"   William   } H. S—
Storr, George, brother to Capt. B. S—
Stow, John D. } of London
"   Mary A. } 1859
Stringer, James, of Worcester
Stratton, William, of Durham 1823–4
Stretton, Mary, *dau.* of Peggy Moore
Streatfield, W. } of Clapham Rise
"   H. H.   } 1851
Street, Elizabeth, *dau.* of John
Stroud, Martha, servant
Stratford, Messrs., of Aldborough
Stuart, Robert, merchant 1820
Stewart, Capt. of the "Glendalough"
Stackhouse Family, of Berks
Sutcliffe, Robert, of Lancashire
Sutherland, Emily, *frmly* Tunstall
Sutcliffe, Phillis, legatee of T. Sykes
Sutherland, Capt. Robert
Sullivan, Mary A., servant 1852
Suter, Mrs. Catherine, of Bermondsey
Summers, Lucy, of Somers-town 1819
Swan, Edward, of Norfolk
Sutton, George, draper, of Dublin
Sweetlow, Eliza
Sweet, Luke, chairmaker
Symoms, John, of Plymouth

Sykes, James, nephew of Thomas
Syoms, John, valet
Symonds, John, of Penzance
Southgate, Anne } *daus.* of William,
"   Mary   } of Southwark
Smythe, Mrs., *frmly* Whitelegge
Studholme, Joseph, of Alvechurch

T

Talbot, Sarah, servant
Tannar, Ann, sister of John, baker
Tait, Andrew B., native of Scotland
Target, Emma S., wife of Felix
Tait, James, tin-plate worker
Taite, Elizabeth, servant
Tapp, William, son of Thomas
Tanner, Mr., of London
Tandy, Charles, native of Dublin
Taylor, Louisa M., niece of J. Davis
"   Charlotte } *daus.* of William,
"   Lydia   } of Glo'cestershire
"   W., Esq., of St. Vincent
"   Ebenezer, ship's steward
"   Elizabeth, *frmly* Finigan
"   George, surgeon 1823
"   Ann, of Lambeth
"   Horatio W., of Bristol
"   James } merchants of
"   David } London
"   James, of Winchester
Tetly, Joseph, of Armsley, Leeds
Tebbutt, Thomas, of Smithfield-bars
Tessier, H. P.
Templer, Elizabeth *o'wise* Collins
Teasdale, John, sen. } farmers,
"   John, jun.   } Clifford
Thacker, Francis, of Chiswick 1819
Thomas, Mr., of London 1818
"   Evan, of London
"   William, of Blandford
Thomason, W., son of Hugh
Thompson, Ferdinand R.
"   Mary, wife of Ebenezer
"   Mary, niece of Colin Anderson
Thomson, William, of Hyde Park
"   William, solicitor's clerk
Thorpe, William, of Ash, Kent
"   William, of London 1818
Thrower, Edward   } children of
"   Mary A.   } William T—
"   Susannah   }
"   Mary, *o'wise* Eade
"   Ann, *o'wise* Richbell
"   Samuel   } sons of
"   John   } James T.

Thrower, Jonathan
"   Jonathan, jun.
Thurston, William } children of
"   Sarah } Susannah
"   Hannah } Thrower
Tidd, Thomas, of Barbican
Tiddie, Miss, governess
Tindall, James } sons of Thomas,
"   William } of Hackney
Tinkler, John, of Grantham
Tonks, Mary Ann
Tod, John, of Madras Artillery 1847
" Emma P., wife of John
Todman, Joseph, of Greenwich
Towers, Mrs. } of London
"   John } 1839
Tounton, John, of Lincolnshire
Topham, Mr., surveyor of Stafford
Tomlins, Francis, of London
Togood, —, valet to B. Lee, Esq.
Tomlins, Eleanor H., of N. America
Townley, John } of Northampton-
"   Elbth. } shire
Trinkler, Ann
Trinkhole, George, of Dorsetshire
Tripp, Mr., of Islington
Troyman, Edw., went to Australia
Tredwell, William, of Pentonville
Trotter, William, son of Thomas T—
"   Margaretta }
"   Maria } sisters of
"   Hannah } Thomas T—
"   Mary, niece of Thomas
"   Robert } brothers of
"   William } Thomas
Truss, John } legatees of John
"   Thomas } T—, of Pimlico
"   Thomas, son of Thomas
Turner, Mary } of Gateshead
"   Alice }
"   Joseph M., of Marylebone
"   James, of Green-alley 1827
"   Mark, legatee of M. Turnbull
"   Mrs. E., of Portland-place
"   Thomas, of Epping
"   Charles H., of Kedleston
Turnbull, Charles, coachman
Turnly, James, of Belfast
Tupper, David H., of Brighton
Tugwell, Humphrey, son of Phœbe
Turtle, James, bank manager
Tucker, W. S., married A. Kingsbury
Turvey, Mary, of Redburn
Turner, John, of Oxfordshire
Twedell, Richard, of Calcutta 1807
Tweed, James

U

Underwood, John, son of Matthew
"   Elizabeth, of Witney
"   Eleanor, of Pimlico
"   John } legatees of
"   Francis } E. Stedman
Utting, John, master-mariner

V

Vaile, Martha Morgan Trigg
Varndell, —, Family of, Berks
Vasey, Lawrence
Vallens, William, of Brentford
Varley, Mary A., *dau.* of Cornelius
Vassey, George, of Berkshire
Victor, Charles, went to America
Ventors, Mary C., of Devon
"   M. C., of Tasmania 1849
Vernon, Edward, of Gibraltar
Vevers, John W., of Hackney
Vincent, James, of Thelnetham
"   Mary, sister of James
"   R., of King's Lynn
"   John, of Cecil street, Strand
"   Harriett, *w* of Col. Thomas
Viner, Mary A., barmaid
Vick, John, son of John and Sarah
Vickall, Mr., of Manchester
Victuller, T. H. J., draper, Chatham
Villock, —, Family
Voutier, Mrs., of the Strand 1858

W

Waldby, Isaac, went to sea
Waller, Martin, of Southwark 1855
Wallis, George J., of Ipswich
Wall, Messrs., brothers of Mrs. King
Walsh, Rev. J. R., *frmly* in the army
"   E. A. J., *frmly* an attorney
Walpole, Mary, *dau.* of Elizabeth
Walford, Nathaniel, builder
Walter, John, of Jamaica
Walch, Richard, son of Andrew
Walpole, Joseph } nephews of
"   John } Richard
Wallace, Robert, of Coldstream 1829
Walcott, Elisha, of Canada 1811
Wallis, Peter, surgeon, London
Wallis, Major W. H.
Walter, Ann
"   Matthew, of Hatton Garden
Walsh, —, widow, of Fenchurch st.
"   Henry W., of Kildare
Walker, James, of Falkirk

ADVERTISEMENTS. 131

Walker, Elbth., *dau.* of Richd. of Herts
" Robert, tallow chandler
" Charles, of Marylebone 1811
" Mary } legatees of
" Matilda } W. Herbert
" Ann, native of Notts
" Thos., of Northamptonshire
" William
" Horatio, of Southwark
" William, of Rugby
Wadge, John, of Great Malvern
Waddilove, Jas. R., son of Margaret
Wait, Sarah
" Betsy } children of Jane W.,
" Lucy } of Midhurst, Kent
" Wm.
Wakeman, Robt., grandson of Robt.
Wakerly, Elbth., *frmly* Bissett
Wain, John, of London 1810
Wakeson, Andrew, of Whitehall
Wade, Thomas, butcher, Durham
Ward, Elizabeth, *frmly* Debnell, s
" Ellen, servant
" Eliza, of Pentonville
" Maria, servant, Scotland
Warren, Robert, footman
Warton, Sarah Elbh. *dau.* of Thomas
Watson, George, seaman, Newcastle
" Levi, seaman, Penrith
Watt, James } of Lodge road,
" William } Regent's Park
Watson, James } sons of Capt. W—
" John } who died at sea
" William
" Sarah, *frmly* Hellyer
" Peter, seaman 1854
" William, of Lincolnshire
Watken, Annett P., *frmly* Mount
Watkins, Thomas, of London
Waters, Mrs. M., of Lambeth-road
Watts, Sarah H., wife of Charles
Waylen, Wm., legatee of M. Gilpin
Wells, William, surveyor
West, Caroline, legatee
Weston, James
" Mary
Wells, Joseph D.
Webb, Thomas H.
Wemyss, Edw., of Algoa Bay, Africa
Welch, Sarah, *dau.* of George
West, John, seaman 1841
Weir, Thomas G., mariner, Dundee
Weatherbeatly, Daniel } Worcester-
" Samuel } shire
Weldon, Thomas, tailor
Wells, Gideon, of Gainesborough 1800
Weller, Mary, *dau.* of Mary Jeynes

Wells, Maria A., niece to C. Kendrick
Weaver, Mary A., of King's Cross
West, John } nephews of Moses, of
" Geo. } Colchester
Welch, James, of Dublin 1817
Weller, Ann, governess, Oxford
Wells, Thomas, of Southfleet
" George }
" Neville } of Marylebone
" Miss }
West, —, Family
Westland, —, Family
Weller, Francis, native of Bath
Weston, Matilda, of Lyndhurst, Hants
Wentworth, Edward
Whales, Robert, seaman 1860
Whatmore, Arthur
Whatoff, John, servant
Wheatley, Joseph, legatee of D. Clark
" Charles, of Hammersmith
Wheeler, Daniel, of Twickenham
" brother to M. Bennett
Whelan, Michael, of Ireland
White, James, son of Sophia
" Mary, legatee of J. Morrison
" Mary, *o'wise* Thornton, of Wilts
" Charles
" Thomas, of Sunderland
" John, *alias* Restorick
" Diana, *dau.* of Jane
" W. H., of Rotherhithe 1825
Whitelaw, David, seaman, of Scotland
Whitfield, Geo., nephew of N. White
Whitrow, Richard } brother & sister
" Mary } to Geo., of Ely
Whitewood, William, fireman
Whiting, Patty, legatee of John Truss
Whiche, Mr., of Ashton-under-Lyne
Wheedall, John
" Alice
Whitingdon, George T., merchant
Whitby, Mrs. Sarah, late of Russia
Whitbrook, Chas. } engineer, went to
" Ann } America
Whittaker, Mary, of Falkingham
Wilding, Jeremiah T.
Wildsmith, Sarah, servant
Willard, Horace } sons of Richard, of
" John } Sussex
Williams, William } of the Minories
" Sarah }
" Martha, of Pembrokeshire
" Jas., seaman, Caernarvon
" Hugh, chemist
" Mary } legatees of J.
" John } Truss
" Thomas, son of Sarah

Williams, Henry ⎫
  "   John   ⎬ sons of Samuel,
  "   Thos.   ⎭ of High Holborn
  "   Wm.
  "   Mary, milliner 1845
  "   Arthur, servant
  "   John, of Hereford 1836
  "   Vine, of Canada 1808
  "   John, nephew of J. Wilson
  "   Oliver, of Wolverhampton
  "   Emma, *frmly* Freeborne
  "   Mrs. M. A., of Birmingham
  "   Hyde
  "   Mary J.
  "   Ann, *frmly* Dallimore
Williamson, Elbth., barmaid
Wilkinson, Joseph, of Hull
Wilks, Mrs. Rebecca
Wilmott, John, son of Francis
Willison, F. A., of Chelsea 1847
Wildblood, William, of Yorkshire
Willmott, Sarah, sister to V. Morris
  "   Henry, brother to ditto
  "   Henry, nephew to ditto
  "   Sarah, wife of Henry W—,
Willcox, Mrs., dressmaker 1852
Willey, Joseph A. C.
Wilde, Charles, of Liverpool
Wilkins, Miss
Wild, Charlotte, *frmly* Watts
Wills, Henry, of Carmarthenshire
Wilkinson, Richd., executor of John
Willoughby, Ann, *frmly* Gostelow
Wild, Elbth. S., daughter of Thomas
Wilson, William, son of John
  "   Clara, *o'wise* Seaton
  "   Eleanor E., wife of J. H. W.
  "   William S., baker, Oxford
  "   John, went to Australia
  "   George E., of Westminster
  "   John ⎫ of Yorkshire, went to
  "   Mary ⎬ America
Wiltshire, Lucy   ⎫ legatees of
  "   Ann Mar   ⎬ J. Truss
Withers, Richard   ⎫ of
  "   James   ⎬ Wrexford
Wittingham, Ann, *o'wise* Daunton
  "   Rich. son of Ann S. W—
Winstanley, Mrs. Elbth. and son
Willsteid, W. H. H., of Southsea
Woblett, George, nephew of Charles
Wood, Thomas, of Salford
  "   John, of Scotland
  "   Mrs., *frmly* of Southwark
  "   Henry, of Australia 1820
  "   Matthias, of Barnsley
  "   James, son of Geo., of Glasgow

Wood, Emma, *w* of Edw., of Stepne
Woodward, Thomas, grocer 1834
  "   John, of Winchester
  "   Samuel, of London
Wooden, Frederick S., of Islington
Woodhall, John, of Nottingham
Woodhouse, Joseph
Woods, Thomas F., of Jersey
  "   Mrs. Mary, of Liverpool
Woolley, Thomas, goldsmith, London
Wormald, Eliza, *dau.* of Jane
Wort, Geo. J. T., son of Geo.
Worley, Isaac
  "   Samuel
Worrall, Jane, *dau.* of John
Wolff, Benjamin, of Devon
Worth, James, of Reading
Worsdell, Sarah, went to America
Worvill, George, of Buckingham
Wrack, John, of London
Wright, George, of Broughton
  "   James, of Hayes
  "   Charles, of London
  "   John, merchant, Honduras
  "   James, native of Paisley
  "   Mrs., niece of J. Stockdale
  "   Edward, of Jamaica 1840
  "   Jane S.
  "   Thomas, broker, London
  "   Geo. N., son of Lieut. W—
  "   John, of Peckham 1825
  "   Eliza, of the Harrow-rd. 1854
  "   John, *frmly* of Gower street
Wreford, Rebecca
Wrake, Michael B., seaman
Wrentmore, William W., of Somerset
Wyllie, Miss E. C., *dau.* of Major W.
Wyeth, John, servant, Dulwich
Wyndham, J. C., of Bristol
Wylie, William, son of Robert

Y

Yates, Jas., son of John, of Hanbury
  "   William, of St. Pancras
Yeats, James   ⎫ went abroad
  "   Charles R. ⎭
Youdan, Elizabeth, *frmly* Everett
Young, H. W.
  "   John, of Norfolk
  "   Ann, servant, Leeds
  "   Thomas T., of North America
  "   Thomas, native of Dorchester
  "   John, of Honduras
Youngh, Thomas, of Preston 1826
Yuill, John, native of Glasgow
Yule, Sarah, *dau.* of Mary Milnes

INTESTATES.

THE FOLLOWING PERSONS HAVE DIED INTESTATE (SINCE THE YEAR 1840) IN AUSTRALIA, NEW ZEALAND, TASMANIA, BRITISH GUIANA, NORTH AMERICA, AND THE CAPE OF GOOD HOPE.

A

Abbott, William
Adams, James
" John
" Samuel
" Stewart J.
Affleck, Harry
Aikman, Edward
Aldenton, Robert
Allen, John
" John
Alexander, Andrew
Alston, James E.
Anderson, Alexander
" Charles J.
" David
" Francis
" John
Angus, John
Arbour, Susan
Archer, Thomas
Armstrong, D.
" John
" Thomas
Arnold, George
" John
" T. G.
Arnott, James
Arthur, John
Asher, Charles
Ashling, Jonathan
Ashworth, Abel
Atkins, John
Allen, James
" John
" William
" William
Allibone, William
Allison, Ellis
Alom, Mary

Anderson, Ann
" John
" Peter
Andrews, Alexander
Archy, Thomas
Armstrong, Thomas
Ashby, Francis
Ashworth, John
Aslett, Solomon
Atherton, Thomas
Atkins, George
" George
" Sarah
" Thomas
Ayers, Samuel
Abbott, Henry
Abel, Thomas
Adams, James
" Peter
" Thomas
Aitken, Charles
Alexander, Donald
Alger, Philip
Allan, Edward
" James
Abbott, Edward J.
Atkins, Richard
Anderson, William
Atkins, Mary
Anderson, Alexander
" George
Armstrong, Mary
" Samuel
Anderson, Bernard
" Alexander
" John
Ashby, John

B

Bishop, John

Blacker, William
Blanch, John
Blackwood, John
Blakely, T. B.
Blassmire, J. E.
Blight, Ralph
Bloomfield, Richard
Blundell, W.
Bocock, Robert
Boland, Patrick
Bondell, James
Boodle, George
Booth, James
Boucher, John
Bourke, Patrick
Boursfield, John
Bowes, Michael
Boyes, Richard
Boyle, Daniel O.
" James
Boys, Edward
Bradford, Edward
Bradley, Charles
" James
Bradshaw, William
Brady, James
Bragg, John
Brame, Frederick
Branson, Charles
Breerton, John
Brickwell, George
Briese, Henrich
Britchley, Charles
Brindle, Moses
Brodie, Andrew
Brogue, Henry
Bloomer, Sarah
Booth, Samuel
Brannen, John
Brogan, Patrick
" Rose

(133)

INTESTATES.

Brown, James J.
" Margaut
" Samuel
" Thomas
Burk, Ellen
" William
Beatty, Margaret
Battey, Margaret
Baxter, William
Baldwin, Alfred
Baker, William
Barnes, John
Barker, William
Bean, Susan M.
Beeson, John G.
Bell, George
Bennett, Elizabeth
Billington, Henry
Bingham, William
Blake, William
Boxer, Richard
Brownley, James
Brown, David
" Francis
" John
Brownley, Jessie
Bruce, John
Boylan, Peter
Burton, Charles
Burnage, William
Bradney, Charles
Bradshaw, James
Bragg, Thomas
Bramhall, William
Brandon, Richard
Brannan, Edward
Breen, Edward
Brian, Simon
Bricknell, Moses
Brignall, Joseph
Bailey, John
" Henry
Baillie, Matthew
Baker, Robert
Ball, John
Barker, James
Barnacle, James
Barnes, Thomas
Barnett, R. H.
Barry, J. C.
" William
Barton, J. H.
Bassett, Thomas
Batty, James
Bayley, James
Beck, John

Beck, Martha
Beckley, William
Beard, William
Beilby, Thomas
Bell, William H.
Bellingham, Thomas
Bennett, Hugh
" George
" Thomas
Bent, John
Bentson, Charles
Bettridge, Mary
Bidders, Joseph
Bishop, Joseph
Black, Thomas
" William
Boddy, Charles
Booth, William
Barrow, John
Bott, Henry
Bourne, John
Bowen, Daniel
Boyd, Benjamin
Boyle, Daniel
" Richard
Boyne, Patrick
Bradford, James
Babbington, Anne
Baker, James
Ball, J.
Barchfeld, J. B.
Barrett, Robert
Becker, William
Blanks, William
Blyth, Benjamin
Brown, James
Buckley, John
Buckton, Henry
Barney, John H.
Bingham, D. H.
Blagg, Charles
Bagg, Samuel
Bailey, James
Bain, David
" Douglas
Balbirnie, James
Bamford, Thomas
Bannister, Charles
Baker, James
Barbauld, Montague
Barclay, Peter
Barnes, John
" George
Barnett, Edward
" Joseph
Barrimore, James

Barry, D.
" George
" Patrick
Barton, George
Bates, Stephen
Baumgartner, A.
Bayley, Thomas
Baylis, Thomas
" John
Beaumont, William
Bees, George
Belcher, Thomas
Bell, James
" James J.
" John
" John
Bergin, Edward
Berry, Joseph
Bertone, James
Betts, Alfred
Bex, Samuel
Birch, Joseph
Britton, John
Broker, Thomas
Broughton, Robert
Brown, George
" James
" James
" John
" Thomas
" William
" William
" William J.
" William W.
Browne, William H.
Brennan, John
Bryant, William
Bryson, William
Bullmer, Benjamin
Bunn, George H.
Bunning, William
Burgess, J. C.
Burke, Martin
" Michael
" Myles
Burns, Patrick
" Terence
Burton, J. H.
Bury, Wilson P.
Butler, William
Byron, Ada E.
Bromley, Richard
Brown, Edward
" Frank
" Jane
" James

INTESTATES. 135

Brown, James
" John
" John
" Mary
" Robert
" Samuel
" Samuel
" Thomas
" William
" William
Bruce, Joseph
Brumley, Kershaw
Bryant, H. R.
" Joseph
Bryce, David
Buchan, Peter
Buckler, Christian
Buckley, Robert
" William
Budden, Philip
Burdett, William
Burgens, Stephen
Burke, John
Burns, Robert
" Peter
Burridge, Henry
Burrows, Robert
Burt, James
Butler, David
Butter, Archibald
Byrne, Peter
Byrnes C.
Babb, Robert
Baker, George
Barry, Francis
Beaumont, William
Blair, Nancy
Blake, Ann
" Thomas
Boyd, Robert
Brown, John
Buchanan, Robert
Burnett, James
Burnham, Cornelia
Brady, James
Brown, Margaret
" John W.
Burdett, George F.
Brown, Charles
Brenan, John M
Bruesing, Charles
Breaden, Mary
Benjamin, Simeon
Briggs, Susan
Burns, John

C

Carter, Henry
" John
" John
" Martin
Cassidy, Henry
" Michael
" William
Castin, George
Castle, William
Challoner, Edward
Chambers, Thomas
Champion, Richard
Chapman, James
" Joseph
Cheetham, J.
Chisholm, Jessie
Chitty, William
Christie, James
" John
Chubb, William
Clapham, J. G.
Clark, William
Clarke, Edward D.
" John
Claxton, William
Clay, Joseph F.
" Richard
Cleary, Thomas
Clelland, Arthur
Clement, John
Clewer, Joseph
Clunes, Gordon
" William
Clerk, Charles
Cobham, George
Cock, Henry
" John
Cole, Samuel
Coleman, James
" James
" John
Collins, Edward
" George
" John
Colstone, William
Comynn, Patrick
Condon, Bridget
Conefry, Hugh
Congalton, Samuel
Connolly, James
Connor, Thomas
" William
Constantine, William
Conway, Patrick

Cooper, Daniel
" Robert
Crichton, John
Cromarty, Robert
Crofton, Henry
Croker, Jacob
Cullen, Patrick
Culling, Charles
Cumberland, William
Cunningham, Richard
Cunninghame, Ter'nce
Curran, Thomas
Curtis, William
Cushion, William
Cutts, Thomas
Caffrey, Ellen
Carr, Catherine
Clark, John
" Mary
Connor, Catherine
Chappell, Samuel
Carville, George
Carroll, Mary
Carey, Susan
Crow, Ann
Carr, Bridget
Costello, Patrick
Cole, George
Crawford, Sarah
Coggins, Catherine
Cole, Isabella
Compton, George
Connay, Ellen
Conner, James H.
Coneskay, Alice
Corcoran, Michael
Coughlin, Catherine
Coulton, William
Creamer, Michael
Croley, Samuel
Caughlan, Jeremiah
Chambers, William
Chapman, John
" William
Chatterly, John
Cheeseworth, Joseph
Chester, William
Cheston, William
Chevin, Joseph
Chrichton, John
Christie, Thomas
" William
Clarke, Henry
" James
" John
Clarkson, Capt. W.

INTESTATES.

Clayton, Edward
" George
Cluff, Richard
Cocker, Edward
Coleman, Patrick
Collins, Charles
" David
" Oliver
" Philip
" William
Condon, P. W.
" Richard
Coulen, James
Connor, Andrew
" James
" James
" John
" Thomas
" Patrick
Conn, Margaret
Conway, Francis
Cooke, Robert
Cooper, James
" John
" Joseph
" Joseph
Coote, James
Cope, William
Corbit, James
Cornish, William
Corrigan, John
Cotten, Patrick
" Timothy
Coultate, Henry
Coulson, George
Cox, Dennis
Crawford, John
Crawley, James
Craig, Robert
Crigan, Patrick
Chevitt, William
Craig, Robert
Caddick, William
Cairns, John
Callagher, John
Callison, Isabella
Cammill, Thomas
Campbell, George
" John
" W. B
Canavan, Charles
Candy, Benjamin
Cannon, Thomas
Carey, Patrick
Carkeck, John
Carleton, George

Carnell, William
Carpenter, Henry
" Joseph
Carter, George
Cagney, Michael
Cahill, Richard
Cain, Patrick
Callaghan, Owen
" Samuel
Cameron, Alexander
" Archibald
" Donald
Campbell, Alexander
" James
" Robert
Cargill, Thomas A.
Carlyle, Worthey
Carne, William
Carney, John
Carr, Sarah
" William
Carroll, Lawrence
" Patrick
" John
Carter, Robert
Carruthers, Robert
Carty, John
Carter, John
Casey, John
Cater, John
Coarney, Samuel
Croton, William
Costelow, William
Cochrane, John
Cummings, Mark
Carstairs, James
Crisby, George
Colmon, James
Cooper, Thomas
" Thomas
Costello, John
Cosgrove, James
Couch, Francis P.
Coulson, Alfred
Coultherd, William
Courtney, William
" W. H.
Cornis, Eliza
Cornish, Alfred
Corbett, Thomas
Cormick, Edward
Craddock, John
Craig, William
Crawford, W. J.
" John
" W. W.

Crawley, Patrick
Cremer, James
Crosbie, James
Cross, William
Crotty, Darby
Cuddy, James
Cumming, James
Cunningham, G.
Currie, Henry
Curtayne, W. T.
Curtis, Joseph
" William
Cuthbertson, James
Cuthbutt, William
Cutts, Samuel
Chatterly, William
Cook, George
Crawford, Donald
Clarke, James
Colbert, Thomas
Cotten, William
Caddy, Joseph
Collier, Aaron
Collins, George
Caldwell, John
Christie, William
Clarke, Archibald
Conn, William
Cook, Thomas
Cormack, Ann
Cagney, Michael
Cahill, Richard
Cain, Patrick
Callaghan, Owen
" Samuel
Cameron, Alexander
" Archibald
" Donald
Campbell, Alexander
" James
" Robert
Cargill, Thomas A.
Carlyle, Worthey
Carne, William
Carney, John
Carr, Sarah
Cambridge, Caroline
Campbell, Hugh
Carmichael, Francis
Christy, John
Clancy, Rev. W.
Clark, Thomas
Clarke, C. S.
" James
Conville, R.
Cramer, John

INTESTATES. 137

Crosby, Richard

D

D'Arcy, Patrick
Daley, James
" John
" Patrick
" William
Dalton, Thomas
Darnell, William
Dart, Henry
Dawes, Robert
Davies, Henry H.
Davis, Henry
" James
" James
" John
" John
" Timothy
Day, James
" John
Delamere, Frank
Dell, Richard
Dennis, Henry
Deoline, Paul
Dick, John
Dickenson, George
Dickinson, Joseph
Dodge, James
Doherty, Richard
Dooling, Miles
Dore, John
Dorina, John
Dowdell, John
Downes, James
Dowling, Lawrence
" George R.
Dowsley, William
Doyle, John
" Peter
" Thomas
Dutton, Samuel
Duncan, John
Durkin Ann
Dowsing, Charles
Deane, Thomas
Dorrington, Stephen
Douglas, John
Downing, Anne
Dunlap, James
Dowling, John
Dainton, Cornelius
Daly, John
Davidson, William
Davidson, W.

Davies, Griffith
" William
Davis, Evan
" George
" James W.
" John
Davison, John
Dartwell, T. W.
Daw, John
Dawe, Richard
Daws, George
Daxon, Arthur
Denning, Alfred
Dennison, John
Dernie, John
Deverill, George
Devonport, Charles
Dewar, Andrew
Dunn, Ann
Durguan, Ellen
Donovan, Patrick
Dalton, Julia
Dalton, Lawrence
Drew, Robert A.
Dalton, Christopher
Devine, Margaret
Dewey, James
Donnelly, Edward
Drew, Nicholas H.
Dunn John B.
Dewing, Thomas P.
Diaper, Alfred
Dignam, Michael
Dingham, George
Dix, George
Dixon, Samuel
Dockray, William
Dodd, Joseph
" Valentine
Dodge, Joseph
Donald, James
Donaldson, Robert
Donnelly, John
" Thomas
Doxey, Edward
Doyle, John
Drakeford, William
Drury, Charles
Duddy, Michael
Dudley, John
Duel, Sarah
Duffey, James
" John
Dufuer, David
Duggan, Joseph
Duncan, Alexander

Duncan, William
" S. H.
Duncanson, Robert
Dunkley, William
Dunn, George
" John
Durant, Charles
Durnford, Thomas
Dye, Moses
Davis, Harris
Dawson, Francis
" William
Downes, Richard
Dunn, William

E

Edington, W. H.
Edwards, D. J.
" Joseph
" Thomas
Egerton, Thomas
Egleton, Richard
Elliott, William
Ellis, Thomas
English, John
" Michael
Entwhistle, James
Everness, William
Evans, Charles
" Esther
" William
Estote, Martin
Evans, David
" Griffith
" H. J.
" Samuel
Everard, George
Ewald, Wilhelm
Eylward Joseph
Eady, Philip
East, Thomas
Earp, Joseph
Edgar, George
Edward, James
Edwards, Charles
" George
" James
" John
" Robert
" Thomas
Elliott, John
Ellis, Alfred
" John
" Thomas
Elsey, John

138   INTESTATES.

Emery, Robert
" William
England, Thomas
Epps, John
Elliott, Maria
Ellis, John
Egan, Stephen
Eat, Daniel
Elligood, Samuel
" William
Elliott, John
Ellis, David
" William

F

Falconer, Daniel
Fauning, Daniel
Farrell, Edward
" Patrick
Faulkner, Charles
Fawcett, William
Fildew, Samuel
Finn, Arthur
" Edward
Finlayson, William
Fisher, James
" Thomas
Fitzgerald, John
" Peter
Fitzpatrick, Patrick
Flannigan, Thomas
Flemming, John
Fletcher, Thomas M.
Flynn, Thomas
" Michell
Forde, John
Forehead, George
Foley, Edward
Ford, Edward
Forster, Miles
" William
Foulkes, Sarah
Fowler, Thomas
" Thomas H.
Fox, Richard
Foxcroft, Henry
Francis, William
Franks, James
Frazer, John
Fredericks, Christian
Freeman, Eliza
" George
French, John
" Thomas
Frith, James

Froggart, Henry
Frost, William
" Daniel
Fry, Richard
Fooks, George
Fletcher, John
Fuller, James
Fussel, Simon
Fettle, Frederick
Fidlar, David
Finnigan, Michael
Frawley, Thomas
Forsyth, John C. B.
Francis, Elizabeth
Foley, Margaret
Frazer, Charles S.
Fabren, Peter
Fagan, John
" Mary
Faircloth, John
Falconer, R. B.
Fardell, Thomas
Farmer, John
" Thomas
Farquhar, Arthur
Farrell, B. O.
" Benjamin
" Daniel
" James
Fawcett, Thomas
Fegan, James
Fenton, George
Fenwick, R. W.
Feren, Daniel
Ferguson, Robert
Fetter, Henry E.
Field, William
Fielder, Thomas
Finch, George
Finlay, Robert
Fitzsimmons, W.
Flat, Thomas
Fleck, Henry
Flemming, Miles
Fletcher, Frederick
" W. J.
Foley, Jeremiah
" Patrick
Foot, Thomas
Forbes, J. A. G.
" William
Ford, Jacob
Forrest, Thomas
Fox, Catherine
" James
" John

Fox, Thomas
" Thomas
Francis, George
Frankland, William
Franklin, John
Fraser, Alexander
" Donald
Fox, Matthew
Flanigan, James
Fallon, Ann
Fletcher, William
Flett, Andrew
Foord, John
Foran, Timothy
Fowler, Joseph
Franklin, Bartholm'w
Friel, John
Furlong, James
Fyfe, John L.
Flay, Susannah
Fraser, Richard D.
Forgerty, Michael
Flynn, William
" Bridget
Frawley, Patrick
Fullerton, Robert
Fury, Michael

G

Garden, Alexander
Gibbs, William
Gibson, James
" Edmund
Giles, Samuel
" Edward
Gnowling, William
Glover, Joseph
Goldfinch, Simon
Good, James
Goodwin, Stephen
Gordon, James
" William
" William
Gorman, George
" John
Gough, Edward
Gower, John
Goulding, Edward
Grace, Charles
Graham, Thomas
Grant, George
Gray, John
Green, Charles
" George
" James

INTESTATES.

Green, Thomas
" Thomas
Greenfield, Charles
Greaves, Charles
Gregor, Rev. John
Gregory, James
" L. B.
Gribble, George
Groves, James
Gumley, Samuel
Guiton, William
Guillam, William
Grant, William
Goddard, Joseph
Griffith, Daniel
Gilmartin, Thomas
Garry, James
Geddes, James
Gordon, John
Grady, Honora
Green, George
Griffiths, Edward
Groat, James P.
Gubble, Samuel
Guild, Alexander P.
Gunning, James
Garratt, James
Getze, John F.
Gibson, Catherine
Gilham, Samuel
Good, George
Gordon, John B.
Gough, George
Grant, Henry
Griffiths, James
Gilchrist, Gordon
" Niel
Gillard, J. G. S.
Gill, John
Gillis, David
Grant, Lachlan
Gray, Alexander
Grey, Magnus
Gulleage, William
Grant, Alexander
Gosling, George
Gaffney, Michael
Gallagher, Matthew
Galloway, John
Galvin, Jeremiah
" Michael
Garvie, William
Gaskin, William
Gaynor, Michael
" Patrick
Genn, Daniel

Gibbs, William
Gibson, George
" James
" William
Gilbertson, James
Giles, George
Gill, George
Gilliam, Joseph
Gilliman, William
Gilliver, Charles
Glanville, George
Glass, James
Gleddon, C. S.
Gleeson, Martin
Glover, Christopher
Goddard, William
Godden, George
Gomm, Absalom
Goodman, Thomas
Gorman, Patrick
Goven, William
Grabham, C.
Grace, William R.
Graham, Sarah
Grant, Charles
" John
" Samuel
" William
Graves, Henry T.
Gray, Charles
" George
Greaves, Henry
Greaney, Anthony
Green, John
" Lewis
" William
Gregg, William
Griffin, John
Griffiths, James
" Thomas
Groves, James
Grumbell, William

H

Haen, Thomas
Hagerty, William
Haggerty, Matthew
Hale, F.
Hales, John
Halfpenny, James
Hall, John
Hallworth, Eliza
Hamilton, James
" John
" Thomas

Hand, Thomas
Hanly, Thomas
Hanson, Jasper
Hansill, Peter
Hardie, Thomas
Hardy, William
Harkins, Charles
Harris, Hugh H.
" James
" William
" William F.
Harrison, John
Hartwick, Joseph
Harvey, Humphrey
" John H.
" William
Hawk, Thomas
Hawkins, Richard
Hawtin, John
Hay, Forest
Hayden, John
Hayes, Benjamin
" John
" Thomas
Haynes, Charles
Hayward, William
Hazlett, John
Healy, Patrick
" Peter
Hearn, William
Hellyer, John
Henderson, D.
" James
" Henry
" John H.
Henry, John
Henshaw, Thomas
Henston, John
Herbert, William
Herbertson, Francis
Hethom, R. H.
Hines, William
Haydon, Edward
Hill, James
Harrington, Sarah
Horsley, John
Hall, John
Hamilton, Ellen
Healey, Thomas
Henson, Abraham
Hickey, Mary
Higgins, Thomas
Hodson, Thomas
Holmes, Thomas
Hornby, John
Hughes, Sarah

INTESTATES.

Hunter, Hugh
Humphreys, C. H.
Harrison, Thomas
Holt, William
Higgins, James
Hinds, Eliza
Hodgkins, Thomas
Harland, Henry
Hogan, John S.
Hartshorn, John
Haylett, Henry
Hillier, William
Hamilton, John
Hobson, Joseph
Hyde, Eliza
Hayer, Edward
Harbroe, John
Herrell, Robert
Holloway, Henry
Hogsett, Thomas
Hownan, Alfred
Hunt, James M.
Hill, Thomas
Hunter, John
Huntsman, George
Hurley, Eliza
" Thomas
Hurst, Henry
Hutchins, Joseph
Hamilton, Capt. J.
Hansen, M.
Hazlewood, Sarah
Hewitt, Thomas
Hickey, Mary
" Michael
Hickinbotham, Mary
Hickling, Thomas
Higginbottom, Edwd.
Hill, Adam
" George
" James D.
Hillier, William
Hilton, Thomas
" William
Hinchley, John
Hinson, Catherine
Hinsworth, Daniel
Hinton, J. H.
Hogan, Patrick
Hogg, David
Holden, James
Holdsworth, W. T.
Holgate, S. W.
Holgate, William
Holland, Harry
" John

Holland, Mary
Holloway, Joseph
" Rob't W.
Holmes, James
" John
Hong, Charles
Hood, Thomas
Hooper, John
" John C.
Hopkins, James
Hopson, Nicholas
Howard, Joseph
Hewell, William
Hughes, Thomas
Hummerstead, J.
Humphries, Robert
Hunt, Robert
Hunter, Andrew
" Ann
Hurcum, George
Hurst, George
" John
Hynd, Thomas
Hynes, John J.
Hernan, John
Hampson, Benjamin
Hands, Samuel
Hanley, Maurice
Haman, Thomas
Hants, John
Harkens, Daniel
Harker, Robert
Harkins, James
Hart, Levy
" Lazarus
" Michael
Harthill, John
Harvey, Thomas D.
" George
Harton, Henry
Haskell, Thomas
Hastings, Caroline
Hatton, John
Hawkrigg, James
Hayes, James
Healey, James
Heenan, A. P.
" Matthew
Hely, Frederick
Henderson, John
Hetherington, Samuel
Hewitt, John
Hexton, James
Heydon, Henry
Hickey, Christopher
Higgins, Thomas

Higgins, John
Higginbottom, John
Hill, James
Hines, John
Hives, George
Hodson, Henry
Holden, George
Holdsworth, Henry
Holland, Thomas
Holloway, Thomas
Holmes, William
Honeyburn, William
Horne, John
Horrigan, Jeremiah
Horton, Geoffrey
Houghton, Charles
Howard, Walter
Howe, Edward
Howie, Robert
Hoxy, John
Hubbard, Charles
Hubert, Samuel
Huggins, William
Hunt, James
" William C.

I

Inglewood, Daniel
Ireland, William
Irvin, Lewis J.
" Robert
Irvine, Joseph
Irving, Henry
Inches, John
Ingram, John
Ingerthorpe, William
Innes, William
Irwin, Simon
Irons, William K.
Ivers, William
Isaac, Edwin
Islop, John

J

Jackson, John
" John
" Thomas
James, W. R.
Javerly, Andrew
Jeffries, John
" Joseph
" Thomas
Jervis, Christopher
" George

INTESTATES.

Jervis, Henry
Jobson, Ann
Johnson, Charles
" George
" Hannah
" Robert
" William
Joice, Thomas
Jones, Alexander
" John
" John
" John D.
" Howell
" Margaret
" Richard
" Robert
" Thomas
Jordan, William
Jacobs, Hester E. F.
James, John
" J. O.
Jones, William
Julian, John
Jones, John
Jobson, Henry
Jayne, John
Jameson, Henry
Jamieson, David
Jones, Jane
Johnson, Richard
Jamieson, John
Jones, Bernard
" Henry L.
" John
Jackson, Joseph
" Peter
" Richard
Jacques, John
Jamieson, Thomas
Jarman, Thomas
Jenkins, Benjamin
" George
Johns, James
Johnson, Frederick
" John
" William
Johnston, John
Johnstone, John P.
" Joseph
Jones, Ebenezer
" Edward
" Evan
" Harry
" Henry J.
" James
" John P.

Jones, Lewis J.
" Richard
" R. W. W.
" Samuel
" Thomas
" T. W.
" William
Joyce, William
Juby, George

K

Kean, Samuel
Kearis, William
Kearns, William
Keckham, James
Kellagher, Martin
Kelly, George
" John
" S. R.
" William
Kelsall, Robert
Kendalin, Michael
Kennedy, Donald
Kennedy, Francis
Kent, William
Kennedy, Patrick
Kenny, John
Kenworthy, Edward
Kerr, Hugh
" William
Kesterton, F. William
Kidd, William
King, James
" John
Kingswell, William
Kirby, Frederick
Kirkham, Joseph
Kingston, William
Kitchen, James
Knox, Walter
King, Thomas
Kirton, W. J.
Kelly, James
Killing, William
Kendal, John
Kealy, David
Keane, John
Kearney, P. H.
Keating, Edward
Keenan, John
" Patrick
Kelly, James
" James
" John
" Michael

Kelly, Patrick
" Richard
Kelty, John
Kemp, Isaac
Kenelly, Jeremiah
Kenny, James
Keefe, Daniel
Kilfol, Owen
Kilfoyle, John
Kilduff, Peter
Killean, James
Kilminster, William
Kidman, William
Kinsela, John
King, Charles E.
Knight, Mark
" William
Kelly, Roger
Kane, William
Kelly, Rosalia
" James
Kirby, James

L

Laball, Sydney
Labot, William
Laird, Alexander
Lake, John
" Thomas
Lamb, H. S.
Lambert, Nathaniel
Lambie, James
Lambshire, Thomas
Lambton, John
Langridge, James
Lankester, James
Lanyon, Richard
Lawrence, Benjamin
" Samuel
" William
Lawrie, Frances J.
" Thomas
Lawton, James
Laxton, William
Layfield, Noah
Leake William
Lee, Andrew
" James
" John
Lenaine, Nicholas
Lennox, Hugh
Leonard, James
Levers, Henry
Lewis, Clement
" David

141

INTESTATES.

Lewis, James
" James
" John
" John
" Morgan
" R. H.
" Sophia
Lillicrop, Richard
Ling, Walter
Lindsay, Robert
Linton, M. D.
Lilster, Henry
Lister, W. H.
Lloyd, John
" John
" William
Logan, Thomas
Lamont, N. C.
Leslie, John
Lewis, John
Landers, William
Langton, John
Livesay, John
Lucas, Samuel
Lloyd, Charles
Lumsden, Leslie
Logan, Robert
" William
Long, George
" William
Loud, John
Love, John
Lovelady, Richard
Lowe, John
" Thomas
Lowther, H. J.
Lumb, Robert
Lumbsden, William
Lynam, Patrick
Lyne, Charles N.
" Joseph
Lyon, Richard
Lyons, John
Laird, Alexander
Lamb, John
Lambe, Henry
Lane, Sarah
" Charles
Larkins, Patrick
Law, James
Leach, William
Leaky, John
Leary, Mary
" Michael
Lear, Charles
Lee, John

Lee, John
" James
" William
Lees, David
Leeson, James
Leighy, Timothy
Leggett, Ann
Lench, Thomas
Lemon, James
Lewis, Henry
" William
Lindsay, John
Lloyd, T. H. L.
Logur, Thomas
Long, William
" John
Loobey, Michael
Low, Henry
Lowe, Richard
Lovell, Anthony
Lucas, Charles
" Thomas
Livermore, John
Lynam, Thomas
Lynch, John
Lyons, Cornelius
" George
Laverty, Ann
Lagger, Jane
Laughlin, Eliza A.
Lawrence, John
Ledde, Daniel
Lee, Henry M.
" James
" Thomas
Leicester, Henry
Leitch, Margaret
Leonard, Michael
Levick, Samuel L.
Lillie, Thomas
Locke, Thomas

M

McAllister, Angus
" James
McBean, George
McClellan, John
" Thomas
McCain, Matthew
McCarthy, Francis
McColl, John
McCord, John
McCrossen, W. B.
McCullock, Hugh
McDonald, Alexander

McDonald, Donald
" George
" Patrick
McDougall, Archibald
" D.
" James
McEllione, J.
" F.
McElligott, Mary
McElligot, Thomas
McEwan, James
McEwen, Moses
McFarlane, Mrs.
" M.
" W. P.
McGarry, James
McGee, Patrick
McGill, Joseph
McGlassen, John
McGlynn, James
McGowan, Patrick
McGrath, Hugh
" William
McGregor, John
McGuire, James
McInnerney, T.
McBeth, Sarah
McClure, William
McIntosh, Alexander
McKinnon, John
McKirdy, Mary
McLaren, William
McNamara, Eugene
Martin, John
Munro, George
McArthur, Duncan
McBride, John
McCann, Michael
M'Cann, Hugh
McCabe, James
McCall, James
McCarty, Dennis
McColl, James
McClymont, James
McDonald, Alexander
" John
" John
McDonough, Charles
McEwen, Daniel
McEncroe, Patrick
McFadden, Archibald
McGarey, John
McGovern, James
McGuiness, John
McGuire, James
McKay, John

INTESTATES. 143

McKenna, Joseph
McKeller, Frederick
McKendray, Edward
McKenzie, Allan
" W. M.
" William
McHue, Ellen
McLoughlan, John
" Patrick
" Edward
McLean, Kenneth
McLeod, Niel
McManus, Hugh
McNamara, Daniel
" Thomas
McMahon, James
McInnis, J.
McIntosh, Alexander
McIntyre, Archibald
" James
McJudure, George
McKay, Alexander
" John
" John
McKennan, John
McKinnon, Alexander
McKenzie, Hugh
McLachlan, John
" Robert
McLean, Donald
McLelland, Donald
McLeod, John
McMartin, Duncan
McMaster, George
McMillan, Archibald
" Malcolm
McMullin, Daniel
McNabb, Jessie
" William
McNeal, Malcolm
McPherson, Donald
" Hugh
McQueen, Peter
Monteith, Patrick
Mitchell, James
McNaughton, James
Maddock, John F.
Mackay, William
Mackie, Thomas
Madget, Edward
Magoveny, Henry
Maltby, Robert
Mannere, Thomas
Mansfield, Richard
Manson, Donald
Marshall, John

Martindale, Ralph
Martin, Edward
" F. G.
" Henry
" Henry
" Thomas
Martins, James
Mason, George
Matthews, Henry
" John D.
" Thomas
Mawdesly, Thomas
Mayhew, W.
Maylan, F. G.
Maynard, Richard
Mead, George
Mears, William
Mee, William
Mercer, James
Mackay, William
McLaughlin, William
Makin, John
Mahon, John
Mansel, John
Mappleback, John
Martin, David
" Jeremiah
Marsh, George P.
Marshall, Peter
Mason, John
Malcham, H. W. C.
Maw, James
Maxwell, William
May, Frederick
Mayhew, William
Meade, James
Meacle, J. C.
Meredith, John
Meyer, W. H.
Miller, Ambrose
" Henry
Marlow, John T.
Marsden, John
McAuley, John
McDonald, William
McGurn, James
Merrey, James
Millan, Hugh
Moore, George
Morris, Thomas
" Michael
Mott, William
Munday, Mary
Munroe, William
Morgan, John J.
Mitchell, Robert

Maddock, Arthur
Madson, James
Moore, Posonby
McBeath, William
Middleton, William
Midforth, Charles
Milards, James
Miles, James
Mills, Henry
" Henry
" William
Milne, James
Milnes, Edward
Millar, George
Miller, John
Minough, James
Minty, Robert
Mitchell, John
" John
" Robert
" William
Miller, Thomas
Miley, Joseph
Mills, James
" Joseph
Minton, James
Minnow, George
Mitchell, David
" John
" Roderick
" William
" William B.
Moncur, James
Montage, James S.
Moody, Jasper
Moor, Henry
Moore, Henry T.
" Thomas
Morgan, Patrick
Morris, Samuel
Morrison, Robert.
Motley, George
Morton, Richard
Mott, Robert
Mould, Arthur
Moylett, Patrick H.
Mundy, T. M.
Munroe, James
Murphy, John
Murray, James
" James
Mustov, Isaac
Myers, Thomas
Moffitt, William
Monk, Thomas
Monahan, Maria

INTESTATES.

Monteith, James
Moreton, Charles
Morgan, David
" John
" Charles
Morris, John
" John
Morrison, Charles
" John
" Robert
Moore, Michael
" John
Mooney, James
Mullen, Catherine
Mullins, John
Munden, George
Murphy, Edward
" Bernard
" William
" William
Murray, John
" John
Myles, Patrick
Myers, Rawson
Mosely, William
McDonald, Ann
Munroe, John
Martin, Catherine
Mitchell, John
May, Stewart
Martin, William
McCall, Rebecca
Myers, Thomas
McKeon, Margaret
McAveny, Thomas
McCartney, Margaret
McCoun, Isabella
McCraw, Peter
McDonald, Maria
McGahan, Patrick
McGlinchy, Michael
McKelvey, James
McKenna, Frances
McLaughlan, Patrick
McManus, Julia
McMenomy, Patrick
McNalty, George
McPeake, Rachael
McSorley, Philip
Malcolm, Joseph
Manay, Mary
Manks, William
Martes, William
Matthews, John
Migham, Sarah
Moore, Mary

Mulligan, Harriett
Mussell, Maria

N

Nash, Sophia
Neale, John
Newton, Ann
" Edward
Nicholson, S. D.
Nicholls, Hugh
Niven, Hugh
Nixen, Edward
Norris, William
Newland, Patrick
Nudds, Robert
Nutkins, George
Naget, Jacob
Napier, Henry
Nelson, Martin
Newman, George
Nibloc, Thomas
Nicholl, Robert
Nixon, Joseph
Norris, Richard
North, Elijah
Nowell, S.
Nunn, Thomas
Norvell, William
Noble, Valentine
Nolan, Bridget
Norris, Augustus
Navine, Hugh
Nicholl, Peter
Napier, Adam
Newman, William

O

O'Brien, Edward H.
O'Connor, John
O'Kell, Thomas
O'Neil, Alice
O'Neil, Francis
" James
Overall, John
Ovens, John
O'Doherty, Michael
O'Donnell, Bryan
O'Hara, Charles
O'Laughlin, Peter
O'Leary, Patrick
O'Neil, Bernard
O'Neill, Thomas
Older, Edward
Orr, William

Owen, Frederick
" John
" Owen
" Samuel
" Thomas
Owens, Thomas
Owin, William
O'Brien, Daniel
" Dennis
" Timothy
O'Connoll, John
O'Connor, Peter
O'Donohue, Thomas **J.**
O'Connor, William
O'Shane, William
O'Sullivan, Phillis
Oathwaite, James
O'Brien, Edward
" James
Owen, James G.

P

Penny, Henry
Pudney, John
Pearce, W. W.
Plyer, John
Power, Robert
Peters, James
Proby, Hugh
Parr, Thomas
Phipps, George
Padfield, Robert
Pagnell, John
Page, George
" Anthony
Paige, James E.
Paine, Charles
Palmer, Robert
Parfit, Jane
Parker, Abraham
Parsons, William
Paterson, John
" William
Perkins, James
Peters, Ann
Pitts, Reuben
Pittron, Isaac
Poltick, James
Potter, George **Thos.**
Powell, Robert
" Thomas
" Thomas
Price, Charlotte
Prince, **Alfred**
Prisk, John

INTESTATES. 145

Pryde, William
Pullen, John
" John
Purtell, John
Purcell, Charles
" John
Pluck, Richard
Paul, Samuel
Powell, William
Parker, Edward
Polkman, Edward
Pollock, William
Poole, Daniel
" Henry
" Henry G.
Poppleton, Edward
Porrett, James
Porter, Henry
Powell, David
" George
" William
Power, James F.
Pratt, James
Preston, John
Price, James
" John
Priest, Thomas J.
Prince, Thomas
Pringle, George
Proctor, Ann
Prosser, Thomas
Purvis, James
" J. G.
Painter, Henry T.
Page, James
Pardy, Thomas
Parker, Henry
" John
" Thomas
Parry, Richard
Parsons, Martin
" Jasper
" William
Parvis, James
Patterson, Donald
" Frederick
" James
" John
" John
Paul, Peter
Paull, Richard
Paxton, Peter
Payne, Daniel
" William
Pearse, Everson
Peck, J. B.

Pender, John
Percival, John
Percy, William
Perkins, Horatio F.
Perks, Joseph
Perry, George
Pettitt, Thomas
Phelan, John
Phillips, James
" W. P.
Philpot, William
Pickering, Robert
Pike, John
Piper, Thomas H.
Pitt, William
Pitts, Walter C.
Parry, Mary
Patterson, James
Perry, John H.
Pick, Jeanette
Phelan, Edmund
Porteous, Richard
Price, Thomas
Paddock, George
Page, Thomas
Paulstone, John
Pedley, Joseph
Perrey, John
Phillips, Thomas
Pilch, Samuel

Q

Quinn, Patrick
Quinlan, John

R

Read, Charles
Reader, Ellen
Reardon, William
" Michael
Reade, Thomas
Redgate, Ann
Redford, William
Rennington, Henry
Reid, Mark
Reynolds, Thomas
Rhodes, William
Richards, Henry
Ramsay, William
Rayall, James
Reddie, William
Rees, John
Reid, George
" John

Reilly, William
Remain, August
Renners, Frederick
Reynolds, Frank
" Joseph
Richards, David J.
" James
" William
Riddle, Isabella
Rielly, Edward
Rigby, Benjamin
" John
Riley, John
Ring, James
" Joseph
Ritchie, Thomas
Rhind, Thomas
Roberts, Francis
" Henry F.
" Hugh
" John
" J.
" Robert
" Richard G.
Robertson, Hugh
" James
Richardson, James
Rix, William
Roach, Walter
Roberts, James
" John
" Stephen H.
Robertson, Duncan
" Alexander
Robinson, Alexander
" Michael
Robson, Andrew
Roche, James
Roe, James
Rogers, William
Rose, George
Rosemary, William
Rosin, William
Ross, John
" George
" John
" Frederick
Russell, Henry C.
Rush, Michael
Ryan, James
" John
" Joseph
" Matthew
" Dennis
" William
Robertson, James C.

146 INTESTATES.

Rowland, Richard
Robertson, Elizabeth
Ryan, Julia
Riley, James
Russell, David
Reck, Susan
Rankin, John
Ryrie, William
Roach, Thomas
Roberts, S. J.
Robertson, James
Rose, William
Ross, Donald
" John
Record, Mary A.
Robertson, John S.
" Hugh
Richards, Elias
Russell, Henry
Ready, John
Reynolds, Mary
Robertson, James
Rowe, Henry
Robertson, James
" John
" William
Robinson, Daniel
" George
Robson, Edwin
Rodgers, John
Rodnell, William
Roe, John
Rogers, John
" Enoch
Rolf, John
Rooney, Patrick
Ross, Ann
" David
" James
" James O.
" John
" Samuel
Rourke, Michael
Rowe, Thomas S.
Rowell, Cuthbert
Rowley, James U.
Rout, Frederick
Roy, Donald
" William
Royall, James
" Julian
Royston, William
Rudd, Thomas
Ruddick, William
Russell, George
" Pierce

Ryan, Joseph
" William
Reed, Rosanna
Riley, Charles
Robertson, James
Roe, Thomas
Ross, Allan
" Margaret
Ryan, John
" Patrick

S

Shannon, Robert
Strong, Frederick G.
Simms, William
Sexton, James
Springfield, William
Spencer, John
" James
" James
Sandford, Benjamin
Shapley, William
Simpson, Robert
Slater, Thomas
Slogan, John
Smith, Robert
Sowerby, John H.
Spry, Col. W. B.
Stephenson, William
Simpson, Horatio
Secker, James
Sharpe, J. F. S.
Salmon, John R. D.
Shea, Patrick
Snead, William B.
Souch, William
Stacey, Charles
Stafford, Thomas
Scanlan, Thomas
Sandys, Catherine
Stuart, Priscilla
Smith, Jane Ann
Stuart, James P.
Stewart, Daniel
Scott, W. H.
Sevill, John
Shea, Patrick
Siddons, Thomas
Smith, Eliza
Stanford, Charles
Sanders, George
Sanderson, James G.
" John
" William
Sangster, John

Sage, William
Salmon, John
Saunders, George
Say, W. H.
Scarce, Richard
Scott, John
" Thomas C.
" Charles
" James
" James
" John
" Peter
" Thomas H.
" Walter
Scotland, William
Scarlan, Matthew
Sedgwick, William
Sefton, William
Senior, Joseph
Shanley, Richard
Shannon, John
Sharpe, Abraham
Shaw, John
" Joseph
Sheddy, C. S.
Sheffield, W. F.
Shelton, John
Shepcott, Joseph
Shepherd, J. H. M.
Sheppard, J.
Shippey, John
Shirley, Caroline
Sharpe, W. S.
Sheardon, James
Shepherd, R. C.
" Joseph
" Robert
Sherwin, William
Shipway, John
Short, James
" Jeremiah
" Richard
Silk, Richard
Simms, Samuel
" Charles
Simpson, James S.
" James
Simpton, Thomas
Sinclair, Duncan
Skews, W. H.
Skey, James
Siddle, Jonathan
Simms, James C.
Simmonds, William
Simpson, John
" John

INTESTATES.

Simpson, Joseph
" Thomas
" William
" William
Sly, John
Slater, William
Slattery, James
Slayter, William
Sloane, John
Smallbridge, William
Smith, Charles
" Charles
" Francis
" George
" Henry
" Henry
" Hugh
" James
" James
" Jarvis
" John
" John
" Joseph
" Ross
" Samuel
" Thomas
" William B.
Smart, William
Smith, Emma
" Eliza M.
" Frederick
" Henry W.
" James H.
" James
" James
" John
" John
" John
" M. A.
" Robert
" Thomas
" Thomas
" William
" William
Snell, Thomas
Snowling, William
Southey, William
Speer, A. T.
Spears, Robert
Sparks, John
Spinks, Abraham
" John
Spratley, John
Spence, Alexander
" John
Spencer, J. B.

Speight, John
Spero, John
Springhall, John
Squires, James
Standing, Benjamin
Stanley, William
Stapleton, William
Steadman, Joseph
Steel, James
Stephenson, George
Stevens, George
" John
Stewart, Alexander
" David
" Henry
" James
" James
" Kirkman
" William
" William S.
Stirling, Andrew
Stoker, James
Stokes, Henry B.
Storey, Edward
Strafford, Eliza
Strachan, Robert
Stringer, Edward
Stroude, William
Stubbs, Thomas
Stack, John
Stanton, John
Stafford, Robert
" William
Starkey, Joshua
Stanwell, Richard
Stewart, Samuel
Steele, William S.
Stephens, Charles
" William
Stephenson, William
Stewart, James
Stone, Edwin
" John
Stubbs, George
Sturmey, Benjamin
Sullivan, John
Summerfield, William
Sugg, Solomon
Suttcliffe, John
Stonehurst, Thomas
Sprent, John
Seeley, Edward
Sullivan, James
" Michael
" Timothy
Summerfield, John

Sweeny, William
Swords, William
Syme, Peter
Symonds, John A.
Scott, Sarah
Semple, Robert
Sharp, John
Shoeman, John
Simpson, William
Soles, George
Sutherland, James
Symes, James

T

Throssell, George
Tindale, John
Tingle, A. A.
Tipple, Thomas
Toole, David
Trainer, Thomas
Trigg, Thomas
Trimnell, Charles
Trenowith, H.
Turnbull, James
Tucker, Henry
Turner, Thomas
" William
Tyacks, Joseph
Tyler, Eliza
Tapper, William
Thompson, Robert
Taylor, J. T. E.
Thomas, Charles
Thomson, Robert
Tweedale, James
Tyte, Samuel
Thatcher, James
Tait, John
Talbot, John
Taylor, E. S.
" John
" Richard
Ternan, M. J. E.
Terrett, R.
Terry, Ellen
" John
" John
" William
Theill, Auguste
Thomas, David
" Evan
" Frederick
" George
" John
" Samuel

148 INTESTATES.

Thomas, Thomas
Thompson, Alex. H.
" G. A.
" James
" John
" John
" J. S.
" Richard
" William
" Francis
Thomson, James
" John
" John T.
" William
Thornhill, William
Taylor, John
" John
" Peter H.
" Joseph
Tegg, James
Telford, John
Tester, William
Tidswell, Joseph
Tindall, Charles J.
Thomas, James
" John
Thompson, James
" Richard
" Thomas
" William
" William
" Thomas
Thorne, George
Tompkins, Jasan
" Susan
Todd, William
Torpy, Michael
Trainer, James
Tripp, Samuel
Tucker, Cornelius
" John
Tunell, Robert
Tappin, George
Turner, Joseph
Tute, Samuel
Tynan, Samuel
Taylor, John
" Sarah
Thompson, Mary
Trotter, Thomas
Tuite, Elizabeth
Talley, Peter J.
Taylor, Charles
Tesser, John
Tinker, Mary
Trevors, Mary

U

Underwood, Henry
Urquhart, Alexander
" John
Ustril, John
Uxay, Mary Ann
Urquhart, Duncan

V

Valentine, John
" William
Vaughan, John
Victualler, —
Viney, Richard
Vicars, George
Venables, Thomas
Vewles, Thomas
Vincent, James
Vansittart, William

W

Ward, James
Whitehead, R. T.
Walsh, William
Watkins, John R.
Watson, David
Wells, Thomas
Whitaker, George
White, William
Warr, James
West, James
Williams, Thomas
" James
" Edward
Watson, Daniel
Way, Dr. John
Wilson, William
Work, James
Wray, James
Wake, William J.
Wakefield, Isaac
Wainfield, John
Wackham, George
Walch, Edward
Wadley, Charles
Waldron, John
Wallace, Nicholas
Ward, Edward
" Joseph
Ware, William
Warren, John
Watkins, William
Waters, William

Watson, James
Waddle, Archibald
Wagner, John
Walker, Charles
" James
" John
" William
Wallace, James
" J. M.
Wallen, James
Walters, Edward
" Frederick
Waunell, John
Ward, Frederick W.
" Rev. G.
" Robert
" William
Warde, George
Warren, James
" John
" Joshua
Waters, Ann
Watson, John
" Joseph
" Thomas
Watts, John
" Samuel
Webb, Henry
" Joseph
" Henry
Weight, John
Welch, Patrick
Wells, Thomas
Wenham, Elizabeth
White, George
" Moses
" Thomas
" Thomas
" Daniel
Whitehead, William
Whiteman, Edward
Webb, John
" Thomas
Webster, John
" John
" Susannah
Wells, Charles
West, John
Whelan, Edward
Whipman, T. W.
White, Alexander M.
" John D.
' George
" Philip
Whitehead, John
Whitehouse, W. T.

INTESTATES. 149

Whitson, Frank
Whittaker, Thomas
Wiewhardt, Carl
Wigley, John
Willards, James
Willcox, W. B.
Wilkinson, James
Williams, Edward
" David
" James
" John
" John
" Morgan D.
" Thomas F.
" Thomas
Williamson, Archibald
" John
" John
Wills, John
Wilson, Benjamin
" James
" John
" Joseph
" Peter
" Thomas
" William
" William S.
Winn, George
Winter, Benjamin
Witham, John
Witson, George

Wilton, W. J.
Wisenden, F.
Wilkinson, George
Williams, Charles
" Daniel
" George
" Henry
" Samuel G.
" Thomas
" William
Wilmott, Thomas
Willway, James
Wilson, Henry
" James
" Robert
" Richard
" Thomas
" James
" Alexander
" Samuel
Wilton, Henry
Worthington, John
Wotherspoon, Oswald
Wright, Benjamin
" James
" George
Winters, William
White, Joseph
Worth, J. W.
Wilson, James
Williams, Horace

Williams, Frank
Welch, Ann
Walch, Matthew
Welch, Anna
Wells, Joseph C.
Willis, Jessie
Wilson, Anna
Wood, James
Woodworth, Augusta
Wormby, James
Wolfenden, Thomas
Wood, E. C.
" George
" James
Woodcock, Louisa M.
Woodhouse, Mary
Wright, Ann
" John
Wyatt, Arthur M.

Y

Young, Jane
" James
" Joseph
Yardley, Thomas
Yates, Gordon
Young, Henry
" John
" John

ADDENDA TO GENERAL INDEX.

A

Adams, James R., living 1838
Adderton, John, baker
Adcock, Mary A., *frmly* Cattley
Adam, William, of Middlesex 1812
Adams, Adam, *d* Scotland
" Jean, *frmly* Crammond
" Charles, *d* Scotland
Agnese, Joseph M. L., *d* London
Ager Charles, *d* Middlesex 1870
Agge, John James B.
Allardice, John G., of London 1857
Alexander, Mary, *frmly* Manning
Allen, Mary
Ambrose, Mary A., *d* Devon 1871
Anning, William, of Axminster
Andrews, John, of Devon
" Captain
Ansell, Solomon, *son* of Thomas
" Sarah, *frmly* Fenn
Anderson, Isabella, *o'wise* Gibson
Andrews, Thomas W., *d* abroad
" James, *d* Surrey
Anderson, John } of Charlestown
" Alex. } 1806
Appleton, Sarah, *frmly* Usher
Apthorpe, Mrs.
Armistead, Henry, *d* abroad 1870
Armstrong, Henry, of Reigate
Arnold, Thomas, *d* abroad
Arkinstall, Joseph, of Staffordshire
Armstrong, George, of Middlesex 1830
Arrowsmith, John, *d* Middlesex 1873
Atkinson, John P., of London
" William } of the Isle
" Kate } of Man
" Christopher W.
" William, of Liverpool
" William George
Ashcroft, James, Sergeant R. A.
Ash, Mrs.
Ashley, Sarah, *d* Wilts, 1869
Austin, John, of Surrey 1830
Aylott, William, *d* abroad

B

Bailey, Lewis, of Northamptonshire
Barton, Alfred, *d* abroad 1859
Badcock, William K., of Taunton
Bassett, Elizabeth, *d* Middlesex 1869
Bardon, Jane, *dau.* of Thomas
Banks, Philip H., of Birmingham
Barrett, William, *d* London 1848
Banks, Elizabeth, *d* Middlesex 1859
Baxter, William James
Barnes, William, *d* Middlesex 1817
Bannister, Henrietta, wife of John
Bagnall, Catherine
Bailey, Samuel, *d* Sheffield 1870
Bates, Mary, *d* London
Bate, Lucretia, of Devon
Barker, John W., *d* Middlesex 1871
Barry, Patrick, of Essex
Bacon, Joseph, of Middlesex 1810
Barnes, W., of Herts
Bacon, Jane, born at Norwich
Bashford, Edward, footman
Barry, James, of Kent
Barton, Samuel } of Manchester
Barton, George }
Barnett, John, W. M., of London
Bawden, Elizabeth, *o'wise* Brown
Batsford, Richard, *d* Essex 1823
Barry, Elizabeth, *frmly* Fox
Barry, William, of Liverpool
Baker, Thomas, of Dublin
Baker, William
Bangley, George, *d* Middlesex 1844
Ball, Herbert
Barnett, James, *d* Scotland
Bathmaker, Joseph, clerk
Bacon, William, of London 1826
Baker, Thomas, of Bristol 1868
Barthelemey, Louis, of London 1856
Bayfield, Sarah, of Haynes 1835
Bass, G. E., of Tiverton
Bass, Edward, of Hawley
Bass, Mrs., of Hounslow
Beard, William, of Surrey 1860

152 ADDENDA TO

Berridge, Thomas, of Ramsey
Beale, Lydia, of Southampton
Beard, William, tailor
Beagham, John, of Kilmainham
Beatty, Michael, of Dublin
Beale, Charles, of Bath
Beaumont, Mrs., *frmly* Sandoe
Berridge, Thomas, of London 1834
Berryman, Mary C., *d* Devon 1871
Berrey, Georgina, Miss
Berrey, Anasttasia, Miss
Beeston, Arthur, of London
Berrie, John, merchant, *d* 1838
Beaudequin, Augustine, living 1818
Beaumont, Henry, *d* London 1870
Beaumont, Ann, of Staffordshire 1830
Beauchamp, James, of Red-hill
Berrey, Margaret, of Jamaica
Bennett, Thomas, of London 1812
Best, Rev. Dr., of Ireland
Beak, Daniel, *d* Gloucestershire 1870
Bennett, Henry, *son* of John
Bertie, Edward, *o'wise* Codwise
Binns, James, of Liverpool 1863
Birket, James, of Lancashire
Birket, John, went abroad
Birnard, Sir John
Billinge, James, *d* Staffordshire 1867
Bird, John, *d* Cumberland 1868
Bingham, Richard, *d* Middlesex 1872
Bishop, E., servant
Blaydon, Charles, of Middlesex 1853
Blissatt, Edward
Black, Mary, *dau.* of Peter
Blackmore, James, *d* America
Bleaze, John, of New Jersey
Blundstone Family
Blundstone, William, of Derby
Blackmore, William
Blackmore, Sarah, of Taunton
Blount, Elizabeth, *d* Middlesex 1873
Blunden, S. A., *o'wise* Cook
Blake, Elizabeth
Blumenthall, Augustine, of London
Blazely, J. T., clerk 1836
Booth, William H., *frmly* of Lynton
Bonaker, William B., *d* Evesham 1869
Bolton, Jane, of Westminster 1850
Borham, James, of Middlesex 1831
Bordenave, Peter, of London
Bourgeous, Madame, schoolmistress
Bousfield Family
Bones, Sophia, *d* Bedford 1872
Box, James
Boothby, Sarah, *o'wise* Smith
Boyle, Ackland, *b* Scotland 1824

Bowyer, Anthony, of Surrey 1825
Body, John, carpenter
Body, Tilly
Brown, Agness
Briggs, Samuel M., of Herts 1840
Brett, Edward, of London 1869
Braddock, C. W.
Britton, Isaac, *d* Kent 1867
Bradley, Thomas, of Dublin
Brennan, John, of Dublin
Brooks, William, traveller
Brown, John, of Middlesex
" John, carver 1850
" J. M., *frmly* Tyrie
Bromley, Eliza, of Shropshire
Brittain, Daniel, *d* Cheshire 1873
" Arthur, of Ireland
Brown, Elizabeth, *frmly* Bawden
" Frances, *o'wise* Harrison
" Henry
Brooks, John G., *d* Surrey 1859
Brown, Maria M., *d* London 1871
Bringloe, John, *d* Suffolk 1829
Breeze, William, of Paddington
Bridgewater, Henry, *d* abroad 1819
Brigden, Julia M., *dau.* of William
Bryan, Henry, *d* Middlesex 1871
Brown, Thomas W., of London 1850
Broadbent, Eliza, *d* Yorkshire
Brown, Sophia S., *o'wise* Harris
" Elizabeth, *d* Middlesex
Bradbury, Anne, *frmly* Edwards
" Eliza
" — of Manchester
Bradley, William, of London 1833
Brown, James, *d* Stirling
Bryant, Mrs., widow
Browne, James H., of London
Bradley, Mary W., *d* 1870
Brewer, Octavius, of Middlesex
Brayshaw, Mary, wife of John
" Ann, wife of James
Brown, Stephen, *d* Middlesex 1870
" Edward, *d* Preston 1820
Bryan, Mary, *d* abroad
Brighouse, Janet, *frmly* Gibbs
Bruce, Thomas, of London 1812
Broderick, Hannah, *d* Herts 1870
Brooks, James, of Somerset
Bridges, Edward, of London
Browning, John, *d* Surrey 1790
Brown, Jemima Dind
Bullman, John, *d* abroad 1839
Bushell, Elizabeth, of Islington 1780
Bullcock, Catharine, widow
Burrow, Emma, of Birkenhead

GENERAL INDEX. 153

Burney, Edward, of Winchester
Bugden, Maria, *o'wise* Wicker
Bushell, Emma, wife of Joseph
Burbridge, Charlotte, wife of William
Burn, Robert, of Oakham
Butler, Eliza, of Kensington
" M., widow, *d* abroad
" W., *d* abroad
Burgin, Thomas, of London 1864
Burnell, Thomas, of London 1850
Butcher, Robert, of London 1825
Butler, Mrs. Mary
Burton, Richard, of Surrey
Bullpott, William, of Middlesex
Buckley, Patrick C., *d* abroad 1872
Burrows, Mary A., *frmly* Wells
Burnell, Robert
Burghope, Mary, *o'wise* Elsworthy
Burton, William
" Richard
Butler, James, *d* abroad 1861
Burwick, Ann, *d* Middlesex 1871
Butler, John, of Dublin
Burby Family
Burge, James B., of Walworth
Butler, George, clerk
Bullman, Joseph, miner
Bussell Family, of London 1828
Buddicombe, Eleanor, *frmly* Harrison
Buck, Angelina, of Jersey 1846
Bucas, Eli, *d* abroad 1857
Buchanan, John, *d* London 1803
" Robert, ship carpenter
Buckle, John, of Surrey
" Elizabeth
Buckley, Michael, seaman R N
Buckingham, J., *d* abroad 1824
Budworth, Richard, of London 1777
Bugg, Jonathan, of Suffolk, *d* 1819
Bull, William, *d* London 1835
Bullock, Henry, of London 1805
Bulput, Catherine
Byrne, Mark, of Dublin
" Jane, *frmly* Wilson

C

Carr, Henry W., contractor
Campbell, Annabella C., of Middlesex
Cameron, Niel }
" Duncan } of America
" Euphemia }
Cable, Eleanor, *d* Middlesex 1864
Cameron, Alexander, *son* of Duncan
Carter, Oscar, of Nottingham
Campbell, James, *d* Surrey 1867

Carter, Richard, of London 1850
Carlaw, George, of Scotland
Campbell, Colin W.
Catlin, Ann, *frmly* of London
Caller, Elizabeth C., *frmly* Freeman
Casterton, William, *d* Middlesex 1848
Catley, Mary A., *o'wise* Adcock
Callam, John, of London
Campbell, Archibald, Captain
" Maria E.
Carter, Robert, *d* Devon
Cameron, James, Sergeant
Carley, William J., went abroad
Carroll, George, of Dublin
Carson, Joseph, of Dublin
Carton, Joseph, of Dublin
Chamberlain, Sarah, of Norfolk
Chesnutt, Robert J., of Cardiff 1856
Chrimes, Hannah, *d* Lancashire 1870
Chapman, Catherine, *d* Kent 1869
" Rosalind A. M. R.
Chadwick, William, of London 1844
Charter, Sarah, of Surrey 1839
Chapman, Alfred, of London 1831
" Joseph, of London 1840
Church, John B., of London 1850
Charters, Benjamin, of London 1810
Chartraine, Carolina, of Turin
Chambers, George
" Frances, *frmly* Woodman
" James, of Westminstr 1828
" Mary, of Cumberland
Child, Sarah, *frmly* Fisher
Chick, Sarah Ann, *o'wise* Rumsey
Childs, Sylvester, of Norfolk
Chinn, Joseph, of London
Cheetham, George, of Macclesfield
Chisnall, Michael, of Dublin
Clark, H. W., of Kinsale
Cleaver, Mary, *o'wise* Gerry
Clare, Elizabeth, *frmly* Lewis
Clarke, Caroline, *d* Scotland
Clapham, Sarah, *w*
Cliffe, Millicent, *frmly* Hill
Clark, James, of Berks
Clack, William, *d* Cambridge 1860
Clark, Sarah, of Leamington 1847
Clark, John, General
Combes, Henry, *alias* Geary
Codwise, Edward, *o'wise* Bertie
Corfe, Mary, of Berks 1780
Cox, Lydia, *d* Sussex 1870
Colepepper, John S. } of Essex
" Bridget } 1810
Cox, Mary, *frmly* Jones
Collis, Kezia, niece of Ann Bull

Cookson, Elizabeth, *frmly* Lansdall
Cooper, Elizabeth, *o'wise* Haylock
Cock, Henry, of Tottenham
Cowen, Elizabeth, *d* Surrey 1870
Conyers, Elizabeth, *d* Kent 1871
Cornish, Harry, *son* of Joseph
Collins, Jane, *d* Middlesex 1861
Coy, Henry, of Marylebone
Conwell, Wm. E. C., of Penang 1828
Coulson, George, *d* Surrey 1871
Collins, Frederick, of Hornsey
Cook, William, of Middlesex 1803
Cook, Charlotte E.
Collick, John, of Kent
Cockman, William } of Middlesex
" Ann } 1838
Cook, William, of London
Collins, James, of Marylebone 1830
Colebrook, Josiah, living 1760
Cole, James, seaman
Coady, Patrick, *d* abroad 1872
Cooper, Ann, *o'wise* Urquhart
Coomb, William H., of Oswestry
Cormick, Mary, *d* Middlesex
Cottell, Ann, *d* Middlesex 1873
Cordwell, Sarah, *d* Surrey 1873
Cottrell, Frances, *d* Middlesex 1873
Constable Family
Cooper, Rachel, wife of Joseph
Cockayne, Henry, baker
Cockrane, William M.
" Alexander
Cowen, Joseph, *d* Liverpool
Connor, Thomas, of Dublin
Connoli, John, of Dublin
Courtney, Bryan, of Kilmainham
Collins, John, of Dublin
Colton, Thomas, of Dublin
Connor, Matthew, of Dublin
Cottrall, George, of Milchett
" Mary
Connor, Albert W.
Coals, Mary, *d* Bristol 1780
Couch, William, of Bristol
Crammond, Alexander, *d* Scotland
Crammond, Jean, *o'wise* Adams
Crang, —, surgeon 1849
Crook, John, *d* Gloucestershire 1857
Cross, Mr., of Islington
Crole, George S., of Knightsbridge
Craig, John, *d* Edinburgh 1837
" James, *d* Scotland 1839
Cremillott, Henry, of London 1840
Crowdy, George, of India Office
Crout, Thomas J., *d* Hants 1841
Crundel, John, of London 1699

Creed, Mary }
" William } of Peckham
" Frances }
Curtis, Jarvis, of Gloucestershire
" Thomas, of Lincolnshire
" Susan, *o'wise* Twell
Culverwell, Richard, of Marylebone
Curling, William
Cummings, James, *d* Liverpool 1870
Cuffley, Benjamin II., of Essex, *d* 1843
Cupples, Theresa Jane
Cusack, Thomas, of Dublin
Curine, William H., of Dorset

D

Davis, Richard, of Middlesex 1824
" Mary, *frmly* Porter
Davies, Jane, *o'wise* Macallister
" Daniel, *d* Cheltenham 1853
" Benjamin
" Samuel
Davis, Charles, of Camberwell
Dands, Joseph, of Bristol
Danson, William, of Bristol 1825
Davison, Sarah J., *d* Middlesex 1871
Dawson, Frederick M., barrister
Davies, Mrs., widow
Day, Mary Ann, *dau.* of William
Davis, Joseph, of London
Day, John, *son* of Thomas
Davis, Alliss, of London 1835
Daviet, Sarah, *d* York 1864
Davidson, James, *d* Scotland 1823
Dallaway, Joseph, surgeon R N
Davey, John B., of Exeter
Dallas, Peter, *d* Glasgow 1872
Dallas Family, of Islay
Deming, Mary A., *w* Hyde Park
Derner, Charles, of Madgeburgh
Derinzy, William R., of Wexford
Debnam, Mary } of Warminster
" John }
Dennent, William
Deeley, Edwin, seaman
Denley, William, servant
Dennis, George, of Mansfield
Dean, Samuel, of London
Deane, Martha R.
D'Espourin, Miss
Deacon, William E., of Reading
Delbosque, Madeline, of Brompton
Demold, Charlotte, *frmly* Gasquet
Delaforce, John, of Surrey 1838
Dixon, Samuel, *d* abroad 1846
Dixon, Elizabeth, *frmly* Scafe

GENERAL INDEX. 155

Dixon, Samuel, *d* Gravesend
Dickie, Charles, of Deptford
Dillon, Amelia, Ann
Dixon, Hannah, wife of John
Dickinson, James, of Lancaster
Dickson, John, of London 1843
Doig, Andrew Wood
" Hannah Charlotte
Dove, Beata, *o'wise* Wicker
Dore, Kesiah, *o'wise* Wicker
Dove, Mary Ann, of Herts
Doyle, Thomas, of Southwark
Douglas, Arthur, of Lancashire
Donkin, G. R., Lieut. R N
Dow, Thomas, *d* Perthshire 1858
Dod, John, living 1760
Dove, Eliza, *w* Middlesex
Douglas, Fredr., born in Shoreditch
Dore, Frank, left England in 1870
Dow, James, of Edinburgh
Doonnan, Charles C., of London
Drausfield, Judith, *frmly* Hill
Drage, John D., of Sutton
Dryborough, Mary B., *d* Kent 1869
Drew, Alexander, of London 1810
Drake, Sarah, *d* Essex 1859
Dugard, Thomas, of Islington
Dunlop, James, *d* Liverpool 1870
Dunn, John, of Truro 1860
Dunneady, Joseph, of Dublin
Duncan, Anna, of Morpeth
Dunn, Frances, *w* 1829
Dugmore, Dorothy A., *o'wise* Thompson
Dubble, William, *d* India
Dyer, Louisa, of Finsbury

E

Eaton, Edmund, *d* Australia 1872
Ebert, Frances, *d* Sheffield 1871
Eccles, David, of Yorkshire
Ede, Charles, of Cornwall
Edie, Robert, of London 1810
Edwards, Thomas, of London 1856
" Harriott, of Sussex
" James, of Middlesex
" Ann, *o'wise* Weeks
" Ann, *o'wise* Bradbury
" Samuel, pensioner
Edmett, Thomas, *d* Kent 1871
Edwards, William, *d* Middlesex
Edgar, Robert, of Newfoundland
Ellis, Thomas, of Essex 1838
Elliott, Janet, *o'wise* Hume
" John, silversmith

Elvin, Joseph, *d* Middlesex 1870
Eley, Mary, *o'wise* Redford
Eldridge, Elizabeth, of London 1825
Elder, Joseph, *d* Birmingham 1870
Elwin, Harriett, *o'wise* Elliott
Elliott, John, of London 1821
Elsworthy, William, gardener
" Mary, *frmly* Burghope
Elsby, John, of India 1841
Elliott, Arscott, of London 1860
" George, of Rochester
Emery, William
" Joseph
Emrie, Margaret E. M. J.
Emwright, John T., *d* Hants 1869
Enson, Mary Ann } of Eltham
" Emma B. }
English, Robert, of London
English, Ann, *frmly* Hillyer
Erratt, Fanny, *frmly* Burbidge
Evans, Richard A.
" Mary Ann
" James, of London 1806
" George Francis
" William } living 1799
" Agnes }
Eyres, Elizabeth, *dau.* of Samuel
Eycott, John N. H., of Gloucester 1857

F

Farra, Joseph, of Liverpool
Fairbairn, Robert K.
Fallon, Jane, *firmly* Bacon
Farmer, Thomas, of Haddington
Farrand, George, *son* of Esther
Faulksham, Mary, *o'wise* Benson
Ferguson, William J., *d* Ireland 1869
Fenton, David, of Middlesex 1825
Fernandez, J. D., of Jamaica
Ffrench, Michael, *d* Middlesex 1843
Finlay, David, of Scotland
Fitzgibbon, Margaret, *o'wise* Macfarlane
F'tzgerald, John G., of Chelsea
Fisher, Sarah, *o'wise* Parker
Findlay, Elizabeth, *w* Isleworth
Fielding, James, of London 1830
Fidkin, Thomas, of London 1820
Fisher, Sarah, *o'wise* Child
Fisher, William, *d* Middlesex 1770
Field, John, *d* Australia
Fioravante, Dominico, *d* Midl'x 1872
Finch, George, lived at Brixton
Fleurriet Family
Fleming, Catherine M., of Dublin

ADDENDA TO

Flower, Eli, of Somerset
Fletcher, Laura, of Brighton
Fleming, Thomas, *d* Middlesex 1871
Foljambe Family
" Jonathan, of Yorkshire
Foster, Hannah, of Faversham
" Charles S., mariner 1812
Fox, Emma, *dau.* of Edward
Folds, Sarah, *o'wise* Walker
Forrest, Mary Ann, *d* Kent 1871
Foster, William C.
Forster, William, of Surrey 1858
Ford, Charles J., tailor
Foster, Charles, of Middlesex 1841
" William, *son* of Charles
Fox Elizabeth, *o'wise* Barry
Frost, Sarah, of Herts
French, Arthur, *d* Ireland 1871
" Family, of Ireland
Frampton, Thomas, of London 1830
Freeman, Ann, *d* Middlesex 1870
Fraser, Hugh, of London
Freke, Thomas, of Dorset 1724
Fuller, George, *d* Norfolk 1854
Fyfe, Edward H., of Liverpool

G

Garratt, Mary
Gardener, Margaret
Gavin, T., *d* abroad 1871
Garratt, William, *d* abroad 1871
Gardiner, Mary, *d* Middlesex 1873
Gardner, Robert, clerk
Gass, John A., soldier
Gair, Richard, of Poplar 1860
Garwood, Mrs., of Hoxton 1864
Gasquet, Charlotte, *o'wise* Denole
Gardner, Ann, of Bath
" Charles Hunt
" Emma Frances
Galley, Thomas, *b* 1757
" William, *b* 1759
" Michael T., *b* 1762
Gerry, Mary, *o'wise* Cleaver
Gerrard, Elizabeth Fanny
George, Sophia, *frmly* Porter
Gibb, William ⎫
" Henry ⎬ of Liverpool
" John ⎪
" Charles ⎭
Gillard, John, carter
Gifford, William, J., *d* London 1873
Gibson, Isabella, *frm'y* Anderson

Gibbons, Margaret, *o'wise* Hackett
Gilchrist, Mrs., servant
" William, of Stirling
Glausser, Anna B., *d* Middlesex 1871
Gladwell, Mrs.
Godfrey, William, of Kent
" Mary, *o'wise* Taylor
Gouldsmith, Mary, *frmly* Marshall
Goldsmith, Laurence R.
Goddard, James, of London 1845
Goodwill, Thomas, of Notts
Goodwin, John, of Dublin
Gordon, David, *son* of Margaret
" Elizabeth, *frmly* McQueen
Gould, Elizabeth, *w*
Gorman, Henry, *d* India
Goldwin, Thomas, of Hants 1810
Gosman, James ⎱ of Scotland
" Alexander ⎰
Goodbody, Robert, labourer
Goodspeed, Mary, *frmly* Wise
Goodwin, J. L., of Pimlico
Grainger, John, painter
Gracie, George, *d* abroad
Grainger, John, *b* 1793
Graham, Rose, *frmly* Smith
Gray, Henry, of Southwark
Gregan, Michael, of Kensington
Grant, William, *o'wise* Burton
Gregory, Barnard, of Middlesex
Grier, Andrew, *d* India
Green, Sarah, servant 1860
Griffin, ——, *d* abroad
Gregory, Ann, of Dublin
Grubb Family, of London
Greenfield, Thomas, *m* 1795
Grey, Mary, *o'wise* Ratray
Griffith, John, of London 1826
Grant, James, Captain
Green, Margaret, *frmly* Heath
" Elizabeth, spinster
" John, of London
Graham, Fowler, of Sunderland
Green, William, of Islington
Gray, John, of London 1721
Grise, Emma R., *b* London 1828
Green, William, *d* Surrey 1870
" George, of London
Gray, David Finlay
Gunnell, John, of London 1830
Guy, James ⎱ of Wilts
" Hannah ⎰
Gurr, Ann. of Brompton
Gunn, Frederick, *d* London
Guy, Francis, of Herefordshire
Gwynne, John, solicitor

H

Hall, Ann, wife of Thomas
Hathaway, Mary E., *frmly* Dodgson
Hasenberg, Henry P., mariner
Haynes, John, *d* Essex
Hall, Mark G., of Yorkshire
Haulbrook, Thomas, of London 1820
Harris, Sophia S., *frmly* Bourne
Hancock, Mary, *w*
" Josias, of London 1868
Handley, Christiana, *d* Surrey 1868
Harrison, John P., *d* Chester
Hayes, John, *d* Manchester 1810
" Samuel, of Lancashire 1808
Hardley, Isaac } of Wittlesea
" William
Hamilton, M. A. P.,*d* Middlesex 1871
Hart, Elizabeth
Harris, Francis K. of Northumberland
" James, born in London
Harding, William H., *d* Surrey
" William, of Somerset
Hall, Thomas William
" Joseph Charles
Hatfield, John, of Westminster 1747
Harding, Henry } of Ireland
" Elizabeth
Harris, Henry, *d* Middlesex 1872
Harden, Thomas, *d* Middlesex 1870
Hazard, William, of Devon 1860
Harrup, Catherine J., of Walworth 1860
Hammond, Thomas, of Bray
Hancock, Mary A., *b* 1808
Hamilton, E. D. F., of Australia 1850
Harrison, Frances, *frmly* Brown
Hall, Joseph C., of London 1860
Hack, Samuel, of Lincolnshire
Hall, Thomas, *d* Cheshire 1845
Haney, Michael, of Ireland
" John
Hawthornthwaite, M., *d* Manchester 1853
Harris, Isabella, *d* Middlesex 1870
Hayner, Elizabeth, *d* Bristol 1870
Haylock, Eliza, *d* Middlesex 1870
Hadfield, Thirza, *frmly* Stafford
Hewlet Family
Herring, John, of London
Heathcote, Joseph, of Warwick
Herbert, Eliza, *d* Middlesex
Heward, Joseph E., *d* Middlesex 1872
Herbert, Charles, of Australia
Heath, George
" Robert

Heath, Letitia
Henderson, J., *d* abroad
Heald, John A., of Lincolnshire
Helsby, John, of India 1841
Henshaw, John, of London 1854
Hewer, Elizabeth E., *frmly* Stuart
Heale, Edgar, of Clapham
Head, Charles, of London 1863
Helm, Susannah, *d* Surrey 1871
Heathwaite, Thos., of Kirkleatham
Healey, Thomas, butler
Hey, Martha, *frmly* Roebuck
Hill Family
Hibbert, Margaret, of Lancashire
Hinksman Family
" John, of Birmingham
Hillyard, Bailey, *d* Wilts 1867
Higgins, Andrew, *d* abroad 1870
Hilton, James, went to America
Hill, William, of Wilts
Hillyard, George, of Oxford
" Richard, of Gloucester
" Samuel, of Bedworth
Hickey, Ellen
" Emily
Hill, Henry, *d* Ireland 1870
Hillyer, Ann, *o'wise* English
Hill, George, of London 1812
" William, of Wilts
Honeycomb, Mary, *o'wise* Cleaver
Howell, John, of Halesworth
Holmes, Robert, yeoman
Hornby, Horatio N., of London 1860
Horwood, Mary, of Lincolnshire
Horne, James } of Edinburgh
" John
Hogan, John, *d* Ireland
Horrabin, Richard, *d* 1859
Holt, William, of Surrey 1780
Hoey, Henry E., *d* abroad
Horne, Edward, *d* Middlesex 1870
Hodges, Elizabeth, *d* Islington 1871
Hogarth, John, of Surrey 1860
Holmes, William, of Middlesex 1824
Hosack, Ann A., *d* 1870
How, Bridget D., *d* Middlesex 1870
Hopper, Margaret
Hodgin, Thomas } living 1760
" Samuel
Howell, Jas., of Camden Town 1834
Horner, Esther, *frmly* Farrand
Hoppe, John, of London
Hodges, John, of London 1842
Howell, John, of Middlesex
Humphries, Mr., of Hornsey Rise
Hutley, John, *d* Middlesex 1866

158 ADDENDA TO

Hunt, Mrs., of Ireland
Hudson, Ann, *frmly* Dodgson
Hutchon, Thomas, of London 1830
Hume, Jane, *frmly* Elliot
Hurrell, Hugh Edward John
Hurst, Elizabeth, *o'wise* White
Hunter, Catherine Mary
Humphreys, George, *d* London
Hyland, Thomas, *d* Ireland 1870

I

Ince, Betty
Illesby, William, of London
Isaacs, Alexander, of Hatcham
Irish, Sarah ⎫
" Catherine ⎬ of Surrey
" Mary ⎭
Irvine, Robert, *d* Scotland 1870

J

Jackson, Elizabeth, *frmly* Hill
Jamaica, unsettled Chancery causes
Jackson, George, schoolmaster
" Sarah A.
Jacobs, William, of Dover
Jackson, Jane, *d* Middlesex 1808
Jeffreys, Mary Maria, of Jersey
Jenkins, Georgina H., *d* Swansea
Jennison, Thomas, lived in Surrey
Jermyn, Emily, of London 1860
Jerningham Edward, of Westminster
Jenkinson, Elizabeth, of Middlesex
Jennings, John, *d* Essex 1841
Jiggs, Daniel, *d* Horncastle 1844
Jones, Carolina M., of Limehouse
" Helena S., *d* abroad 1872
" William, of Carmarthen
" William, of Bath
" Mary Ann
" Sophia, of Pentonville
" William, private 10th Foot
" John, of Tottenham
" William C.
" Thomas, of Islington
" Charles, of Herefordshire
" George
" Samuel, *son* of Edward
" Frederick, of Southwark
" Edward, of Ruthin 1854
" Robert T., of Ipswich
Johnson, Sarah, *d* Suffolk 1795
" Alexander, of Surrey 1860
" Thomas, of Warwickshire

Johnson, Mary, *d* Hereford 1869
" Cornelius, *d* Stepney
" Ann
" Lorenzo C., of Stepney
Joyce, Charles, of Lancashire
Joynt, Mary, of Mile End
Judge, Elizabeth A. ⎫ of London
" Joseph ⎭ 1823

K

Keen, Lieut. W., *son* of Robert
Keay, Mary Ann, *d* Dumfries 1870
Kettlewell, Thomas, of Yorksh. 1803
Kean, James, of London 1848
Kemp, Ann, *d* Middlesex 1871
Kersopp, Christopher, of Newcastle
Kelly, Margaret
Kenny, Edward William
Kean, William, *b* in Wales
Kemp, Jacob ⎫ of Southwark 1780
" Mary ⎭
Keane, William, *d* abroad
Kempton, Sophia, of Shoreditch 1860
Kennedy, Mary, *d* abroad 1872
Kerr, Jonathan D., of Edinburgh
King, Samuel, *d* Surrey 1867
" Maria, of Suffolk
" Charles M., *d* Surrey
Kingston, Mary, *d* Middlesex
King, William, of London
Kidd, W. J. P., *d* Scotland 1870
Kinton, Janet, *d* abroad 1872
Knight, Elizabeth M., of Bromley
Knott, Harry, went to America
Kyan, Ellen, *d* Guernsey 1870

L

Layde, James, of Clevedon
Lawson, Cæsar, *d* Southport 1869
Lauder, William, *son* of John
Lardner, Ann
Langley, Henry, joiner
Lacy, Edward, *d* Kent 1871
Lawson, Alice, widow
Lambert, ——, *d* abroad
Lawes, Mary A., of Middlesex 1864
Lane, Robert C., of Devon 1870
Lawrence, Emma, servant
Larchin, Mary, *d* about 1810
Lawdey, Charles A.
" Frances M., of Middlesex
Lavender, John, of London
Laskey, James, of Middlesex

GENERAL INDEX.

Laskie, David J., *d* Middlesex 1868
Lane, William, of Clerkenwell
Lessley, Charles, butler 1818
Leavesley, Dorothy, *d* Cheshire 1869
Lediard, M. F. A., *d* Leiscest'she 1868
Leiscester, Frederick Rev.
Lee, Edward F., of London
Leicester, Peter, of Manchester 1835
Lee, Thomas, of Birmingham
Levitt, Lewis, of London 1832
Lee, James, of Yorkshire 1849
" Caroline, servant
Leach, Charles, of Kent
Lewis, Eliza, *o'wise* Clarke
Litchiquary, Mary
Llewellyn, Anna M., *o'wise* Martin
Lock, James, of Putney 1831
Lonsdale, Maria F. L.
Logan, Mary, *w* of James
Lowe, William, *d* abroad
Lodder, Thomas, *d* Middlesex 1871
Longhurst, Samuel, *d* Yorkshire
Lowrie, Jane, *o'wise* Phillips
Lowe Family
Loran, Kate, of London
Low, William, *d* India
Loughlin, John, gunner R. A.
" Michael, of Dublin
Loughran, James, of Dublin
Lanigan, James, of Scotland
Luxford, William
Lushington, Anna N., of Matlock 1844
Lynne, Jane, of Bognor
Lyle, William G., of London

M

Mawson, Percival, went abroad
Matthews, John, of Walworth
Martin, Anna M.
Mason, Anna M., *d* Middlesex 1869
Martin, Thomas, of Clerkenwell
Matthews, Ruth, of Bristol
Martens, Sophia D., of Margate 1868
Main, James, *son* of Edward
Manning, Ann, of Notts
Matthews, James H., of Middlesex
Manning, Anna, *o'wise* Hentley
Mangin, Warren G., *d* Middlesex 1871
Mangin, Samuel H.
Manning, Mary, *dau.* of John
Mayne, Mary, of London
Martin, Elizabeth, *frmly* Wood
Mason, Henry Swaine
Maxwell, Mary Ann, *d* Kent
Maltman, Gavin, of Scotland

MacIntyre, ——, of Mile End 1867
Marrin, Walter, of Ireland
Maidwell, Francis, *d* Suffolk 1871
Mackenzie, Elizabeth, of Paris
Martin, Mary Jane, *w*
" David, of Whitechapel
Margrove, Rachel, *d* Middlesex 1872
Manning, Sarah, *d* 1865
Mawer, William, of Gateshead
Mann, Abraham, of London 1830
Mahon, James, of Dublin
Maguire, Patrick, of Dublin
Mason, John } of Dublin
" George }
Malyn, Henry, of Middlesex 1824
" Mary A., *frmly* Porter
Markham, Sarah, of Ireland
Mahony, Joseph R., of London
Macallister, Jane, *d* Doncaster 1870
Maslen, William J., *d* Surrey 1870
May, William
Marshall, Mary, *o'wise* Goldsmith
McNabb, Henry, *d* Lancashire 1856
" Family, of Tyrone
McLerman, Roderick
McFarlane, Margaret, *d* London 1866
McLay, Helen, *o'wise* Spiers
McKernan, John, of Dublin
McEwen, Jonah, of Glasgow
" Family
McViccar, Duncan, *d* 1866
McNeal, Daniel, of London 1810
" Family, London
McHugh, Lydia, *frmly* Wilkins
McPherson, John, *d* India
McConnell, R. C., *d* India
McCrummen, Norman S., *d* 1871
McArdle, Charles, surgeon
McQueen, Elizabeth, *o'wise* Gordon
McEwan, John, *d* America
" James
McKerroll, Isabella
Merredith, Michael, *d* Middlesex 1865
Mellor, Frances M., of Australia
Meredith, Elzbth. M., *d* Surrey 1872
Mercer, Andrew, *d* Canada 1871
Meacher, Esther, *o'wise* Roy
Mears, Mary, *dau.* of Thomas
Metcalfe, William, *d* Surrey 1836
Meighan, Richard, of Kevin's Port
Miers, Samuel, *d* Leeds 1866
Miller, Charlotte, of Bray
Millner, John, of Dublin
Miller, Clara, *frmly* Ward
Mitchell, Ann, *frmly* Tomlinson
Millbanke, Elizabeth, of Kent 1860

ADDENDA TO

Mitchison, George B., *d* Surrey 1871
Mills, Richard, of Tarring
Miles, John, *d* Middlesex 1866
Miller, James, of Scotland
Milne, John G.
Molineaux, William, printer 1834
Moses, Moses, of London 1856
Morley, Matthias, of Southwark 1830
Morcombe, Elizabeth, of Taunton
Morgan, Margaret, *d* London 1865
Morley, Robert, solicitor 1790
Morgan, David, of Dalston 1870
Morton, J., of Australia 1856
Molyneaux, Edward, *d* before 1828
Morgan, William, tin-plate worker
" Margaret, *dau.* of Ann
" Phillip, *d* Herefordshire
Monk, Daniel J., of Middlesex 1810
Morgan, Cornelia, of Bristol
Moore, G., *d* abroad 1863
Motham, Charles, of London
Mouat, Henry, *d* abroad
Moss, Elizabeth, *d* Surrey 1870
Morine, George, of Doncaster, *d* 1872
Morley, George, *d* Yorkshire 1866
Morrison, Sarah, *w* of Thomas
Morris, Joseph, *d* Ramsgate
Moore, Thomas, *son* of Isaac
Moodeey, Richard, of London 1699
Moreton, Samuel H., *d* Liverpool 1869
Moore, David, *b* in Edinburgh
Morse, Robert, *son* of John
Murphy, Humphrey, of 17th Regt.
" Barnaby, of Dublin
Murray, Robert, of London 1835
Munro, Hugh, *d* abroad
Mullett, John, of Chelsea 1860
Munro, William, railway contractor
Murney, George
" Edward
Myers, Thomas, of E I C Service

N

Nash, John, *d* Bristol 1822
" William, living 1848
Naylor, ——, *d* abroad
Newnes, George
Newman, William S., *d* Chester 1872
Nest, Eliza, of Gloucester
Nee Family
Nelson, William, *d* abroad
Negri, Lucie, *o'wise* Phillips
Newman, John, of Chelsea
Nee, Edward, of London 1813

Neucabie, Henry S., *d* Lincoln 1869
Nicholas, Sarah, *d* Worcester
Nicholson, Theodocia
Nish, Thomas M., of Glasgow
Nolte, John A., merchant
Norris, William, *d* Bath 1832
Norton, Henry, *d* Middlesex 1843
Norman, Eliza, *o'wise* Gardner
Nudd, James, of Norfolk
Nugent, William S., *d* abroad
Nye Family

O

Oaks, Mary, *frmly* Tomlinson
Oakley, William W., of Clerkenwell
O'Brien, Emma Eliza, *w* 1836
" John of Dublin
" Thomas F., seaman
" John, of Ireland
Ockerby, James T., of Hull
O'Farrell, John, of Dublin
" Andrew
Ogilvie, Francis M., *frmly* Oldfield
Ohren, Margeret
" Emma
O'Keefe, Arthur, of Dublin
Okey, Thomas, of Bristol
Olivant, Betty, of Lancashire 1869
Oldfield, James, *d* Middlesex 1857
Oldroyd, Mary, *wife* of Thomas
Oldham, Thomas C., of London
Olding, John, of Southampton
Ommanney, John, of Hants 1768
Ormiston, Robert, of Edinburgh
Oxford, Thomas, *d* Lancashire 1810
Osborne, Elizabeth, of Kent 1835
" Mary Ann, *d* Staffordshire
" William, of Northampton
O'Sullivan, John L. } of North
" Susan R. } America
Otter, Denis, *son* of William
Owen, Henry Hugh, *d* abroad
Oxley, Charles, of Camberwell

P

Patterson, Charlotte, *d* Middlesex
Parker, Eleanor E., of Hoxton 1862
Parry, Elizabeth, *w* London
Parker, Sarah, *frmly* Fisher
Page, Ann, *d* Surrey 1855
Parker, Eliza P. W., of London 1840
Paull, Frances, *frmly* Andrews
Paterson, Thomas A., of Putney

GENERAL INDEX.

Page, Elizabeth, of Kent
Paine, Richard, lived in Walworth
Park, Diana, *d* abroad
Parker, Mrs., *o'wise* Rawlinson
Payne, William, *d* America
    " Family
Paling, Catherine, of Northamptonshire
Paine, Sophia M. C.
Parrot, Louisa C.
Parsons, Elizabeth, *d* 1862
Palmer, Sarah, of Surrey
Paske, John C., *d* abroad
Park, Marian, *wife* of Adam
Palmer, Thomas R., *d* Middlesex
Pain, John H.
Palmer, Isabella
Parkins, ——, sheriff 1829
Patterson, William, of Kevin's Point
Parker, Robert W., *d* Manchester 1872
Paterson, Henry
Penaluna, Thomas, *d* Kent 1871
Peterson, T., of Liverpool
Pearcy, Matthew, of London 1828
Perl, Jacob M., of London 1865
Pearse, Agnes, of Middlesex 1852
Peacock, Amelia, of Camberwell
Pearce, James E., *d* Middlesex 1869
Peacock, Isabella, servant
Percival, James, of Cheshire *d* 1806
Pearson, Eve, *d* Surrey
Peché, Charles, *d* Middlesex 1828
Pearce, M. A., *d* abroad 1868
Pitkin, Hannah, *d* Bucks 1869
Pine, Agnes Miller, *w*
Pilkington, Diana
    " George, of York
Pike, George, of Kent 1815
Pither, Charles, of Hants
Pick, William, of Yorkshire
Pickworth, William John
Pillar, Anna M., *d* Surrey 1872
Pilcher, James, of Chelsea
Pittman, Frederick, of Sandwich
Pickett, William, *d* Middlesex
Phelps, Philip H. F., *d* Sussex 1872
Phillip, Robert, *d* Scotland 1868
Phillips, John, of Carmarthen
    " Thomas, *d* Australia
    " William, of Surrey 1840
Phillip, Jane, *o'wise* Lourie
Phillips, Herbert, servant
Plowden, Edmund W. C., *d* Kent 1865
Plowman, John, *d* Middlesex 1852
Plomer, Thomas, of Dorset

Porter, John, artist
Pointon, Francis, *d* Herts 1866
Powell, Elizabeth, *frmly* Wheeler
Potts, John, quarter-master
Porrall, Richard, of Yorkshire
Potter, Sarah, *d* Surrey 1869
Porter, Amelia A., of Islington
    " Mary A., *o'wise* Malyn
    " Mary, *o'wise* Davis
    " Sophia, *o'wise* George
Postle, Edward, *d* abroad
Prigent, Mary Frances C.
Priest, Ellen, *d* Bristol 1870
Prosser, Mary, *d* Brecon 1870
Pretlove, David, *d* London 1834
    " Hannah, *d* Middlesex 1872
Pullen, George
    " Samuel
Pursey, Joseph, of Canterbury
Putley, Francis, of Surrey
Purshouse, Mrs.
Pyne Family
Pyle, Edward, of Newcastle

R

Ratray, Mary G., *d* Middlesex 1873
Randall, Richard
    " Ann, *o'wise* Wagstaff
    " Edward, groom
Rawlinson, Alexander
Ramsay, William, of Edinburgh 1826
    " Margaret, *d* Glasgow 1872
Reynolds, Elizabeth, *frmly* Wheeler
Rennolds, Susan, of London 1825
Read, Cordelia A., *d* Surrey 1871
Redford, Mary, *frmly* Eley
Reeve, Thomas, of London 1834
Reader, Richard, of Kent
Rea, Jane, of Kent, *d* 1818
Reilly, Bernard, *d* Ireland, 1871
    " Edward } of America 1869
    " Margaret }
Reid, Catherine, *frmly* McEwen
    " William, of Glasgow
    " John J., *d* Surrey 1873
Reilly, Valentine, of Ireland
Reid, Miss A., of Bristol
Reynolds, Louisa, servant
Rennie, Ann, *d* Middlesex 1873
Reid, John, cabinetmaker
    " George
Rhoads, Mrs. John
Richardson, Henry, *d* Middlesex 1869
Rishworth, Thos., of Middlesex 1844
Ritchie, Nicol, of Newcastle

Ridge, Priscilla, *d* Surrey
Richardson, John A. B., of Essex
Ritson, Daniel, of Liverpool
Richards, John, of Exeter
Rose, George F., *d* Middlesex 1872
Robertson, William, *son* of Andrew
" David, of London 1812
" Alexander
Roberts, William, of Marylebone 1845
Robertson, Thomas, of London 1835
Rose, Ellen, of London 1860
Robinson, Eliza, *d* Kent 1866
Roughton, John, *d* Notts 1819
Robb, Robert, *d* London 1870
Rolls, Edward John, of London
Roberts, William, of London 1843
Ross, David, Doctor of Medicine
Rossiter, Elizabeth, *d* Bristol 1871
Roughton, Francis, of London
Robertson, John, *d* Scotland 1870
" John, *d* about 1740
Rowles, Byron G., *d* abroad 1861
Roule Mrs. Mary
Robertson, James, of Penrith
Rose, John of London
Roodhouse, Robert, of Wakefield
Roy, Esther, *frmly* Meacher
Rushton, Ann, *d* Warwickshire 1871
Rushby, Jane, *dau.* of Thomas
Rumsey, Sarah A., *frmly* Chick
" William, of Bath
Rubidge, Eleanor, of Camberwell
Russell, William, of London
Rumbold, George Samuel
Rule, James, of Edinburgh
Rudden, Ann, *d* Surrey 1870
Rushby, Jemima, *o'wise* Hough
Ryder, Mary Ann
" Andrew

S

Salmon, John, of Jamaica 1810
Sanderson, Henry, ship steward
Savell, William, *d* Middlesex 1858
Sayers, Robert, *son* of Sarah
Sanders, John, of Brenchley
Sayer, Lydia, *o'wise* Wade
Sadler, Edward T., *d* India
Saunders, William, *d* Gloucestershire
Sansbury, John, *d* Middlesex 1853
Sayers, Benoit, of London
Savage, Henry A., *d* abroad 1861
Saunders, Robert, of Australia 1865
Sawden, Elizabeth, *frmly* Bellby

Sayer, Matilda, of Middlesex
Sabine, Charles, of London 1836
Salomson, Samuel, of London
Sandys, John W., *d* London
Sandford, Edward, *d* London
Savage, Charles, of Whitechapel 1831
Sambourne, Edward M., of London
Saer, Margaret } of Caermarthen
" James }
Sclater, Thomas, *d* Greenwich 1835
Scarth, Elizabeth, *frmly* Tomlinson
" Henry W., *d* London 1811
" Henry, *d* Surrey 1870
Scott, Walter, *d* Beds, 1843
" John, of Cumberland
" Mary Ann, *w*
Scholes, George, of Yorkshire
Seheberras, Jane, born 1823
Scott, William, lived in Surrey
Sellers, Harry B.
" William, J. B.
" Selina M.
Selby, Thomas, of Brompton
" Catharine, *d* Leicestersh 1869
Seed, William, of Lancashire
Seggie, Peter, of West Calder
Sevestre, Julia } of
" Henrietta C. } Calcutta
Sell, Thomas }
" Anne } of London
" Mary }
Sheriden, John, of Kilmainham
Sheppard, Elizabeth, living 1760
Shaw, Thomas H., of Bedminster
" Ann H., *d* 1871
Sharland, Elizabeth H., of Devon
" Thomas V., *d* Devon 1870
Shirra, David, of Edinburgh
Sherratt, John, of Aberdeen
Shaw, Hannah, *frmly* Hill
Shepherd, John, *d* Cheshire 1871
Sharp, Martin, captain
Shepley, George S., of Lancashire
Sherman, Amy, of Chiswick 1780
Sienesi, Joseph
Simpson, Mrs., *frmly* Stewart
Siddely, J., *d* abroad
Sikes, George, of Dublin
Silvester, W., baker
Slyman, Anne, *d* Middlesex 1873
Slight, Thomas, *d* Hunts 1871
Sleap, Elizabeth, *o'wise* Dixon
Slattery, Mary, *d* Surrey 1872
Smith, James W., of London 1830
" Rose, *o'wise* Graham
" William, of London 1810

GENERAL INDEX.

Smith, Margaret A., of Sussex
" George, *d* London 1843
" Thomas, of Ryde
" John, of Hereford
" Thomas, lived at Leeds
" Mrs., of Southwark
" George, went abroad 1854
" Henry, coachman
" Courtney, of London
" James, *d* Westminster 1873
" Robert, Lieut-Colonel
" Jane, *o'wise* Hurst
" Mary, of London
" William, *d* Middlesex
" William P., of New Zealand
" Ann, of Westminster 1817
" Mary E., *d* Somerset 1870
" George, *d* Middlesex 1842
" John G., *d* Surrey 1861
" James, of Dublin
" Charlotte, of Middlesex 1860
" Janet M., of Middlesex
Smallbones, George B., *d* abroad 1873
Smart, Joshua, of Essex
Smyth, Henry, *d* Sandown 1867
Smart, John, of London 1820
Soper, James, of Brighton
Sowden, William, went abroad
Spellar, Mary, of Kent
Spry, Matthew, of Exeter
Spintall, Mary, *o'wise* Cottrall
Squires, Mary, *o'wise* Bryan
Steele, Richard, *d* abroad 1866
Story, Mary, of London
Starr, Joseph } resided
" Rebecca } in America
Street, Family of Pinner
Stroud, Edward A., of Berks
Starling, James, of Essex
Stone, Henry
Stannard, W. B., grocer
Stephens, Stephen, of London
Stewart, Mary A., of Hackney 1857
Steele, George, *d* abroad 1872
Stanley, Eleanor, *d* Middlesex 1872
Stephens, Robert, Rev.
Stanford, William, *d* Chester 1872
Staples, Robt. P., of Middlesex 1837
Steele, George, of Dalkeith
Stobie, John, of Dumfermline
Steel, Lieut. Royal Marines 1812
Stow, Ann, *wife* of William
Strong, Henry, of Surrey 1848
Stratten, James, of Middlesex 1780
Stafford, T., *o'wise* Williams
Still, Henry, born 1824

Still, Charles, born 1821
" Edmund, born, 1827
Steel, Robert H., of Suffolk
Sterne, Henry L., of Jamaica
Stewart, Margarey, *d* Scotland 1872
Sutherland, William
Swaine, Bennett, of Lincolnshire
Swanton, Francis, of London
Swann, Anna, of London 1830
Symes, Charles P. } of Dorset
" William }
Sym, Elizabeth, of Scotland
Sykes, Judith, *d* Yorkshire 1828
Sumption, John, *d* Middlesex 1847

T

Talver, John, *d* Devon 1837
Taylor, Thomas, of Kent
" James, *d* Scotland 1842
" William, of Marylebone
" Richard T. W., *d* Cornwl. 1817
Tait, Margaret, of London 1828
Tarleton, John E., *d* Kent 1849
Taylor, John, *son* of Thomas
Tarleton, William, of Tasmania
Tayler, Richard, of London 1830
Tart, Obadiah
" Mary, *frmly* Wheeler
Taylor, James, *d* Middlesex 1872
" John, *d* Middlesex
" Joseph, of Glo'ster
" Esau, *son* of Thomas
Terry, James, of Bath
" Robert, *son* of John
Tepper, Jabez, *d* Middlesex 1871
Thompson, John, tobacconist
" Emma, of Homerton
Thomas, William, tailor
Thurnell, William, of London
Threlfall, Elizabeth, *frmly* Seed
Thomas, Robert, *d* abroad
Thompson, Samuel, of London 1820
Thornton, Thomas, of Sussex
Thompson, James, servant
Thurlow, Thomas
Thomas, Mrs., of Marylebone
Thompson, Mary, of Middlesex
Thomson, Andrew, of Selkirk
Thompson, Dorothy A., *frmly* Dugmore
Thompson, Mary }
" Alfred } of Pimlico
" George }
Thomas, Anna M., *d* Kent 1872

Tippler, Robert, of London 1850
Tilley, John, of Charleston 1806
Tiley, James, of Bath
" Matthew
Tibbenham, John, *d* Suffolk 1854
Tindall, Jane, *wife* of George
" Margery, *wife* of John
Titcombe, Jane P., *d* Surrey
Tobin, Michael, *d* Ireland 1866
Townsend, Sarah, *frmly* Wright
Towers, John G., of London
Todd, Henry J., of London 1846
Tomlinson, John
" James
" Samuel
Tovey, James T., *d* India
Toker, John Rev.
Tripe, Anthony Rev.
Trollope, Frances, *d* abroad 1872
Turnville, Ann, of Clevedon
Turncock, Hannah, *w*
Twiss, Charles Edward
Twell, Susan, *frmly* Curtis
Tyas, Esther, widow

U

Uholamb, Frederick W., of Pimlico
Ullathorne, John
Upton, William, *d* Middlesex 1872
Urquhart, C., *d* abroad 1870
" Ann, *frmly* Cooper
Usher, Samuel, *d* Middlesex

V

Valentine, George C.
Vaters, John, of Frome
Venton, John J. } of Plymouth
" Francis J. }
Vickers, James, of Peckham
Viney, Alfred, of Kidderminster

W

Watson, John, *d* 1831
Ward, Thomas, *d* 1836
Watson, Catherine, *d* Scotland 1870
Ward, Nathaniel, of Wisbeach
Waters, Robert, of London 1831
Warn, Elizabeth, of Poplar
Ward, Emma } *daus.*
" Catherine } of Thomas

Wade, Lydia, *o'wise* Layer
Watts, Elizabeth, *d* Middlesex 1872
Warcup, William, *d* Yorkshire 1872
Watkins, Jeremiah, of London
" Family
Wallace, John, of London 1845
Warren, Alfred, of London 1865
Wakefield, John Davis
Wagstaff, Ann, *o'wise* Randall
Ward, James, sergeant 35th Foot
Wallace, William, of W. Indies 1820
Wandby, Arthur J., *d* Middlesex 1872
Wandy, George, *d* 1862
Waring, Henry
" William
Warner, Simeon, of Kent
Wagstaff, Ann R., of London 1843
Wayne, Richard, went abroad 1760
Wallis, John, *d* Surrey
Waters, Robert, of Middlesex
Warwick, Emmanuel
Warde, John, of Berks
Watkins, George, of London
Wardell, James R., of London
Ward, Eleanor, of York 1845
Watson, William, of Leeds
Ward, Eliza
Ward, Thomas William
Wakerhill, Elizabeth, *d* Berks 1870
Watts, Caroline A., *d* Devon 1866
Webster, John C., *d* Sussex 1850
Webb, Bethia, *d* 1800
Wells, William, of London 1839
Webb, Mary, of Birmingham
Webster, William F., of London
West, Martha
" Anne
Welham, Joseph, of Suffolk
Wederburn, Thomas, of London
Webb, Edward
West, Thomas, of Oxford, *d* 1872
Weir, John
" Marion
Weaver, Charles } of Essex
" Henry }
Weston, Charles H., of Bow
Wells, Daniel, of Sussex
West, James, engineer
Waterhall, Laetitia, of Melbourne
West, Martha, of Battersea
Welburn, Benjamin, of Hull
" Charlotte
White, Robert
" Nathaniel
Wheeler, Charles, *d* Middlesex 1869
White, Thomas, of Surrey

Whittan, Thomas
" John } of York
" Joshua
Whur, Cornelius W., *d* abroad 1866
White, George T., of London 1843
Wheeler, Mary, *o'wise* Tart
" William, *d* Shropshire 1815
" Elizabeth, *o'wise* Powell
Whitehead, Jonathan, *d* Essex 1873
" John
Williams Family, 1824
" John, of Hammersmith
Widger, John } of London
" Amey
Wilkins, Sarah, *d* Surrey 1870
Wilson, Agnes, *o'wise* Evans
Williams, Edmund, *d* Dorset 1873
" William } of London
" Jane   1805
Wilkinson, Janet, *wife* of John
Williams, William, *d* London 1824
Withers, Mary, went abroad 1855
Wiltshire, Harriet E., *d* Hants
Wilson, Martha, *d* Middlesex 1872
Wilkinson, Mrs. *w*
Willers, William, living 1760
Wishart, James
Wilkins, Lydia, *o'wise* McHugh
Wilson, Mary, *d* Cheshire 1872
" Alexander, of Cumberland
Williams, James, *d* Liverpool
Wilkie, James, *d* abroad 1825
" David, *d* Middlesex
Willdigg, Hannah
" William
Winn, Elizabeth, *frmly* Smith
Winterbottom, John
Wicker, Daniel, *d* Isle of Wight
Wilson, Alexander } of Carlisle
" Thomas
" John, of Liverpool
" Jane, *o'wise* Byrne
" Robert, *d* abroad 1759
Williams, Williams, *d* Cardiff 1859
" Isaac, of Yeovill
Willey, Catharine M., widow
Williams, George, *d* Kent 1868

Williams, Thomas, *d* Surrey 1862
Wise, John, *d* Berks 1851
Williams, Maria, *d* Middlesex
" Francis
" Augustin
Woods Family, Cheshire
Wood, Elizabeth, *o'wise* Martin
Woodroff, Thomas
Worlding, Elizabeth M., *d* Middlesex 1835
Woodward, Edwin, *d* Middlesex 1871
Wood, John, *d* Northamptonshire 1870
" Charlotte, of London 1848
" William Henry, cooper
Woodman, Charles
" Mary
Wood, John, of Edinburgh
" Alexander
Woods, James P., of London
Wood, Susan, ser**v**ant
" John, *d* Yorkshire 1872
Wright, Charles, of Whittlesea
" Ellen, of Southwark 1850
Wrigglesworth, James, of Southwark
Wyatt, William H., of London 1848
Wylie, Alexander, of Scotland
Wyatt, A., of Brompton
Wymas Family
Wymas Family

Y

Yates, Catherine
" Frances E., *frmly* Symendson
" Matthew L., living 1816
" Francis, of London 1840
Yeatts, John
" Alexander
" Jane
" Maria
Youatt, William, surgeon
Youart, Frank, shoemaker
Young, Robert, of Surrey
" George W., of Essex 1860
" William, *d* Essex 1870
Yoxall, John George

www.ingramcontent.com/pod-product-compliance
Lightning Source LLC
Chambersburg PA
CBHW020307170426
43202CB00008B/523